D1071846

Edna Ferber's Hollywood

TEXAS FILM AND MEDIA STUDIES SERIES
Thomas Schatz, Editor

Edna Ferber's

HOLLY

American Fictions of Gender, Race,

J. E. Smyth

foreword by Thomas Schatz

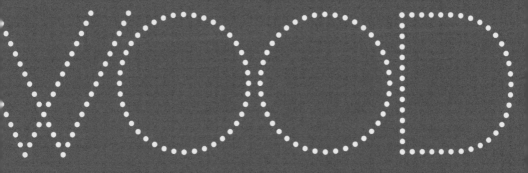

and History

University of Texas Press, Austin

Requests for permission to reproduce material
from this work should be sent to:
    Permissions
    University of Texas Press
    P.O. Box 7819 ·
    Austin, TX 78713-7819
    www.utexas.edu/utpress/about/bpermission.html

∞ The paper used in this book meets the minimum requirements
of ANSI/NISO Z39.48-1992 (R1997) (Permanence of Paper).

Library of Congress Cataloging-in-Publication Data
Smyth, J. E., 1977–
    Edna Ferber's Hollywood : American fictions of gender, race,
and history / J. E. Smyth ; foreword by Thomas Schatz. — 1st ed.
        p.   cm. — (Texas film and media studies series)
    Includes bibliographical references and index.
    ISBN 978-0-292-71984-2 (cloth : alk. paper)
    1. Ferber, Edna, 1887–1968—Film and video adaptations. 2.
Ferber, Edna, 1887–1968—Knowledge—Motion picture industry.
3. Women in the motion picture industry—United States. 4. Historical fiction, American—Film and video adaptations. 5. Motion
pictures—United States—History—20th century. 6. Racism in
literature. 7. Sex role in literature. I. Title. II. Series.
    PS3511.E46Z895 2010
    813'.52—dc22   2009020099

Contents

mong the literary giants of early twentieth-century America whose works were adapted into Hollywood movies, few, if any, cut a larger figure than Edna Ferber. From her breakthrough success in 1924 with the best-selling Pulitzer Prize–winning novel *So Big*, which became a major motion picture that same year, to the pinnacle of her career with *Giant* three decades later, Ferber enjoyed a remarkable run of successful novels—and a few hit Broadway plays, including *Dinner at Eight* and *Stage Door* (co-written with George S. Kaufman), which in turn became hit movies. Ferber, in fact, was the top-selling woman writer of the twentieth century, and one clear measure of her impact on Hollywood was that just three of her best-selling novels—*So Big*, *Show Boat*, and *Cimarron*—generated eight movie adaptations from 1925 to 1960.

Although Ferber's stature with the New York literati earned her a seat at the legendary Algonquin Round Table, literary critics and scholars have consistently undervalued or overlooked her work—due, no doubt, to its popular and commercial success, as well as to its obvious appeal to women. And perhaps not surprisingly, that critical neglect has extended into film studies. Despite the impact of her writing on the movie industry, and despite the scholarly interest in film adaptations of the work of such Ferber contemporaries as William Faulkner and John Steinbeck, film scholars, as J. E. Smyth points out, "have persistently ignored Edna Ferber."

Until now, that is. With *Edna Ferber's Hollywood*, Smyth eradicates decades of inexplicable indifference toward what she aptly terms the "historic partnership" between Ferber and Hollywood. Smyth mounts a convincing case that "Ferber's relationship with Hollywood was arguably the closest and most profitable experienced by any twentieth-century American writer," and also that the novelist provided the movie industry with some of the richest, most complex, and most challenging story material that it had ever taken on. Actually, Hollywood could ill afford *not* to buy the rights to Ferber's fiction, given her massive popularity with precisely the audience the studios sought to attract. But after spending record sums for the rights to these "presold story properties," particularly the historical novels with their unconventional (to say the least) female protagonists and their revisionist, vaguely subversive accounts of America's past, producers were often at a loss about what to do with them.

Smyth deftly combines social history, cultural theory, and industrial and textual analysis in *Edna Ferber's Hollywood*, making brilliant use of primary materials culled from multiple Hollywood studio archives as well as Ferber's own papers. While the book is not a biography, we do glean a strong sense of the personal life of this extraordinary woman—a small-town Midwesterner with enormous professional ambition, an ardent feminist and deeply proud Jew, and a resolute "old maid" (her term) who might easily have been cast as the protagonist in one of her own novels were it not for her ascetic lifestyle. But Smyth's focus throughout is firmly fixed on Ferber's professional career and her long, difficult, and endlessly fascinating relationship with the movie industry. Smyth takes us deep inside the Ferber-Hollywood partnership, providing an engaging and insightful account of the complex and inevitably byzantine adaptation process at every stage. This process begins with the writing itself, of course, as Smyth traces the conception, the actual creation, and the reception of Ferber's novels. Such a discussion is altogether necessary to an explanation and assessment of Hollywood's transformation of those novels into movies, which is Smyth's ultimate concern, and her analysis of this process of cultural production is so thorough and detailed that *Edna Ferber's Hollywood* stands as an invaluable case study not only of Hollywood film adaptation, but of both literary and motion picture authorship as well.

The Edna Ferber that emerges here is an enormously gifted writer and an astute observer of the American experience, but also a canny businesswoman and skilled literary entrepreneur. Ferber realized quite early in her career, for instance, that the serialization of her novels, prior to their publication, in national women's magazines like the *Ladies Home Journal* and *Cosmopolitan* not only provided additional revenues but significantly enhanced the value of subsequent iterations both in print and on screen. Ferber also came to understand the trademark value of her name—what we now term "branding"—and carefully cultivated that value in both the publishing and motion picture industries. Furthermore, she controlled the press coverage of her professional life and her work, and closely monitored the marketing of her books. Ferber also demanded (and usually received) "possessory credit" on film adaptations of her writing. This ensured the prominent display of her name in the credits as well as on posters and in other publicity for the movie versions of *Show Boat*, even though they were based on Florence Ziegfeld's Broadway musical production of Oscar Hammerstein's stage adaptation—which in fact was quite faithful to Ferber's very serious historical narrative. Readers should also note that most of the publicity for the 1960 remake of *Cimarron* referred to the film as *Edna Ferber's Cimarron*.

Unlike Steinbeck, Faulkner, Fitzgerald, and many others among her prominent contemporaries, Ferber rarely ventured into screenwriting; she scarcely needed the income, nor did she want the headaches. A steadfast New Yorker and a solitary writer, Ferber had little time for the ways of Hollywood and the workings of the movie industry. Nonetheless, she made an effort to engage in all aspects of the adaptation process, from the negotiation of the screen rights, to the writing and endless revising of the screenplay (usually by multiple writers), to the actual production and even the marketing of the films. And in her ongoing interaction with producers, writers, and studio executives, Ferber exerted whatever influence she could once Hollywood's filmmaking machinery began grinding away. This was invariably a trying experience for Ferber, which is scarcely surprising given the vagaries of movie making and also, crucially, the challenges involved in translating many of her novels—particularly her signature historical sagas—into commercial films.

Smyth's deepest interest is in the historical novels and the "Ferber films" that they generated. These "fictions of gender, race, and history," as Smyth puts it in her subtitle, consistently invoke a crucial, fundamental paradox. On the one hand, best-sellers like *Show Boat*, *Cimarron*, *Come and Get It*, *Saratoga Trunk*, and *Giant* had established audience appeal and seemed well suited to Hollywood's long-standing investment in American frontier epics, biopics, and women's pictures. On the other hand, Ferber's novels consistently employed narrative elements and themes that directly countered Hollywood's "way of seeing" history, human agency, and the American experience. The novels' female protagonists were scarcely subordinate to male history-makers or victimized by social conventions and conditions, as Hollywood typically would have it, but instead actively "drove the course of American history." Moreover, notes Smyth, "race and gender were often intertwined within her national portraits"—most notably in Ferber's inclusion of mixed-race heroines, one of her favored narrative devices.

On a deeper level, Ferber's historical novels dealt with not just the disappearance but the destruction of the American frontier, and with the exploitation of women and racial and ethnic minorities in the process. Thus, Ferber the novelist was both a revisionist American historian and something of a "new feminist" writer. Ferber the Hollywood trademark was another matter, however. These essential qualities of Ferber's historical fiction clearly presented problems for the movie industry, given its penchant for a more triumphalist view of American history, and a history more securely in the hands of great white males. The studios and major independent producers who bought the rights to Ferber's novels appreciated their narrative and thematic complexity as well as their presold story value, but they also recognized the realities of the movie marketplace, the nature of the mainstream moviegoing audience, and the fundamentally conservative (if not reactionary) bias of the movie industry at large. Thus, the adaptation of Ferber's historical fiction was particularly fraught, and the negotiations, permutations, and altercations involved in translating her novels to the screen were as intensely conflicted and dramatic in some cases as the novels themselves—perhaps more so in the case of *Come and Get It*, the description of which is one of the livelier episodes in Smyth's engaging narrative.

Both the degree of Ferber's involvement in this process and the eventual outcome—i.e., the movie adaptations themselves—varied considerably from one project to the next. Smyth charts these developments in vivid detail, always privileging Ferber's semi-detached but never disinterested perspective. Ironically enough, the most successful and satisfying of Ferber's Hollywood experiences came relatively early and involved adaptations of her historical novels: Hammerstein's brilliant stage musical version (he wrote the play's "book" as well as the lyrics) of her 1926 novel *Show Boat*, which became a Broadway hit in 1927 and a movie hit for Universal in 1936, and the adaptation of her 1929 novel *Cimarron* by RKO in 1931, which won multiple Academy Awards—including best picture and best adapted screenplay (by Howard Estabrook).

Things rarely went so well with subsequent adaptations, which for the next quarter-century kept Ferber intermittently preoccupied and continually exasperated. Indeed, another telling irony that Smyth effectively conveys is that, as Hollywood's notion of the "Ferber film" steadily coalesced, the revisionist and feminist underpinnings of her novels were increasingly compromised. This was most acute in the 1950s, which saw a remarkable Ferber revival with remakes of *So Big* and *Show Boat*; the publication of two more best-selling historical novels, *Giant* (in 1952) and *Ice Palace* (in 1958), that were immediately adapted into big-budget, big-screen Hollywood movies; and a lavish 1960 remake of *Cimarron*. In each of these last three films, which marked the culmination of the Ferber-Hollywood partnership, the novel's female protagonist was either marginalized, as with the female principals in *Giant* and *Cimarron*, or effectively eliminated as a central character, as in *Ice Palace*.

Giant provides Smyth with the most compelling instance of this contradictory cultural process, and her chapter on that particular adaptation is in many ways the centerpiece of *Edna Ferber's Hollywood*. Both the novel and the film were monumental hits—even in Texas, where they were also widely reviled—and of course the film was an immediate sensation, due in part to the untimely death of James Dean (who was killed just after filming ended). Without question, it was *Giant* that finally secured the Ferber brand in Hollywood, but at considerable cost to her artistic vision and historic sensibilities. Smyth is astute enough to recognize, however, that the decision by producer-director George Stevens to counter the proto-feminist critique implicit in the characterization of the film's protagonist (played by Elizabeth Taylor) with the redemption of her cattle-baron husband (played by rising star Rock Hudson) and the rugged appeal of Dean's maverick wildcatter—and thus to ultimately "rehabilitate" the patriarchal order—was crucial to *Giant*'s success.

The release of *Cimarron* and *Ice Palace* in 1960 ended the Ferber-Hollywood partnership, completing a trajectory that traced the rise and fall of Hollywood's classical era as well as Ferber's career. (*Ice Palace* was her last novel.) J. E. Smyth is keenly attuned to these parallel arcs, and in that sense *Edna Ferber's Hollywood* tells the story of both the novelist and the movie industry that so successfully exploited her work. But Smyth's ultimate achievement in this remarkable book is firmly situating Ferber alongside novelists like Hemingway, Steinbeck, and Sinclair Lewis, whose writing provided not grist for the moviemaking mill but source material for some of the most significant films that Hollywood has ever produced.

THOMAS SCHATZ

Acknowledgments

he British Academy funded my research in Madison, Los Angeles, Boston, and Austin, and I would like to thank the board for its early support of this book. I am also indebted to Harry Miller of the State Historical Society in Madison, Wisconsin, for his help locating material in the massive United Artists Collection and Ferber's extensive papers. Special thanks are due to the Houghton Memorial Library at Harvard University, J. C. Johnson of Boston University's Howard Gotlieb Archive and Research Center, Lauren Buisson of UCLA's Arts Special Collections, Steve Wilson of the Harry Ransom Center at the University of Texas, Austin, the staff of the special collections at Brandeis College, the staff of the Warner Bros. Archive attached to the University of Southern California, the staff of the University of Southern California's Cinema-Television Library, and the staff of the Margaret Herrick Library of the Academy of Motion Picture Arts and Sciences.

Ned Comstock and Barbara Hall were, as always, invaluable resources. Part of the pleasure of working at the University of Southern California's Cinema-Television Library and the Academy of Motion Picture Arts and Sciences Library is certainly their knowledge, generosity, and kindness. It is hard to believe that I have known them now for ten years. Sitting in their empires, reading through a stack of scripts, and breathing the Southern California air conditioning are some of my greatest pleasures. I am especially indebted to Ned for keeping me informed of new finds in the collection, and for recommending Heika Burnison as an offshore research assistant. Heika helped immeasurably in the final stages of this book.

The director of the Margaret Herrick Library, Linda Mehr, negotiated access to the Samuel Goldwyn papers, and I would like to thank her and the Goldwyn family for their assistance. Jenny Romero, Faye Thompson, Sarah Weinblatt, and Sarah Shoemaker all gave advice and located archival material when teaching duties prevented me from travelling to the United States. Colleagues Mary Beltran, Camilla Fojas, and Patrick Major helped me think about Hollywood's involvement in visualizing mixed-race Americans more broadly. The editorial staff of *American Studies* published an earlier version of my work on Ferber and *Giant* and very kindly permitted me to reprint a substantial amount of that material here in Chapter Six.

I would also like to thank Robert Sklar and Dudley Andrew for their consistently good advice. Jim Burr, Thomas Schatz, and the editorial staff of the University of Texas Press have been invaluable in the final stages of the book—incisive, supportive, and patient. Tom's early reading challenged me in many ways, and I am especially grateful for his insights regarding Ferber's relationships with Lillian Hellman, Anzia Yezierska, and other Hollywood screenwriters.

Finding time to write when you are a new mother is next to impossible, but Evelyn and Peter Smyth, Zeynep Talay, and Patrick Major helped me find it. This book is dedicated to Zachary.

Edna Ferber's Hollywood

1.1. Ferber and James Dean conferring on the set of *Giant*, 1955.

one

Edna Ferber's America and the Fictions of History

dna Ferber wrote vividly of the first time she saw a film: "It was in 1897 that I glimpsed the first faint flicker of that form of entertainment which was to encircle the world with a silver sheet. We all went to see the new-fangled thing called the animatograph," she recalled. "It was hard on the eyes, what with a constant flicker and a shower of dancing black and white spots over everything. But the audience agreed that it was a thousand times more wonderful than even the magic lantern."[1] Twenty years later, Ferber made her first sale to Hollywood—*Our Mrs. McChesney* (1918), her first coauthored play (with George V. Hobart). Metro Pictures purchased the screen rights of the play for its original Broadway star, Ethel Barrymore. A year later, independent director and producer Hobart Henley adapted Ferber's short story "A Gay Old Dog."

Ferber did not discuss these early transactions with Hollywood. In the first part of her two-volume autobiography, published in 1939, she remembered her "first film sale" more dramatically. In 1920, she sold the rights to her semi-autobiographical novel, *Fanny Herself* (1917), to Universal.[2] She used the money to finance the writing of her first major historical novel, *The Girls* (1920). As Ferber recalled, her first Hollywood paycheck was "an unimposing sum." But the buyer was Irving Thalberg. At this point, Ferber had no agent or lawyer, and met directly with Thalberg. He was a complete shock to her. Expecting him to follow the stereotype of "larger gentlemen smoking oversized cigars" (or to look like his boss, pioneering film producer Carl Laemmle), she was amazed to find "a wisp of a boy, twenty-one, so slight as to appear actually frail . . . High intelligence, taste and intuition combine rarely in Hollywood or elsewhere."[3] It was her first and only dealing with Hollywood's "boy genius," although she would meet many more filmmakers, forming close relationships with Samuel Goldwyn, who produced *Come and Get It* in 1936, and, later, director-producer George Stevens (*Giant*, 1956).

Ferber's attitude toward Hollywood was complex. On the one hand, she was fascinated with its iconic stars, glamor, and the artistry of a handful of great filmmakers. She admired some like Thalberg, Goldwyn, Stevens, screenwriter Howard Estabrook, and actor James Dean for their drive, ambition, self-invention, and commitment to their work (Fig. 1.1). It was a commitment she shared. Yet she was repelled by Hollywood's "ghostlike" persona—where the flowers had no scent and the people were overplayed personalities rather than individuals.[4] After selling the rights to *Fanny Herself*, she remained in the Los Angeles area for several months to write her next novel. But it was difficult to write a story of women in post–Civil War Chicago while she was stuck in Hollywood's cultural desert. As she commented, "About the town, its life and its people there was in 1920 a crude lavishness that had in it nothing of gusto. It wasn't American, it had no virility, it sprang from almost pure vulgarity." Ferber expected the "pioneering" new industry to possess something of California's nineteenth-century spirit. But, she complained, "There was about it none of the lusty native quality of the old gold-rush camp days. Offended by it, and bored, too, after the first glance or two needed for complete comprehension, I retreated gratefully into the work-walk-read routine of escape."[5]

That year, friend and colleague William Allen White had shared his less-happy studio experiences with her. Though White had made a little money from the sale of his popular short story "A Certain Rich Man," according to him, the screenwriters had transformed it into an almost unrecognizable, tawdry romance. He fumed, "The way the others put your stuff up and the way they tear the heart out of a creation, I don't care to have them. I'd rather have nothing and get the picture across as I conceived it than to have many thousand dollars and get the story all balled up." He continued, "I don't like to have a movie butcher go in and mangle my stuff."[6] White was neither the first nor the last writer to complain about Hollywood's adaptation of his work, but Ferber's experience was different. Although admittedly she had not made much from her first sale to Thalberg, it was the start of one of the most influential and profitable historical relationships in twentieth-century American culture. Ferber was one of America's most prominent historical novelists, a writer whose uniquely feminist, multiracial view of the national past deliberately clashed with traditional narratives of white masculine power. Hollywood filmmakers paid premium sums to adapt her controversial best sellers, creating some of the most memorable films of the studio era—among them *Cimarron*, (1931), *Show Boat* (1936), and *Giant* (1956). Her historical fiction resonated with Hollywood's own interest in prestigious historical filmmaking aimed principally but not exclusively at female audiences. Ferber, like many Hollywood filmmakers of the studio era, projected a hybrid historical vision that challenged prescribed boundaries between low and high culture, history, fiction, and cinema, and gender, race, and power. This book is the story of that historic partnership.

The Ferber Franchise

In *A Peculiar Treasure* (1939) and in her second volume of autobiography, *A Kind of Magic* (1963), Ferber focused on the writing and the Hollywood afterlives of her historical fiction. It was an impressive body of work. When *So Big* won the Pulitzer Prize in 1925, Warner Bros. had already released the first of its three adaptations of her novel. *Show Boat* (1926) was to have a life of its own on Broadway beginning in 1927 before Universal made the first of its two film versions. Counting the later MGM film musical, three versions of *Show Boat* were released between 1929 and 1951. *Cimarron* was first a number one best seller in 1929 and then the number one film of 1931. It was reckoned one of the industry's most impressive critical and popular masterpieces for years before MGM made its own version in 1960. *Come and Get It* (published 1935; released 1936), *Saratoga Trunk* (published 1941; released 1945), and *Ice Palace* (published 1958; released 1960) were adapted only once, but each was marketed and reviewed as a prestigious "Ferber film" and helped define the industry's attitude toward American history during the studio era.

Ferber's Broadway plays also served as the basis for several major films of the 1920s and 1930s, but in her autobiographies, she virtually ignored both her collaborative work with George S. Kaufman and Hollywood's smaller-scale silent-era adaptations of her modern short stories. The story "Old Man Minick" (1924) was filmed by Paramount in 1925 (*Welcome Home*) and by Warner Bros. in 1932 (*The Expert*) and 1939 (*No Place to Go*). In addition, Ferber and Kaufman produced a trio of successful plays about American performers. *The Royal Family* (1928) was so evocative of the Barrymore theatrical dynasty that Ethel Barrymore nearly sued the duo. It was a guaranteed hit for Paramount in 1930, retitled *The Royal Family of Broadway* and starring Fredric March. *Dinner at Eight* (1932) became one of MGM's most star-studded productions a year after its Broadway opening, showcasing John Barrymore as a ravaged actor among a cast of New York social climbers. RKO quickly purchased *Stage Door* (1936), releasing an adaptation starring Katharine Hepburn and Ginger Rogers in 1937. All three plays and films are elegantly paced and loaded with Kaufman's stock-in-trade cynical repartee. Their protagonists and supporting casts are glamorous, frenetic, strained, grasping, and frequently vapid—obscure actresses trading insults in an overcrowded boardinghouse, socialites and players jockeying for momentary supremacy, egomaniacal siblings hamming it up onstage and off. Kaufman had won the Pulitzer Prize in 1932, and the duo's work was also critically respected. Kaufman's biographer Howard Teichmann speculates that while Kaufman supplied the deadly dialogue, Ferber brought depth, variety, and drama to the partnership.[7]

Once produced by Hollywood, the film versions of the plays were critical and box-office successes, but unlike the adaptations of her novels, they were not known as "Ferber films" or even prominently reviewed as "adapted from the play by Edna Ferber and George S. Kaufman." In fact, New York theatre critics always gave Ferber second billing to Kaufman.[8] Broadway publicity subtly undercut Ferber's influence, and some playbill photographs show Ferber watching while Kaufman edits their script.[9] Even in Hollywood, Ferber's name was not always mentioned in reviews of *The Royal Family of Broadway*, *Dinner at Eight*, and *Stage Door*; in fact, neither of the playwrights' names appears on the posters and ads for *Stage Door*.[10] Ferber seems to have responded in kind; she did not discuss the plays in her autobiographies beyond a perfunctory acknowledgment of their existence. As she remarked of *Stage Door*: "It was rather good but not frightfully good."[11]

But Ferber's reputation in Hollywood did not depend on her collaborations with Kaufman, and therefore they are not the focus of this book. While Kaufman always worked with another playwright and had only one successful stint as a credited coscreenwriter, Ferber was a filmmaking gold mine.[12] Although she worked only once as an uncredited screenwriter (*Giant*) and once as an uncredited script vetter (*Come and Get It*), Ferber's historical novels became some of Hollywood's most profitable films. The studios did their best to make her a screenwriter. Even when the demands of wartime production curtailed historical projects between 1942 and 1945, studios were busy negotiating for future Ferber works. In 1944, MGM offered her $375,000 over a period of three years to write one new film a year. According to the contract, she could remain in New York. As agent William Herndon wrote to her, "The content and quality of the original would be entirely up to you . . . I don't know how you feel about this, Miss Ferber, but such homage, to my way of thinking, is absolutely startling."[13]

Hollywood critics and journalists were equally aware of her power. As the *Los Angeles Times* commented during the production of *Giant*: "While it may be 15 years since Edna Ferber visited Hollywood, her influence even in later days has been strong in the films. It has been tremendous when you view it in full perspective, for no fewer than nine of her creations have been made into motion pictures and some of them several times."[14] After her death, in 1968, when seven years had passed since a new Ferber film was in theatres, the trade papers reminisced about her ability to engineer landmark contracts and hefty film rights. *Weekly Variety* recalled, "When agent Leland Hayward sold Edna Ferber's *Saratoga Trunk* to Warner Bros. in 1941 for $175,000, he also established a precedent in the sale of literary properties to motion pictures. It was the first time that such a deal called for all rights to the property to revert back to the author after a stated period. In the case of *Saratoga Trunk*, this was for eight years, although renewed twice, for five and eight years. Hayward also came close to securing the negative rights for his client."[15] The writer went on to comment that only recently had top stars like Cary Grant managed to secure rights to the negative.

But in many ways, Ferber was a star on a par with Grant. No other American writer had such a sustained, successful relationship with the industry during the twentieth century.[16] Between 1918 and 1960, no fewer than twenty-five films were made from her work. While Zane Grey's novels and short stories were adapted more frequently during this era, the majority of the films were low-budget westerns produced for a specific genre market. The renewed interest in prestige westerns during the 1930s, generated largely by the successful adaptation of Ferber's *Cimarron*, did not include Grey's stories. Most of Ferber's work, in contrast, was lavishly produced and advertised to a broad spectrum of viewers. Although several of her contemporary short stories during the 1920s became fairly pedestrian variations on the filmed themes of love, money, and adultery, Hollywood's main interest in Ferber lay in her historical novels. In fact, her career as one of America's most popular writers spans the classical Hollywood era and parallels the film industry's obsession with national history, panoramic narratives, social and political controversy, and financial success.

With the introduction of sound to cinema in 1926–1927, Ferber's reputation in Hollywood rapidly expanded. Arguably, the new medium transformed and reenergized historical cinema more than any other Hollywood genre, giving greater prominence to the many meanings of the projected and spoken word.[17] During the 1930s in particular, American historical cinema (sometimes referred to as Hollywood "Americana") dominated critical and box-office polls. In their different historical contexts, *Cimarron* (RKO, 1931), *So Big* (Warner Bros., 1932), *Show Boat* (Universal, 1936), and *Come and Get It* (United Artists, 1936) both reflected and commented upon the nation's fascination with its varied past. Ferber's historical novels also made a critical connection between prestige filmmaking and female audiences.[18] Her heroines had an unconventional dynamism, echoed later by Julie Marsden (*Jezebel*, 1938), Scarlett O'Hara (*Gone with the Wind*, 1939), and Phoebe Titus (*Arizona*, 1940). During the Second World War and the heyday of the war genre and propaganda film, the studios wisely avoided producing Ferber's often-critical appraisals of American history and female-driven narratives. But *Saratoga Trunk* (Warner Bros., 1945), *Show Boat* (MGM, 1951), and *So Big* (Warner Bros., 1953) responded to the industry's renewed faith in the allure of history and the costume picture to draw female audiences. *Giant* (Warner Bros., 1956) arguably represented the apex of Ferber's influence in Hollywood; the author would also serve as an unofficial screenwriter and a very well publicized producer. The film's phenomenal success spurred MGM and Warner Bros. to make more Ferber films, but *Cimarron* (MGM, 1960) and *Ice Palace* (Warner Bros., 1960) reflect more of the industry's increasingly frantic search for bigness and novelty in the age of impending studio collapse than of Ferber's feminist, even multiracial America.[19]

The Critical Legacy

Despite their massive popularity with the American public, Ferber and Hollywood's "Ferber films" have been neglected in contemporary academic criticism.[20] Mary Rose Shaughnessy's study, the first attempt to assess the spectrum of Ferber's feminist literature, fails to examine Ferber's historical interpretations, use of racial minorities, and relationship with Hollywood.[21] Niece Julie Goldsmith Gilbert's popular biography reacquaints audiences with Ferber the celebrity author, but like Marion Meade's more recent collective biography of 1920s women writers, *Bobbed Hair and Bathtub Gin*, it focuses more on the author's New York social life than on her historical novels and Hollywood successes.[22] While Jerome Kern and Oscar Hammerstein's musical adaptation of Ferber's *Show Boat* is well known to popular and academic film criticism, Ferber's novel is less studied.[23] Only one of Ferber's written works has received any major attention: *Cimarron* (1929) is the subject of several accounts of western history and prestige filmmaking.[24] But aside from this, literary scholars and film historians have ignored the writer and her impact, possibly put off by what Joan Shelley Rubin terms her "middlebrow, mass-cult success."[25] I would also argue that Ferber's interest in American historical narratives rather than in modern literary style and characterization has lowered her in the eyes of academic critics. She seems almost a generation apart from contemporaries F. Scott Fitzgerald and Ernest Hemingway. Fitzgerald was particularly offended by her work, refusing to read *So Big* despite editor Maxwell Perkins's recommendation. Jealous of her big sales and generous reviews, the anti-Semitic writer sniffed that Ferber was "the Yiddish descendant of O. Henry."[26] Ferber responded in kind, remarking to editor Ken McCormick of Doubleday: "I suppose that, like Scott Fitzgerald, you have to be dead to be good. I'll oblige, sooner or later."[27]

Other male critics shared Fitzgerald's distain, even if not his anti-Semitism. More often, Ferber was attacked for her portraits of multiracial America; Stanley Vestal raged that *Cimarron* (a novel with a mixed-race protagonist and family) had no respect for western history's "racial standards."[28] Nearly thirty years later, reporter Lon Tinkle damned Ferber's portrait of Texas white supremacists: "You aren't writing *Uncle Tom's Cabin*."[29] Like Harriet Beecher Stowe a century before, Ferber used the form of a family melodrama to expose the history and contemporary legacy of American racism.[30] Ferber's America was inherently multiracial, but it was her feminism that made many

American men see red. Texan Sam Nugent disliked all of Ferber's work because "only the women are worth their salt! It is obvious that Miss Ferber's contention is that men may be attractive, but only in the sense that children are attractive. She seems to feel men are only excess baggage in her tidy little feministic world. Thus in her books, without exception, women are the builders, men are picturesque—but really useless."[31]

Although some female literary critics, like Margaret Lawrence, Mary Rose Shaughnessy, and Diane Lichtenstein, have promoted Ferber as a feminist icon and the first woman to write about successful, even heroic American women, she does not have the critical status accorded to other female American novelists, like Kate Chopin, Edith Wharton, and Willa Cather.[32] Shaughnessy has suggested that Ferber is out of step with late twentieth-century feminist criticism precisely because her heroines are not victimized by the patriarchy.[33] Ferber succeeded in writing the "androgynous" books that British novelist and critic Virginia Woolf had sought in *A Room of One's Own* (1929). Ferber herself resisted being labelled a writer of "women's fiction" and its association with contemporary romantic melodrama. Her turn to historical fiction may have been one means of casting off any limiting gendered critiques of her work. Doubleday's marketing strategies, which stressed the "epic," "heroic," and "panoramic" historical appeal of her work rather than the characters' romance and glamor, reinforced her image as a writer of serious American historical literature.[34]

Contemporaneous critic William R. Parker's complaint in the *English Journal* targeted her popularity, productivity, and, more subtly, her preferred genre of historical fiction. According to him, her work was "too capably made, like the imitation antiques that come from Grand Rapids."[35] Parker was particularly annoyed by influential critics like William Allen White, who argued, "Of the first dozen chroniclers of the America that has grown up in this twentieth century, authentic reporters of American life, Edna Ferber would be in the first five if the rating were made on popularity, artistic accuracy, and a deep understanding of the American scene."[36] White, like Ferber, was a small-town newspaper reporter who made good marketing small-town American values to an increasingly urban America. Both were masters of America's powerful mass-cultural market, and had little tolerance for elitist highbrows who damned success—especially when it was American made.[37]

In one of his glowing appraisals of her work, White quoted Ferber: "'I wish America would stop being ashamed of its art . . . It's time we stopped imitating . . . Let us write in the American fashion about America.'"[38] Despite

White's sense of Ferber as an "authentic reporter of American life," she preferred to write about America's past rather than its present. Ferber embraced the romance, the pain, and the conflict of American history. Critics like Parker called it "crudeness." Dorothy Van Doren had another name for it—Ferber's writing was perfect for the movies.[39] In a review of her novel *Great Son* in 1945, *Time* profiled this relationship: "*Great Son* . . . is the dependable Ferber brand of slickly written, cinemadaptable Americana . . . The success of *Great Son* is assured. The Literary Guild alone is printing 450,000 copies, *Cosmopolitan* has serialized it, and Broadway producer Mike Todd has reputedly paid $200,000 for the movie rights."[40] These faint sneers bothered Ferber, who was quoted in the same article: "'What's wrong with writing a book that lots of people buy? . . . My God, there's no point in writing it if you don't sell your stuff.'" Samuel Goldwyn could not have said it better. Ferber and Hollywood were made for each another. They were American cultural entities that thrived on mass audiences and publicity; they were frequently condemned by critics for their "crude," lowbrow popularity; yet they both successfully used American history as a means of elevating their prestige.[41]

Until recently, critical appraisals of classical Hollywood's historical genre concurred that on-screen national history was dead, white, and male, and reflected an old-fashioned, heroic view of the past.[42] Although a majority of biopics released during the classical era focus on the exploits of conventional American heroes (*Abraham Lincoln*, 1930; *Silver Dollar*, 1932; *Diamond Jim*, 1935; *Sergeant York*, 1941; *Buffalo Bill*, 1944; *My Darling Clementine*, 1946; *The Magnificent Yankee*, 1950; and *The Spirit of St. Louis*, 1957, to name only a few), unconventional women dominate Hollywood adaptations of historical fiction. Women like Ramona Moreno (Helen Hunt Jackson, *Ramona*, 1928, 1936), Scarlett O'Hara (Margaret Mitchell, *Gone with the Wind*, 1939), Sabra Cravat (*Cimarron*, 1931, 1960), Selina Peake (*So Big*, 1925, 1932, 1953), and Magnolia Hawks (*Show Boat*, 1929, 1936, 1951) all sprang from the historical imaginations of American women. More than any other author, Ferber was responsible for making American women an integral part of Hollywood's projection of history. Ferber's version of American history was not a celebration of masculine ingenuity, strength, and hard work. Instead, it was American women who dominated her narratives, making decisions, overcoming romantic disappointment and social prejudice, achieving public fame. As her niece and biographer Julie Goldsmith Gilbert noted in 1978, "[Ferber] was a precursor of the Women's Liberation Movement by depicting every single one of her fictional heroines as progressive originals who doggedly paved large inroads for themselves and their 'race.' Her male characters, on the other hand, were usually felled by their colorful but ultimately ineffectual machismo."[43] An advocate of many progressive social and political policies, Ferber hoped that her work and example would transform contemporary gender imbalances. She commented in 1959: "The world so far . . . has been run by men, and it's not very pretty. Perhaps the women ought to use their powers, begin running things. They bear the children, rear them, keep the household budget. They may get us out of the woods yet. Men have dominated for thousands of years. It is only since 1920, when women were granted suffrage, that the female has had any rights."[44]

Ferber's feminist counterhistories even tackled the racism dominating western and southern historical narratives; indeed, race and gender were often entwined within her national portraits. Her studies of American racism cover discrimination against African Americans and mulattas in the postbellum South (*Show Boat*, 1926; *Saratoga Trunk*, 1941) and Mexican Americans in twentieth-century Texas (*Giant*, 1952). Her portrayals of Native Americans in *Cimarron* (1929) and *Ice Palace* (1958) go beyond the frontier myths of noble savages, vanishing Americans, and marginalized characters. Ferber was the only important American author to create mixed-race heroines who were active historical protagonists rather than passive, tragic mulattas or voiceless, vanishing Americans.[45] Most scholarly work on race and gender in classical Hollywood cinema, best exemplified by the work of Daniel Bernardi, Linda Williams, Susan Courtney, Richard Dyer, and Gwendolyn Audrey Foster, insists that the studios merely reinforced prevailing racial and sexual ideologies and stereotypes.[46] Often, Hollywood's alleged racism coalesced around its two dominant historical genres, the western (*The Plainsman*, 1936; *Stagecoach*, 1939; *The Searchers*, 1956) and the Civil War epic (*The Birth of a Nation*, 1915; *So Red the Rose*, 1935; *Gone with the Wind*, 1939). Both Ferber and Hollywood framed American history primarily within the nineteenth- and early twentieth-century West and South, regions that embodied complex texts and images of racial and sexual dramas. But when adapting Ferber's work, studio-era Hollywood filmmakers foregrounded the history of a multiracial, multicultural nation, often interrogating the visual and historical ambiguity of racial difference and the insidious nativistic and misogynistic social codes upholding the myth of white America. *Show Boat*, *Cimarron*, and *Giant* focused on these themes and would become some of the most prominent American historical films of the classical era.

Yet despite the critical and box-office acclaim of Ferber's adapted works and even the long-standing interest in Hollywood's adaptation of American literature, film scholars have persistently ignored Edna Ferber. Of all her contemporaries, only the novelists William Faulkner and John Steinbeck had careers that were in any way comparable. But while eight of Faulkner's novels and short stories were adapted for the screen, only *The Long Hot Summer* (1958) was a hit with critics and audiences. Faulkner was better known as an unsuccessful, frequently uncredited screenwriter for Warner Bros. and Twentieth Century-Fox during the thirties and forties. Steinbeck was responsible for four screenplays, and his work served as the basis for ten films, including the Academy Award–winning John Ford picture *The Grapes of Wrath* (Twentieth Century-Fox, 1940) and Elia Kazan's adaptation of *East of Eden* (1955), set in early twentieth-century California. But while he commanded high fees for movie rights, his films (*Of Mice and Men*, 1939; *The Moon Is Down*, 1943; *The Wayward Bus*, 1967) did not always receive the same prestige treatment and box-office receipts of a Ferber picture. Warner Bros., MGM, Paramount, RKO, United Artists, and Universal all produced Ferber films, but Steinbeck sold his work mostly to Fox and later to Warner Bros. Nevertheless, Ferber is only a footnote in contemporary film history, while the Hollywood careers of Faulkner, Steinbeck, and even the failed novelist-turned-screenwriter F. Scott Fitzgerald have been the subject of several studies.[47]

But long before twentieth-century American fiction and films became the subjects of critical inquiry, Edna Ferber's name meant something to readers, filmmakers, and audiences. Studio executives treated Ferber with respect because they had to; in addition to winning the Pulitzer Prize in 1925 (for *So Big*, 1924), she was routinely at the top of *Publishers Weekly*'s best-seller lists. No other writer secured such favorable terms for film rights and publicity. In addition to commanding the highest prices for her work (*Cimarron* cost RKO $125,000 in 1930, and *Giant* and *Ice Palace* also netted her percentages of the films' grosses), Ferber received television, radio, and copyright reversion on most of her work. Beginning in 1924, clauses in all of her contracts required that each time the studios advertised a film title based on her work, they also had to mention her name. So "Edna Ferber" appeared on almost every piece of studio film publicity, from posters to syndicated press articles. Film credits not only gave her a separate writer's title all to herself (when usually the original writer's name appeared on a shared title beneath that of the screenwriter), but also introduced the film with her name and the studio's (for example, "Warner Bros. Presents Edna Ferber's *Giant*"). Ferber knew that her relationship with the studios was a happy partnership because it was based on mutual exploitation. Both she and Hollywood made national history sell and helped each other reap high profits. In her autobiographies, Ferber devotes pages to her novels and their adaptations by various Hollywood studios, and it is through her historical novels that we begin to understand her long-term relationship with Hollywood.

Women Writers, Readers, and Filmgoers in Modern America

As remarkable as Ferber was—as a writer, historian, and Hollywood player—she drew upon the legacies of best-selling women writers, social crusaders, professional and popular American historians, and filmmakers. To a certain extent, Ferber's career and influence can be triangulated with the perspectives of nineteenth-century novelists Harriet Beecher Stowe (*Uncle Tom's Cabin*, 1852) and Helen Hunt Jackson (*Ramona*, 1884); journalist and historian Ida Tarbell (*The History of Standard Oil*, 1904); historical novelists Ellen Glasgow (*Battleground*, 1920), Willa Cather (*My Ántonia*, 1918), and Margaret Mitchell (*Gone with the Wind*, 1936); historians Mary Beard and Mari Sandoz; and popular Jewish novelists and playwrights Fannie Hurst (*Imitation of Life*, 1933), Anzia Yezierska, and Lillian Hellman. While the historian Julie Des Jardins recently examined American women historians' impact on academic social and cultural history, an analysis of Ferber's career reveals the wider impact of women on the popular dissemination of national history.[48]

Hollywood had a long-standing investment in female writers, including top-earning screenwriters Anita Loos, Frances Marion, and Jeannie Macpherson. During the studio era, Hollywood writers adapted a wide variety of material for fiction films, ranging from Broadway plays to popular biographies and history to best sellers and widely read articles in major journals like the *Saturday Evening Post* and the *Ladies' Home Journal*.[49] Much of this work was written by women, including Ferber's Jewish colleagues Anzia Yezierska and Lillian Hellman. Although Ferber was not a screenwriter, she, Yezierska, and Hellman worked for Samuel Goldwyn (Fig. 1.2). Goldwyn hired Yezierska briefly in the 1920s to adapt her successful *Hungry Hearts* (1923) and *Salome of the Tenements* (1925; starring Jetta Goudal).[50] Film historians are more familiar with Hellman's career as a playwright and screenwriter, though, surprisingly, there have been no in-depth studies of her work since 1983.[51] Although an-

1.2. Ferber posing with Samuel Goldwyn in Hollywood, 1935.

ticommunist witch-hunting curtailed her influence after the ill-fated Goldwyn production *North Star* (1943, released by RKO), for ten years she produced
some impressive work for Goldwyn and Warner Bros., adapting her plays
alone or in collaboration with Dashiell Hammett (*These Three*, 1934; *The Little
Foxes*, 1941; *Watch on the Rhine*, Warner Bros., 1943) and revamping old scripts
like *The Dark Angel* (1925; remade by Goldwyn in 1935).

Compared with Ferber's, both Yezierska's and Hellman's influence in Hollywood was short-lived. Although they dealt with major social issues like the
lives of immigrants and the urban poor, the exploitation of women, anti-
Semitism, and, in Hellman's case, fascism and the Second World War, they
were mainly writers of contemporary America. While Ferber, the historical
novelist, proved more adaptable and enduring to filmmakers and audiences

in her own generation, Yezierska and Hellman would eclipse Ferber in the late twentieth century as icons of American feminist literature and, in Hellman's case, liberal Hollywood filmmaking.

In the 1930s, Hollywood bought the work of writers such as Fannie Hurst (*Imitation of Life*, Universal, 1934 and 1959, and *Back Street*, Universal, 1932 and 1941), Elizabeth Madox Roberts (*The Great Meadow*, MGM 1931), Edith Wharton (*The Age of Innocence*, RKO, 1934), and Margaret Mitchell (*Gone with the Wind*, Selznick, 1939). In the 1940s, writers such as Ethel Vance (*Escape*, MGM, 1940), Jan Struther (*Mrs. Miniver*, MGM, 1942), Marcia Davenport (*Valley of Decision*, MGM, 1945), Kathleen Winsor (*Forever Amber*, Twentieth Century-Fox, 1947), and the estate of Marjorie Kinnan Rawlings (*The Yearling*, Twentieth Century-Fox, 1946) all made lucrative studio deals.

What distinguished Ferber from these writers? Quite simply, none of these women sold as much, for as much, as Edna Ferber. With the exception of *American Beauty* (1931) and *Great Son* (1945), all of Ferber's historical novels published between 1924 and 1958 were adapted as major motion pictures. Many were remade more than once. Ferber was an astute businesswoman. She maximized each book's potential readership by first serializing it in a key national periodical such as the *Woman's Home Companion*, the *Ladies' Home Journal*, or *Cosmopolitan*. It was a smart strategy, for Americans read magazines in huge numbers. As Robert and Helen Lynd note in their study of an average American town (*Middletown*), in 1923 the 9,200 homes in the town (later revealed to be Muncie, Indiana) consumed 20,000 copies of each issue of commercially published weekly and monthly periodicals.[52] Three in ten of workers' families and nine in ten of those from the business class took three or more magazines. The Lynds found powerful evidence of "the way periodicals operate, probably even more powerfully than books, to shape the habits and outlook of the city."[53] The *Ladies' Home Journal*, *McCall's*, and the *Woman's Home Companion* were taken in one in five of Middletown's 9,200 homes. Between two hundred and five hundred homes took *Collier's*, *Cosmopolitan*, and *Good Housekeeping*. These journals all contained fiction authored by women and often intended for female audiences, who, the Lynds revealed, had constituted America's main reading population since the nineteenth century.

Doubleday did not object to Ferber's decision to serialize before publication. Publishers were rapidly discovering that although the number of American readers had grown since the late nineteenth century, most were library readers.[54] Wealthy women were the largest group of book buyers in America, but as leisure time and disposable income increased for most Americans following the First World War, publishers worked to capture new book-buying audiences from the middle and working classes. A book had a better chance of becoming a best seller if it reached a wider audience.[55] The audiences were, as the Lynds discovered, reading magazines and going to the movies. For a book to succeed in postwar America, it had to be marketed and exhibited in a variety of cultural venues. It also had to appeal to women, who now formed the heart of motion-picture audiences.[56]

Following the serialization of Ferber's work, which typically would be spread over a six-month period, Doubleday would heavily market the book, pushing a variety of editions and even selling reprint rights to different presses. Sometimes, Ferber would substantially change the novel's ending (as she did with *Come and Get It*), managing to recapture magazine readers who otherwise would not have bought the book version. More than any of her other Hollywood novels, *Come and Get It* focused on a hero's rather than a heroine's struggles. Ferber may have been aware that this novel had less appeal to her contingent of women readers.

Beginning in the 1920s, studios bought Ferber's work in part because she reached an audience that often went to the movies. In turn, Doubleday recognized that Ferber films added substantially to the novels' sales. Ferber usually managed to sell the film rights to her work during the initial serialization period, so that when her book finally did hit the stores, newspapers and trade papers would carry multiple articles and blurbs about her book and the film. During and after film production, Hollywood and Doubleday would negotiate a variety of hard- and paperback film editions—the most important with Grosset and Dunlap, which had been publishing classic and contemporary literature illustrated with film stills since the early twentieth century.[57] After the war, in an attempt to attract filmgoers as potential readers, dust jackets and paperbacks displayed scenes from the films with stars like Ingrid Bergman and Gary Cooper (*Saratoga Trunk*, 1946 editions) or Elizabeth Taylor and James Dean (*Giant*, 1957 editions). So while Hollywood profited from Ferber's best-selling status, the Hollywood films generated yet another cycle of publicity and revenue for Ferber and Doubleday.[58]

But astutely, she never trusted the film industry completely, reading the *Hollywood Reporter* and *Variety* religiously in case producers tried to capitalize on her name or her works.[59] Ferber never let producers read her work in advance and never gave interviews on her works in progress, all too aware of how Hollywood might infringe on her historical territory. In the midst of writing *Great Son* (a novel about nineteenth- and twentieth-century Seattle, which was purchased by Mike Todd but never filmed), she wrote to agent Leland Hayward, worried about a reference in the *Hollywood Reporter* about a new film on Seattle history: "Can you find out for me something about it? Without, I mean, having it leak out that I want to know. I'd hate to think that all my work might be for nothing," she anguished. "Can you let me know the period, the background—modern or otherwise—so that I may know whether I'll have to abandon my book. I think I have some rather good material and I'd hate to throw it all in the wastebasket."[60] Ferber was not just a born worrier; she knew that historical novelty was one of the secrets of her success in Hollywood.

The "Middlebrow" and Historical Fiction

Ferber's unrivalled business acumen helped make her America's top-selling female writer, according to the literary magazine the *Bookman*, which began publishing "best-seller" lists in 1895.[61] She was by no means the first best-selling female writer. Mary Johnston and Ellen Glasgow were both impressive precursors, often writing historical novels. In 1900, Mary Johnston had the number one best seller with *To Have and to Hold*, and she made it to number four in 1902 with *Audrey, Sir Mortimer* in 1905, *Lewis Rand* in 1908, and *The Long Roll* in 1911. Ellen Glasgow made the list with *The Deliverance* in 1904 and *The Wheel of Life* in 1906, and even beat Ferber's *Come and Get It* in the top ten list some thirty years later. Of all the writers on the list from 1900 through 1960, only turn-of-the-century novelist Winston Churchill outperformed Ferber, making the top ten nine times. Yet Ferber's seven best sellers were published between 1924 and 1958, when the publishing market was more competitive. As Alice Payne Hackett pointed out, *Publishers Weekly*, the main measuring stick after 1912, only lists books "distributed through the trade"—those sold through bookstores and purchased by libraries.[62] Copies of Ferber's books sold by mail order or by book clubs (and she was a regular pick of the Book-of-the-Month Club and the Literary Guild) were not included. If *Publishers Weekly* had recorded all of Ferber's sales, she probably would have been off the charts. But Ferber was so highly regarded that even the first instalment of her autobiography, *A Peculiar Treasure*, was rated number eight in the top ten for nonfiction for 1939. That year was a competitive one for nonfiction and memoirs; ironically, Ferber's book was narrowly outsold by Adolf Hitler's *Mein Kampf.*

But being a best-selling author does not guarantee long-term literary regard; in fact, American cultural critics almost always equate popularity with mediocrity. Indeed, Ferber's reputation has been in decline since her death. Just as film-studies scholars have paid more attention to Faulkner, Steinbeck, and Fitzgerald, literary historians have neglected Ferber in favor of her peers Willa Cather and Edith Wharton. Even Fannie Hurst has been revived, in large part because of her status as the author of *Imitation of Life* (1934), one of the earliest films to depict the dilemma of a mixed-race African American.[63] But Ferber's interest in the history of racial mixing and mixed-race protagonists endured throughout her career. Unlike Hurst, she did not simply dabble in the theme.

Although in 1925 she won the Pulitzer Prize for *So Big* and many critics routinely compared her favorably with Cather and Wharton (also Pulitzer Prize winners and best sellers), by 1952, the year of *Giant's* publication, Ferber was relegated to being only one of many popular writers in Edward Wagenknecht's massive *Cavalcade of the American Novel.* Even though Wagenknecht noted that the "thirties witnessed the first great revival of historical fiction since the turn of the century," Ferber was not mentioned.[64] While Cather's work merits an entire chapter, including a section on her attitude toward the American past, Ferber is relegated to a few sentences in the index. They are not flattering:

> Edna Ferber exemplifies the popular novelist of twentieth-century America whose books are usually best-sellers. Among others in this class are Kathleen Norris, Mary Roberts Rinehart, Janet Ayer Fairbank . . . Fannie Hurst, Frances Parkinson Keyes, Taylor Caldwell, and Marcia Davenport. All of these women have aimed at mass circulation and have consequently concerned themselves with themes which interest the average reader and handled them in a manner which the average reader can comprehend. They attempt little or no technical experimentation, and their principal appeal is to readers of their own sex. But they all know how to tell a story, and some of them sometimes produce a book which interests even readers of quality fiction.[65]

Wagenknecht's brand of criticism, with its misogynistic dismissal of female writers and popular women's fiction, is indicative of the kind of highbrow criticism advocated by Clement Greenberg and Dwight MacDonald.[66] MacDonald, in fact, would later foreground Ferber as a "masscult" blot on the American cultural landscape. In the opening sentences of "Masscult and Mid-cult" (1960), the conservative social critic damns her work as part of a mas-sive "parody of High Culture" and the descendant of "'servant-girl romances.'" Ferber was masscult personified because of her mastery of the modern mass media (Hollywood), her status as a best seller, and her "indifference" to critics like him. But like many advocates of high culture, MacDonald seemed am-biguous about the standards that define American "art."

Some critics appreciated the energy, vitality, and unique Americanness of the new "arts," including Gilbert Seldes and filmmaker Charles Chaplin, self-proclaimed "high lowbrows."[67] In later years, the influence of postmodern deconstructive criticism undermined the canons of critics like Greenberg and MacDonald. Once-reviled popular female novelists like Fannie Hurst are now studied as part of courses in literature and film studies. Academic engage-ments with film noir during the 1980s and 1990s elevated Raymond Chan-dler and Dashiell Hammett to artistic genius and even made Mickey Spillane's Mike Hammer thriller *I, the Jury* a subject of serious criticism.[68] For at least half a century, there has been widespread interest in rediscovering formerly spurned works of mass culture, whose authors compete in American studies courses with former icons of high culture like Fitzgerald, Hemingway, and Cather. Ferber, however, continues to be marginalized, largely because she is not, contrary to MacDonald, a true emblem of masscult. She is a much more dangerous writer: a middlebrow.

Ferber's historical research and writing, her popularity with critics like White and William Lyon Phelps, Hollywood's prestigious adaptations of her work, mark her as the consummate middlebrow. As Joan Shelley Rubin notes, middlebrows are not popular in the bifurcated world of American cultural criticism. Academics "have thus reified and perpetuated the conventional dichotomy between 'high' and 'popular' culture, overlooking the interaction that went on between the two."[69] Middlebrows retain some of the nineteenth century's faith in literary standards, intellectual argument, and Victorian self-improvement. During the first few decades after the First World War, they even created canons of their own in journals like the *Saturday Review* and in-stitutions like the Book-of-the-Month Club, making high culture accessible to the public. The Book-of-the-Month Club, launched in 1926, helped make *Show Boat*, *Cimarron*, and *Giant* best sellers. Middlebrow culture was not always such an unpopular topic. Van Wyck Brooks was perhaps the first American critic to call for "a genial middle ground" between elitism and low materialism in American culture. Women, as Margaret Widdemer writes in "Message and Middlebrow" (1933), were the backbone of this group.[70] They were the majority of the readers who supported culture by buying books and attending lectures. They would become Ferber's major audience.

Although it is difficult to pinpoint the gender demographics of Ferber's American film audiences, several critics, including Tino Balio and Steve Neale, have noted the connection between "prestige" filmmaking and women's films produced during the studio era.[71] Ferber's adapted works arguably represented the apex of this important production area. But it was not just Ferber's Pulitzer Prize and the admiration of populist critics like William Allen White that set her above female novelists like Marcia Davenport, Elizabeth Madox Roberts, Fannie Hurst, and Kathleen Winsor. Critics of Ferber's generation believed that her status as a serious American historical novelist and social critic set her apart from other best-selling writers. Her tendency to write about traditionally "masculine" historical topics like the American West also helped her win over male audiences and prevented critics from labeling Ferber adaptations "weepies" or "women's melodrama." Many of her staunchest supporters acknowledged Ferber's powerful female protagonists and female fan base but insisted that she was a national writer whose historical material transcended gender.

Similarly, though Ferber was proud of her Jewish heritage and spoke at length in her autobiographies about early confrontations with anti-Semitism during her midwestern childhood and later sojourns as a reporter and writer in Chicago, New York, and Europe, the protagonists of her historical novels are not Jewish Americans.[72] While respected female Jewish American writers like Emma Lazarus and Anzia Yezierska combined narratives about Jewish culture and family with themes of assimilation and American identity, Ferber's characters are largely secular Christians.[73] Although sympathetic Jewish characters like Schultzy (*Show Boat*) and Sol Levy (*Cimarron*) populate her American landscape, she did not write ethnic American histories about Jews. Instead, she subsumed her American Jewish "outsider" identity and heritage in dramas involving discrimination against mixed-race, Native, African, and Mexican Americans. But in writing principally about the history of ordinary American women, Ferber retained another dimension of her identity as an American outsider (that is, as a working woman), channeled and marketed it to a wider and undoubtedly more sympathetic reading and viewing audience. If, as Ferber believed, America was "the Jew among nations," then women were Ferber's chosen people. In 1963, she argued that women "have had to be smarter in order to survive . . . They are smarter for the same reason that Jews are often considered smarter than non-Jews. Hounded and bedeviled and persecuted, granted few rights and fewer privileges, they learned—the rejected Female and the rejected Jew—perforce to see through the back of their heads as well as through the front of their heads."[74]

Although Edna Ferber's America was a history of its outsiders and was often fiercely critical of the white male establishment, her supporters promoted her as an American institution. In 1954, Vincent Starrett of the *New York Herald Tribune* defined her as America's preeminent historical novelist and admired her impact on Hollywood: "For Miss Ferber is first of all an exciting story-teller." Her novels are "sentimental, pictorial, and resistlessly 'readable'. (I am sorry for critics who find these virtues negligible!) But they are realistic, too, when realism is called for; and they contain a social criticism that hasty readers do not catch. Above all, I would painstakingly point out, they are American; for Miss Ferber is one of the most enthusiastically American of contemporary novelists."[75] Starrett defended Ferber as both a consummate storyteller and an incisive historian. Yet here was the great irony: the historical perspective that distinguished Ferber from other writers also undermined her authority as a serious historian and novelist.

Women and the Historical Tradition

Though Ferber's popularity as a historical novelist and her ability to master various forms of twentieth-century media are unrivalled in her own generation of writers, American women had a long history as best-selling authors during the nineteenth century. This was in part due to their status as consumers of culture after 1850. As literary historians Nina Baym and Ann Douglas have pointed out, American women led the publishing market throughout the nineteenth century. Elite writers with abstruse literary qualities like Herman Melville and Nathaniel Hawthorne may dominate critical appraisals of American fiction during the nineteenth century, but it was female authors who truly approached the modern concept of a best seller. As Baym writes, "It is widely agreed that since the middle of the nineteenth century, no book can hope for popular success if it does no attract large numbers of women readers, because women were and are the majority of readers in America."[76]

Women's fiction usually tells the story of a young woman who has to make her own way in the world without the usual familial, social, or economic supports to cling to. They are stories of struggle, success, and accomplishment—even if, quite often, though not always, the ultimate accomplishment and conclusion of the tale is a happy marriage.[77] But most of the novel deals with the heroine's struggle to conquer an insecure, indifferent, and even hostile world. As Ann Douglas writes, "Sentimental 'domestic novels' written largely by women for women dominated the literary market in America from the 1840s through the 1880s. Middle-class women became in a very real sense the consumers of literature. The stories they read and wrote were themselves courses in the shopping mentality, exercises in euphemism essential to the system of flattery which served as the rationale for the American woman's economic position."[78] But as Nina Baym argues, many more show women working and achieving within the capitalist system—a path that Ferber would later take.

Ferber read voraciously as a young woman, and it is very likely that Susan Warner's *The Wide, Wide World* (1850) was one of her early influences. The book was the first of the best-selling domestic novels about the unwillingness of a young girl (Ellen Montgomery) to participate in the wide world of economic competition. Ellen's father is an ineffectual man who loses both a lawsuit and his income, so Ellen must work. Ironically, something similar happened to Ferber when her father, Jacob, an unsuccessful storekeeper, went blind. Although her mother, Julia, tried to run the business, take care of her husband, and raise her two girls, Ferber's dreams of finishing college and attending dramatic school were over. She went to work as a reporter, and turned novelist and short story writer when a brief illness prevented her from continuing her reporting job. The savior of the Ferber family finances was another single working woman, Emma McChesney.[79] Emma and later Selina Peake in *So Big*, Magnolia in *Show Boat*, and Sabra in *Cimarron* went to work when the traditional patriarchal structures failed—but these women thrived on the experiences.

Harriet Beecher Stowe's *The Minister's Wooing* (1869) contained a precedent for *Cimarron*'s relationship between Yancey and Sabra. The heroine, Mary Scudder, also must fend for herself. As Douglas writes, "It is the men in her world who are, economically, at best unreliable, at worst downright shiftless." Mary's mother supported a visionary but profligate father. Later, she and her mother look after the local minister, who cannot take care of himself or his flock. "Mrs. Stowe is offering an economic critique here, if a symbolic one,"

Douglas argues. "The male poets and preachers think while their women work."[80] This pairing of a weak man with a strong woman would become the mainstay of Ferber's America. But Ferber's closest connection to Stowe was through *Uncle Tom's Cabin* (1852). After the publication of *Show Boat*, critics frequently linked Ferber's name with Harriet Beecher Stowe's. The first half of Ferber's novel is structured around the exposure of a mixed-race actress during the postbellum South. This woman, Julie Laverne, is the heroine's best friend and confidante, and the rest of the novel resonates with their physical, cultural, and spiritual closeness. The references to Stowe continued with *Giant*'s revelation of contemporary Jim Crow laws in Texas, although many irate Texans used Stowe's name as a curse rather than a compliment. Filmmakers also saw her as Stowe's heir. Harry A. Pollard, who had directed the lavish 1927 version of *Uncle Tom's Cabin* for Universal, was assigned to direct the first production of *Show Boat*, in 1928. In early 1944, producer Arthur Hornblow was planning another remake of *Uncle Tom's Cabin* (with Paul Robeson), and agent Leland Hayward reported, "He and I were talking about writers for it and I said the one perfect person in the world to write it would be Edna Ferber. He agrees entirely."[81]

Ferber's novels also commanded a social power akin to Stowe's. The story of President Lincoln and Stowe's first meeting, in which he credited her book with precipitating the Civil War, is well known.[82] But Ferber's presentation of prejudice against Mexican Americans prompted some prominent Texans to attack the book, undercut its reviews in major periodicals like the *Saturday Review*, insinuate that the author was a communist, and even censor George Stevens's film in its Latin American runs. Later, Ferber's writing on Alaskan race relations and the exploitation of the territory had a direct influence on the congressional decision to grant statehood. Governor Ernest Gruening would later call *Ice Palace* "the *Uncle Tom's Cabin* of the crusade for statehood."[83]

Stowe allegedly did a great deal of historical research on American slavery, but her 1852 best seller was not a historical novel but a contemporary melodrama. While many of the nineteenth-century best sellers were contemporary novels about good conduct and self-sacrifice, a few very prominent women made their names as writers of historical fiction, including Lydia Child (*Hobomok*, 1824; *The Rebels*, 1825), Catharine Sedgwick (*Hope Leslie*, 1827; *The Linwoods*, 1835), and Helen Hunt Jackson (*Ramona*, 1884). These writers created heroic female protagonists. In addition, like Ferber's future work, *Hobomok* and *Hope Leslie* both deal with women's relations with other exploited minority groups; Hope Leslie even rescues a young Native American woman from prison. Helen Hunt Jackson created a powerful mixed Native American heroine, something Ferber would develop in *Cimarron* and *Ice Palace*.

Although many female novelists of contemporary fiction raised the tone of their romantic quests with discourses on theology and morality, these were subjects long associated with the "women's sphere." Even Stowe's unique use of a serious political issue in *Uncle Tom's Cabin* was cushioned within a sentimental morality tale with exaggerated, melodramatic characters and situations. In contrast, history drew a select group of novelists into a realm hitherto dominated by men; history was a means of "elevating" the cultural value of women's literature, though, as Bonnie Smith points out, female historians suffered constantly under male charges of incompetence and amateurish research and writing: "Amateur writing came to be seen as in some way fit for women—women who made their living by writing for the marketplace, outside the more exclusive professional institutions of history. This kind of market-driven work was interpreted by later professionals as base, catering to low reading tastes, and distinct from the high-quality work of affluent men outside the academy. Women were the quintessential amateurs, who dealt with the market; men, the appropriate professionals, who served more lofty ends."[84] Like her predecessors, Ferber would also use the historical novel to her advantage, capitalizing on the middlebrow trend for cultural elevation. Doubleday's publicity and syndicated interviews emphasized the meticulous historical research behind the best-selling narratives. Ferber's intellectual, high-culture cachet was dependent upon her use of American history, but ironically, she would suffer at the hands of critics who attacked both her lack of literary style and overly "colorful," hybrid, amateur women's history.

This disdain for female historians and historical novelists dates from at least the late nineteenth century. When Ferber was born, in 1886, the American historical profession was undergoing a serious transformation. More and more, male writers of history were consolidating the writing of history as a masculine profession. Women had long been respected national historians. Mercy Otis Warren's *History of the Rise, Progress, and Termination of the America Revolution* (1805) was published in multiple editions, and Martha Lamb, author of *The History of the City of New York* (1877–1881) and editor of the *Magazine of American History*, was one of the most widely read historians of her generation.[85] But with the redefinition of history as a "professional" rather than a "popular" field, women were increasingly robbed of their historical authority.

They were excluded from universities, denied access to archives, and refused membership in learned historical societies. Scientific, Rankean-derived historiography demanded endless facts and archival research and tended to focus on the "masculine" realms of diplomatic and political history. Underlying this national reconstruction of the profession was the long-standing popular veneration of the great male life. Female historians lacked the credentials for such work, and because of their propensity to examine social and cultural history, they were dismissed as popular, unreliable historians.

Douglas argues that female historians and historical novelists have suffered greater professional exclusion in the United States than in Europe because "in a country like America whose historical identity rests on a short series of self-conscious crises, the exclusion of women from the historical life of the culture is particularly acute. American history does not reach back into an irrecoverable past; hence it nowhere takes on in retrospect the aspect of process which interweaves it inexorably with social life. We have marble busts of all our great leaders . . . men keep public records; women seldom figure in them, much less keep them."[86] But female historians often rejected both the style and content of these rigid patriarchal narratives and biographies, writing historical novels that "express discreetly veiled hostility to the very history they were apparently extolling."[87] While Catherine Sedgwick created fearless, unconventional fictional heroines, female historians pursued social and cultural history as a historiographic antidote to great men and endless battles.

By 1900, women were not only infiltrating the American Historical Association and low-level university positions across the country, but also writing popular and professional history and historical fiction that conflicted with both areas of masculine historiography: the dry, ivory-tower lists of facts and the popular heroic masculine biography. Women impacted American history at every level—as elementary school teachers, journalists, and novelists. Julie Des Jardins comments, "Often their bottom-up methods for the dissemination of social and cultural history mirrored their insightful methods of historical analysis. As marginal figures to the historical profession, many represented pasts of Americans marginalized by race, class, ethnicity, or gender in ways that scholars have little acknowledged." Women were more inclined to take a critical historical perspective: "Whereas men often viewed the American past superficially as one of perpetual progress, these women peeled back the layers to see it as a patterned prevailing of power."[88]

In 1917, historian and educator Lucy Salmon speculated in *What Is Modern History?* that recent nativist paranoia instigated by patriotic groups revealed the prevailing ignorance of ethnic history in American schools. The history of America, Salmon argues, is a narrative of racial and ethnic mixture: "How can we deal with the melting pot in America unless we know that races have always mingled and intermingled? . . . I have always felt that our great strength as a nation has come from the mingling of the many races."[89] Ferber was not the only historical writer to share Salmon's perspective on the American past. During the 1920s and 1930s, female historians increasingly focused on issues of race, gender, and national history. Native American historians Angie Debo and Mari Sandoz and women's historian Mary Beard were Ferber's ivory-tower equivalents, exposing the racist practices of the federal government and the patriarchal structures of American history.[90]

But though Beard was fairly well known through her collaborative histories with husband Charles Beard (*The Rise of American Civilization*, 1927), her individual work was not as widely read. Debo was next to unknown until her death. In contrast, Ferber had a readership numbering hundreds of thousands. However, both Mari Sandoz and Ferber traded on their historical hybridity on many levels. Like Ferber, Sandoz specialized in highlighting controversial aspects of American social history, reaching many mainstream readers. Like many of Ferber's historical novels, Sandoz's *Old Jules* (1935) was a "middle-brow" selection of the Book-of-the-Month Club. But while Ferber's historical fiction covers a broad landscape of racial, ethnic, and gendered conflicts, Sandoz focuses on the experience of Native American men in imaginative biographies and social histories, setting Native American masculinity in opposition to the dominant narratives of the white West. As Suzanne Clark notes, "In book after book about the Great Plains during the Cold War, Sandoz promoted a revulsion against assimilating national high-handedness, questioned the recording of Western history, and promoted sympathy for the alternative histories of the American Indian."[91] In spite of Sandoz's harsh critiques of the U.S. government, *Old Jules* (1935), *Crazy Horse* (1941), and *Cheyenne Autumn* (1953) reached wide audiences, and ten years after its publication, when pro-Native American westerns were more fashionable, John Ford filmed *Cheyenne Autumn* (1964) with actor Richard Widmark. Both Ferber and Sandoz wrote counternarratives of the American West that reached mainstream audiences, and Sandoz's work on *Cheyenne Autumn* arguably influenced Ferber in the last decade of her working life.[92]

But Ferber's closest friendship with another female historian was with Margaret Leech (Mrs. Ralph "Peg" Pulitzer), whose work on postwar Washington won the Pulitzer Prize in 1942 and 1960.[93] Although Ferber and Leech corresponded regularly throughout their lives, they did not discuss American history, social criticism, or their books. True, they had different historical interests; Leech was primarily a political historian and a biographer of prominent American men. Ferber chose to keep her thoughts about American history and the role played by women and minorities in its development to herself—with one major exception. She communicated her historical vision to Hollywood.

Edna Ferber's Hollywood

Ferber's novels and Hollywood's adaptations of her work confront the major issues facing American identity and society in the nineteenth and twentieth centuries: the disappearance of the frontier, the rise of immigration, the ongoing exploitation of women and racial and ethnic minorities, the crisis of historical relativism, and the nation's enduring fascination with its own past. Ferber herself was bewitched by America's history and what she saw as its "violent, varied . . . insular, spectacular" qualities.[94] In many ways, Ferber remained a nineteenth-century American, her progressive political and social attitudes coexisting with a modern, critical perspective on the past and a mastery of the postwar media. But her historical perspective was always controversial.

This book contextualizes Ferber's work and her cinematic legacy within four historiographic areas: the roles of American women in history, literature, and cinema; classic and more recent perspectives on mixed-race Americans; Hollywood's commitment to American historical filmmaking; and finally and most crucially, classical Hollywood's long-term investment in the adaptation of her work. *Edna Ferber's Hollywood* locates the writer's reputation and impact on Hollywood through an intertextual historical analysis of her writing, literary publicity, reception and criticism, legal negotiations and contracts, private letters, interviews, annotated screenplays, production correspondence, studio publicity, audience previews, national critical reception, and, where possible, domestic and foreign box-office reports. While the writing of history is itself an exercise in adaptation, Ferber's career pushed the meaning of the term to its modern media limits. Her revisionist historical novels were in turn adapted and reenvisioned by countless Hollywood filmmakers in multiple remakes that added new layers of cultural context, historical argument, and images of American race and womanhood to her original narratives.

Edna Ferber's Hollywood is not a traditional literary biography or analysis of Hollywood adaptation. Each chapter focuses upon one or two of Ferber's historical novels and the subsequent film versions, and these do proceed in sequence according to the books' initial publication dates. The structure is not intended to give priority to the literary text over the subsequent film versions, as do many traditional adaptation studies.[95] Indeed, such a structure would hardly suit Ferber, a writer distinctly outside the canons of American literature and historiography—and proud of her status. As I argue here, Ferber's writing cannot be considered in isolation from Hollywood and its complex networks of projecting and marketing American history. Each chapter explores a unique set of critical and historical contexts that impacted the historical narratives.

In addition, each chapter is deeply connected to a particular aspect of historiography, literature, and social history affecting the American West and South. Ferber and Hollywood shared a biregional historical vision of America. While the cinematic preoccupation with the West and the South has produced its share of ideologically conservative, misogynistic, and racist historical films, Hollywood's commitment to Ferber represented a large investment in American counterhistories. With this in mind, I have organized the first few chapters to alternate between the revisionist westerns *So Big* (Chapter Two) and *Cimarron* (Chapter Four), on the one hand, and the equally revisionist southern-belle epic *Show Boat* (Chapter Three), on the other, until Chapter Five, which examines both the frontier history of *Come and Get It* and *Saratoga Trunk*'s mixture of western and southern themes. In Chapter Six, *Giant* integrates the two regional perspectives with the Jim Crow treatment of Mexican Americans. It is significant for me to end the book with *Ice Palace*, not only because it was Ferber's last book and the last Warner Bros. film that came out of their historic partnership, but also because *Ice Palace*'s history as a cultural entity links the theme of the end of the frontier with the dying Hollywood studio system.

Part of Ferber's uniqueness certainly lay in her ability to connect the revisionist historical trends in American social and cultural historiography during the first half of the twentieth century with the cultural power of Hollywood. She was, in many ways, the ultimate middlebrow, mediating the worlds of traditional and revisionist history, history and fiction, high art and mass culture. Edna Ferber's America was inherently multiracial and multiethnic; it was a woman's as well as a man's country; it was struggle, conflict, intrigue, disillusionment, poverty, and racism. Edna Ferber's Hollywood was a testimony to the power, challenges, and contradictions of middlebrow culture. The filmmakers capitalized on the historical prestige of a Ferber adaptation, carefully presenting the historical authority of a woman, a novelist, and a Jew. Her critical perspectives on the past, race, and gender also fit with Hollywood's own ambition to produce a national historical genre that appealed to women.

Although essentially an American author, Ferber's fan base was international. Fellow Doubleday writer and fan Rebecca Reyher wrote to her shortly after the run of *Giant*, quoting a woman from Ceylon: "'It's a story that appeals to Ceylon. The rich Benedict family, thinking themselves better than everyone else coming down in the world. The poor man getting ahead, and the son marrying an Indian girl, and the brown baby being the one to carry on the family name!'" Reyher continued, "They ought to have a revival of *Show Boat* here regularly, they would eat it up in all the coloured countries."[96] The dramas of race, gender, and nation appealed to women around the globe. Yet like so many American female historians and novelists, Edna Ferber's fame and legacy have been disparaged by a misogynistic critical culture. It may seem surprising that Hollywood, often defined as a hegemonic culture industry driven by male fantasies, should have championed Ferber's work for so long. Perhaps Hollywood's reputation, like Edna Ferber's, demands a new perspective.

two

The Life of an Unknown Woman

SO BIG, 1923–1953

n 1924, when Edna Ferber published *So Big*, she was one of America's most successful serial fiction writers. Her modern stories of divorced mother and midwestern saleswoman Emma McChesney had made her a household name among female readers. She published her first novel in 1911, and a few years later sold the semiautobiographical *Fanny Herself* (1917) to Universal Studios. In 1920, she wrote her first historical novel, *The Girls*, a chronicle of three generations of middle-class Chicago women and their struggles for personal and financial independence from the Civil War to the aftermath of the First World War. Although Ferber had slowly constructed a large and loyal group of female readers, she had not yet produced a best seller in the emerging national book market and had made only tentative forays into Hollywood.

But with *So Big*, Ferber achieved three major breakthroughs. The novel proved to Hollywood that Ferber's work was worth serious investment, initiating a four-decade filmmaking partnership with Warner Bros. She became increasingly known as the nation's most popular writer of American historical fiction, with a decided interest in generational novels focusing on the experiences of women. Perhaps most surprisingly, *So Big* won the Pulitzer Prize for fiction in 1925, beating the more modish work of Joseph Hergescheimer (*Balisand*) and the war fiction of Laurence Stallings (*Plumes*). With a Pulitzer Prize to her credit, critics were less apt to blithely dismiss Ferber as "a woman's magazine writer" or "a lady novelist." However, since then critics have debated whether the best-selling author really deserved an award designed to create and authenticate a canon of great American literature. Others have dismissed the book because of its enduring popularity with Hollywood.

Arguably, literary standards mattered little to Ferber. A developed character was, for her, one who exhibited the complex and contradictory qualities of his or her historical era; a good plot was not literary ingenuity—it was simply good history. Most crucially, in an era dominated by experimental fiction (Gertrude Stein); modernist themes of adultery, addiction, and disillusionment (Ernest Hemingway, F. Scott Fitzgerald); and distinctions between high art and mass culture (George Jean Nathan), *So Big* returned to the nineteenth century and the life of an unknown woman in a cutthroat capitalist economy. Neither fashionable nor famous, Ferber's heroine was simply a brave widow and mother struggling for independence and spiritual survival in a culture that placed little value on integrity, simplicity, or faith in oneself.

Yet *So Big* also profited from the expanding media culture of the postwar era. Initially, Ferber had no hopes for her story of a poor Illinois truck farmer named Selina Peake. As she recalled some fifteen years later, "I wrote it against my judgment; I wanted to write it." She added, "Nothing ever really happened in the book. It had no plot at all, as book plots go. It had a theme, but you had to read that for yourself between the lines." If anything, she argued, "it was a story of the triumph of failure."[1] She sent it off to the prestigious publisher Doubleday with misgivings and even apologies, telling Russell Doubleday: "I think its publication as a book would hurt you, as publishers, and me as an author."[2] As she later wrote, "Who would be interested in a novel about a middle-aged woman in a calico dress with wispy hair and bad teeth, grubbing on a little truck farm south of Chicago?"[3] But Russell Doubleday loved it, and the press mass-marketed the book, selling hundreds of thousands of copies in the first year alone.[4] *So Big* became the unlikely publishing phenomenon of the 1920s.

This chapter, the first critical look at Ferber's best-selling historical novel, focuses on several key issues: *So Big*'s status as both a mass- and multimarketed best seller and a product of the 1920s middlebrow cultural hierarchy;

Ferber's construction of a uniquely feminist, critical view of American history and its western pioneers; and Ferber's and Selina's rejection of modern American materialism and other dominant values of the 1920s. Perhaps the greatest irony of *So Big*'s popularity was that Ferber made thousands of dollars on Selina's rejection of wealth, power, and the modern fascination with public success. While Selina talked of the uniqueness of an independent artistic American vision, Ferber made those very qualities saleable commodities by the postwar culture industries. This ideological contradiction resonates more broadly with what Lynn Dumenil and other historians identify as postwar America's defining modern and antimodern cultural perspectives.[5] Ferber's novel embodies the era's conflicted attitudes toward the frontier myth, immigration and cultural pluralism, working women and mothers, and creativity and material success. But this chapter is also the history of Ferber's relationship with Warner Bros. (which would also produce *Saratoga Trunk*, *Giant*, and *Ice Palace*), her most important association in Hollywood. For decades, the studio would make hundreds of thousands of dollars adapting and remaking "Edna Ferber's Pulitzer Prize–Winning Best-Seller" for female audiences, carefully balancing its high-art themes and reputation with its mass appeal. It is perhaps a measure of Ferber's reputation that a novel "without a plot . . . or action" could hold Hollywood's interest for twenty years. But *So Big* initiated a Ferber genre of women's historical fiction that would form a significant component of Hollywood film production through the 1950s. Selina's anonymity, ironically, helped make Ferber famous.

Ferber: At Odds with 1920s America?

Scholars have long emphasized the ideological transformation of America in the 1920s, the postwar rebellion against Victorian "conformity" in literature, music, and lifestyles. But the romantic images of the Lost Generation and short-skirted flappers were hardly representative of mainstream America. More recent research has acknowledged that the forces of modernity (industrialization, immigration, urbanization) stretched far back into the nineteenth century and that even the arts, the position of women, and conventional morality had begun to change by the 1890s. However, the economic, social, and cultural transformations of the 1920s, bracketed by the aftermath of the First World War and the onset of the Great Depression, were very real. American industry adapted the mass-production techniques learned during the war for a domestic consumer market. Robert and Helen Lynd's sociological study *Middletown* (1929) chronicles the rapid changes in the work of men and women, transportation, leisure, education, and marriage. But the Lynds conclude that however quickly America was transforming into a modern consumer society, many nineteenth-century values were slower to change: "Bathrooms and electricity have pervaded the homes of the city more rapidly than innovations in the personal adjustments between husband and wife or parents and children."[6]

More recently, historian Stanley Coben argued that the 1920s witnessed "the first strong nationwide rebellion" against Victorian values, but "the powerful assaults launched against Victorian culture during the twentieth century failed to replace most essential aspects of that culture with durable values, concepts, and institutions derived from the severe critiques."[7] Although Coben's main bastion of nineteenth-century Victorianism is confined to the rise of the second Ku Klux Klan, other historians and cultural critics have provided a more nuanced picture of the modern-antimodern dialectic operating in America after the war. Resistance to "modernity" was reflected not simply by religious fundamentalism, anti-immigrationism, and the resurgence of the Klan. As Joan Shelley Rubin points out, despite most historians' adherence to the belief in the twentieth-century decline of "the genteel tradition," the rise of middlebrow culture and new public cultural hierarchies represented the persistence of the Victorian belief in great literature and art, self-improvement, and intellectual and spiritual values.[8]

I would also argue that Edna Ferber's ability to market American history and old-fashioned "pioneer" values to 1920s audiences demonstrated the persistence of Victorianism in America. But too often, as in the work of Coben, Victorianism is confused with the repression of women, religious hypocrisy, social conformity, and racism. To many in Ferber's generation, Victorianism meant individuality, self-reliance, a strong work ethic, and a commitment to social improvement. Ferber's body of work and even her own lifestyle celebrated these very qualities. Her lifelong writing regimen; her commitment to strenuous daily exercise; the historical qualities of endurance, independence, and change she explored in her novels; and the lives of her imagined Americans, including *So Big*'s Selina Peake, were testimonials. It is easy to see why Ferber's three personal American heroes were Ida Tarbell, Jane Addams, and Theodore Roosevelt.[9] Ferber shared Roosevelt's commitment to the "strenuous life" and the legacy of the nation's pioneer heritage without necessarily adhering to his racial convictions.

But perhaps most crucially, Tarbell and Addams were feminist icons to women of Ferber's generation. Tarbell and Addams spent their lives trying to improve the condition of working-class Americans suffering from the effects of modernity. Tarbell shared Ferber's background as a crusading reporter and, throughout her career, combined a commitment to the betterment of the lives of urban women and children with popular historical writing—her biographies of Lincoln were some of the best known of the early twentieth century.[10] Addams's work on behalf of suffrage, maternal care, and child labor would cause conservative Americans (many of them women) to malign her as "one of the enemies of our government" and a communist. Although far less subject to such criticism, Ferber's work, which celebrated the modern effects of immigration, racial and cultural mixing, and working women and mothers, made her vulnerable to anticommunist witch-hunting.[11] In addition, though Addams is best known now as a leader in the Progressive movement, she also believed in the power of women's collective and individual memories to uphold and challenge the social order.[12] Like Ferber, Addams saw women's vision of the past as essentially different from that of men. By the 1920s, these three Americans, like Ferber's heroine, belonged to another era. But Ferber believed that Selina's life was crucial for the modern generation to read about and understand.

So Big and the Frontiers of American History

Ferber did not become a best-selling author by accident. An astute business-woman, she maximized her potential readership by serializing *So Big* in the *Woman's Home Companion* from December 1923 to March 1924 in anticipation of its publication in book form on 1 March. The journal had one of the largest readerships in America, and like the *Ladies' Home Journal* and the *Saturday Evening Post*, routinely published fiction and human-interest articles by nationally renowned writers, including Zane Grey and F. Scott Fitzgerald. But Ferber had an advantage over her male peers: she wrote about women, and most American readers in the 1920s were women. With serialization, she reached women of all ages who otherwise did not read literature or could not afford to buy her novels.

As the author of the well-known Emma McChesney stories, Ferber was arguably one of the most highly paid magazine writers in the country. Serialization rights for *So Big* commanded $35,000. Like Emma, Selina was the centerpiece of Ferber's narrative. In fact, the original title appearing in the magazine was *Selina*, emphasizing the narrative as a fictional biography. Ferber disliked her final title, *So Big*, but changed it only because calling the work *Selina* seemed "a lazy way out of the difficulty."[13] In addition, female authors during the Victorian era routinely titled their works with the first names of their teary-eyed, timid heroines, and Ferber may have been wary of designating her book as simply "women's fiction."

So Big narrates the life of Selina Peake, the daughter of a debonair, cultured professional gambler. As a child in the 1880s, Selina was toted all over Europe and America, but she settles outside Chicago after her improvident father is shot in a gambling house. Simeon Peake was a dreamer, and although he provided his daughter with a deep love of life and beauty, he could not support her financially. With few options open to poor young women, Selina goes to work as a schoolteacher in High Prairie, a Dutch settlement south of Chicago. She intends to work there for only a couple of years before qualifying to teach at a city school, but isolation, loneliness, and pity drive her to marry impoverished truck farmer Pervus DeJong. For years, DeJong resists all of Selina's suggestions to adopt modern farming methods. It is only after his death that she is able to carry out her plans to make the DeJong farmstead an independent producer of high-quality vegetables, thereby ensuring her survival in an increasingly competitive market. In the meantime, the diminutive, stylish young lady is bowed, coarsened, and aged by working in the fields. But Selina is still happy. Although she has a deep love of the earth, she works in order to give her son, Dirk (nicknamed "Sobig"), all the advantages possible. More than anything else, Selina wants to bequeath her vision of life and her love of beauty to her son. Unfortunately, she lives to see him give up architecture for the more lucrative and fashionable field of bond selling, have an affair with a married flapper, and be labelled one of the generation's "jeunesse dorée."

So Big was the first of Ferber's novels to consider the legacy of the pioneer woman in the development of the nation. Ferber was fascinated not only by Selina's physical impact on the land and the economy but also by her intellectual and spiritual gifts. But as Ferber indicates, Selina's son does not inherit these more abstract qualities. While Dirk blindly follows the path to wealth, it is her former pupil Roelf Pool who is inspired to leave High Prairie for Europe. Years later, a world-renowned sculptor, he returns to visit her. Selina's lifework survives in Roelf. Ironically, Roelf even physically resembles Selina more than her own golden-haired son does. Selina's "fine great dark eyes" and "dark abundant hair" are shared by Roelf, first described by Ferber as a "dark, handsome sullen boy" whose eyes could blaze with beauty.[14] When Selina sees him on her first evening in High Prairie, she is "inexplicably drawn" to the quiet outsider. Although Roelf is Dutch, he is as different from his blond, plump family and bovine neighbors as Selina. He is the only other person in the Dutch settlement to find the abundant landscape beautiful, the only one to create things for people's pleasure, and the only other person interested in reading books (the first time she sees him, Roelf is struggling to read the dictionary by firelight—a modern Lincoln).

Arguably, Ferber's belief in pluralism is what connects her to the more overtly modernist writers in 1920s America. Walter Benn Michaels's study of postwar American literature looks beyond the traditional Lost Generation canon to include writers like Zane Grey (*The Vanishing American*, 1925) and sociologist Edward Sapir among its case studies.[15] While Michaels argues for a more complex definition of modern American literature in the 1920s, he presents, with the exception of Willa Cather (*The Professor's House*, 1925), an exclusively male canon, which ignores the best-selling work of Edna Ferber and other middlebrows.[16] In addition, as literary scholar Donna Campbell points out, Michaels's proposal that "the great American modernist texts of the '20s must be understood as deeply committed to the nativist project of racializing the American" is flawed without any consideration of Ferber's work. According to Campbell, Ferber's work "confronts the nativism of the 1920s" through "the theme of exogamy or intermarriage," portraying heroines who are racially linked to other, darker ethnicities.[17] But Ferber's challenge to the racialization project of 1920s literature was even more subversive. While writers like Fitzgerald and Cather were preoccupied with defining a racially pure American, Ferber was fascinated with historicizing ethnic and racial mixing as a means of dramatizing the future of America. Racial mixing was not simply a condition of the postwar era, to be either celebrated or lamented—it was part of the nation's history.

Selina is the first of these "dark" heroines, but hers is a spiritual and intellectual, rather than an overtly defined ethnic or racial, difference. Selina's forebears may have come from New England, but her outlook on life is as different from that of the High Prairie Dutch as it is from those of the fast-paced cosmopolitans of the Lost Generation. When she first arrives in High Prairie, Selina is struck by the complacency and even vacancy of the people around her. Sex roles are rigidly defined. Men make decisions about the farm; women are silent. But women work in the fields like men as well as in the house. They are drudges like poor Maartje Pool, who, though only twenty-eight, looks like an old woman. When Selina asks the High Prairie men about fertilization and farming methods, they stare at her, speechless, for "in High Prairie women did not brazenly intrude thus on men's weighty conversation."[18] Later, when she tells Pervus they must drain some waterlogged acreage, plant different crops, and make use of the new farming techniques she has been reading about, he merely laughs at her: "What was good enough for my father is good enough for me."[19] It is Selina, a woman and an ethnic outsider, who advocates change and development.

Set apart from the people of High Prairie both physically and intellectually, Selina is a courageous but lonely woman. High Prairie, Illinois, is not the Wild West of *Cimarron* and *Come and Get It* and *Ice Palace*, but Selina is a frontierswoman. Ferber first describes her heroine as working like a man in the fields, and periodically alludes to her "pioneering" characteristics: "You saw a young woman in a blue calico dress, faded and earth-grimed. Between her eyes was a driven look as of one who walks always a little ahead of herself in her haste." Her hands "were usually too crusted and inground with the soil into which she was delving."[20] She wears men's boots and her husband's old hat, and is the first woman to drive her vegetables to the Haymarket in 1890s Chicago. Although Selina's wilderness is now a food-growing garden, supplying the demands of elite Chicago, women have little power in the community and are often lonely. Only the Widow Paarlenberg and Selina have any measure of power. The widow's position derives from her husband's property and her status as a single woman. Selina, interestingly, speaks out before, during, and after her marriage to the impoverished and ignorant farmer Pervus DeJong, but achieves autonomy and productive change only after his death.

Many feminist historians of women on the American frontier have argued that "instead of freeing women from social constraints, the West 'isolated women from other women, heightened their vulnerability to men, and increased their domestic work load.'"[21] Certainly, it was Selina's sense of personal and physical isolation that caused her to mismarry the stolid Pervus DeJong and wreck her youth with hard work. Selina sees this not as a tragedy, but rather as an opportunity to embrace life, the landscape, and America's glorious future for productivity. In Selina's world, women work harder because they do the work of both sexes, but unlike men, they can succeed at doing all sorts of work. When Pervus objects to Selina's leaving her domestic space to work in the fields with him, she responds, "Nonsense, Pervus. Working in the fields is no harder than washing or ironing or scrubbing or standing over a hot stove in August. Women's work! Housework's the hardest work in the world. That's why men won't do it."[22]

In discussing nineteenth-century women's writing about the West, the historian Brigitte Georgi-Findlay points out that women's more circumscribed domestic sphere and interests "can be read not only as the basis for a female countervision to male fantasies of conquest and possession, but as in fact, complementary to them: the ideal of domesticity, read in a context of empire building, also functions as an instrument for imposing cultural and social control and order upon the 'disorderly' classes of the West."[23] In *So Big*, Ferber acknowledges that Selina's background and domestic pursuits—reading about farming; appreciating literature, art, and beauty; talking; improving the aesthetic and practical appeal of her home and garden—help transform her dilapidated farm into something modern, productive, and beautiful and even help Roelf escape High Prairie's prescribed roles for men. It is Selina's drive for improvement that makes her a success and leads the way in the modernization of agriculture in the Midwest; the woman does make the wilderness a garden—but a useful and successful garden nonetheless. Ferber's heroine is therefore the impetus behind traditional frontier development. Selina is not interested in social control or in maintaining the exacting standards from back east, but in agricultural progress, growth, and the preservation of the American spirit, aims that continue to be associated with masculine frontier development. In her understanding and spiritual kinship with the productive land ("Cabbages are beautiful," she affirms, finding beauty in what others consider pointless toil), Selina resembles her masculine pioneer forebears. However, the men of her generation have lost this understanding. Selina even articulates this connection, forming her own philosophy of American development: "As cabbages had been cabbages, and no more, to Klaas Pool, or, to Pervus, these carrots, beets, onions, turnips, and radishes were just so much produce." But, Ferber continued, "Selina sensed something of the meaning behind these toiling, patient figures, all unconscious of meaning, bent double in the fields for miles throughout High Prairie."[24]

While the outsider Selina embodies pioneering spirit and drive, the High Prairie Dutch immigrants seem to perpetuate the mistakes of their European forebears. Women are kept to their minimal domestic roles, and men keep to their fathers' farming methods, regardless of financial loss. With the exception of Roelf, High Prairie Dutch Americans are stolid and static. Though possessing highly valued racial features (health, golden hair, and blue eyes), they are not pioneers. Their modern descendants, such as Dirk, become bond salesmen, concerned with social form and reputation but not with nurturing the spirit. *So Big* was written at a time when a concern with race had become crucial to preserving "American" identity. The Immigration Act of 1924 (the Johnson-Reed Act) necessitated a racial mapping of the American population that would be used to determine future immigration quotas. Taking the 1890 census as a baseline, the act cut the percentage of new immigrants to 2 percent of each nationality accounted for in the census. Lawmakers hoped that they could return America to a purer form of pluralism—with as few of the new southern and eastern European immigrants as possible.[25] In this ethnic equation, the Nordic-featured immigrants of High Prairie were the desirable population. Yet as Ferber indicates, they are culturally barren, lacking the vividness and perspective of the darker Selina and Roelf.

Throughout her career, Ferber would return to the theme of American immigration and racial mixing as the key to continued national strength, but *So Big* presents perhaps her harshest critique of the pioneer image and its racial dependence on Nordic peoples. Her heroine resists categorization as a traditional frontier character. She is both a woman and a New England–born outsider among European immigrants. Ferber was not the first to write critically about women's situation in the developing West. Laura Ingalls Wilder and Rose Wilder Lane, as well as Willa Cather, described women's drudgery and loneliness and their lack of personal, political, and economic control, even over their own property. Cather's novels about the European immigrant communities of the Midwest, *O Pioneers* (1913) and *My Ántonia* (1918), both focus on female "outsider" protagonists and offer significant alternatives to the myth of the masculine frontier. But Ferber is arguably more concerned with linking her heroine's life to the nation's historical trajectory. In all of Ferber's historical novels, her heroines act within distinct historical contexts rather than self-enclosed fictional communities or mythic spaces.

In William Handley's study of Willa Cather, he argues, "Cather's resistance to the more invidious forms of Americanization and her celebration of immigrant farmers is also the result of her distaste for her culture's alignment of masculinity with racialized nationalism, especially through marriage."[26] Like Ferber, Cather resisted traditional white masculine myths of the frontier; the historian Frederick Jackson Turner disliked her work because Cather was too sympathetic to unassimilated "non-English stocks." Handley continues,

"The 'country' of the plains offers a feminized agrarian alternative to masculine 'America.' Her Naturalism suggests not only her belief that Nature will have the last word, but also her desire that women, less invested in masculine myths and denied power, will have the last word on narrating the West's true history."[27] Ferber's Selina shares this reenvisioning of the American frontier landscape and the role of women in developing that ideal.

For all of Selina's pioneering character, she is no feminist. She is first and foremost a mother. After former friend Julie Hempel discovers her selling vegetables door-to-door in Chicago, the Hempels want to help her and Dirk financially. Selina refuses at first, explaining, "I wanted him [Dirk] to have everything. Beautiful things. I wanted his life to be beautiful. Life can be so ugly, Julie. You don't know."[28] She continues, "My life doesn't count, except as something for Dirk to use . . . I'm here to keep Dirk from making the mistakes I made."[29] Throughout Ferber's career, the author would create strong heroines who were married mothers—notably, Sabra Cravat (*Cimarron*) and Magnolia Hawks (*Show Boat*)—but Selina is the most maternal of all her characters, the woman most dependent on the welfare of her child.

In many ways, Ferber's portrait of working mother Selina Peake responds to the tensions facing women in the 1920s. Although women had won the vote after generations of struggle, very few were elected to Congress or state legislatures. The National Woman's Party and other middle- and working-class women's groups were polarized by the relative benefits of the proposed Equal Rights Amendment. Women continued to vote, but not in the numbers predicted, and the massive "housecleaning" of politics predicted by suffrage advocates did not occur.[30] The dominant image of American women in the 1920s continues to be the flapper—liberated, certainly, but hardly a powerful political figure. While many historians have pointed out the failure of the women's movement to build an effective political base after ratification of the Nineteenth Amendment, in 1920, some have argued that feminism survived as "social feminism."[31] The passage of the Sheppard-Towner Act in 1921, which provided some federal funding and state aid for maternity services and child care, was a case in point. Theodore Roosevelt had called for a children's bureau back in 1909, but there were many opponents of progressivism or any social-security measure to protect women and children. Since the women's movement was the most vital political organization pursuing progressive reforms in the early twentieth century, opposition to progressivism often included opposition to suffrage. During and after the war, this opposition often charged its supporters, including Jane Addams, whom Ferber greatly admired, with communist subversion. But the facts about America's poor maternity care were very real. As J. Stanley Lemons points out, studies revealed that the United States had "unusually high rates" of infant and maternal mortality. During the war, childbirth deaths increased from 16,000 to 23,000 a year, and more than 250,000 infants died each year. The women's movement lobbied for the passage of the Sheppard-Towner Act as the first major indication of its political validity. The law eventually passed (although Congress allocated far less than the four million dollars originally stipulated); however, the Child Labor Amendment was rejected.[32]

Ferber's book, essentially a story of a hardworking mother's sacrifice and dreams for her child, resonated with the struggles of social feminists in the 1920s. But when Selina's son, Dirk, becomes merely part of the modern money- and flapper-chasing crowd, Ferber indicates the failure of modern society to bolster the efforts of mothers. Contemporary America may have celebrated the liberated woman, but Paula, Ferber's archetypal flapper, is unfaithful, unemployed, scheming, and idle. Dirk may have escaped toil and death in the world war (he arrived in Paris two months before hostilities ended), but only to become a fashionable college student and bond salesman. Ferber had little sympathy for the modern age's self-indulgence. Ferber observes that after the war, Dirk said that "the war had disillusioned him. It was a word you often heard uttered as a reason or an excuse for abandoning the normal. Disillusioned."[33] Later, she compares that manicured, college-educated generation with their fathers—America's rough, uncouth, vital immigrant buccaneers of nineteenth-century business. These older men have strong hands marked by hard work. "Those hands," Ferber continues, "whose work had made possible the symphony orchestras, the yacht clubs, the golf clubs through which their descendants now found amusement and relaxation."[34] Similarly, Selina's rough, dirt-crusted hands have provided Dirk with his advantages. Although not embarrassed by his farming mother, he inherits nothing of her vision. This, for Ferber, was the tragedy of modernity and American history.

Canonicity and the Pulitzer Prize

Female critics responded enthusiastically to Ferber's new book. In Chicago, Fanny Butcher had nothing but praise for Ferber's creation of Selina, revelling in the history of an "unknown" woman whom "no drudgery or misfortune could subdue."[35] Lena Morrow Lewis was particularly perceptive, commenting in the *New Leader*: "Life does not proceed on the theory of a deep and mysteriously laid plot. Neither does Edna Ferber's latest novel, *So Big*. It runs along just like life itself with its bits of charm, its sombre realities, its dull and all but unbearable moments, its victorious triumphs."[36] Ferber deliberately chose a nonchronological, episodic, even amorphous narrative structure as a corrective to the chronologically ordered, prescriptive success stories of American men. While Lewis admired the feminist subtext of the unconforming biography, others were bemused by Ferber's unusual "artistic" turn.[37]

Lewis appreciated other aspects of the book's feminist discourse: "If one desires to know the tragedy of a woman of vision and ambition tied to a dull clod of the earth, you get it in this story. Fortunately the man dies in time to leave the woman still young enough to do something worthwhile with her life. All the things the husband said were impossible and impractical she succeeds in doing." But she also commended Ferber's value as a social historian of America, writing, "No one who wants to know the story of Chicago's growth and the changes in the farm country near by, the continual conflict between the people of vision and the folks who never get away from the material grind of life, can afford to miss this book."

More often than not, women reviewed *So Big* for the major papers and journals, indicating Ferber's perceived status as a writer with a unique feminist outlook.[38] But colleague Laurence Stallings, one of the few men to review the book, saw Ferber as part of an elite group of female American novelists, which included Willa Cather and Zona Gale.[39] *So Big* reminded him of Cather's *My Ántonia*, and Stallings continued, "Our women are better novelists and better poets than our men. Perhaps they shall try their hands at history presently. And perhaps this too will sparkle with a native flavor. Miss Ferber, in her novelist's way, is an historian, with an observing wit and a gusto for the American scene that is the best characteristic of the mid-Western writer."

A few years later, literary historian Margaret Lawrence considered Ferber to be America's "supreme feminist" and a writer on par with Jane Austen, the Brontës, and George Eliot.[40] Ferber's style and material were totally American. "There is nothing in her stories borrowed from Europe," Lawrence writes. Just as she borrowed nothing from literary forebears, so her heroines are independent of men and described "at the height of their powers." Selina, like all of Ferber's heroines, is "not dependent upon men for the adequate conduct of [her] life . . . In all of Edna Ferber's work there is an undercurrent of dissatisfaction with men which is characteristic of all the general writing of the modern School of Femininity in its current phase."[41]

Yet Ferber's work stood apart from all other historical fiction and contemporary women's fiction. Her Emma McChesney stories had laid the groundwork for a solid national readership, but *So Big* made Ferber one of the most popular writers in America. Doubleday marketed the book as both a runaway best seller and a work of great literature. The publisher noted both that "every week for more than a year this book has sold more copies that many new novels ever sell" and that it was the "best American novel since Willa Cather's *My Ántonia*."[42] After reading *So Big*, Betsy Greenebaum of the *Chicago Evening Post Literary Review* wondered, "Will she land in the ranks of the more pretentious craftsmen? Or among the inveterately commercial writers? Both ways still remain open."[43] But as Ferber would later complain, writing a successful historical novel diminished an author's critical stature in America. Parodying her literary position in her 1939 autobiography, she wrote that the author "may find shelter in the Mauve Decade, the Civil War period, or the Covered Wagon days. From this excursion into the past he emerges with a Nostalgia Novel which is offered as a sedative to a jittery world. It is called the Escapist School of writing."[44] Ferber knew she was out of step with the rest of modern American literature and revelled in her difference. *So Big* was an unabashedly historical novel, and Ferber did look back with nostalgia on prewar America. At least one major critic sympathized with Ferber—William Allen White.

Ferber won the Pulitzer Prize for *So Big* in 1925 thanks largely to the unflagging support of William Allen White. The critic, a longtime friend and reporting mentor of Ferber's and a proponent of democratized culture, was furious to learn that Doubleday had not submitted a copy of the book to the Pulitzer committee.[45] Doubleday was certainly aware of the book's phenomenal sales. Around 11,500 advance copies were printed, and then beginning the week of 1 March, *So Big* sold on average of 3,000 copies a week through the new year. By the end of January, it had sold 144,268 copies, "a record of continuous sales so remarkable" that White was flabbergasted at the publisher's omission.[46] But the two other judges that year, Professor Jefferson B. Fletcher of Columbia (chairman) and Professor O. W. Firkins of the University of Minnesota, felt otherwise. They preferred Joseph Hergescheimer's *Balisand* and future Hollywood screenwriter Laurence Stallings's war novel *Plumes*. White, however, was bored with war literature and found Hergescheimer's book stylistically impressive but empty of content: "Hergescheimer's novel is better written but its theme is trivial and unimportant . . . My feeling about the award is that the novel should be of significance."[47] Ferber's faith in pioneer values and her revulsion against postwar materialism also appealed to hundreds of thousands of American readers, many of whom had not moved to the cities, experienced the First World War and its aftermath of "disillusionment," or fled to an artistic exile in Europe.

White was from Emporia, Kansas, and he treasured the small-town, small-farm environment as the heart of the country. His paper had a mass following in America, even with people who had never been to Kansas. Humorist Will Rogers, another midwesterner (from Oklahoma), helped popularize and nationalize the midwestern outlook as distinctly American. As Carl Becker, a historian and longtime resident of Kansas, later wrote, "The Kansas spirit is the American spirit double distilled. It is a new grafted product of American individualism, American idealism, American intolerance. Kansas is America in microcosm."[48] White felt, with his usual populist convictions, that the public should have some say in what constituted great literature. Fletcher partially agreed, and wrote to the Pulitzer committee: "Again, there is no disputing the strong emotional appeal and lively narrative interest of *So Big*. On the other hand this very appeal to the feelings is at times, as it seems to me, a little raw."[49] Fletcher liked both *So Big* and *Balisand*, but admitted that the second half of *Balisand* was not that good. However, Firkins disliked *So Big*, and was in favor of either *Plumes* or *Balisand*.[50] Fletcher felt that in view of their deadlock, the award should be abrogated that year. It was an unusual proposal, but indicated the growing crisis in organizations purporting to determine the standards of high American art and mass culture. White was upset: "I am, however, a little bit fearful that our refusal to make an award will be misunderstood."[51]

For a while it seemed as if the only alternative to deadlock was for White to give into Firkins and allow *Balisand* the prize. But in a passionate letter to Pulitzer head Frank D. Fackenthal, White wrote, "Miss Ferber's thesis was one badly needed in America and one which was dramatized with much skill. The contention of her book is that America needs creative spirit in something besides finance; that we should express ourselves in beautiful things—beautiful architecture, beautiful lives and that beauty is the sad and vital lack of America. Hence, I stood for *So Big*."[52] Fackenthal showed the letter to the trustees of the Pulitzer Prize, and persuaded by White's eloquence and perhaps jaded by the glut of disillusioned but stylish fiction, they did something almost unprecedented. Although the committee selected *Balisand*, the trustees overruled it and gave the prize to Ferber. White gleefully recounted his coup to Ferber on April 28, 1925.[53]

Several female writers had previously won the Pulitzer Prize for literature, including Edith Wharton (*The Age of Innocence*, 1920) and Willa Cather (*One of Ours*, 1922). However, Ferber was unique in that her popular appeal won out over two entries with more overtly modernist themes—social decay and wartime disillusionment. While her work may have seemed "raw" compared to that of the more stylish Hergesheimer and Stallings, her characters plain and verging on the anonymous, and her narrative static, White recognized that so were the lives of many of her readers.

Only a year later, he would join Henry Seidel Canby, Dorothy Canfield Fisher, Christopher Morley, and Heywood Broun as judges for the newly established Book-of-the-Month Club. Ferber's work (*Show Boat* would be one of their first selections) represented what White loved: uniquely American literature that conformed to no canon but that of the public. As literary historian Joan Shelley Rubin comments, White "remained basically a nineteenth-century figure yet departed furthest of all the members on the board from the genteel tradition's conception of the critic's role."[54] White was a lifelong supporter and publicist of the Progressive movement. But rather than insisting on educating the masses with elite literature it ought to read, White believed in a democratized American culture in which critics and ordinary readers educated each other. He liked books that exemplified some aspect of the American past, but was also sensitive to the need for books to be saleable. According to Rubin, he "was an effective promoter of consumer values even as he functioned simultaneously as an emblem of the past."[55]

White had long seen Ferber's value as an American writer. As he wrote in the introduction to a collection of her short stories: "She is the goddess of the worker. And from her typewriter keys spring hard-working bankers, merchants, burglars, garage-helpers, stenographers, actors, travelling salesmen, hotel clerks, porters and reporters, wholesalers, pushcart men, wine touts, welfare workers, farmers, writers—always doers of things."[56] In *So Big*, Ferber wrote a story that celebrated life and the spirit, not success. She also wrote a story that appealed to female readers. As one fan, Hannah Sintow of Vancouver, wrote, "I have just read *So Big* and I want to thank you for the great pleasure it has given me, the clean beauty of it, and the greatness of Selina, are there any such women now-a-days? But of course there are, it is a privilege to meet one in a book, and must be a greater to meet one in real life, but perhaps we do, and have not all the gifts of recognizing one, or looking beyond externals."[57] Finnish immigrant Saimi Fassett confided to Ferber that the author had reminded her of her own experience and pride in her family. Selina was very like Fassett's mother, and like many women, "she has never had the opportunity to give voice to what is within her."[58] Ferber had inspired Fassett to write about her own mother one day.

The book's historical value lay in Ferber's rescue of a great American woman from anonymity. It recognized and valorized female courage, endurance, and resourcefulness. But ironically, Ferber's Pulitzer Prize citation reads: "For the American novel published during the year which shall best present the wholesome atmosphere of American manners and manhood."[59] Equally ironic, given the book's attitude toward material success, Ferber made hundreds of thousands of dollars on the sale of the book. Even her serial contracts with major magazines became more lucrative. Editor Gertrude Lane of the *Woman's Home Companion* informed Ferber in August 1925 that she was raising her next serial contract from $35,000 to $45,000. "Neither you nor I anticipated quite the sensational success of *So Big*," she wrote.[60]

Ferber and Warner Bros., 1924–1932

As Ferber admitted, *So Big* did not have plot or action or a glamorous protagonist, yet Hollywood made three versions of it between 1924 and 1953. She made them pay for the privilege. Although Ferber sold the motion picture rights to Warner Bros. for $20,000 soon after publication—and before she was awarded the Pulitzer Prize (which certainly would have raised its potential value)—the introduction of sound in 1927 meant that Warner Bros. also had to purchase sound rights to her novel if it wanted to remake the film. So when Warner Bros. planned another version in 1931, it had to pay Ferber another $20,000.[61] But Ferber's contracts were not only about money; she also insisted that any "so-called 'teaser' advertising or the issuance of special publicity and/or exploitation," no matter how small, would mention her name.[62] While writers like Stephen Vincent Benét and F. Scott Fitzgerald were content to work as unsuccessful Hollywood screenwriters while abusing the studios' artistic standards, and others like Fannie Hurst and Ernest Hemingway were content to take the money and run, Ferber was interested both in maximizing the subsequent film profits and in wielding a measure of authorial power. Regardless of how many films based on her novels Hollywood released, Ferber was determined that audiences would know them as "Edna Ferber's."

Ferber also made it quite clear that she was selling only the motion picture rights. During the negotiations for the sound-rights contract, her lawyers wrote to Morris Ebenstein of Warner Bros. legal department: "She is perfectly willing to let you have picture rights (talking and silent) in the present version of the book and also in any future revision of the book made by her, but she cannot agree to letting you have talking picture rights of the version of a dramatization which might be made by some one else."[63] In other words, Ferber demanded control of dramatic, musical, radio, television, and even screen rights for future *So Big* adaptations. By 1938, she had so exhausted the legal department by defending her financial rights to *So Big* ventures that Morris Ebenstein wrote to executive Jacob Wilk, "All our radio rights in *So Big* expired on December 8, 1934, and the lady now has uncontrolled radio rights in her great masterpiece."[64]

Ebenstein might have been snide, but Ferber's unconventional "masterpiece" mattered to other departments in the Warner Bros. hierarchy. What it lacked in conventional action, it made up in character, and the role of Selina was a potential hit for the star-oriented production and marketing techniques of Hollywood. However, Selina was not a glamorous figure, and usually filmmakers resisted adapting narratives that required the principal female star to age. Generational novels were often modernized and compressed, such as Universal's first version of Ferber's *Show Boat* (1929) and MGM's 1951 remake. But all of Warner Bros.' adaptations of *So Big* remained faithful to Ferber's novel, carrying Selina from girlhood to old age.

Although prints of the original film are lost, *So Big* was a major Warner Bros. production. Directed by Charles Brabin, it was released on 28 December 1924. John Bowers, John Gilbert's rival as a homegrown romantic lead during the 1920s, played Pervus. Ben Lyon was Dirk, Wallace Beery was the earthy Klaas Pool, and Jean Hersholt played August Hempel, the wealthy father of Selina's childhood best friend. Top star Colleen Moore won the role of Selina (Fig. 2.2). It was a major prestige effort for the studio in the days before *Don Juan* (1926) and *The Jazz Singer* (1927) made it rich, but Warner Bros. was allegedly reluctant to cast Colleen Moore as Ferber's heroine. *So Big*'s theme was so at odds with Moore's youthful, glamorous image that the studio feared it might detract from her future worth as a star. But the star of *Flaming Youth* (1923) and *The Perfect Flapper* (1924) wanted the challenging role. As Moore re-

clockwise from top left: 2.1. Poor, hungry, and shabby Selina and Dirk trying to sell vegetables (*So Big*, Warner Bros., 1924); 2.2. Colleen Moore as Selina (*So Big*, Warner Bros., 1924); 2.3. Radishes are beautiful (*So Big*, Warner Bros., 1924); 2.4. Selina teaching Dirk in the fields of High Prairie, Illinois (*So Big*, Warner Bros., 1924).

called, after starring in four comedies, "I longed to play a dramatic part for a change . . . The role of Selina, who ages in the story from sixteen to sixty, was a challenge, and I wanted to prove I could play it. I was a big enough star now to demand the story I wanted, and it was given to me."[65] Executives may have cast Ben Lyon as Dirk in an effort to preserve some of their chemistry from *Flaming Youth*. If it was an unusual film for Moore, it was equally unique for 1920s Hollywood—there was no glamor or fame for Selina, only the struggles of single motherhood and financial survival (Figs. 2.1, 2.3, 2.4, and 2.5). Moore knew the film would not be a big box-office hit like her usual, ultramodern fare, but she, like Warner Bros., wanted the prestige Ferber's protagonist and a historical production could give.

Adelaide Heilbron's script reinforces a sense of the past with photographic and textual references to the narrative's historical context. These textual superimpositions not only set the overall historical period, but placed Selina's life and doings within its framework. The script begins: "On a vignette close-up of the cover of an album containing stereopticon views. Tooled in leather on the shield—centered on the cover—are the words 'VIEWS DURING THE TRAVELS OF SIMEON PEAKE AND HIS DAUGHTER SELINA PEAKE. 1875–1888.'"[66] Heilbron then planned a close-up of Selina's hand "holding an old fashioned stereopticon set with a photograph out of focus—the sliding focus moves slowly back until the picture comes in sharp and clear."

Selina's hand orders a series of dated travel images of the Riviera, Paris, and finally Chicago in 1888; she puts them in focus, and it is from her perspective that we see the course of her early life (Fig. 2.6). It was a remarkable way for the studio to retain the structure and discourse of Ferber's "biography" of Selina. Rather than beginning with an omniscient male gaze on her life, Selina authors her own vision. This is her album, which we are looking at through her eyes. The sorts of documents that chronicle her life are uniquely feminine—personal photographs. The script also makes use of Selina's letters and writing to structure the narrative. This is the sort of material that dominated American social history written between 1875 and 1888. The historian Julie Des Jardins identifies this as an era of social and cultural history authored principally by "amateur" women writers.[67] Selina is exhibiting the era's awareness of personal history.

Heilbron even retains Selina's feminism. Her father is still the glamorous but insolvent gambler. When her father mentions money troubles, Selina offers to work: "Now I'm equipped to be a self-supporting woman! If you're

above: 2.5. Moore deglamorized (*So Big*, Warner Bros., 1924); *below*: 2.6. Selina and her father looking at their past (*So Big*, Warner Bros., 1924).

worried about money, I'll get a position as a school teacher." Although her father refuses, it is not because he does not think women should work, but because teaching would not give her the intellectual stimulation and rich personal experience he believes she deserves: "[T]hat means getting into a rut—I want you to go everywhere—to realize that life's just a grand adventure." But her father also says that he wants her to see all kinds of people and places: "The more people you see, the more things happen to you, the richer you are—EVEN IF THEY'RE NOT PLEASANT THINGS."[68] Selina is fortunate to have a parent who validates all kinds of experiences rather than promising a spurious happy ending.

The first two-thirds of the script follows Ferber's book, although Heilbron eliminated Roelf as a character in order to simplify the narrative. After her father's death, Selina goes to work for both financial and personal fulfilment. When her wealthy friend Julie begs Selina to "give up this dreadful idea of earning your own living and come with Pa and me," Selina replies, "'I can't be dependent upon anyone—not even you—Julie.'"[69] And though she does marry Pervus, first described as looking like "a Greek God," a title card acknowledged that this was no Prince Charming but a man "narrow of vision." Later, when he reprimands her for dancing in the fields in front of her son, she responds angrily: "You're a coward, Pervus, a coward! Like all High Prairie your only thought is work-work-work—Never any play." Even Ferber did not give her young, married Selina this assertive a voice. Selina is a constant advocate for "modern methods" on the DeJong farm, but as in Ferber's book, change and prosperity do not come until after Pervus's death. Like Ferber's heroine, she braves the disapproval of the male farmers of High Prairie ("A woman cannot go by Haymarket to sell vegetables with men") as well as the shock of Chicago prostitutes, who remark, "You ain't tellin' me YOU run that farm—come to market alone, raise the kid—'neverything? . . . Ain't a woman a fool to work like that—what does SHE get out of it?"

The last third of the script deals with "So Big" (Dirk) and his entanglement with Paula, the married daughter of Julie Hempel. The studio evidently thought that it could handle adultery narratives with more panache than Ferber, and, in doing so, abandoned the author's portrait of modern failure. Dirk became a more attractive figure than in the book and gained elements of the artistic dreamer, Roelf. Rather than being merely a boring bond salesman or successful banker, Dirk became an architect for a new financial building. The independent young sculptress, Dallas O'Mara, was transformed into a temporarily spurned love interest of Dirk's. Dirk runs off with the more exciting Paula, but eventually he returns home to his mother and Dallas. Instead of revealing the emptiness of modern American wealth and consumerism, the final sequence titillates audiences with a conventional, melodramatic modern love triangle.

The film was plainly marketed as a woman's picture, a Ferber film, and a vehicle for Colleen Moore. Mordaunt Hall of the *New York Times* admitted that it lacked a conventional dramatic plot, but enjoyed the film's attention to historical detail and characterization. While he commended Moore's heroic Selina, Hall found the men less than impressive. Pervus was "an industrious skinflint, lacking in initiative and imagination," and Ben Lyon's performance of Dirk was especially unsympathetic.[70] Mildred Spain of the *New York Daily News* also liked the historical portions and dismissed the studio's invented modern romance, but saved most of her praise for Moore's standout performance.[71] Yet many were bewildered by the star's serious change of pace. Theatres everywhere tried to cover the incongruity, advertising "Colleen Moore in her greatest historic achievement." It was the first but not last time that Ferber's work would be labelled a major Hollywood actress's "greatest historic achievement," yet *So Big* did not net Moore any more "serious" period roles. Her next films were *Sally* and *We Moderns* (1925). Although a critical success, embellishing Warner's and Moore's prestige, *So Big* was not the usual million-dollar Moore sell-out.[72] So why did the studio make a film so at odds with current taste and star expectations? Perhaps executives hoped to be as pleasantly surprised as Gertrude Lane and Russell Doubleday had been by *So Big*'s popularity. Perhaps its historical content, small-time success, and old-fashioned heroine appealed to audiences worn thin by the hedonism of *The Plastic Age* (1925).

Film historian Miriam Hansen has speculated on the power that female spectators had during the silent era and has even argued that in cultivating stars such as Rudolph Valentino, Hollywood producers catered to a "female gaze."[73] Although *So Big* lacked a sense of visual empowerment through the fetishization of the male body (something that would have almost guaranteed its box office), the film confronted the courage ordinary women needed to survive their dull marriages and aging bodies. Although there may well have been an element of masochism involved with watching and identifying with Selina's deteriorating body and physical exhaustion, identifying with Selina's small spiritual triumphs may have mitigated female audience members' sense of personal powerlessness and anonymity. This ordinary women's picture catered to another aspect of an empowered female gaze.

Over the next few years, Ferber published *Show Boat* and *Cimarron*; Warner Bros. was outbid for them by the smaller Universal and RKO. Although studios did not make many expensive American historical films during the silent and early sound eras, those that were made attracted a lot of attention and occasionally big box-office profits during the Depression.[74] In the early 1930s, Ferber adaptations—even remakes—were hot properties, and Warner Bros. decided to remake *So Big*. But the studio was unsure whether it actually owned the talking rights to Ferber's book. So in April 1930, it made a quick, inexpensive short of a scene from *So Big* as "a test case on the question of the necessity of our buying sound rights where we had previously bought the silent right to make a picture of the novel."[75] Ferber and her lawyers threatened suit, and the studio quickly drew up a contract that paid Ferber an additional $20,000 for the sound rights.[76] The short must have infuriated Ferber, since it dealt with a new scene by Beatrice Van and Richard Weil in which Dallas and Paula argue over Dirk. It was a tawdry means of advertising the story's potential as a sexed-up tale of adultery.[77] Starring Helen Jerome Eddy, the short would have served as an audience appetizer before one of Warner's new A-feature releases.[78] But the studio's test case also conditioned audiences for the next *So Big*.

In the meantime, *Cimarron* had won multiple Academy Awards and been the biggest grosser of 1931. The film had also spurred an industry-wide interest in American historical cinema.[79] Warner Bros.' decision to remake its silent version of *So Big* represented an awareness of Ferber's work as historical and box-office material. But in 1932, Hollywood was still recovering from its worst year yet of the Depression, and the film was made on a budget. With the exception of Barbara Stanwyck (Selina), studio contract players dominated the cast. But some of the contract players were remarkable, including Bette Davis (Dallas O'Mara) and George Brent (Roelf).

J. Grubb Alexander's script follows Ferber's book, but invests Selina's life with more biographical details than Heilbron's silent version.[80] It begins with a scene from her birth and her mother's subsequent death. The finished film even embellishes its historical context with a text foreword about Chicago, "the gateway of the great West." The text foreword, first used extensively in sound-era historical films such as *Cimarron*, would soon become one of the most prominent elements of the genre. In *So Big*, the text subtly prepares audiences for the story of a different kind of pioneer woman, one who conquers her own wilderness of poverty, loneliness, and cultural isolation. The second feature film is far more preoccupied with Selina's quest for beauty than the first, which cut Roelf Pool from the narrative. In one sequence, Dallas, remarking on Selina's significance as a pioneering American woman, says that she wants to paint American portraits: "Not portraits of ladies with a string of pearls and one lily hand half hidden in the folds of a satin skirt . . . I mean character portraits of men and women who are really distinguished looking—distinguishedly American—like your mother."[81] Rather than focusing on Dirk's sexual transgressions with the married Paula, the film concludes with the happy reunion of Ferber's two "pioneers," Selina and Roelf. They talk before a window through which tractors and farm hands are seen working her neat and prosperous farm. While Selina admires Roelf for sculpting the great men of Europe, Roelf focuses on her great American life—"full, rich . . . successful."

The film was one of Warner Bros.' prestige pictures for 1932, but was still made in just under a month. Shooting started on 11 January and finished on 3 February; after some trimming, the film was released as an eighty-one-minute feature. Warner Bros. had given Ferber director approval (a rare decision granted to any writer), and she had no objections to William Wellman (*Wings*, 1927; *Beggars of Life*, 1928; *The Public Enemy*, 1931).[82] Ferber and Wellman would share a credit title, but Ferber would get top billing, even over Wellman, as the creator of *So Big* (Fig. 2.7).

Overseen by production chief Darryl F. Zanuck and producer Hal Wallis, the film capitalized on both the recent trend in American historical and biographical films (*Abraham Lincoln*, 1930; *Billy the Kid*, 1930; *Alexander Hamilton*, 1931, *Cimarron*, 1931; *Silver Dollar*, 1932) and the audience's continued interest in adaptations of Ferber's novels.[83] However, the filmmakers' commitment to Ferber's novel and its depiction of a heroic woman is difficult to assess. Although Wellman included scenes showing Selina's intelligent interest in new farming methods and an argument between her and Pervus about the running of the farm, the studio cut a significant amount of Wellman's footage depicting Selina's struggles against male prejudice in the Haymarket and with the police.[84] The final script, stills, and Wellman's shooting records indicate that *So Big* was to have included Selina's discouraging day at the Haymarket and the abuse and threats she received from a Chicago cop for peddling vegetables without a license. These cut scenes included dismissive remarks from

Italian immigrant vegetable buyers—"Vegetables is for sell to woman, not to buy from"—and a sequence in which a cop manhandles Selina, telling her and young Dirk, "I've a good mind to run you in . . . Get out of here."[85] While Alexander and Wellman showed Selina's battles against misogyny and masculine authority, Zanuck must have been wary of the implications of showing a cop harassing the heroine and her child as poor vagrants. Too many Americans had recently suffered similar treatment in the Depression. Instead, the released film skims over Selina's solitary hardships and toil, jumping from the night before Selina's first selling day in Chicago to a montage of tractors and expanding fields.[86] The impoverished underdog succeeds, and civic authority is untarnished.

Nevertheless, Wellman maintained a powerful sense of female solidarity, using Selina's hands and handclasps with other working women as a visual theme throughout the film. The first instance involves Selina's white, unscarred, seminary-schooled hand meeting that of Maartje Pool (Roelf's overworked mother). Mrs. Pool, though still young in years, looks worn, white, and dead, her nails chipped and her blistered hands caked with dirt. Later at the Haymarket, Selina will meet Mabel, a Chicago prostitute who, out of pity, tries to give Selina money to get a room for Dirk. Though Selina refuses charity, she is kind, and the two shake hands in mutual respect. Finally, in the last few moments of the film, the older Selina looks at her work-worn hands (Fig. 2.8). Roelf, a successful artist who has absorbed her attitude toward life and beauty, pays tribute to her by kissing them.

The 1932 narrative retained Ferber's theme, so central in the 1920s, of art versus soulless materialism; however, the filmmakers also saw *So Big*'s continued relevance to contemporary American issues. The studio was not simply remaking the property; research files indicate that the narrative was expected to resonate with the heartbreaking problems so many American farmers were enduring in 1932. Screenwriters read what Selina Peake would have read in 1931, the *Thirty-sixth Annual Report of the Illinois Farmers' Institute* (30 June 1931), which concluded: "The farmers are all broke." The pamphlet acknowledged that modern innovations of the past decade had certainly helped U.S. agriculture, but that poor conditions were preventing any change from occurring.[87] The writers and director emphasized the connection between irresponsible business practices in the 1890s and 1920s and Selina's personal tragedy. Simeon Peake's "business," according to his adoring daughter, is "the market."[88] When he goes bust, Selina has to fend for herself. Later, in the 1920s, after

above: 2.7. Ferber's name above Wellman's (*So Big*, Warner Bros., 1932).
below: 2.8. Roelf (George Brent) gazes at Selina's (Barbara Stanwyck's)
hands in the final scenes of *So Big* (Warner Bros., 1932).

Dirk has abandoned architecture for the more lucrative world of bonds and stocks, Selina asks suspiciously, "What are bonds?" When he explains that "everyone" buys them, she responds, "I don't. Probably because whenever I had any spare money it went back into the farm for improvements."[89] The criticism was plain to many American viewers in 1932. Although only one in thirty Americans held stocks and bonds, they were partly responsible for initiating a crash that destroyed the livelihoods of thousands of farmers who had never heard of bonds. In focusing on the deprivation and struggles of a woman with a young child, *So Big*, in its 1930s context, added a feminine dimension to "forgotten man" narratives.

Critics appreciated this second feature-length version. The *Motion Picture Herald* wrote: "Warner has remade Edna Ferber's *So Big* for the talking screen with Barbara Stanwyck in the virile part of a typical American mother whose simple life epic is the backbone of America's greatness . . . The Ferber classic should not disappoint those who enjoyed the silent version, comment indicated." The film's historical context was not the only attraction. The reviewer acknowledged that it was not a typical Hollywood film:

> Plot is not the important thing in *So Big*. It is characterization, the revelation of plain folk doing the things they think, striving always toward a goal of useful citizenship. It revolves around a mother who struggles to make a farm pay, and whose greatest problem is a son who, dissatisfied with farm life, wants to become a "big businessman" in the city. It goes back to the days when farm life was drudgery, but brings it up to the day of the tractor, the radio, the automobile, paved highways and so many other conveniences which have radically altered rural life.

The reviewer commended both Stanwyck and director William Wellman for "carrying the episodic story along."[90]

Again, it was the lead actress's performance as Selina and Ferber's reputation as a best-selling, Pulitzer Prize–winning author that the studio and critics saw as the heart of the "epic of American womanhood." Press campaigns pushed stories emphasizing the two female "creative geniuses," and Stanwyck was quoted, "I am more enthusiastic over this part than any other I have ever had, either in pictures or on the stage. I feel that Edna Ferber's story and heroine have an epic quality that is truly great, and that I am privileged in being able to bring them to the talking screen."[91]

So Big was a breakthrough film for the actress. When Stanwyck made *So Big*, she was a rising independent contract star, perhaps best known for her partnerships with director Frank Capra (*Ladies of Leisure*, 1930). Stanwyck had occasionally played a historical figure; her performance in Capra's *The Miracle Woman* (1931) was loosely based on the life of evangelist Aimee Semple McPherson. Like Selina Peake, McPherson was another 1920s woman who embodied the era's modern and antimodern characteristics, catering to Americans' desire for a rigorous, old-time, fundamentalist faith, but fulfilling that desire through the modern radio industry.[92] But though Stanwyck was well known, *So Big* arguably contributed to making her a bigger star. Only a year later, she went on to make the notorious *Baby Face* (1933) and *The Bitter Tea of General Yen* (1933). And though many would later praise her Academy Award–nominated performance in Samuel Goldwyn's adaptation of *Stella Dallas* (1936), Stanwyck first developed her performance as a self-sacrificing mother in *So Big*. Perhaps most significantly for a glamorous young female star of her calibre, she allowed herself to age, to look pale, tired, lined, desiccated, and bent with work. Although Colleen Moore had done the same thing in 1924, she could not entirely overcome her image as the ultimate flapper. Stanwyck's body of work and Depression-era Hollywood's increasingly popular genres about downtrodden misfits and unknown men and women (*Little Caesar*, 1931; *The Public Enemy*, 1931; *I Am a Fugitive from a Chain Gang*, 1932; *Jenny Gerhardt*, 1933; *The Gold Diggers of 1933*, 1933) made her the ideal Selina.

From History to Nostalgia

Although it was normal for studios to reread old literary acquisitions and scripts in order to assess their future value, Warner Bros. kept an extremely close eye on *So Big*. Perhaps Ferber's interest in contracts kept them vigilant. In 1936, only four years after their last successful remake, story reader Dorothy Robinson commented, "This is a valuable piece of property. With skilful treatment, it can be made into a fine picture. The characters are real and interesting; the story is convincing. It offers an important role for an actress— Bette Davis perhaps." Robinson's comments do not merely indicate her ignorance of production history, but also show the continued perception of *So Big* as a prestige property for the studio's biggest female star. By 1936, *So Big* cast member Bette Davis had become one of Warner Bros.' top stars. Ironically, she had first drawn national critical attention to her acting ability by playing

Mildred in *Of Human Bondage* (RKO, 1934), another unglamorous role in which her looks deteriorate from disease and drugs.

Warner Bros. sat on Robinson's report, turning its attention to dozens of other historical projects before wartime production intervened to curtail the cycle. In 1943, screenwriter and newly promoted producer Jerry Wald was planning yet another version of the film, but one that transformed much of Ferber's material. Instead of being a pioneering modern farmer, Selina would become a symbol of the American schoolmarm and an inspiration for future generations of boys (a female Mr. Chips, perhaps). Writer Jo Pagano (whose last project had been the Hopalong Cassidy film *Leather Burners*, 1943) thought Wald's idea "revolutionary" and jumped at the chance of working with Wald.[93] It would certainly have been "revolutionary" for a Ferber film. No studio had ever dared to alter her material to such an extent, whether from fear of legal retaliation or the outrage of loyal fans. In Warner Bros.' last publicity campaign for a Ferber adaptation, lead articles claimed that "Edna Ferber has a 7,000,000 reader following who are waiting to see her Pulitzer Prize novel on the talking screen."[94]

But Wald's change represented the growing wartime and postwar backlash against women working in "male" occupations. The icon of 1940s wartime motherhood, Mrs. Miniver (*Mrs. Miniver*, MGM, 1942, starring Greer Garson), never works. In the prominent Selznick drama *Since You Went Away* (Selznick, 1944), stay-at-home mom Anne Hilton (Claudette Colbert) goes to work only when she absolutely has to—for the war effort. *Mildred Pierce* (Warner Bros., 1945) portrays a divorced mother (Joan Crawford) making a career in prewar America, but it brings her personal disaster. While Bette Davis's strong performance in *The Corn Is Green* (Warner Bros., 1945) indicated that the role of a schoolteacher could be both professionally and financially rewarding for star and studio, the film was a faithful adaptation of a recent Broadway success. Fundamentally changing *So Big* would have serious implications. In the original novel and first two films, Selina is shown not only working in a traditionally male occupation during peacetime, but also scientifically improving agriculture when men were sticking to time-tested but failing methods. Women were modern advocates for change; men were traditionalists. Limiting Selina to the role of schoolteacher, one of the very few and poorly paid occupations open to women in the nineteenth century, would seriously curtail Ferber's feminist exploration of women's work. However laudable the history of American female schoolteachers, theirs was a conservative occupation, repetitive, and geared to the development of young male minds.

Yet while Wald attempted to give Selina some semblance of autonomy with a prominent voice-over, Pagano did not like this idea: "The use of Selina's voice as a narrative overtone is, I think, considerably overdone." Pagano realized their new script would "alter basically Edna Ferber's story," but he thought that Wald's script would give "an emphatic point to the picture" for another reason: Wald had moved the time period forward and carried Selina's life as a teacher through 1943. *So Big* was to be a war picture![95]

Wald evidently saw his and Pagano's intervention in Ferber's material in large terms. While in the midst of other projects, he continued to work on the screenplay with Pagano. Wald's script, dated 11 February 1944, begins with a foreword that places Selina within a distinct historical frame: "The story of Civilization is written in the lives of its school teachers. In their hands rests the responsibility—and privilege—of moulding the lives of future citizens. This is the story of a woman who helped bring Freedom into the classroom. Her name was Selina Peake. We all owe her a debt of gratitude."[96] Wald placed Selina's story within Hollywood's historical cycle; forewords had become one of the key elements indicating the intellectual seriousness of the genre.[97] But Wald also did some major editing of Ferber's text, killing off Dirk as a young boy, focusing on Roelf, and adding a love interest for Selina following Pervus's death. Wald tried for months to get the studio to commit to producing his new script. Although Wald wrote to Jack Warner that star Ida Lupino was "terribly excited about it," she had "read only the book" and was probably less than impressed with Wald and Pagano's story.[98] A year and a half went by, and Wald tried again, suggesting actress Eleanor Parker or Alexis Smith for the role and calling *So Big* "a great women's story."[99] Warner Bros.' wartime productions were nearly finished, and Wald's advice to develop women's properties was certainly sound. Pagano also pushed Wald to change the title to *Selina Peake*, arguing, "There is nothing more interesting on the marquee than a title which suggests an interesting woman—witness *Mrs. Miniver* and *Stella Dallas*, etc."[100] It was Selina, not her failure of a son, who would bring women audiences to theatres.

But Wald knew Pagano was getting ahead of himself; the studio still balked at remaking the film. Toward the end of the war, Jack Warner had scaled back on the studio's annual releases, and profits were soaring.[101] Although Warner may have had his doubts about *So Big*'s future, Wald was committed to what he saw as a prestige women's picture. He wrote to producer Steve Trilling: "For sometime now I have had completed the Temp Script on a rewrite of *So Big*. . . . If Ferber wrote this story today you'd be happy to pay a quarter of a million dollars for it and think you were getting a bargain."[102] He continued in desperation, "Isn't it possible for somebody to read it and give an opinion on it?" But three years later, Warner Bros. still had not come to a decision. Wald again wrote to Trilling: "As you well know, Edna Ferber's *So Big* is an American classic; and it is so complete with great conflict and emotional scenes that whoever plays the role of the girl can't help but become a big star."[103] He had been considering newcomer Patricia Neal for Selina, but in March, when he received word that longtime Warner actress Jane Wyman (*The Lost Weekend*, 1945) wanted the role, he thought he finally could get the picture moving.

Wyman was currently starring in Wald's latest production, *Johnny Belinda*, and he predicted that her performance would soon give her clout enough to dictate her roles to Jack Warner. He wrote to Warner, "Everyone these days is trying to secure good woman stories. Again, I call your attention to the script I have on *So Big*. As you know, Jane Wyman read the script some time ago and is most anxious to do it. I doubt very much whether you would have trouble in getting a top female personality for this story. What would you like to do about it?"[104] Although Warner made a note to commit to the picture with Wyman, he was in no hurry.[105] In the meantime, Wyman won an Academy Award for her performance in *Johnny Belinda* (released in September), and Wald won the Irving Thalberg Award for his work at Warner Bros. The two did not work together on *So Big*. It took an additional five years before audiences saw the last remake, and by then, Wald was involved in other projects.

However, Ferber was not plagued by Hollywood's postwar tendency toward indecision and inaction. In 1947, she allowed CBS to have temporary radio rights to make a version of *So Big*. In all of her studio contracts, she retained radio and even television rights. Even during the 1920s, when television was still in experimental stages and shown only in public venues, Ferber recognized its future value as a private entertainment medium. So while Warner Bros. fiddled with potential remakes, CBS broadcast an hour-long radio version of her novel.[106] The script, adapted by Addie Richton and Lynn Stone, was remarkably faithful to the material, and CBS gave the work a careful advertising campaign. Former Warner Bros. actress Joan Blondell starred as Selina. *So Big* was promoted as a "magnificent chronicle" and a modern classic, and aired in the prime-time adult slot of 9:30 p.m. The story continued to draw audiences in many media, and as the book reached its twenty-fifth anniversary, Ferber began to consider future dramatic productions.

Eventually, Jack Warner put a new series of writers on the script; he did not feel comfortable with Wald's massive revision of Ferber's narrative. Selina remained a truck farmer, but the studio wanted to update the time frame. In August 1950, Edith Sommer told research director Carl Milliken about her new script project: "I have been assigned to experiment with a new version of Edna Ferber's *So Big*, for Henry Blanke. We are attempting to begin the story in 1920 and end it in 1950 or 1951, as opposed to the original version which began in 1890. We want to be certain that in changing the period for this story we do not lose the flavour of Miss Ferber's book."[107] Modernizing to such an extent certainly would have undercut Ferber's critique of the materialistic 1920s, but it is interesting to speculate whether Blanke perceived a parallel between the two "successful," money-making postwar periods. Like the 1920s, the period after the Second World War was dominated by economic expansion, consumer spending, and an increasingly conservative political culture. Eventually, perhaps wary of potential complaints from Ferber, the studio decided to begin the story in 1898 instead of 1920.[108]

In the meantime, Warner Bros.' legal department made sure that the studio still retained the film copyright. In October 1951, Ferber renewed the copyright on the novel, and Doubleday continued to release new editions of the book. Warner Bros.' attorneys noted to Roy Obringer that "they still have complete picture rights with respect to renewed copyright," but that Ferber retained full television and radio rights.[109] When the project again moved forward in June 1952, Warner had assigned writer John Twist to the project. Twist's script used many structural devices long associated with the historical film genre. The script embraced Ferber's nonchronological format, but viewed Selina's life in flashback. The script opens with Dirk, Dallas, and Roelf discussing the old Selina in 1929.[110] Twist retained Ferber's analogy between Selina and the pioneer women of earlier centuries and preserved Alexander's lines from the 1932 film. Dallas remarks: "'She's like the women who came over on the Mayflower. Or crossed the continent in covered wagons. That magnificent jaw-line—and those eyes, all lit up with lights—from somewhere—inside.'" But the revised final script's most obvious historical touch was its opening foreword; an unidentified narrator begins, "In the delirious decade of the 'Twenties' everything was changing but New Holland, that small district of truck farms on the outskirts of Chicago. Some of its people still remained as Dutch as the Netherlands, and its fields were still as green as the lowlands of Amsterdam. One had only to drive the few miles from the city and look at it to see the past."[111]

Unfortunately, as this opening sequence foreshadows, Selina was also portrayed as part of that unchanging past, a bit of quaint nostalgia not particularly relevant to the modern world. Although filmmakers like Walter Mac-Ewen saw Selina as the center of the narrative ("I think we would be much better off to take this story for what it is, the saga of Selina"), they were reluctant to pursue Ferber's portrait of an independent thinker.[112] Instead, the filmmakers accentuated Selina's connection with her father, attributing her attitude toward life and beauty to him alone. Selina's first words are a quotation of fatherly wisdom. They even did their best to rehabilitate the patriarchal authorities in Selina's life. Her father, an itinerant gambler in the novel and earlier films, is by 1950 a fabulously rich Chicago businessman famous enough to be painted by John Singer Sargent. His impressive, black-suited portrait hangs over the mantel in Selina's childhood home (Fig. 2.9). Although he does "go bust," it is not through shady business practices. Pervus, once a stupid, stolid, prejudiced man, becomes a shy but romantic farmer, bringing Selina flowers on his way home from the markets. Even the town minister of High Prairie loses his pious misogyny. While in 1924, 1925, and 1932, Ferber's reverend had objected angrily to Selina's plan to sell vegetables in the Haymarket following her husband's death, the 1953 version has him generously offering to drive her wagon!

It seems that time had rubbed the rough edges and sexual conflict off Ferber's original. The earlier film versions had focused on Selina as a feminist advocate for innovations in American agriculture and had portrayed the father as an irresponsible but charming ne'er-do-well, the husband a clod, and the minister a judgmental busybody. That the third version should weaken Selina's individualistic streak is slightly surprising, given Wyman's own star status in Hollywood in the early 1950s. But despite her Academy Award and reputation as an articulate, career-oriented actress, Wyman achieved her greatest film successes while playing unhappy, lonely women (The Yearling, 1946; The Blue Veil, 1951) and victims, like the deaf rape victim in Johnny Belinda and, later, the blind widow in Douglas Sirk's remake of Magnificent Obsession (1954).

One could argue that postwar Hollywood was more invested in rehabilitating the patriarchy and defusing the tensions between men and women than in championing a pioneer feminist. Jane Hendler has made this argument about George Stevens's production of Giant (1956).[113] After all, on its surface, this period tale of a self-sacrificing mother had an enduring and harmless sweetness. The studio kept fan letters that reinforced the film's new identity as a classic American morality tale. A twelve-year-old boy from San Francisco

2.9. Selina (Jane Wyman) with her father's portrait in *So Big* (Warner Bros., 1953).

wrote to the studio: "Miss Ferber's books are always wonderful reading material especially this one." Pastor Murley Severtson of Pequot Lake, Minnesota, agreed, and asked for more films like *So Big*, for "in doing so you will make a real contribution to the culture and the progress of our country." But Mrs. Robert Iott of Deerfield, Michigan, was more pointed, "If all movies were of this calibre, I'm sure your industry would have nothing to fear from television."[114] For these viewers, Ferber was both prestige for the studio and a cultural standard, someone who educated children and adults about the nation's great past. She was a bastion of traditional American values.

Yet however much the studio may have clung to this good publicity, even the third remake of Ferber's novel did not mask all of *So Big*'s historical tensions. Myths of the complacent, untroubled 1950s are no longer historically tenable. As film and cultural historians have pointed out, the "radical upheaval" in American ideology was especially powerful and polarizing for women after the Second World War, manifesting itself in countless postwar pictures that "complemented and challenged" Hollywood's roles for women.[115] Ferber's text had promoted an independent feminist vision in the 1920s and during the Depression. In the novel and the first two full-length film versions, one sees the grimness of Selina's life and her struggle. She is an impoverished, downtrodden woman, forced to marry an unimaginative, mediocre man and to mother an equally blighted, materialistic son. Other female novelists had followed similar narrative patterns, which endured throughout the studio era.[116] Yet *So Big* is a rather unusual women's melodrama in the context of 1950s culture. Selina sees herself as neither an unhappy woman nor a victim; she is active, self-sufficient, and even cheerful. She does not need men in order to be happy or successful. By the end of the 1950s, in spite of the many films that had portrayed independent working women (*Rear Window*, 1954; *Three Coins in the Fountain*, 1954; *Designing Woman*, 1957; *The Best of Everything*, 1959), women living happily without men were almost unheard of in Hollywood; the industry had no visual vocabulary to convey Selina's spiritual independence and small-time success.[117] So certain romantic adjustments were made to highlight "little Lina" and her passion for the blond giant, Pervus (the stolid but golden-haired Sterling Hayden). But the film projects very conflicted images about feminine independence and fulfillment. Despite attempts to bolster the male roles and curtail Selina's nonconformism, Warner Bros. retained a measure of Selina's personal autonomy and preserved some of Ferber's discourse about American success and failure.

Warner Bros. treated its third version of Ferber's work as a high-profile production. The involvement of Wyman and director Robert Wise virtually guaranteed box-office profit in 1953. The film suffered some initial delays, since Wise was working at Twentieth Century-Fox until late December 1952.[118] Shooting began on 16 February and ended 1 April, only three days behind schedule. Publicity was garbled, sending two very different messages about the film. On the one hand, the posters and lobby cards tried to market the film as a typical romantic drama, emphasizing the sexual attraction between Selina and Pervus, with headlines such as "He stood there so big. Love had come, intense, unashamed—She was ready to forget she'd ever been a lady" and "A love so big . . . this was what she wanted—and nothing anybody said could change it!"[119] These turgid lines were supported by photographs of Hayden grabbing Wyman by the shoulders as they stared into each other's eyes. It was quite a contrast to the advertising for the 1932 version, which had headlines reading "She took all life had to offer . . . Edna Ferber's epic of American womanhood."[120] But articles in the 1953 press book mention Ferber, the Pulitzer Prize, and great literature.[121] The lead story read "*So Big*, based on Edna Ferber's Prize Novel Due," and another article called her "one of U.S. Top Authors." Most of the articles mentioned the Pulitzer Prize and did their best to capitalize on Ferber's status. But in doing so, the studio was obeying the terms of its own thirty-year contract with Ferber. The film was billed as "Edna Ferber's *So Big.*"

Critics' opinions were mixed but, like the original reviews of the book, focused on Selina (Jane Wyman). The *Los Angeles Daily News* called it "mild, but Wyman strong," while Lowell Redellings of the *Hollywood Citizen News* found it "inspiring" and even quoted the California Congress of Parents and Teachers: "Edna Ferber's Pulitzer Prize–winning novel as motion picture deserves a top prize, also."[122] Evidently, educational and cultural groups were pushing the film for children and young adults. *Cue* did an in-depth review of the film and its antecedents and reminded audiences of its adult themes: "Edna Ferber's novel of struggle, hardship and the eternal battle between beauty and materialism was an instant success when it made its first appearance nearly 30 years ago," it began. "It won a Pulitzer Prize and in no time at all became a popular American classic. Its long and detailed story of the well-to-do Chicago girl who at the turn of the century lost father and fortune, and built a new life among the Dutch farmers outside the city, was filled with typical Ferber dramatic touches." The reviewer continued: "Today the simple moralizing of Miss Ferber's drama about the woman who, despite a lifetime of struggling to survive, felt it more important to create beauty than material wealth, seems rather naïve—but it was strong stuff back in the surging 1920s. Not that Miss Ferber's premise isn't, within reason, sound enough today," he added. "But as projected here on film, the story seems to have lost some of its penetration and elemental power; it has become a celluloid sob story with several good scenes but mostly with more surface than substance, more soapy sentimentality than solid significance."[123]

Newsweek agreed: "In its third film translation, Edna Ferber's Pulitzer Prize novel of 1925 emerges as a long series of sentimental episodes, with Jane Wyman giving a good, clear performance against quite an ordeal by screenplay." Twist's script was "superficial and embarrassing. And, in general, the human and professional elements of Edna Ferber's narrative deserve a sophistication of treatment which they are far from getting here."[124] The message was clear: Despite the novel's old-fashioned, rather sexless narrative, Ferber and her work had a certain status in Hollywood. Updating the story with romantic melodrama may have been an effort to attract box office, but it did not work. The film only cleared $2 million in domestic rentals.

But the major film periodicals, less aware of the original novel and its previous film versions, blamed Ferber's material for its "old fashioned" themes. *Variety* commented, "It's [*sic*] basic flaw is that it attempts to cover too much, resulting in an episodic quality and in flat surface character delineations. The problem it poses—to toil for monetary returns or to create 'beautiful' things for a sense of inner satisfaction—appears old hat in today's coin-happy society."[125] The *Hollywood Reporter*'s Nat Kahn titled his review "Edna Ferber Story Too Old-Fashioned" and wrote: "*So Big*, in the main, seems rather old-fashioned in its writing in 1953, and it plays that way." But while the script was "rambling, unexciting," he acknowledged that the Ferber original was a vital work of American literature.[126]

Although Ferber did not publicly condemn any of the *So Big* versions, she resented the third version, since Warner Bros. paid her nothing for it. MGM had exploited *Show Boat* in a similar manner in 1951, and while Ferber had learned to negotiate far better contracts since the publication of *Cimarron* in 1929, it galled her that the studios owned the rights to two of her most famous books outright. Perhaps she would have enjoyed knowing that Warner Bros. legal executives approached their third adaptation with trepidation, largely fearing that they had to renew their film rights with Ferber for any remake.[127] But as she complained to film critics Bosley Crowther (*New York Times*) and Otis Guernsey (*New York Herald Tribune*), the rights to *So Big* had for many years been "out of my hands."[128] She even claimed that she had no prior knowledge of the remake until reading the reviews. This seems unlikely, given her careful consultation of the trade papers over the years.

But Ferber really resented Warner Bros.' repeated exploitation of *So Big* as well as the way the studio used her name and novel without adequate payment. At the Paramount Theatre in New York, one exhibitor lured audience members by offering free tickets to those who brought along a copy of her book.[129] Since Ferber maintained all publishing rights, she found this outrageous. But Ferber's self-portrait as a victim of studio exploitation was not completely valid. After all, she allowed Doubleday to negotiate film tie-in editions of the book (except when the royalty was too low), capitalizing in a small way on renewed interest in the narrative.[130] Ferber also tried to get *So Big* turned into a play or musical in the early 1950s, since she still owned the dramatic and musical rights.[131] She may have hoped that producer Robert Fryer of CBS would purchase the motion picture rights from Warner Bros., and that eventually she could buy back the rights following the dramatic production or at least earn a percentage on any future remakes. But she acted too late: Warner Bros., already in the midst of the third version, was "inclined to take a dim view of the proposition."[132]

Ferber wanted to get as much money and publicity as she could from her novels. Critic Heywood Broun had noticed *So Big* and its author's commercial and artistic contradictions back in 1924: "I gather that Miss Ferber feels that beauty is something which belongs almost exclusively to those engaged in certain set pursuits, which may roughly be classified as 'the arts' . . . But no man or woman is an artist merely by virtue of his calling." "Perhaps Selina should not be expected to realize that," he argued, "but at least Miss Ferber ought to know. I don't think she does, for in *So Big* the young bond salesman first comes to the devastating conviction that Philistinism and Babbittry have captured him when he meets a young woman artist who gets $1,500 for each advertising poster which she draws."[133] Would Dirk and Ferber have felt the same if Dallas and Roelf Pool had been poor, struggling artists? Would Selina have approved of her creator's creative materialism? But Ferber's experience with *So Big* represented only a part of her thirty-year negotiation with Warner Bros.

three

Making Believe

how *Boat* is perhaps Ferber's best-known work of histor-
ical fiction, but ironically, most Americans remember
the Oscar Hammerstein–Jerome Kern musical adaptation rather than Ferber's original text.¹ Apart from selling Florenz Ziegfeld the musical rights to her novel in
1926, Ferber had no role in the creation of the libretto,
but because of her business foresight, her name would
always be linked with any publicity for the musical and subsequent films. Ferber's novel of Magnolia Hawks Ravenal's experience in the post–Civil War
South considered three major issues that held Hollywood's attention for decades: romance, race, and performance. In Ferber's novel and, to a certain
extent, Hammerstein's libretto, "making believe" leads to unhappiness and
loss of independence. Magnolia's transformation from a romantic, compli-
ant young wife into a mature, self-reliant single mother, artist, and business-
woman following her abandonment by husband Gaylord Ravenal represents
Ferber's demystification of the southern belle myth. *Show Boat*'s critique of
traditional romance and marriage was an odd choice for Broadway and Hol-

lywood producers, who during the 1920s depended on a steady crop of contemporary love stories. However, the original Broadway production (1927) and the first two Hollywood adaptations, released by Universal in 1929 and 1936, retained much of Ferber's narrative about the performance of romance and the presence of working women in vaudeville and on Broadway. Ferber's chronicle of Julie Laverne's experience as a mixed-race woman and her exploration of the post–Civil War segregation of African Americans posed additional problems for Hollywood screenwriters intent on challenging the censors.

Part of *Show Boat*'s uniqueness in American cultural history lies in Ferber's treatment of the tragic mulatta—Magnolia's childhood friend and showboat actress Julie Laverne. American literature is populated with many mixed-race heroines, some of them extraordinarily beautiful and courageous, like James Fenimore Cooper's Cora Munro (*The Last of the Mohicans*, 1826), but all of them doomed to loneliness, exile, or death. The trope persisted after the Civil War, made more painful by the historical realities of racism and segregation in the North and South.[2] Julie partly conforms to the traditional stereotype, which was increasingly visible because of the popularity of southern historical fiction between 1880 and 1926, but like Ferber's southern belle, Magnolia, she also possesses revisionist elements. For a few years, while they live and work aboard the *Cotton Blossom*, Julie and Magnolia are like sisters, and Ferber explores the full implications of their lives after Julie's expulsion from the troupe for violating southern miscegenation laws. Ferber's twin heroines— both thin, graceful, dark, and romantic; both actresses with gifts for singing African American music—reveal the instability and cruelty of race as a marker of American difference.

In many ways, it is tempting to compare Ferber's historical novel and its popular visual legacy to Margaret Mitchell's *Gone with the Wind*, begun shortly after the publication of Ferber's novel in 1926, but published ten years later, which was also when James Whale made the second of *Show Boat*'s three film versions.[3] Mitchell's heroine, Scarlett O'Hara, also shares close relationships with African Americans and racial and class hybrids in the antebellum and postbellum South, and she too was dark, unconforming, and passionate.[4] But Ferber's work has another connection with the history of American women's fiction in its similarities to Harriet Beecher Stowe's *Uncle Tom's Cabin* (1852). Following the publication of *Show Boat*, many critics compared Ferber to Stowe, whose best-selling narrative of slaves' lives was the greatest publishing phenomenon of the nineteenth century. Like Stowe, Ferber was a best-selling writer who capitalized on an expanding publishing market fuelled largely by female readers. They also shared a belief in history's ability to affect contemporary society. Film historian Linda Williams even argues that Ferber's characters mirror Stowe's melodramatic racial types: Magnolia is Little Eva grown up, Jo and Queenie are like Uncle Tom and Chloe, and Julie is "an amalgam of the ravaged Cassie and the passing-to-escape Eliza."[5]

While Stowe created dramatically exaggerated racial types in order to persuade an American population of the ills of slavery, Ferber, along with librettist and screenwriter Oscar Hammerstein, appropriated the well-known melodramatic mechanisms of "performance" to expose American entertainment's twin fantasies of race and romance. Gender, race, and power shift within the evolving history of popular entertainment. Although less impressed with *Show Boat*'s rendering of race, literary historian Lauren Berlant argues that as a product of the dominant culture industries of publishing, musical theatre, and film, "*Show Boat* delivers a meaningfully incoherent account of whether white women represent a subaltern class in America."[6] But a closer look at Ferber's novel and Universal's second production reveals a coherent and even incisive portrait of America's mixed-race history and the fictions of race and gender in vaudeville and cinema.

Making Believe and Miscegenation

Ferber began researching showboat culture in 1924. At the time, she and her producer, Winthrop Ames, were weathering difficulties in launching her first coauthored play with George Kaufman, *Old Man Minick*. When Connecticut theatres continued to be half empty during tryouts, Ames suggested lightly that the company hire a showboat next time and float around in search of audiences, never bothering to get off the boat.[7] Ferber was fascinated by Ames's description of the floating theatres that had entertained country people who otherwise would never have seen a performance. Historian Martin Ridge explains the showboat phenomenon as a uniquely American entertainment form, arguing, "The expanding frontier left a thin veneer of culture in its wake, a people starved for social contact and entertainment."[8] While many small towns had theatres for local amateur players, only the showboats regularly brought professional entertainers to out-of-the-way ports. Samuel Drake's company went from New York to Kentucky in 1815, using the Allegheny

River. But it was English immigrant acting families like the Chapmans who transformed the art of showboat performance in the years before the Civil War. William Chapman's Covent Garden Theatre background brought theatrical professionalism and a working-family atmosphere to American frontier entertainment. As years passed, communities eagerly awaited the return of the troupe. A weakened southern economy temporarily slowed the rebirth of the showboat business following the war, but Gus French, a middle-aged, former small-town businessman, tried his hand at building a floating theatre, and with the help of his wife, Callie, the first licensed female pilot on the Mississippi, the business grew throughout the 1880s and 1890s.[9] Competitors would build bigger boats, but a French "New Sensation" was still patrolling the rivers until 1907. That year, French's widow, Callie, the troupe's manager since French's death five years earlier, finally sold the boat to showman A. B. Price. Although the novelty of bigness and live performance lasted for a few more years, Callie French was wise to get out of the business when she did. By the early decades of the twentieth century, another form of popular entertainment was competing for audiences in even the smallest American towns: the movies.

Winthrop Ames was under the impression that the age of the showboats lasted from the 1860s to the 1880s and that they no longer performed on the rivers. But Ferber discovered that, like the old-fashioned immigrant farms in *So Big*, these anachronisms had persisted into the 1920s. At last Ferber could combine her love of theatre and performance with her historical writing: "Here, I thought, was one of the most melodramatic and gorgeous bits of Americana that had ever come my way."[10] She was even more inspired since American historians had all but neglected the showboat, despite its being a purely national phenomenon: "It was unbelievable that this rich and colorful aspect of American life had been almost completely overlooked."[11] Ferber's research on the history of showboats lasted a year, during which she spent weeks in libraries tracking down obscure references to showboat culture and enjoyed several days aboard the *James Adams Floating Theatre* in the spring of 1925—her hosts were all longtime Ferber fans. Her narrative would focus on a family that owned and operated a boat over several decades. Ferber saw the story in her mind as a series of vivid images: "At the very thought of the Mississippi there welled up in me from some hidden treasure-trove in my memory or imagination a torrent of visualized pictures, people, incidents." As she reminisced in her autobiography, "I don't to this day know where that river knowledge came from. Perhaps, centuries and centuries ago, I was a little Jewish slave girl on the Nile."[12]

Ferber's self-casting as a slave girl on another river in another time evokes the source of her deeper interest in American showboat culture: the heritage of African American slavery and racism in theatre history. Curiously, in her autobiography, Ferber deliberately prefaced her discussion of the showboat project with an account of her first hands-on theatrical venture: *Old Man Minick*. The company was a bit "daring," even by the standards of New York in the 1920s, because it hired an African American actress to play a black maid, rather than a white woman in blackface. "White and colored actors did not then ordinarily mingle," Ferber recalled. "The stage has grown in that direction, at least."[13] As she put the book together in the spring of 1926, her major research question seems to have been whether black and white actors performed together. Certainly, audiences were segregated from the beginning. As Philip Graham points out, an 1831 woodcut of the Chapmans' first showboat shows "a small gallery at the bow (the rear of the theatre) for colored people."[14] The most popular boat on the antebellum Mississippi, G. R. Spaulding's *Banjo*, specialized in a "nigger show" (minstrel show), with both black and white performers in blackface, but as Graham acknowledges, "with such a program on board the *Banjo* would not dare play south of Cairo [the southernmost town in Illinois]."[15] Despite the accelerating popularity of minstrel shows in the mid-nineteenth century, audiences and most troupes remained segregated, even in the North. After the Civil War and the legal enforcement of segregation, many African Americans migrated north to Chicago and New York. The mixed-race minstrel show had something of a revival in these cities at the end of the century, and black, white, and mixed-race women also participated, either corked up or powdered to pass. Although showboat programs often had short melodramatic skits, African American and white southern songs, and minstrelsy, long narrative dramas, particularly about race, were less frequent. Augustus French's decision in 1897 to put on *Uncle Tom's Cabin* (on northern rivers only) was the only time he gambled on a full-length drama in his career as a showman. But adaptations of Stowe's narrative were fairly frequent in northern waters after the turn of the century.

Ferber also asked Charles Hunter, the manager and brother-in-law of the *James Adams*'s owner, about how the antimiscegenation laws worked in the South. As Hunter wrote, he knew of quite a few cases of white women married to black men and vice versa, although interracial marriages were far less common in the South because of the laws: "But I can't say as much for the southern men, between me and you there is plenty of mixed blood in the South and it isn't all confined to the lower classes by any means." He even told her of a case twenty years earlier in Charlotte, North Carolina, in which a white man legalized his connection to his mixed-race wife (a showboat actress) by drinking her blood before the sheriff could convict them of miscegenation. They called such mixed-race women "yellow girls." This one, Hunter remembered, would sing for the customers, "powdered until she was almost white."[16] It was allegedly a black man who told the police of the illegal marriage. Hunter never discovered what happened to her. He wrote bitterly, "There is many a father sitting down stairs among the whites with a daughter in the gallery among the colored."[17]

Ferber would incorporate this real miscegenation case, making it the centerpiece of Magnolia Hawks's childhood memories onboard the fictional *Cotton Blossom*.[18] *Show Boat* would entwine the lives of its two showboat actresses, Julie Laverne, the mixed-race actress and early role model for Magnolia Hawks, the daughter of a showboat owner, and Magnolia herself, who would use Julie's music and experience to fashion her own theatrical career. Ferber's previous novel, *So Big*, revolved around a heroine who was a cultural oddity in her hometown, and *Show Boat* also pursued themes of racism, nativism, and cultural difference by coloring Magnolia as vividly as Julie. Although Ferber's preface to *Show Boat* claims that it "is neither history nor biography, but fiction," her remarks were simply a way of protecting herself from lawsuits. Just as with *So Big*, she chose a historical period that was still a part of some living memories, and therefore the potential subject for slander suits. Ferber was proud of her research, but she knew that historians rarely made the best-seller list, particularly when their work was weighed down with a bibliography and footnotes. But like her two heroines, Ferber's approach to writing about the past was a hybrid, a mixture of theatricality, memory, and women's history. Just like Selina, Julie and Magnolia were women who were excluded from the realm of public history and national memory. Even by traditional theatre-historical standards, they were not important enough to be the subject of biographies. But *Show Boat* made their experiences integral to American popular culture.

The Tragic Mulatta

To a certain extent, Ferber uses classic stereotypes to describe Julie's mulatta background. She is passive, indolent, graceful, and beautiful.[19] Her eyes and hair are dark, but her skin is pale and sallow. While on the showboat, she even has a marmoset, or pet monkey, which she keeps close to her like a child. When she is about to be exposed by the sheriff of a small southern river town, Ferber writes that there was "a strange resemblance" between her expression of wide-eyed terror and the marmoset's.[20] Although mainstream historians virtually ignored the experiences of mulattas and mestizas (mixed-race Native American or Mexican American women) until the late twentieth century, biracial women have a long history as protagonists in American literature. While mixed-race African American and Native American men are almost without exception demonized as atavistic and insane, white authors have approached mixed-race women with more frequency and sympathy.[21] As Suzanne Bost points out in her study of mixed-race literary representation, "Throughout popular culture and literature, debates about the nature of mixed-race identity are mapped out on the body of a woman because thinking about racial mixing inevitably leads to questions of sex and reproduction."[22] Women also have the unique ability to embody the past, present, and future of American multiracialism. Mixed-race women not only are the product of white male rape and exploitation of Native and African American women, but also have the potential to bear mixed-race children. Over time, racial mixture is therefore rendered a natural, integral component of American development and not a result of aberrant male violence.

In American literature, light-skinned "mixed" heroines are frequently indistinguishable from their white sisters, challenging the validity of race as a visual and cultural category. Many mixed-race heroines in nineteenth-century literature act in contemporary dramas about slavery and the myth of racial purity that structured American exceptionalism (*Clotel*, 1853; *Zoe*, 1859, etc.). But others are set distinctly within the American past. The first mixed-race heroine in American literature was Cora Munro, James Fenimore Cooper's tragic West Indian–Scottish heroine in *The Last of the Mohicans: A Narrative of 1757*. According to literary historian Cassandra Jackson, Cora formed the pattern for future mulatta heroines: she was graceful, modest, brave, beautiful, passive, resigned, and doomed.[23]

Although Julie shares in much of the tragic mulatta heritage in American literature, Ferber complicates the notion of race and culture with her double, Magnolia. Ferber's opening chapter describes the birth of contemporary Broadway actress Kim Ravenal on her grandfather's showboat on the Mississippi River. The scenes of birth and motherhood are dominated by women: Parthenia Hawks, Magnolia's bossy New England–born mother; the midwives (who "snigger" at the clumsy inadequacy of the male doctor's modern ways); and Magnolia. First described as "white," "limp," "slim," and "passive," the weakened Magnolia seems an unlikely Ferber heroine.[24] She refuses food from her mother, but allows her husband to help her. Ferber describes the thin figure with her black hair "spread so dank and wild on the pillow." One of the greatest ironies of *Show Boat* was the name of its heroine. Though a seemingly pale and passive southern belle, overcome by the pains of childbirth, Magnolia is no literary stereotype. On the opening page, Ferber notes that Magnolia never fit the standard image of the nineteenth-century actress: "In a day when the stage measured feminine pulchritude in terms of hips, thighs, and calves, she was considered much too thin for beauty." Throughout Magnolia's childhood, Parthy tries to make her daughter into the ideal obedient child. She fails to normalize Magnolia's Huckleberry Finn-esque river, curb her love of African American culture, or curl her mass of long, "almost black" straight hair.[25] Parthy might as well have tried turning Topsy into Little Eva. For of all the characters in *Show Boat*, Magnolia most resembles Julie Dozier— ironically, the only other "almost black" character in Ferber's cast.

It is soon revealed that Julie is half black and half white. Her mother was an African American woman from Mississippi. But until a jealous boat worker tells the sheriff in the town where she was born, no one can see Julie's black blood. A classic tragic mulatta, Julie is pale enough to pass for a white woman in both the North and the South. Married to the white Steve Baker, she is Magnolia's closest friend while she grows up on the *Cotton Blossom*. When Magnolia first sees Julie walking down the street near her house, Ferber notes that "her eyes were deep, and dark, and dead." She is carelessly dressed in a trailing black gown with a matching veil, "imparting a Spanish and mysterious look."[26] The initial description of Julie matches James Fenimore Cooper's image of Cora in the wilderness, her face hidden by a seductive veil.[27] Julie and Magnolia exchange smiles immediately, for "a filament of live liking had leaped." Magnolia's enjoyment of the ease and variety of river life matches

Julie's. And like Julie, who was "a natural and intuitive actress"—undoubtedly because of her need to survive in a black-white world—Magnolia too is drawn to the fantasy of the stage.[28]

They are not merely spiritually kin, but also visually linked. Julie's eyes are "deep-set and really black," and although Magnolia's haven't yet acquired their dark, mournful romantic experience, they too are dark. When she spies Julie kissing Steve, Ferber describes Julie's "slimness" and "limp" form, paralleling her initial description of Magnolia recovering from Kim's birth.[29] Both are described as having "sallow" coloring and dark hair.[30] When she and Julie run off to look for berries and flowers on riverbanks, Parthy scolds significantly, "Now keep your hat pulled down over your eyes so's you won't get all sunburned, Magnolia. Black enough as 'tis."[31] Later, when Julie is hiding from discovery in her room, refusing to play in her hometown, Ferber describes her dark, dank hair tumbled wildly about her. Pale and listless on her bed, Julie again oddly takes on Ferber's initial description of Magnolia.[32] Shortly thereafter, when the sheriff forces Andy to dismiss Steve and Julie, Magnolia is the only one to excoriate the sheriff. After her angry outburst, the sheriff remarks to Parthy and the rest of the company, "Well, women folks are all alike . . . I kind of smell a nigger in the woodpile here in more ways than one."[33] According to him, Magnolia is so close to Julie that there may be more than one racial subterfuge on board the boat.

After Julie leaves the showboat, Magnolia runs after her, wanting to say goodbye. At first Julie runs away from the girl, fearful of meeting her again with the public recognition of their racial separateness between them. But when Magnolia dissolves into tears, Julie runs to comfort her one last time, and Ferber writes, "When finally they came together, the woman dropped on her knees in the dust of the road and gathered the weeping child to her and held her close, so that as you saw them sharply outlined against the sunset the black of the woman's dress and the white of the child's frock were as one."[34] While Lauren Berlant argues that Ferber reveals the ongoing racial divide in the South by expelling the mixed-race Julie from the white showboat, transferring "the narrative energy of romance" to the young white Magnolia, more than romance and plot structure have been transferred.[35] In this sequence, the black of Julie's dress and the white of Magnolia's become "as one." Ferber's vivid language evokes their shared spiritual and blood ties, visualizing the significance of their shared experience. Julie embraces Magnolia as the mother

that Magnolia has never known. While Parthy is cold, calculating, and big-
oted, Julie is warm, wise, and generous. She shares her experience and love
with Magnolia as would a mother.

The scene is prefaced by Steve's physical taking of Julie's blood, which
would become the melodramatic centerpiece of the musical libretto. But in
this exchange between women, the embracing women, represented by their
black and white dress colors, share, blend, and become one. Rather than
Steve's melodramatic act, this scene between the women is the most important exchange of blood and color in the novel. For in it, Magnolia symboli-
cally takes on Julie's racial history, her knowledge of African American songs,
and her romantic tragedy. While some critics have viewed Magnolia's career
as a white singer of black songs as another white commodification of black
music and theft of racial history, for Ferber, Magnolia has become part of Julie's blood.[36] Even before their final exchange, Magnolia has begun to absorb
African American teachings. "An excellent mimic," she sings like her two
teachers, Queenie and Jo, with "her head thrown slightly back, her eyes rolling or half-closed, one foot beating rhythmic time to the music's cadence."[37]
She even sings with a "Negro overtone." While Parthy tries to force Magnolia
to practice proper music, the girl wants only to learn in the showboat kitch-
en from her surrogate family. Ferber describes Jo, Queenie, and Magnolia as
a complete, happy family unit: "Filled with the healthy ecstasy of song, the
Negro man and woman and the white child would sit in deep contentment in
the show boat kitchen."[38] Parthy could break them apart, but only temporarily. In James Whale's film adaptation, Julie becomes the fourth member of
this family—another mixed-blood teaching Magnolia black ways—but here
Magnolia is the child in a true family unit. When Julie leaves the showboat,
a new mixed-blood actress, Magnolia, takes her place. Magnolia's name and
her resemblance to that white flower are typical Ferber ironies. Magnolia is
neither as fragile nor as white as the pristine southern flower.

The second half of Ferber's novel concerns Magnolia's career as a showboat actress—first alone, when she creates quite a following as the *Cotton Blossom*'s ingénue lead—and later opposite her future husband, Gaylord Ravenal.[39]
From the first, Ferber describes him as a master of pretense. Although dressed
in the shabby remains of once-fine clothes and with a crack in his shoe, Ravenal poses as an elite and cultured man of leisure, looking down his "aristocratic nose" at both Andy and the *Cotton Blossom* when the former asks him to
join the company as the juvenile lead.[40] From a distance, his clothes impress

Magnolia, but he does not hold up so well under close scrutiny.[41] Later, after he joins, he also works on the stage scenery, imparting the same "at a distance beauty" to landscapes. As Ravenal explains to the company, which has grown used to trees that are meant to look like trees at any distance, "It isn't supposed to look like a forest . . . It's supposed to give the effect of the forest."[42]

Ravenal does well in showboat productions, which treasure beauty and illusion. Magnolia, like the audience, is bewitched by a man who plays both onstage and off, and, under the influence of the company's standard melodramas, falls in love with her leading man. As Ferber writes, "Their make-believe adventures as they lived them on stage became real."[43] Though some moments of her life on the boat resemble scenes of traditional melodrama— from Julie and Steve's exchange of blood to her stolen nocturnal meetings with Ravenal—Magnolia soon discovers that happy endings do not exist and that the only way to escape poverty, fear, and loneliness is to work and become independent.[44] Although initially attracted by the color and excitement of 1880s and 1890s Chicago, Magnolia is gradually disillusioned as Ravenal gambles away her inherited share of Andy's *Cotton Blossom*.[45] The romance of make-believe wears off without money, and the colorful images of Chicago life become "shadows, sinister, menacing, evil" as she learns to despise her ineffectual husband.[46]

But Ferber's heroine is no feminist; she returns to work only after Ravenal has left her. Significantly, Parthy's threatened visit precipitates his abandonment of the family. He cannot stand to have the New England widow who always resisted his charms point out his failure as a businessman, husband, and father. He stays out all night and returns, drunk, with alleged winnings bankrolled by his friend and city madam, Hetty Chilson. Magnolia examines his sleeping unlined face and sees its bland lack of character or strength.[47] When she returns the money that morning, Magnolia meets a "genteel" black-gowned assistant with ivory skin whom she recognizes as Julie. Julie flees from Magnolia in horror, but their meeting inspires the destitute Magnolia to do as Julie had once done years before. She tries to enter vaudeville. On her way home, she goes into a variety theatre and asks for an audition. Borrowing a musician's banjo, she sits down onstage, throws her head back "as Jo had taught her," and begins to sing the songs she learned as a child. Magnolia's meeting with Julie has not only given her the nerve to pursue an independent career, but also created a parallel public perception of her mixed-race origins. She is so convincing that the manager, assuming she is black, asks her, "You a nigger?" When she says no, he replies, "Well, you cer'nly sing like one. Voice and—I don't know—way you sing . . . I've seen 'em lighter 'n you."[48] The man is a seasoned manager, and yet she fools him, momentarily "passing" as a mixed-race woman.

At this time, vaudeville was one of the few entertainment venues in which black and white players could mix. Cakewalker Aida Overton Walker and comic Bert Williams were major vaudeville headliners, and many mixed-race and white women participated in minstrel-show skits, either in blackface or powdered to "pass." However, as M. Alison Kibler points out, "Managers clearly accepted white women's challenges to vaudeville's ideal womanhood far more readily than they tolerated black performers' attempts to cross the racial lines in vaudeville."[49] Women did not have to be attractive to become minstrel stars, and in profiting from their comic ability, they usurped the traditional province of male vaudevillians. As Kibler argues persuasively, "Racial disguises provided the raw material both for white women's upward mobility and for a feminine subtext of vaudeville's past."[50] While black women and large white women such as actress May Irwin could successfully play the conventional mammy stereotype on stage, more troubling to vaudeville managers and audiences were light-skinned mulattas who masqueraded as whites, or attractive young white actresses like Josephine Gassman and Leona Thurber, who blacked up and danced enthusiastically with her troupe of black "pickaninnies."[51] But while blackface was often the road to individual success for actresses and chorus girls, white women's increased presence in and patronage of high-class vaudeville as the century wore on created a gentrification of minstrelsy. White women in fancy ball gowns often sang sedately without a cohort of black children to liven things up.

Ferber spends very little time discussing Magnolia's struggle and eventual success as a singer; we do not know whether she sang in blackface or in a ball gown to polite high-end vaudeville audiences. Most of the novel follows her preparation for stardom, in which she performed a variety of melodramatic skits. And the African American musical heritage that is integral to her training stands in stark contrast to her daughter Kim's education in convent and dramatic schools. The modern teachings, like Kim's own career, are "so artificial, so studied, so manufactured."[52] While Magnolia appreciates all forms of theatre, from showboats to vaudeville to Ada Rehan and Sarah Bernhardt, Kim is carefully prepared to perform for a certain type of audience. She arguably represents the final gentrification and homogenization of mass culture in the twentieth century. As entertainment culture forms its boundaries around separate audiences, Kim becomes part of "this new crop of intelligent, successful, deft, workmanlike, intuitive, vigorous, adaptable young women of the theatre." But "there was about her . . . nothing of genius, of greatness, of the divine fire." Ferber hints that Magnolia's life and career were more nourishing and magnificent because of their "mixture" of elements.[53]

Show Boat remains Ferber's most enduringly popular novel, and perhaps because of this and the romantic beauty of the Kern-Hammerstein musical, many critics have tended to downplay its social criticism.[54] Contemporary reviewer Louis Kronenberger loved the book for being "gorgeously romantic" and for making a lost era "live again," but acknowledged that "this is little else but an irresistible story."[55] Ironically, he seemed so caught by the aura of period romance that he missed Ferber's sharper historical commentary. Ravenal was "that most engrossing and romantic character of all." Kronenberger paid no attention to the book's racial subtexts, critique of modern entertainment, or cast of dominant woman characters. Ferber herself remembered the novel through the haze and color of the musical; in her 1963 memoir, she writes that *Show Boat* "never was intended to be more than an authentic and romantic novel of Americana" and lacked any "underlying theme or purpose." Musical theatre historian Miles Kreuger, while obviously enthralled by the various versions of the narrative, believes that the novel "is quite frankly escapist romance with no hidden social meaning." This seems a remarkable statement to make, given Kreuger's awareness of *Show Boat*'s racial subtext. Even Mary Rose Shaughnessy, whose work acknowledges Ferber's feminist portrayal of women attaining self-respect and independence, notes that "it does not contain the social protest of her other novels."[56]

Only Lauren Berlant differentiates the textual and musical narratives, arguing that Ferber's original was a far more complex and racially nuanced portrait of America. Berlant contends that the novel *Show Boat* "follows the dissolution of the American color line into the linked crossover dynamics of the Harlem Renaissance, modernist youth culture, and middlebrow entertainments."[57] While Ferber's novel "discloses some of the mechanisms by means of which subaltern activity and in particular the public history of African Americans have been expropriated for the purpose of creating a 'modern' American culture, one that might flaunt a rich past while feeling free from accountability to the past's ongoing activity in the present," Berlant argues that the musical and films "have made the text a classic vehicle for amnesiac narrative, an authentic piece of kitsch history."[58] Ferber's rich multiracial America is reconfigured by the visual-culture industries into a more simplified black-and-white world. While Berlant does acknowledge that the play and film versions "give richer, more elaborate, and more nuanced subjectivities to the African-American characters" than the novel does, she contends that these new adaptations banish African American subjectivity to the past. The narrative primarily follows Magnolia and, later, Kim; the African American characters Jo and Queenie are static and relegated to Magnolia's childhood. They do not sing their music; instead, it is used and performed by white entertainers. But Ferber and her adaptors were just as concerned with another "subaltern" class and its history of service to white men—women. According to Berlant, Ferber's interest in women's history was transformed by Hollywood into "white women's history," and "love plots and domestic fantasies come to saturate the narratives of experience with which women of a certain class identify."[59]

While Berlant's claims for the discursive differences between Ferber's historical novel and the ensuing visual adaptations are persuasive, she pays less attention to the dynamics of Ferber's multiracial America, the nuances of racial mixing, the performativity of race, and Ferber's belief in women as the carriers of historical experience. While *Show Boat* certainly focuses more on Magnolia's life than Julie's, their histories are linked. Ferber and, later, Hammerstein do not simply transform women's history into "white women's history," but focus on Magnolia's mixed cultural, romantic, and racial inheritance from Julie. The three filmed versions of *Show Boat* differ surprisingly in their handling not only of Ferber's historical narrative, but also of the relationship between Magnolia and Julie. They chart not only the changes, from 1927 to 1951, in Hollywood's attitude toward visualizing America's theatrical past, but also the persistent instability of racial difference and heterosexual romance.

Rehabilitating Romance

Ferber spent a year writing *Show Boat*, finishing it in early 1926. Soon after it appeared in the April edition of Gertrude Lane's *Woman's Home Companion*, Hollywood studios started bidding for the rights. However, Ferber held off the film sale to Universal until Doubleday published it in book form that September. Since the novel was an early Book-of-the-Month Club pick (courtesy of William Allen White) and best seller, Universal knew that it already had a ready-made film audience. Given the popularity of the book, even before being adapted as a musical, it is surprising that Ferber accepted Universal's offer of $65,000. She signed the contract October 26, 1926, and never ceased to regret that she hadn't held out for a higher price or for copyright reversion. Though Ferber would receive an additional $20,000 for each of the remakes of the musical, this was a pittance compared with what she might have obtained. Soon after, she hired attorney Morris Ernst to handle her affairs with the studios.

One of the studio's story readers, R. B. Willis, commented that the novel was a "dramatic narrative life of a show-boat actress," but completely ignored Julie and the film's racial melodrama.[60] Despite praising it as a "brilliant, entertaining piece of work, wonderful character drawing, colorful life," Willis concluded that the novel was merely a superficial, historically worthless narrative: "It's just a story, it isn't significant, it isn't TRUE, however plausible the author's genius makes it. Despite story's drama and color there is doubt in my mind if this is practicable." The reader also found Ferber's feminist perspective unsettling. Although Willis was convinced that the Mississippi River "is a man's river, not a woman's" because "it is the 'Father of Waters,'" "two women over-shadow the whole story—Parthy and Magnolia. The latter is much like the River, indeed, but the former is not." Ferber's story, if adapted, could not remain so woman oriented: "What will be needed then for picture purposes will be to augment the male roles, especially Andy's and Ravenal's in the river part, to an equality with the female roles to escape this otherwise feminine over-balance." But the real need was to rehabilitate the failed romance between Ravenal and Magnolia. Willis suggested that Ravenal turn up on the showboat at the end, meeting Magnolia by chance: "They're both middle-aged and can forgive. He's not all a swine; he deserted her mainly because he'd shamed them both, dragging her down low."[61]

But before Universal could adapt a version of Ferber's book, she arranged a deal in November 1926 for its adaptation as a musical. Florenz Ziegfeld, in a major departure from his usual annual spectacles of scantily but artistically clad beauties (the Ziegfeld *Follies* series), produced the Jerome Kern–Oscar Hammerstein stage version. Initially, Ferber "resented the idea" that one of her works was thought to be good material for a Broadway musical.[62] As Miles Kreuger has pointed out, until *Show Boat*, the American musical had dealt with no more pressing social issue than whether the poor girl could marry the rich boy.[63] Plots were negligible. In addition, transforming *Show Boat* into a musical went directly against the grain of Ferber's novel, in which the melodramatic showboat plots (where love and truth are always triumphant) are juxtaposed with the harsher realities of river life. The audience and the players found only temporary relief in make-believe. As Ferber described one typical performance: "They knew that things in life did not happen thus. But they saw, believed, and were happy . . . They forgot the cotton fields, the wheatfields, the cornfields . . . The women forgot for an hour their washtubs, their kitchen stoves, childbirth pains, drudgery, worry, disappointment. Here were blood, lust, love, passion. Here were warmth, enchantment, laughter, music."[64] More than in the case of straight dramatic plays or photoplays, audience belief and commitment to the plot of a musical depends on a suspension of reality. This is particularly true of the integrated musical, in which performers break into song and dance and remain in character, as, for example, when Fred Astaire sings Cole Porter's "Night and Day" to Ginger Rogers in *The Gay Divorcee* (1933, RKO)—or as in much of *Show Boat*. As Jane Feuer and Rick Altman point out, in movie musicals, particularly the integrated variety made in the classical era and dominated by MGM, characters break into song and dance unconsciously—as if doing so were the most natural thing in the world.[65]

Turning *Show Boat*'s entire narrative into a self-contained performative world, a spectacle of white consumption of black culture, does undercut much of Ferber's critique.[66] However, as Miles Kreuger argues, Hammerstein's libretto is remarkably faithful to the details of Ferber's book. It focuses on Magnolia's twin abandonment by Julie and Ravenal and on her indomitable life. Hammerstein also understood the way stage melodrama inflected Magnolia's life offstage, and he moved the site of Julie's racial unmasking from her bedroom to a rehearsal on the stage of the *Cotton Blossom*. From the beginning, Hammerstein made the discovery of Julie's black blood the centerpiece of the first four scenes. Early versions of the script reveal that Hammerstein felt it necessary to "demonstrate the exact moment in which Pete confirms that miscegenation is illegal in Mississippi." Although a musical scholar such as Kreuger considers this merely a rather clumsy and old-fashioned "scene of convenience," it is also evidence that Hammerstein took the story's racial text seriously.[67] His major transformation of the Julie-Magnolia relationship occurs in the second act. While Ferber arranged them to meet by chance in Hetty Chilson's house—two casualties of the sexual and financial enslavement of women—Hammerstein has Julie give up her headliner status in a Chicago club to boost Magnolia's career. This performative parallelism reinforces Julie's status as a tragic mulatta. Audiences took to the plot devices, and *Show Boat* had an impressive run on Broadway and later on the road.

Universal's first version was made just as Hollywood began the awkward transition to sound (*The Jazz Singer* was released in October 1927). Although the studio could have avoided the problem of adapting a musical as a mostly silent film by focusing exclusively on Ferber's narrative, the adaptation does not follow the novel closely. Charles Kenyon's script, developed slowly between March 1927 and April 1928, retains Julie and her close relationship with Magnolia, but avoids all mention of race or miscegenation![68] Kenyon describes Julie (Alma Rubens) comforting Magnolia after a fight with her mother. Magnolia responds in a title: "Julie—I wish you were my mama."[69] But when Magnolia announces that her great ambition is to become an actress "like Julie," her mother (Emily Fitzroy) fires Julie. Julie's departure is thus managed as a fight between two women over the mothering of a young girl. It is Julie's implied low morality as an actress combined with maternal jealousy, rather than Julie's mixed-race blood, which instigates her departure ("I'm not going to have my daughter corrupted by showboat trollops like you!" Parthy declares).

The script does make some effort to project Magnolia's gradual coming-of-age and her hard-won independence from both mother and husband. The adult Magnolia (Laura La Plante) eventually becomes an actress, defying her mother's wishes, but unlike the motivation provided in Hammerstein's more romantic libretto, her decision now has nothing to do with Julie's departure or the gambler Gaylord Ravenal's propitious arrival. Instead, the gambler (played by the elegant Broadway actor Joseph Schildkraut) appears when Magnolia is already well established by her father as "the greatest living actress on the Mississippi." They do not develop careers together; instead, Ravenal takes her from both family and career. Ravenal is every bit Ferber's vain dandy and mercenary hypocrite. Following Andy's death in a storm and Magnolia's decision to sell her share of the boat to Parthy, Ravenal spends all of his wife's money. After several humiliating years, Magnolia, in one of the film's few sound sequences, decides to send her daughter to a convent, adding that she herself will be "going to work . . . going back to the stage" (Fig. 3.1). He laughs nastily and derides the showboat as a "mud scow."[70] But Ravenal is unable to find work, even on a mud scow. Magnolia's scorn is made even more apparent to audiences in the sound sequence: "If you're too much of a gentleman to do a little honest work now and then, I'll have to do it," she sneers.

Magnolia returns to the stage (billed as a "Coon Shouter") and becomes a success without her hapless husband, but Universal evidently agreed with Willis that the romance needed to be repaired. The script follows Hammerstein's libretto, reconciling the couple in middle age, following her retirement from the stage. The implication was clear: women could work and become successes, but not if they wanted to preserve their marriages.

It was a troubled production. Although the studio hired Harry A. Pollard, fresh from directing the racial melodrama *Uncle Tom's Cabin* (1927), Pollard collaborated in Kenyon's whitewashing of the miscegenation narrative. Since sound was rapidly replacing silent film production, music director Joseph Cherniavsky integrated a series of spirituals into the sound track and composed new love songs for Magnolia.[71] Pollard's first version contained nothing of the Kern-Hammerstein score because the studio had been unable to secure the musical rights. While Pollard edited a silent (1 hour 54 minutes) and a slightly longer partial-sound version (2 hours 11 minutes), Carl Laemmle's attorneys continued to negotiate with Ziegfeld, Kern, Hammerstein, and Ferber. Universal executives were caught between wanting to capitalize immediately on *Show Boat*'s current vogue as a best seller and a successful musical, and negotiating the rights to reproduce parts of a libretto still under the control of Ziegfeld. Eventually, in January 1929, Universal purchased the musical rights from Ziegfeld, Kern, Hammerstein, and Ferber (who had retained a percentage in the musical rights and retained the novel's stage rights) for $100,000.[72]

But even with the rights, the studio still could not scrap Pollard's first version and film a faithful adaptation of the musical. Instead, Pollard was forced to reshoot and insert Kern-Hammerstein songs where he could in the existing sound print. Thus, it is Magnolia who sings "Ol' Man River" to white audiences in a Chicago club, not Joe.[73] In fact, Pollard's version virtually whitewashed the text's racial themes and cut any sequences with secondary black characters Joe and Queenie. The script originally opened with Joe (Stepin Fetchit) and Queenie (Gertrude Howard) teaching Magnolia (Jane La Verne) the songs that will help maintain her career years later.[74] In the final film, Pollard merely shows the troupe approaching a river town, punctuating the scenes with portentous intertitles like "The Mighty Mississippi—dark and moody." Black or mixed-race characters have no connection to Magnolia at all.

With the best of intentions, Universal also filmed a panchromatic opening sequence of Ziegfeld's stage stars performing *Show Boat* hits, but New York

above: 3.1. Magnolia (Laura La Plante) telling a threatened Ravenal (Joseph Schildkraut) that she is planning to go to work to support their daughter (*Show Boat*, Universal, 1929); *below:* 3.2. "White Noise": Laura La Plante as Magnolia in *Show Boat* (Universal, 1929).

film critics reacted scornfully to the musical preamble. Creighton Peet asked, "Can't the main film stand on its own?"[75] Evidently many felt otherwise. In the *New York World*, Quinn Martin wrote "There is no end of unnecessary, pointless material grafted into the running story."[76] Richard Watts, who would later praise other Ferber adaptations, dismissed it as "tedious."[77] Pollard and Kenyon's work had been damaged by the transition to sound and by Universal's rush to shoot the film before obtaining the musical rights, but the fact remains that neither filmmaker paid much attention to Ferber's racial text, instead crafting the film as a bittersweet period romance. Sime Silverman wrote for *Weekly Variety* that Pollard's film had very little of the Kern-Hammerstein libretto but that it was no more faithful to Ferber's work: "The story follows the book as it pleases."[78] Although Silverman derided the film's length and poor editing, he thought that the new scenario's plot device bringing "the small time gambler back to his Magnolia at the finale" was "one of the best bits." He also noted that Paul Whiteman's band played at the Globe premiere, solidifying the narrative as a white appropriation of black music. Whiteman's band was the best-known jazz band of the period, but the all-white ensemble capitalized on watered-down adaptations of original work from King Oliver and Louis Armstrong. Arguably, La Plante's performance as Magnolia reflects this white appropriation of black culture. Fair haired and pale, and making no attempt to imitate black performers or diction, La Plante's Magnolia lacks both the narrative and the physical connection to Joe, Queenie, and the mixed-race Julie (Fig. 3.2).

A White Woman Passing as Black? Irene Dunne and Show Boat (1936)

Universal had plans to remake *Show Boat* as early as 1933, but production was delayed until 1935. In January, the studio announced that Charles Winninger, the original Captain Andy Hawks, and Irene Dunne, who had first attracted RKO's attention while touring as Magnolia in 1929, were ready to make the film. In the meantime, executives had hired playwright-screenwriter Zoe Akins to write the script. Producer Carl Laemmle, Jr., may have thought that he had hired a writer in sympathy with Ferber's work. Both were successful female writers, often specializing in period material (Akins's *Old Maid* was a Civil War drama), and Akins's *Morning Glory* had been a big hit for RKO, earning Katharine Hepburn her first Academy Award. Hammerstein was brought in only after Akins's scripts were rejected.

Although initially reluctant to hire a green screenwriter, Universal decided to use Hammerstein out of a desire to capitalize on the success of the Broadway musical, and also out of a sense of the historical value of the novel. Hammerstein's original libretto had preserved *Show Boat*'s sense of nineteenth-century American and theatrical history, and during the 1930s, Hollywood was in the midst of a historical revival, partially fuelled by Ferber's work.[79] Many of these films celebrated women in American entertainment history, particularly Mae West's series of films at Paramount and Darryl F. Zanuck's productions such as *The Bowery* (1933), *She Done Him Wrong* (1933), and *Belle of the Nineties* (1934).[80] In addition, the text of *Show Boat* had attained an almost historical importance in the minds of its filmmakers. Laemmle tried whenever possible to sign actors who had been involved in the original Broadway or London productions or in U.S. road tours of the musical. The casting was therefore an attempt to remain faithful to the narrative and its cultural history. Besides Winninger and Sammy White (Schultzy), Helen Morgan, veteran of the original Ziegfeld production, was cast as Julie. Paul Robeson, star of the London production, re-created his role as Joe. Even Hollywood newcomer Allan Jones (Ravenal) had starred in a St. Louis production of *Show Boat* in 1934.

While Universal's first film focused on Magnolia's romance with Ravenal, cutting Julie out almost entirely, Hammerstein's screenplay, written six years later, preserves most of the structure of his original libretto. Both of Hammerstein's narratives for *Show Boat* focus on the experiences of Julie and Magnolia. The film adaptation opens with Pete's ominous threats to expose Julie, Julie's "swift terror" when Queenie recognizes her African American song, the miscegenation sequence, Magnolia's failed romance and rising career, and Julie's decline. It also preserves the dual-generation format, contrasting the rich entertainment experience of Magnolia with the more mundane, gentrified Broadway of her daughter, Kim (Sunnie O'Day). Hammerstein even includes a gimmick linking the screenplay to Ferber's novel. At one point, Kim asks her guests whether they have read Edna Ferber's *Show Boat*. Evidently, it is a biography of her mother, and Kim tells her audience that everything Ferber wrote about Magnolia is true.[81] Hammerstein, at pains to preserve Ferber's exposure of racial injustice and romantic myth, bolsters the novel's authenticity with this reference to Ferber. It was not "just a story" or a colorful romance, but an entertainment biopic.

As in Ferber's novel and the Ziegfeld production, Julie's experience dominates the first half of the script. When the sheriff informs Andy that he has a "miscegenation case" aboard, he is totally bewildered. It is not simply that it is a big word, but one totally foreign to his vocabulary. His incomprehension serves to alert the audience about the definition of racial mixing, and gives the southern laws regarding it almost a foreign or non-American quality.[82] After the sheriff goes, reassured that Andy will send Julie and Steve away, Magnolia tells her father to ignore the "law": "Nobody'll know about them in the next town," she pleads. "Julie's my friend."[83] Ravenal is also rehabilitated to a certain extent. In Hammerstein's final script, Andy does not die, and therefore Ravenal does not take Magnolia's money from the proceeds of the showboat. It ends with Magnolia reconciling with her husband.

Compared to the 1929 scripts, Hammerstein's version has a more nuanced delineation of the racial and sexual undercurrents in Ferber's book. The script notes that in the first glimpse of the showboat people, Andy and Magnolia are on the upper deck while "Julie, Steve, Joe and others on lower deck."[84] When Queenie catches Julie singing "Can't Help Lovin' Dat Man" to Magnolia and remarks, "Sounds funny fuh Miss Julie to know it," Hammerstein and director James Whale followed the shot with one of African Americans singing the same song outside on the riverbank.[85] Julie's knowledge of the music, which Queenie implies is an African American song, confirms Julie's racial heritage. Magnolia takes easily to the lyrics and the shuffle, horrifying Parthy (Helen Westley) when she sees Magnolia fitting in so well with Queenie (Hattie McDaniel), Joe, and Julie below decks.

Hammerstein's major departures from his 1928 libretto are an additional romantic duet between Ravenal and Magnolia, "I Have the Room above Her," and Magnolia's blackface number as Matilda Hill in "Gallivantin' Aroun'." While the original musical contained an elaborate sequence set in Chicago during the 1893 Columbian Exposition, in his screenplay, Hammerstein was far more interested in historicizing Magnolia's career as a singer and actress. He cut the Chicago sequence and added a historical montage later on, adding weight to Magnolia's life after Ravenal. Although Ravenal is not the sneering opportunist of the 1929 film, Hammerstein had far less sympathy for him than in his 1928 libretto. The Columbian Exposition sequence was the only one to depict Ravenal in a fairly good light, as he and Magnolia showed Andy and Parthy the splendors of the "white" city.[86]

However, the early romance between Magnolia and Ravenal is every bit as innocent and bewitching as Ferber and the original musical production described it. The two "Make Believe," and then fall in love during a spate of performances, their stage life gradually taking control of their offstage existence. Dunne's Magnolia even loses some of her tomboyish vivacity of the earlier sequences as she transforms into one of the innocent romantic heroines of nineteenth-century literature and theatre. But when she does try to step back into reality, asking the amorous Ravenal how he intends to support her once they marry and leave the showboat, he puts her in her place: "Magnolia, it is not the place of a gentlewoman to share her husband's business worries. I will provide for you. You must trust me, dear." Beneath the fantasy of theatrical romance lies its financial basis: chauvinism and hypocrisy. The scene is followed immediately by a new sequence, in which Magnolia has her baby without any white male help, including that of a doctor or her husband. Instead, Ellie (Queenie Smith), Queenie, Joe, and Parthy help her. But while Kenyon showed Ravenal laughing at Magnolia's plans to work and become a success, Hammerstein's Ravenal simply disappears, hoping in his last letter to her that she will return to her parents. Only after he has left and the marriage is over does Magnolia plan to work. She does not go back to her parents, abandoned and defeated, as Ravenal had intended.

Universal's second version of *Show Boat* was the studio's big prestige effort of 1936. But the trend toward expensive historical pictures came at a bad time for Universal, still on the verge of bankruptcy.[87] Studio founder Carl Laemmle and his son Carl Jr. were being forced out by corporate interests, and may have hoped that a successful prestige production would save the studio. It certainly was both a critical and popular success, with Irene Dunne receiving much of the praise. By 1936, Dunne was the actress most closely associated with the work of Edna Ferber. Dunne had starred in the 1929–1930 road-show production of *Show Boat*, and even then, many reviewers preferred her to the original Broadway Magnolia, Norma Terris, as did Edna Ferber, who, according to Dunne, told the actress personally that she "was the ideal Magnolia."[88] Dunne went to Hollywood soon after her successful road performance, and RKO put her under contract in April 1930 at the then-impressive salary of $1,000 a week and the stipulation that her "name will appear in type larger than any other female player, and as large as the featured male player."[89]

Although she missed being cast in Universal's first version of *Show Boat*, her second role in Hollywood was as Ferber's Sabra Cravat in *Cimarron*. Dunne had campaigned vigorously for the part in RKO's biggest film of 1931, perhaps hoping that another Ferber success would boost her career, since audiences seemed temporarily bored with filmed musicals.[90] It was not the last time that an actress would save her career with a Ferber role; in addition to receiving rave reviews for her performance as Sabra, Dunne was nominated for her first Academy Award. Soon she became one of the most popular actresses in historical films, specializing in American period productions like *The Silver Cord* (1933), *Ann Vickers* (1933), and *The Age of Innocence* (1934). But though Dunne was initially brought to Hollywood because of her singing success in *Show Boat*, musicals had been out of favor since 1929. By 1933, Universal had abandoned a planned *Show Boat* remake to be directed by Frank Borzage and starring Dunne. But as the decade wore on, other studios began to develop period musicals as a component of the lavish historical genre. Dunne's success in the Warner Bros. production *Sweet Adeline* (1935), about a famous theatrical star, may have reassured Universal that the time was right for *Show Boat*.

Shooting began in December 1935 and continued through the second week in March. Whale allegedly exposed over fifty hours of film, driving the production hundreds of thousands of dollars over budget and worrying the cast and executives that the English director had lost control of the project.[91] But according to film and musical critics, Whale's version is the most faithful to both Hammerstein's and Ferber's original portraits of multiracial America.[92] The opening credits are composed of a massive revolving paper cutout of the showboat performers advertising their wares on a main street, and emphasize the old-fashioned performative basis of showboat acting and the cardboard-cutout nature of their characters. Again, the film is presented as "Edna Ferber's *Show Boat*," although Hammerstein is given a separate writing title. Whale's version connects the showboat's brand of entertainment to working-class southern African American audiences in the opening frames. "Ol' Man River," later sung by Paul Robeson (Joe), accompanies the credits and carries over into a dissolve of the *Cotton Blossom* on the Mississippi. The next shot shows a black stevedore (Eddie Anderson) gleefully exclaiming, "It's the show boat!" while a crowd of men, women, and kids runs down to the dock to meet the boat. The opening shot is therefore linked to the perspective of an African American (Fig. 3.3).

Later, Whale experiments with the idea of African American perspective. As Paul Robeson sings "Ol' Man River," the camera pivots 360 degrees around his body before panning in on his profile as he sings the first verse. The lyrics lead to a series of internal point-of-view shots showing Robeson enduring the racial inequalities of the Jim Crow South. The canted frames and angled shots differ dramatically from Whale's camera practices for filming the white romance and melodrama. When filming the showboat actors during a per-

above: 3.3. Black point-of-view shot: Eddie Anderson spotting the showboat first (*Show Boat,* Universal, 1936); *below:* 3.4. Irene Dunne (Magnolia) with her white props (*Show Boat,* Universal, 1936).

formance of the old chestnut *Tempest and Sunshine,* Whale includes a series of shots of the audience, emphasizing the reflexive aspect of the performance. But Whale goes further, including shots of the African American audience watching from above. At one point, Whale positions the camera behind the African American spectators' heads to look down at the drama from their point of view. He repeats this practice several times throughout the film: during Magnolia's number "Gallivantin' Aroun'," and when Julie is exposed as a mixed-race woman during a rehearsal.

The first half hour of the narrative follows Hammerstein's script and focuses on the mixed-race melodrama. The first time we see Julie (Helen Morgan), she is one of the lead attractions of the shore parade, riding in a carriage and dressed in an elaborate white satin dress and hat. No longer Ferber's character lead, she is now the "Sweetheart of the South" and the company's leading lady. As Andy introduces her, Whale cuts to a group of lovelorn white men, eagerly looking up at her in the carriage. As in Hammerstein's libretto, Andy underscores that his boat is "just one big happy family"—but he always says it with a definite sense of irony. The first time he utters this cliché, it is to cover up Pete and Steve's public brawl over Julie; the second incident occurs as he tries to weather Parthy's dislike of Julie. This family component, always essential to a Ferber historical novel (but absent from the original text of *Show Boat*), underscores not only the concept of race and the American family, but also the film's ties to the American historical genre, which had successfully narrated American history from within the microcosm of the family unit since at least D. W. Griffith's *Birth of a Nation* (1915).

Although as Lauren Berlant points out, Whale preserves Ferber's and Hammerstein's sense of African American musical culture and its transference to Magnolia, the opening sequence somewhat compromises Ferber's creation of Magnolia and Julie as narrative doubles. When Julie and Magnolia meet in the kitchen to discuss Ravenal, Julie's dress is black, mimicking Helen Morgan's lustrous dark hair and eyes. But Irene Dunne, who, according to contemporary publicity, was a "medium brunette" and had appeared as a brunette in *Cimarron*, has a lighter wig on and wears a white print dress.[93] In fact, throughout her stage career on the showboat and later in Chicago, Magnolia wears props of whiteness—white dresses and even blond wigs (Fig. 3.4). Arguably, this artifice would not be necessary for a performer who was unquestionably white. Furthermore, in this early sequence, Magnolia proves that she can shuffle as well as any black riverfront worker, and even leads Joe, Queenie, and Julie outside to perform for the black spectators (Fig. 3.5).

In the next sequence, those same African Americans run up to the theatre windows to watch Steve and Julie's melodramatic scene with the sheriff. Joe is the only African American to observe the scene from inside the theatre, but he observes from the segregated gallery. Whale does not bowdlerize the racial sequence; the exchange of blood is important enough to merit a close-up of Steve cutting Julie's hand. But Whale does not linger on the tragedy, pushing the romance between Magnolia and Ravenal even before the mixed-race couple have left the boat. When Magnolia tries to kiss Julie, she resists; nor do the two meet outside the boat. Whale cut Ferber's scene in which Magnolia and Julie embrace, their dresses and forms blending into one color. Instead

above: 3.5. Magnolia (Irene Dunne) shuffling with Queenie (Hattie McDaniel), Julie (Helen Morgan), and Joe (Paul Robeson) (*Show Boat*, Universal, 1936); *below:* 3.6. Magnolia (Dunne) in blackface (*Show Boat*, Universal, 1936).

of uniting in the natural world outside, they part in a theatre, in the midst of a stage-bound melodramatic rehearsal. While Ferber sought to render their closeness as natural, Whale and Hammerstein approached the fictions of whiteness from another angle, positioning the "miscegenation scene" within a public performative space.

Magnolia soon takes over Julie's part as Lucy in *Tempest and Sunshine*, but ironically, she is far less convincing as the innocent white heroine than Julie. "Gallivantin'" is certainly Dunne's liveliest number as Magnolia. After Magnolia's girlish but stiff performance as the put-upon white heroine in *Tempest and Sunshine*, she performs a role with which she feels much more at ease— that of Matilda Hill, a young black woman who has been off in town seeing other men. Whale goes out of his way to show the mechanics of fabricating blackness. We see Magnolia backstage in the process of blacking her face, and during her number, the camera lingers in close-up on her exaggerated black face and batting eyelashes (Fig. 3.6).

Historian Michael Rogin criticizes blackface numbers in Hollywood cinema as "white noise," moments in which white artists perform black music, displacing and sublimating the history of slavery and oppression.[94] Many critics echo Rogin, attacking the cultural "theft" of blackface. However, on one level, the film is merely affirming the historical context of showboat performance and the historical adaptation of Ferber's novel. Blackface minstrelsy was a key element of showboat programs, in which both black and white, male and female actors blacked their faces. Furthermore, as M. Alison Kibler argues, critics like Rogin have tended to avoid the more complicated issues raised by women appearing in blackface. While Jewish performers like Jake Rabinowitz (Al Jolson) in *The Jazz Singer* (1927) could erase their ethnicity and enhance their claims to whiteness and capitalist success, women performers continued to perform the dual masquerades of femininity and race while remaining subservient within the mass cultural system of success.[95] Blackface was both a liberator from the confines of white femininity and a marker of inescapable subaltern status. Sharing, rather than theft, dominated this exchange. This is particularly true of *Show Boat*, for unlike Jake in *The Jazz Singer*, Magnolia has familial and visual ties to African Americans.

Also, as Linda Williams argues persuasively, "there can be no genuine, uncontaminated white or black cultural identity and autonomy in a culture so permeated by crossracial posing."[96] Ferber's novel and Hammerstein and Whale's film both push this sense of cultural and racial mixture, yet Williams views Magnolia as a white character only. But Magnolia's performance in blackface solidifies her spiritual, as well as her physical, connection to African American music and people. While Williams discusses Helen Morgan's ladylike, almost prim rendition of "Can't Help Lovin' Dat Man" as the performance of a mixed-race woman "passing as white," Magnolia, as Julie's narrative double, performs "Gallivantin'" as a mixed-race white woman passing as black.[97] Although Magnolia is much more natural as a black woman than as a standard white heroine, her male backup dancers are less convincing as African Americans. Andy and his stagehand try to manage the number's special effects—a rising moon and a bird flying past it—but as with the singer and dancers, Whale reveals the artifice behind the number.

Hammerstein's addition of "Gallivantin' Aroun'" to the narrative solidifies Magnolia's attachment to things African American.[98] But her theatrical career changes as she climbs the cultural ladder. When she auditions in Chicago years later, she will sing the song Julie once taught her—"Can't Help Lovin' Dat Man." Yet when she attains stardom at the Trocadero, she sings the old white chestnut "After the Ball" in a flounced white ball gown. In Ferber's novel, Magnolia's career is marked by both race and class; throughout her career, she remains a singer of African American songs in vaudeville. However, on-screen, she is transformed into a high-toned Broadway actress. The social stigma of vaudeville's working-class reputation is gone, and a montage of playbills shows her appearing as a sweet, pristine heroine in the nineteenth-century women's melodramas, *Wild Roses, Princess Caprice, Pink Lilacs*, and *Bluebell*.[99] Yet Magnolia is no icon of high culture; the saccharine titles of her hit plays construct her as a tintype of feminine masscult, held in as much contempt by modernist critics as Ferber's own fiction![100]

Hammerstein acknowledges that Magnolia's rise to stardom represents a rejection of the more challenging feminine and racial masquerades of her youth aboard the showboat. Whale pursues these themes, juxtaposing Magnolia's career with Broadway's own rejection of its complex theatrical past. A generation later, Magnolia's daughter Kim performs on Broadway, and the musical libretto concludes with Kim's number "It's Getting Hotter in the North," which the actress plays in southern blackface (echoing her mother's performance in "Gallivantin' Aroun'"). However, Whale and Universal replaced the sequence with a moonlight-and-magnolias period number that even more cunningly parodies Magnolia's "Gallivantin'." Magnolia strummed a banjo to the upbeat lyrics; Kim's version is a polite minuet.

While Lauren Berlant argues that Kim's original jazzy song "both links and sunders the music from its lived context" of African American history and contemporary urban culture, Hammerstein's new number for the 1936 film continues his and Whale's subtle critique of modern theatrical entertainment, nostalgia, and theatre's white memory.[101] This modern version of "Gallivantin'" caters to modern mass culture's taste for nostalgia (as displayed in films such as *So Red the Rose* [1935] and *The Gorgeous Hussy* [1936]) and embraces the comforting stereotypes of plantation life in which blond, white-skinned, white-crinolined girls relaxed on verandas while black slaves stayed on the margins, humming spirituals. Ironically, the black lyrics that Magnolia once sang are gone—this is merely an instrumental number stripped of its voice. The *Motion Picture Herald* noticed Hammerstein's "contrast" between old and new media and their treatment of race, printing a photo spread that juxtaposed scenes from the showboat and Broadway "Gallivantin'" numbers.[102] However, critics paid far more attention to Dunne's performance in blackface than to any other song, with the possible exception of Robeson's rendition of "Ol' Man River."[103] Her fancy Broadway career was ignored.

Hammerstein and Whale were almost as committed to challenging the performance of romance and women's sexual enslavement to men as they were to critiquing race relations. Though reviewers and, more recently, cultural and film historians have focused on Robeson's singing of "Ol' Man River," debating whether the sequence contains the seeds of black militancy, Helen Morgan's second solo performance of "Bill" directly addresses women as the other great subaltern class in America.[104] Curiously, the sequence acts as a kind of narrative pair with Robeson's song. Both performers lounge as they sing (Joe whittling on the docks, Julie slouching on a piano), and both sing of the lows of being black or a woman, tied to the "white boss" or to a romantic entanglement with a mediocre man. But while the black stevedores sing the chorus with Robeson, actively pushing bales and barges with grim faces, Julie is accompanied in a very different manner. As she sings, Whale's camera slowly pans across another silent chorus. Singers, dancers, and cleaning women all stand, transfixed, some crying, as they listen to Julie sing (Fig. 3.7). Though all are white (or perhaps pale enough to pass, like Julie), they too understand and sympathize with her song. While "Ol' Man River" narrates the unchanging sadness of the lives of black (male) Americans, "Bill" acts in narrative counterpoint, telling of women's unchanging service to men.

Although Magnolia's life is the focus of *Show Boat*'s historical narrative, her story is not simply the heroic success story of a determined, confident

3.7. The women's lament: Julie's audience watching her sing "Bill" (*Show Boat*, Universal, 1936).

protagonist—a format frequently used in the popular masculine biopic cycle (*Abraham Lincoln*, 1930; *Sutter's Gold*, 1932; *The Mighty Barnum*, 1934; *Diamond Jim*, 1935).[105] Hammerstein and Whale stop short of portraying Magnolia as Ferber's self-motivated survivor. Although Whale's heroine goes to work singing and later acting (refusing the charity of her parents onboard the showboat), she is no suffragist or protofeminist, as were so many of her real contemporaries.[106] Instead, as in the Broadway libretto, her old friend and showboat colleague Schultzy advises her to get a job and helps her get it (with some unknown help from Julie). When it seems as if she is about to fail in her first number at the Trocadero, it is her father who helps her succeed, giving her stage directions from the audience. Shortly thereafter, we see him managing her career as an innocent icon of mediocre plays. With the exception of Julie, it is white men who help Magnolia attain stardom.

Show Boat capitalized on the growing historical trend in Hollywood that had been fostered by adaptations of women's historical literature (*Little Women*, 1933; *The Age of Innocence*, 1934; *Ramona*, 1936), including Ferber's works *So Big* and *Cimarron*.[107] Reviewers were ecstatic, most singling out Dunne's performance as the film's highlight. *Variety* in particular mentioned her ability to portray Magnolia's transformation over a period of thirty years: "Irene Dunne maintains the illusion of her Magnolia throughout—from her own secluded girlhood; into sudden stardom on the *Cotton Blossom*; and later, as a more mature artist."[108] The *New York Times* even did a feature article on Dunne, outlining her biographical similarities to Ferber's heroine.[109] But though *Show Boat* was dominated by its female star and her appeal to female audiences, many reviewers went out of their way to avoid labelling it a "woman's picture." Instead, the *New York World-Telegram* linked the film to Hollywood's other great national epic, *Cimarron*: "Universal has done right by our great American classic—*Show Boat*—a grand pageant of song, sentiment, and loamy nationalism—the finest piece of filmic folklore since *Cimarron*."[110] Nevertheless, both films, labelled "national" epics, were the product of women—Dunne as star, Ferber as originator. Even the *New York Times* focused on Ferber's novel rather than on Hammerstein and Kern, proclaiming, "We have reason to be grateful this morning, for it has restored to us Edna Ferber's Mississippi River classic, *Show Boat*."[111] Given the film's obvious appeal to women through female-driven narratives, family melodrama, and top female stars, the reviewers may have slanted publicity in the hope of attracting male audiences.

The Nonintegrated MGM Musical

Regardless of the film's popular and critical success, it could not save Universal from bankruptcy. It was the last film that Carl Laemmle would present at his studio. After Universal went into receivership, executives generated money by auctioning off the studio's most profitable films and rights. MGM bought the screen rights to *Show Boat* from Universal in April 1938, along with many other Universal properties.[112] The new contract dissolved the old agreement between Ferber and Universal on 26 October 1926 and Ziegfeld, Ferber, Kern, and Hammerstein's musical contract for the first musical version on 17 January 1929. The contract allowed the first two film versions of *Show Boat* to stay as Universal properties, but sanctioned future Loew's productions after May 1940.

Ferber was furious with the contract. Hammerstein and Kern, who had a controlling interest in the threesome's 15 percent share of the net film profits over $125,000, had agreed to it. MGM later acquired *Cimarron* in a similar manner. Essentially, there would be no fees for any potential remakes. MGM writer George Wills began writing a treatment for a remake of *Show Boat* in 1944 as MGM anticipated its postwar film lineup. More than any other studio, MGM specialized in musicals.[113] Producer Arthur Freed and director Vincente Minnelli's most recent venture, *Cabin in the Sky* (1943), had an all-black cast. But *Show Boat*'s themes of segregation and miscegenation, as well as the heroine's broken marriage, did not really fit with MGM's typical musicals. Freed and Minnelli's *Meet Me in St. Louis* (1944) was a period musical more in tune with white middle-class memories of turn-of-the-century America. But like many MGM musicals—particularly those with a period setting (*The Harvey Girls*, 1946, for example)—*Show Boat*, at least in Wills's early drafts, concentrates on women's perspectives. The script begins with a subjective personal narration by Magnolia: "When I was a little girl on the Mississippi I'd often think—if I could be a river I'd like to be this one."[114] Warner Bros. had introduced the personal-recollections-of-a-star touch in the George M. Cohan biopic *Yankee Doodle Dandy* (1942). Some parts of *Show Boat*'s historical context are more equal than others, however. Although Wills retains the bare bones of the mixed-race melodrama and Julie's eviction from the showboat, he is less interested in the patterns of Ferber and Hammerstein's racial drama.

Instead, Wills emphasizes the white romance between Magnolia and Ravenal, airbrushing Ferber's lonely but determined heroine. Magnolia may act as a narrator, but she lacks the self-possession and grit to survive. Ravenal, in contrast, is reconstructed as a dutiful husband. He fetches the doctor during Magnolia's confinement. He is not a gambler; their poverty is portrayed as something unfortunate and unlucky. And when he finally does leave her, she blames herself alone, "I must have done something very wrong." She does not then become the great entertainment success; instead, she returns home, beaten, to her family. Andy then tells her that Ravenal went back to run family plantation but became sick. Her narration takes over again: "There was only one thing wrong—he tried to take care of me—and I should have been looking after him."[115] So much for Ferber's attempt to critique traditional romance and sex roles! MGM would never demystify romance if it could avoid doing so.

Wills was taken off the project, which was shelved until the late 1940s, when musical director Arthur Freed took over the project. By then, MGM had already tested part of *Show Boat* in the Kern biopic *Till the Clouds Roll By* (1946), and musicals formed over 25 percent of MGM's output. However, MGM's record of projecting racial and ethnic diversity in musicals was mixed, despite the studio's enormous genre output. Although Lena Horne appeared as Julie in the short version of *Show Boat* within *Till the Clouds Roll By*, Frank Sinatra sang "Ol' Man River" in a white tuxedo. Veteran screenwriter John Lee Mahin focuses on Julie's racial status, but he uses obvious racial stereotypes to mark her has black. He begins the script with Julie toting a monkey on her shoulder. As she stares at the river, the boat hand Pete fails in some crude sexual blackmail. When she resists him, he hints at her mixed status, calling her "zebra gal." Julie's dangerous racial ambiguity, emphasized by Hammerstein, is gone. Julie betrays her fear of exposure when she says to Captain Andy, "Don't you think it would be better—as Steve suggested—if we went on down to Booneville?"[116] Julie is again the classic tragic mulatta, but whereas Kenyon avoided the issue and Hammerstein obscured it, Mahin identifies her straightaway by her monkey, Pete's comment about her black-and-white skin, the initial description of her "dark brooding eyes," and, more subtly, her passivity and failure to assert herself or her desires. As the famous Julie Laverne, she could have asked Andy more directly to choose another performance locale. Instead, she intimates that her desire comes only from her support of Steve, her husband.[117]

Lauren Berlant points out that MGM's version does not include Queenie's recognition of Julie's African American song or, therefore, her cultural recognition of Julie's kinship.[118] Hammerstein made this explicit, and even Magnolia becomes a part of the dark showboat family, quickly adapting to the music and dance. It is interesting that the early scripts indicate that MGM intended to avoid this sequence. Although Julie and Magnolia sing "Can't Help Lovin' Dat Man," they are alone. No one of African American descent comments on their performance. Also, the song has a quicker tempo, and when Magnolia joins in the chorus, it has a pristine, singsongy quality. There are no somber blues in the song. It has been bled white.[119] But curiously, Mahin planned that following Pete's betrayal, the public exchange of blood, and the sheriff's threats, Andy would beg Julie to finish the show. In effect, Steve and Julie thwart the miscegenation law, but only so that Andy is not hurt financially.

Mahin also planned a new song, one in which Julie disparages her dark blood and implies that her best moment was when Steve saw the "whiteness" in her: "I was a lost and forlorn type, / A wish-I'd-never-been-born type of girl. / A pearl of no great price was I."[120] It continues somewhat ambiguously: "I want to be no one but me. / I am in love with a lover who likes me the way I am! / I have my faults, he likes my faults / . . . He may be wrong, but if we get along, / What do we care, say we?" At the end, Julie seems to embrace her "faults," but only because of the love of her white man. Mahin notes that after singing it, her eyes are "proud and defiant and tragically happy" and "she reaches around and Steve takes her hand, holding it in both of his."[121] Although Julie is shown going onto the stage in the final version, director George Sidney cut the song with its suggestive lyrics.[122]

Julie remains Mahin's tragic mulatta till the last, but though Magnolia does not absorb Julie's closeness to black music, she absorbs some of her passive tragedy. After her marriage to Ravenal, she occasionally criticizes his profession and his failure to provide for her, but Sidney toned down much of the dialogue. Magnolia does not assert herself as a mother concerned for her child's welfare or decide to pursue a career on her own. She remains passive and dependent upon men. Although she meets her father during an abortive attempt to sing at a Chicago nightclub and succeeds with his help, she throws away future success. Andy, exhilarated with the applause for his daughter, cries, "Well, you can be thinking of yourself from now on! Why after tonight, you can go on to be a big star—you can go on to New York and—." She interrupts him, "No, Poppa—there's going to be somebody else now . . . a baby."[123] She goes home to her parents. Hammerstein and Ferber's Magnolia had too much gumption for this, but MGM's heroine remains a dutiful wife and mother. Even after she returns to the *Cotton Blossom*, there is no indication that Magnolia resumes acting. In a supposedly neat narrative tying-up, a poor, dissolute Julie (who has obviously paid for her racial makeup) persuades Ravenal to return to his family. Like so many MGM films, it concludes with tears and a kiss.

Arthur Freed and director George Sidney had big plans for the production. However, as the scripts indicate, they were wary of Ferber's narrative of racial prejudice and miscegenation. Though *Show Boat* is fundamentally about issues of race and gender, MGM's integrated musical largely obliterates Ferber's racially integrated narrative. As Sean Griffin points out, while MGM often took the lead in producing integrated musicals in the 1940s and early 1950s (like *Meet Me in St. Louis*, 1944), it excluded black and other minority performers in order to create a "utopian" picture of America.[124] Even the rare all-black *Cabin in the Sky* (1943) segregated the performers. Griffin also astutely points out that when racial issues became important to integrated movie musicals in the 1950s—as in *Carmen Jones* (1954), *The King and I* (1956), and *South Pacific* (1958), for example—"intriguingly, MGM did not make these films—they were all made at Twentieth Century-Fox."[125]

Although Sidney took notes on the original text, none of the pages describing Julie's race or Magnolia's closeness to her were underlined.[126] Mahin's script handles the legal aspects of miscegenation with gloves, describing the entire sequence in a full shot, avoiding any close-ups showing Steve piercing Julie's finger and drinking her blood (Fig. 3.9).[127] The drama, details, and horror are minimized because the audience does not know where to focus. In addition, Freed had cast southern-born Ava Gardner in the role of Julie, despite the fact that MGM had African American actress and Julie-veteran Lena Horne under contract.

Although there had never been an African American or mixed-race Julie in a full-length *Show Boat* before, Helen Morgan's casting in 1936 did not arouse any controversy, since she had a long association with the musical. Sallow and dark haired, she seemed the ideal counterpart to Irene Dunne's lighter coloring. Yet casting Gardner and Kathryn Grayson (Magnolia) as the two female leads was not a mere MGM whitewashing of the script. Both actresses had similar pale coloring, and Grayson's brown hair was darkened and curled to match Gardner's naturally curly black hair. So whether he intended it or not, Sidney made the two women doubles. In some sense, there is no way to tell them apart except through their speaking voices. While Gardner was a throaty alto, Sidney dubbed her with Annette Warren's soprano, so her screen singing voice is almost indistinguishable from Grayson's somewhat shrill soprano. While in earlier versions the difference between Julie and Magnolia was emphasized in both appearance and voice, in MGM's film there is no difference between the two women in the opening sequences. The filmmakers avoided leaving any visual traces of race on Julie, thereby rendering her mixed blood irrelevant except as a social construction. Therefore, in some key ways, MGM's version unwittingly is the most critical of racial differences and miscegenation laws. But after Julie's unveiling, her coloring and closeness to Magnolia start to deteriorate. By the time Julie meets Ravenal aboard a gambling boat, her skin has taken on an almost yellow tinge. Poorly groomed, in a stained red dress, she travels in white society, but is now visually marked as a racial and moral degenerate.

Furthermore, while earlier productions had spread the star power of their casts, Ava Gardner was far and away the film's biggest star (Fig. 3.8). Howard Keel (Ravenal) was a relative newcomer; his only major hit had come in *Annie Get Your Gun* (1950). Though Grayson had been in films as long as Gardner (both since 1941), Gardner was a major star who had by 1951 played opposite

left: 3.8. Studio publicity focusing on Ava Gardner (*Show Boat*, MGM, 1951); *below:* 3.9. The almost unnoticeable case of mixed blood (*Show Boat*, MGM, 1951).

Clark Gable (*The Hucksters*, 1947), Robert Taylor (*The Bribe*, 1949), James Mason (*East Side, West Side*, 1949), and Robert Mitchum (*My Forbidden Past*, 1951). Preview audiences concentrated their positive comments on Gardner's performance.[128] Though a reviewer for the *New Yorker* joked that "Ava Gardner, playing the mulatto girl, is subjected to such close scrutiny by the camera that her handsome face often takes on the attributes of a relief map of Yugoslavia,"[129] excessive close-ups were MGM's way of highlighting its major star.

Spectacles of MGM Publicity

When Ferber was forced to sell her share of the rights to *Show Boat* to Loew's/ MGM, she also lost the sort of publicity that she prized. Although all her other contracts made the studios include her name with any mention of the title, MGM's trailer does not display Ferber's name. Instead, it focuses on the musical aspects: "Music the whole world loves! By Jerome Kern and Oscar Hammerstein II." It was advertised as "the biggest musical Metro-Goldwyn-Mayer EVER made! And that means the biggest show you've ever seen!" Publicity hyped the color and "Jerome Kern's Immortal Songs." Hammerstein, interestingly, was given short shrift in the publicity compared with Kern. Was this because the studio was not using Hammerstein's old screenplay and wanted to downplay the film's ties to Universal? If so, it followed MGM's tendency to disregard authorship. Shortly before the film was released, Ferber grumbled to editor Ken McCormick, "What harm the motion pictures have done to this country these past years. Most of the world has formed its opinion of us through these idiotic films."[130]

Although vestiges of Ferber's old contract with Universal forced MGM to keep her name along with Hammerstein's and Kern's on all posters, MGM placed Ferber's name in the smallest print, far below the title, stars, and other filmmakers.[131] While the studio press books for other Ferber films contain articles on the historical background, Ferber, and the stars' and other filmmakers' research for the production, MGM's is full of articles on its major stars, Gardner, Keel, and Grayson. While some of the racial and cultural knowledge of African Americans was certainly lost in the 1951 version, Gardner's tragic mulatta dominated the film publicity and most of the close-ups. In 1936, Helen Morgan was definitely subordinate to Irene Dunne, but in 1951, Gardner's Julie was the film's most glamorous star. The film synopsis mentions that Julie (Gardner) is forced to leave "because it is discovered she is part Negro and married to the white Steve Baker (Robert Sterling)," but the real focus was on Gardner's costumes and makeup. One major headline was "Trying to De-Glamorize Ava Gardner Hollywood's toughest Make-up Job!" Gardner also dominated the wider product marketing, appearing in ads for Lustre Crème Shampoo and Lux Soap. Although there was less emphasis on Grayson, articles on her also emphasized dress and spectacle. Even Howard Keel was turned into something of a dandy, as one of the articles noted: "Keel has more *Show Boat* wardrobe changes that his two leading ladies."[132]

Unsurprisingly, the other versions were downplayed. None of the previous *Show Boat* players—even Paul Robeson—was mentioned, although MGM built up his successor, William Warfield, in a feature article. But publicity headlines emphasized the filming in Technicolor and the new musical numbers, linking the property with MGM's other big musical spectacles, *The Harvey Girls* (1946), *The Barkleys of Broadway* (1949), and *An American in Paris* (1951). It outdistanced all of these films at the box office, however. *Show Boat* was the second-highest domestic grosser of 1951, making $5.2 million.[133]

Critics, familiar with the earlier two versions and the frequent Broadway revivals of Ziegfeld's original production, admired the scenery, but were nostalgic. New York critics in particular gave only guarded praise to MGM's new box-office giant. The *New Yorker* titled its review "Old Perdurable" and praised the music even MGM could not change. But one can detect a tone of criticism in the Hollywood reviews. The *Hollywood Reporter* began, "A whole new generation has grown up since *Show Boat* last appeared in a wonderfully faithful version by Carl Laemmle, Jr. Arthur Freed's production takes more liberties with the story."[134] But while New York critics emphasized the Kern-Hammerstein score as the bedrock of *Show Boat*'s appeal, Hollywood critics measured MGM's version in terms of its faithfulness to the Ferber story. While the *Hollywood Citizen-News* was happy that the emphasis was not on the plot but "the production numbers," *Weekly Variety* liked it because, it claimed, "there has been no tampering with the basic line of the Edna Ferber novel."[135]

But more recent critics disagree. Miles Kreuger is particularly critical of MGM, dismissing Grayson's Magnolia as "vapidly virginal" and commenting that in compressing time and focusing on just the first-generation romance between Ravenal and Magnolia, the "emphasis is placed upon domesticity rather than majesty."[136] He is particularly critical of the famous miscegenation scene, in which Steve Baker sucks blood from his wife's finger, arguing that Sidney's version destroys the meaning of the act. While in the 1936 version and in Ferber's novel, the sequence is given center stage, literally stopping the rehearsal for the evening's melodrama, hardly anyone notices Steve's act in 1951 because it occurs offstage during a real performance when no one else is looking: "Only a viewer familiar with *Show Boat* can figure out what is happening." In MGM's sanitized version, instead of using a knife, emphasizing the barbarity of the laws and his fierce love for Julie, he uses a pin. As Kreuger remarks, "Sidney seems eager to get on quickly with the more picturesque cupids of his love story, rather than dwell on racial troubles."[137]

Berlant concurs with Kreuger, but focuses on MGM's transformation of an earlier sequence, included in Hammerstein's versions, in which Julie's mixed-race status is nearly discovered by Queenie: "Prior to Queenie's intervention, the song Julie sings appears to expose her intimacy with the ordinary tragic disappointments of love; but recast as an artefact of racial history, it comes to reveal her criminalized racial and sexual identity to the audience."[138] But more than this, Magnolia's ease below decks with her real family and her understanding of African American dance and song give her knowledge of this history. "As might be expected," Berlant argues, in MGM's version the song is entirely extracted "from its racial context and is likewise transported from the basement kitchen to the public deck of the boat." Queenie and Joe are not present to recognize or participate in the song, and therefore "their knowledge of the racial archive is irrelevant to what becomes an impromptu scene of female bonding over love's complexities." In comparison with the 1936 version, MGM's film enacts a kind of "national amnesia," by "displacing the 'race' crisis onto a love story at every moment it can, and by refusing to specify what Ol' Man River knows."[139]

Yet in MGM's version, Gardner is the principal star, and she, as Julie, becomes the carrier of history. She, rather than Queenie, knows the origins of her music. Rather than focusing on the historical context as had Whale's version, Sidney concentrated on the learning and transference of the music. It happens so easily between Julie and Magnolia because they are romantic doubles in the film. While one can certainly argue that MGM's version evacuates race from its historical discourse, this film sequence also suggests that race is a social construct that discloses difference only through the violent imposition of the law. It is the transference of knowledge between women that really matters. Later, it is Julie who instigates Ravenal's return to Magnolia, repairing the marriage with a clipping from Magnolia's past. Julie has kept her own archive of Magnolia's life, or even her family album, staying close when Ravenal abandons them. Though it is the romantic white heterosexual couple that travels freely down the river in the final sequence, leaving mixed-race Julie stranded on the shore, the shot lingers on her when the strains of "Ol' Man River" return for the credits. As a mixed-race woman, Julie knows what Ol' Man River knows, far better perhaps than a white or black American would.

Ferber's novel and Whale and Hammerstein's version, in contrast, did not see the "erasure of history as the cultural dominant of American modernity."[140] Magnolia's knowledge of the river and of racial prejudice preserves some of this history. But critics have persisted in seeing *Show Boat* in all its forms as harmless entertainment. Shortly after the publication of the second instalment of Ferber's autobiography, in 1963, W. G. Rogers commented,

> Her attitude toward Negroes is only one of her unwavering liberal convictions. Muckraker Ida Tarbell was one of her idols, and there's a wide streak of unconventional Tarbell daring in the Ferber thinking ... Her novels were written as protest, she says, but adds "loving protest." She exaggerates their social vigor and bite. "Ol' Man River," to her is "a compassionate and terrible indictment of the white man's treatment of the Negro." Jerome Kern and Oscar Hammerstein wrote a moving song, but with more moonlight and magnolia than revolt, and no one ever came away from *Show Boat*, book or musical, determined to fight segregation.[141]

Show Boat will inevitably disappoint latter-day critics looking for black militance and rejection of white culture. Ferber and her adaptors were less interested in polarizing race than in exploring America's mixed-race heritage. The twin histories of Ferber's two "leading ladies" reveal American women and African Americans' shared history of bondage to white men and the varied performances demanded by popular culture.

four

Marking the Boundaries of Classical Hollywood's Rise and Fall

CIMARRON, 1928–1961

erber reflected once, "I have always thought that a writing style should be impossible of sex determination. I don't think the reader should be able to say whether a book has been written by a man or a woman."[1] She was proud that her novels "could never be designated as feminine writing in theme, characterization, style or attack. They were written by a cerebral human being who had a knowledge of the technique of writing and of the human race. . . . When the writer obtrudes in a work of fiction it is bad writing."[2] Despite the fact that she created such powerful female protagonists, Ferber insisted on the irrelevance of her gender as an author, perhaps believing that a "feminine" perspective might seem to depreciate the overall quality of her ideas and literary authority (or impact her sales). But the stakes were arguably higher for Ferber as a historical novelist. Many critics, both male and female, drew specific attention to Ferber as a female historical novelist, sometimes to praise her surprisingly unromantic historical perspective and attention to detail, and sometimes to denigrate her work as highly colored, inaccurate, and catchpenny. In

Hollywood, the difference was often measured by whether critics referred to her work as "historical Americana" or "melodrama."

Ferber's authority as a respected American historical novelist was most hotly contested when she wrote about the West. Although *So Big, American Beauty* (1931), *Come and Get It* (1935), and *Saratoga Trunk* (1941) invoke various aspects of the frontier experience and the pioneer myth, only *Cimarron, Giant,* and *Ice Palace* are true western novels, taking place within recognizable western territories. *Giant* and *Ice Palace,* her final works, are set within the twentieth-century West, and play somewhat daringly with the notion of frontier spaces, race, and gender roles. *Cimarron* is unique for a number of reasons. It is the only one of Ferber's western novels to span the nineteenth and twentieth centuries. It also uses a series of well-known historical events to generate the frontier experience of its two protagonists. It contains all of the traditional symbols of the frontier, and is structured by two major binary conflicts: the ongoing racial clash between white settlers and the Osage and Cherokee tribes in Oklahoma, and the similar struggle between wilderness-loving Yancey and his sunbonneted civilizer wife, Sabra. *Cimarron* was also the first of Ferber's novels to be both praised and condemned for its historical perspective. Ferber's "attack" on traditional myths of western historiography was too unfeminine for some male historians and critics, who reacted angrily to her and the book's astonishing popularity.

But *Cimarron*'s life in Hollywood would arguably be more remarkable than its status as the country's number one best seller in 1929. The first adaptation of her book by RKO, in 1930–1931, became one of the industry's great historical films, not only initiating a prestigious cycle of national historical cinema during the sound era, but also shaping the style, structure, and discourse of cinematic history.[3] Years after its release, film critics and filmmakers would cite the film as the zenith of prestige filmmaking. It was inevitable that Hollywood would try to remake the film, and thirty years later, MGM released its version of Ferber's work. The differences between the two films are striking, but they illustrate in microcosm the transformation and, in many senses, the decline of the American film industry.

A New Feminist History of the West?

Ferber knew nothing of Oklahoma history until friend and colleague William Allen White suggested that she might find it an interesting topic for her next novel: "I knew literally nothing of Oklahoma," she confessed. "I didn't know when the Indian Territory had become a state; I had never heard of the land rush of 1889."[4] White and his wife also told her of the "fantastic story's" most ironic aspect: Native Americans were forced onto the poorest land in the territory—"You couldn't raise anything on it. And the reason turned out to be that it was the richest oil land in America."[5] Although Ferber loved combining historical research with her writing, she was reluctant to write anything about the West. Ferber's oft-quoted response was, "No, the story of Oklahoma is a man's job."[6]

More than any other historical territory, the American frontier was dominated by men. Although women had written about the frontier and the westward settlement since at least the seventeenth century—Mary Rowlandson's 1682 captivity narrative was enormously popular—their work was rarely classified as a historical contribution. Instead, women's writing was labelled memoir, travelogue, or captivity narrative. As Julie Des Jardins points out, "Their lack of recognition as historians suggests that while women in the West benefited from greater literary opportunities in the twentieth century, western history in particular developed into a staunchly masculine field, in both content and perspective."[7] Although during the late nineteenth century, some female historians and memoirists published popular books about the frontier, by the twentieth century the reputations of George Bancroft and Frederick Jackson Turner overshadowed all other names. Even nonprofessionals like Theodore Roosevelt and popular historians and novelists like Courtney Riley Cooper, Emerson Hough, and Walter Noble Burns gave support to the idea that frontier history was a man's business. Historical fiction was also overwhelmingly authored by men—Owen Wister (*The Virginian*, 1902), Rex Beach (*The Spoilers*, 1906), Jack London (*The Call of the Wild*, 1903), Zane Grey (*Riders of the Purple Sage*, 1912), and Hough (*The Covered Wagon*, 1922), to name only a few. In 1928, the work of Mari Sandoz, Flora Seymour, and Angie Debo was all in the future.

Nonetheless, Ferber liked a challenge and took White's advice. She spent the spring of 1928 in Oklahoma, researching in the state library and interviewing old-timers who recalled the white settler "runs" of 1889 and 1893. The research and writing would occupy her for a year and a half. She absorbed both the "blood and thunder tales" of the pioneers and the history of the Oklahoma Indians. Ironically, Ferber often described traditional pioneer history as a mixture of fiction and fantasy, while she valued the Native American past for its historical value. In her description, the early years of white settlement in Oklahoma were "as fine an example of minority persecution and injustice as an historian would care to see."[8]

But Ferber also disliked the traditional narratives of western history, and she found the newly oil-wealthy, white Oklahoma population narrow and self-satisfied. As she wrote to her family in New York, "The longer I stay here the more bewildered I am . . . There's enough stuff, God knows, for a ten volume novel. But some of it has been done, much of it is bad man, Indian, pioneer stuff that is an old story. Oil makes me tired. The only angle that interests me from a story standpoint is the rich oil Indian."[9] She lunched with Chief Lookout of the Osage Tribe and briefly entertained the idea of writing about the exploitation of the Oklahoma tribes and the theft of oil lands. But, she wrote, "I honestly don't know whether I'll ever write anything about it. I hate historical stuff and 'western' stuff. I'll have to let it settle awhile in my mind, and see what happens."[10] In another letter, she derided the overly dramatic quality of the history: "It's movie stuff. It's like an old-fashioned western—the kind of thing I'd walk out on if they were doing it at the Harper or the Rivoli. All but the rich Osages, which give a new and fantastic angle to the thing. But the frontier days, and the territory rush for land, and the oil, and all that—I don't see how that could be done with any freshness."[11]

Ferber was interested in new perspectives on the West, though, and in addition to researching the Osage and other tribes, she went to Watonga to meet pioneering newspaperwoman Elva Shartel Ferguson ("I have a hunch that she will have stuff that interests me.").[12] By that time, Ferber had already been caught by the tales, and her original frustration with the staid white masculine history changed to worries about how she would balance traditional narratives with the perspectives of women, Native Americans, and other western minorities. "I hope to heaven I'll be able to weave the whole forty years into some sort of pattern," she wrote.[13] Ferber remained in Oklahoma a bit longer for research, but found it difficult to tolerate much of the white Oklahoma elites. Their hospitality was mixed with an undercurrent of benign pity toward a "woman scribbler" and a barely disguised anti-Semitism that made Ferber feel like one of the Indians. She later would write to Mary Austin, "Oklahoma I hate and loathe, stern and stem, people and habits, towns and country, up and down, forever and ever."[14] She put the hatred to good use, narrating the successes and legends of women, Jews, Native Americans, and racial hybrids.[15]

Although "Cimarron" was the nickname of her male protagonist, Yancey, *Cimarron* was the story of Yancey and Sabra Cravat. They were another one of Ferber's mismatched pairs, but each exemplified the powerful and contradictory drives of the American frontier. Yancey was a dreamer. It was he who persuaded the carefully brought-up Sabra to leave sedate Wichita, Kansas, for the unknown territory of Oklahoma. He was a gunfighter, cowboy, rumored half Cherokee, and, more recently, newspaper editor and proprietor. Yancey belonged to a long line of frontier heroes, descendants of Cooper's Leatherstocking who helped tame "wild country" and thereby consigned themselves to the past.[16] Sabra, on the other hand, was the practical power behind frontier settlement. She brought the structure of white civilization west and turned the proverbial wilderness into a garden. Indian hater, bigot, social dictator—she wrote and ran Yancey's paper, managed her house, brought up her children, and was elected to Congress. When she took root in western soil, she flourished, and Yancey ran as far as he could go to other frontiers—the Cherokee Strip, Alaska, Cuba, even the western front of Flanders during the First World War. Ferber's novel was unusual in that it gave equal weight to the experiences of both Sabra and Yancey. Most literature about the frontier focused on the exploits of men and marginalized or ignored the presence of women. As Richard Slotkin argues, the frontier myth symbolized the masculine racial clash between white and red.[17] But this fabrication of American ideology did not simply sanction the ethnic cleansing of Native Americans—it all but wiped out women from the history of the West.

Leslie Fiedler defines the West of classic American literature as the place "to which White male Americans flee from their own women into the arms of Indian males, but which those White women, in their inexorable advance from coast to coast, destroy."[18] Within this ideological paradigm, women were the scapegoats in paradise. Men discovered the idyllic wilderness, then women domesticated it and took it away from them. As historian Brigitte Georgi-Findlay argues, "The feminist revision of the frontier myth has exposed the androcentric bias underlying the pastoralization of America—a bias that either neutralizes women completely or colonizes them as captives within the story of the male innocent."[19] The great irony is, of course, that women were the practical impetus behind frontier expansion. It was they who actually fashioned the wilderness into a garden. Ferber understood this well: "Grimly Sabra (and in time, the other virtuous women of the community) set about making this new frontier town like the old as speedily as possible. Yancey, almost single handed, tried to make the new as unlike the old as possible. He fought a losing fight from the first."[20] But rather than taking sides in this battle of wills, Ferber was critical of both frontier icons.

To a certain extent, Ferber's historical novel anticipates many of the revisionist historiographic arguments about the frontier as a masculine space. With *Cimarron*, Ferber offered a new perspective on western history, one that privileged the perspectives of two groups often ignored in traditional accounts of the frontier—women and Native Americans. Ferber's portrait of the American pioneer woman was one of her most complex. Unlike Elizabeth Ellet or many of the late twentieth-century historians who sought to idealize the western woman (see, for example, Dee Brown's *The Gentle Tamers*, 1958), Ferber also critiqued her image. She would claim repeatedly that she was presenting a critique of the female pioneer, and that those who praised her heroic portrait had not understood the novel. As she wrote in her autobiography, "*Cimarron* had been written with a hard and ruthless purpose. It was, and is, a malevolent picture of what is known as American womanhood and American sentimentality. It contains paragraphs and even chapters of satire, and, I am afraid, bitterness, but I doubt that more than a dozen people knew this. All the critics and hundreds of thousands of readers took *Cimarron* as a colorful romantic Western American novel."[21] William Lyon Phelps was one of the few who did understand Ferber's alleged intent: "Many reviewers said that *Cimarron* and *American Beauty* were written for the 'pictures'—that *Cimarron* was a straight romantic story, with the wife held up as the 'purest type of American womanhood'; if they could only have known how Edna Ferber hated her!"[22] Rudyard Kipling, a Ferber fan, agreed, writing to her publisher, "How well she describes the merciless pressure of the respectable women pulling their men folk into line—like mothers chasing up bad boys which, indeed, I suspect all men are."[23]

Donna Campbell's more recent critical interest in *Cimarron* builds upon Ferber's remarks, arguing that Ferber's portrait of Sabra is a sustained attack on the hallowed image of the female pioneer, and that "reviewers and fans ignored Ferber's ironic tone and the grim humor with which she saw the triumph of the sunbonnets."[24] According to Campbell, "readers instead responded with expectations shaped by the conventions of the pioneer narrative: a civilized woman reluctantly comes to a Western land, remaining to tame it into a domestic territory suitable for statehood."[25] While mainstream culture had begun to publicize the image of the female pioneer, it was a recent addition to the pioneer legacy.[26] Although women were often a part of movie westerns, like Molly in *The Covered Wagon* (Paramount, 1923), they were almost always marginal figures, passively reacting to the hardships of weather, homemaking, and motherhood. Their presence on the frontier never directly challenged the patriarchal structures empowering men and containing women. While Bess Streeter Aldrich's *A Lantern in Her Hand* (1928) may have prepared audiences to view Sabra as a noble "Prairie Madonna" and domestic civilizer, Aldrich's novel was hardly typical of the frontier narrative.

Sabra does wield domestic and civic power beyond anything in the emerging prairie-Madonna literature. Although undoubtedly "indifferent to art and literature, narrow-minded, racist," Sabra is not "utterly conventional."[27] Campbell misses Sabra's ability to shape Oklahoma history, to manipulate the masculine frontier, and even to do the work of men. In many ways, Sabra seems closer to Constance Lindsay Skinner's heroine in *Becky Landers, Frontier Warrior* (1926) than to any prairie Madonna.[28] Left the head of her family after the murder of her father and the capture of her elder brother by Indians in Revolutionary-era Kentucky, Becky hunts, traps, and even participates in a raiding party on Kaskaskia. Instead of finding empowerment in the domestic economy, Becky successfully challenges the social and sexual order on the frontier at its most basic level: she hunts and kills Native Americans.

In *Cimarron*, Sabra's civic power derives from both her public work as a newspaperwoman and her management of the domestic sphere. One job publicizes the other. As Brigitte Georgi-Findlay points out, "The domestic can be read not only as the basis for a female countervision to male fantasies of conquest and possession, but as in fact, complementary to them: the ideal of domesticity, read in a context of empire building, also functions as an instrument for imposing cultural and social control and order upon the 'disorderly' classes of the West."[29] But Sabra's manipulation of the press and her power over an avid female newspaper readership connect her—like Ferber—to the masculine public space. Like her creator, Sabra is also deeply concerned with Oklahoma's pioneer legacy and with helping to craft its history, areas traditionally exploited by men.[30] Despite Ferber's insistence on her critical portrait of Sabra, she also admitted that Sabra was "my own dramatizing of myself" during her youthful days as a struggling reporter.[31]

But if Campbell is right in stressing that Ferber intended only a harsh critique of the female pioneer, one could argue that Ferber was unconsciously playing into the hands of traditional history, in which women were the harbingers of eastern civilization and the destroyers of all that was uniquely free and "American." For all of Sabra's racism and efforts to cleanse frontier society, was she not also a successful working woman and a pioneer in her own right? Ferber was subtler in her critique. On the first page of *Cimarron*, she begins with an excerpt from Yancey's public eulogy for the American frontierswoman:

Rough hair, and unlovely hands, and boots with the mud caked on them. It's women like her who've made this country what it is. You can't read the history of the United States (all this he used later in an Oklahoma Fourth of July speech when they tried to make him governor) . . . without learning the great story of those thousands of unnamed women . . . women in mud-caked boots and calico dresses and sunbonnets, crossing the prairie and the desert and the mountains enduring hardship and privation. Good women, with a terrible and rigid goodness that comes of work and self-denial.

Both Yancey and Ferber could admire their strength and bridle under their single-minded righteousness. But Yancey's speech also cunningly prepares the way for Ferber and her new feminist historical perspective on the West: "Their story's never really been told. But it's there, just the same. And if it's ever told straight you'll know it's the sunbonnet and not the sombrero that has settled this country."[32]

Although Yancey's rhetoric may indeed represent some of Ferber's revisionism, she does not take his remarks at face value. As Heidi Kenaga argues, Ferber's aside, in which she remarks that Yancey "reused" this rhetoric for a political purpose, "links this discourse to the nationalist rhetoric implicit in this historical chronicle."[33] His perspective on the American frontier is determined by his own political agenda and the way he manipulates his audience. Just as Ferber herself rejected the traditional masculine history she first encountered on her research trips to Oklahoma, so in her novel she complicates the masculine ideology's attempts to appropriate and incorporate women into its bombastic, self-congratulatory narrative.

Although Ferber undoubtedly suggested women's exclusion and complicity in the frontier legacy through her complex portrait of Sabra, she was equally critical of protagonist Yancey Cravat. However, contemporaneous and more modern critics have been more reluctant to see her critique of

Yancey. Campbell tends to focus on Ferber's ironic portrait of Sabra while leaving the romantic Yancey untouched: "Throughout the novel . . . Yancey has staunchly defended the territory's outcasts . . . fighting for Indian citizenship and property rights during the debates over statehood."[34] Kenaga astutely points out Yancey's constant flow of "nationalist" historical rhetoric, arguing that by portraying Yancey talking about rather than accomplishing his alleged feats on varied frontiers, Ferber "foregrounds the importance of storytelling and mythmaking to the institutions of pioneer culture."[35] But even more importantly, by investing Yancey with overblown, excessive rhetoric, Ferber reveals the discursive fakery and masculine aggrandizement essential to traditional western historiography. Further, Yancey is arguably just as much a frontier hypocrite as Sabra. While Yancey does defend Indian citizenship and land rights throughout much of the book, he also helps white settlers take the Cherokee Strip after he made the 1889 run. After fleeing the civilization of Sabra's home, he runs to Alaska to exploit Native land, and even joins Roosevelt's Rough Riders in Cuba, where the racial discourse of the frontier got a new lease on life. But Ferber renders Yancey's actions even more problematic. Yancey Cravat is a mixed-blood Native American. So while Sabra is an unabashed white racist for most of her life, arguably using her racial distain and domestic power as a means of social control in a masculine space, Yancey spends much of his life exploiting his own people.[36]

Ferber's decision to write a western with a mixed-blood American protagonist was rare but not unprecedented. While writers since James Fenimore Cooper had created white male protagonists who understood Native Americans' culture, adopted their dress and language, and even associated with them, they were always careful to mention the character's biologically pure white racial status. Even Hawkeye (Leatherstocking) repeatedly told other white settlers that he was "a man without a cross."[37] Although there were noble Native American figures (Uncas), racially mixed heroes were almost nonexistent. Yancey Cravat possesses many elements traditionally associated with the western hero of American literature (he is eloquent, persuasive, relatively honest, an advocate of underdogs, and, at least early in his career, a figure of renown on the frontier). However, he does not belong in this tradition of white hunter-heroes, which has been exhaustively documented by Richard Slotkin, men who "knew Indians" so well that they often adopted their culture, but were still responsible for the racial battles that ended in the near extinction of Native Americans. Ferber made Yancey's mixed status even more explicit by using Yancey's nickname, "Cimarron," as the title of her book. The Spanish term was used to denote racial mixing on the frontier.

Within the first few pages, Ferber describes Yancey's racial ancestry: "They say he has Indian blood in him. They say he has an Indian wife somewhere, and a lot of papooses. Cherokee . . . They said evidences of his Indian blood were plain; look at his skin, his hair, his manner of walking."[38] Yancey is one of the few to speak Spanish and Cherokee, and when confronting an enemy, he utters a Cherokee death cry. Yet when one gunfighter calls him "Cim," making a public reference to his "wild and unruly" racial heritage, Yancey is alert and ready to kill. He may wear a dazzling white hat, but what lies beneath it is a darker color.

As Harry Joe Brown has pointed out, mixed-race Americans remain "spectral" characters in American literature because "scholars have tended to interpret these texts dialectically, as negotiations between self and other, colonizer and colonized, white or Indian, unwittingly excluding in-between figures like the mixed-blood who confound this binary picture of race and culture."[39] Mixed-bloods were arguably far more problematic than full-blooded Indian characters because "whereas the full-blood Indian could be restricted to America's prehistory or history, could be safely combined in the past, the mixed-blood Indian belonged very much to the present and quite possibly to the future of America."[40] While "vanishing Americans," well known in the literary tradition from Cooper to Zane Grey (*The Vanishing American*, 1925), could be enveloped within American mythology because they had "vanished" from the racial makeup of America, mixed characters endured. Yancey not only survives through the 1920s, but also has a daughter and a son, the latter also named Cimarron, who carries on the mestizo tradition by marrying an Osage woman. Although back in 1884, Helen Hunt Jackson created a highly popular mestiza heroine, Ramona Moreno, Ramona eventually flees the United States for Mexico.[41] Her mixed-race child with her Indian husband dies of a fever. Jackson implies that there could be no future for Native or mixed-race Americans in the United States. In contrast, as Mary Dearborn argues, Ferber presents mixed marriages as true "American" cultural partnerships, in which both heritages endure.[42]

Ferber resisted turning Yancey into either a tragic figure or a traditional hero. Throughout the narrative, she contrasts Yancey's racial and masculine identity with that of other men on the frontier and even compares his physical beauty with Sabra's. Ferber's description of his dark complexion and hair also combines feminine elements such as his long eyelashes ("like a beautiful girl's"), his feet ("small and arched like a woman's"), and his hands ("slim, pliant, white").[43] Yancey has never worked with his hands, revealing the fraud behind his frontier rhetoric. A cattleman or farmer would at least bear the marks of sun and calluses. While Ferber mentions Sabra's embarrassment at wearing her Wichita finery around the ladies of Osage, Yancey reassures her. She describes Yancey in his "broad-brimmed white sombrero, his high-heeled boots, his fine white shirt, the ample skirts of his Prince Albert spreading and swooping," competing with Sabra's elaborate dress.[44] Like many Native men described in women's diaries and memoirs of frontier life, Yancey is a bit of a dandy. His swarthy complexion and Cherokee war whoops function with his Prince Albert coat, impeccable white hat, and elaborately tooled high-heeled boots. He is no Virginian with dusty chaps, a battered hat, and an unassuming demeanor.

Yancey's dandyism may be read as a potential feminist racial critique. As Georgi-Findlay argues at length in her discussion of women's frontier writing, many white women criticized Native men as lazy, overdressed, and unmanly while taking the part of downtrodden Indian women: "The way Indian men are aestheticized and feminized in women's texts illustrates how discursive conventions of colonialism can work in the service of women's empowerment." She continues, "Together with the representation of Indian women as victims of Indian patriarchy, the description of Indian men as effeminate dandies or aesthetic objects forms part of the rhetorical de-legitimation of Indian cultures . . . in white women's western writings."[45] Sabra's evident distaste for the Indian men she meets in Oklahoma can be read as her manipulating the expansionist rhetoric and frontier discourse in order to gain a foothold of feminist empowerment in this space.

But this also affects her relationship with her husband, who does not support his wife and children, and even with other men, who cannot do jobs as thoroughly as she. Fairly early in the novel, Sabra awakens to her husband's masculine failings: "She had been bred to the tradition that the male was always right, always to be deferred to. Yancey . . . had always treated her, tenderly, as a charming little fool, and this role she had meekly—even gratefully—accepted. But now . . . these last three weeks had shown her that the male was often mistaken, as a sex, and that Yancey was almost always wrong as an individual."[46] While Ferber cast a critical eye at white men bent on expansionist adventuring, Yancey's racial status and masculinity are implicated in the unstable power structures of the frontier. Sabra must look after both the household and the paper while Yancey runs off on further adventures.

Circling the Wagons: The Reception of *Cimarron*

Several years after *Cimarron*'s publication, Ferber alleged that almost no one understood her attempt to critique America's frontier myths, although many reviewers had recognized and applauded her efforts. As E. F. Edgett remarked, "It is obvious that Miss Ferber must have drawn upon her imagination as well as upon the printed records that she doubtless made the starting point of her story, but her imagination blends so well with the fact that we seem to be reading the accounts of an eye witness." Edgett went further, taking aim at popular western history: "If we want to read about life in Oklahoma in the not so very long ago, we may seek it in Miss Ferber's latest novel, and we shall find it there in much greater abundance and with more truth than in many books that yet are fiction even though they do not wear its label."[47] The *New York World* also singled out Ferber's historical talents for special praise: "The Oklahoma land rush of 1889 has long been awaiting the imaginative historian."[48] But others found the novel's historical content distracting and even detrimental to its literary qualities. As Harvey Fergusson of *Books* wrote, "Her immense mass of material is never sufficiently fused and moulded by any clear emotion. The characters are often buried under piles of facts and seldom attain to a convincing reality. This book contains a fine intention, a conscientious effort, a good deal of dullness and not a little absurdity. In spots it shows powers of observation and imagination which do not get much exercise, chiefly, I believe, because Miss Ferber has chosen a remote and unfamiliar subject."[49]

Other critics, like Dorothy Van Doren, seemed determined to disparage the book as merely a colorful evocation of the West.[50] Although Van Doren admitted that Ferber's "irresistible protagonist . . . is the West—mad, the West of infinite distances, of men and horses, of six-shooters and blankets, of mud huts and red 'likker,' the West that Oklahoma was forty years ago," she seemed uncomfortable with narratives that focused on history and narrative background rather than on characters. "I never get inside Yancey's skin; I never penetrate, indeed, beyond his white sombrero and his Prince Albert. I never feel that he is more than an actor to whom the great panorama of a civilization that is rolling out behind him is no more than a scene in a play," she complained. But Van Doren failed to realize that Yancey has no interior—he is merely an empty frontier myth, with plenty of style.

While many critics appreciated Ferber's historical elements, and some even praised her revisionist perspective, most were reluctant to acknowledge her critical portraits of Yancey and Sabra. The *New York Times Book Review* tried to make as much of Yancey as possible, and dwelled on his romantic persona without actually questioning his iconic image: "The story is told chiefly through the experience of Yancey Cravat and the young wife who went with him from their home in Kansas . . . This Yancey Cravat is by all odds the best of Miss Ferber's creations, and one of the most picturesque figures in the whole range of American fiction. Gaylord Ravenal of *Show Boat* is pale beside him."[51] However, it is Sabra who dominates the review:

> Sabra belongs in the line of Miss Ferber's indomitable, executive women whom she endows with strength beyond that of their men, and Sabra is to repeat their history . . . It is Sabra who takes over the day-to-day management of the paper he founded and builds it up, Sabra who finally embarks on the political career he distained and thrust away from him. She enters Congress and as we take our leave of her, it is hinted that she may become governor. Yancey's life, despite its glamor, runs a descending scale, his end at once heroic and pathetic. To Sabra belongs the sober triumph.

But even though the reviewer chronicled her success, his praise was grudging: "There is a taint of feminist thesis about these women of Miss Ferber's which makes them somewhat synthetic and not wholly convincing." Evidently American literature had no vocabulary adequate to describe the heroic woman.

While *Cimarron* was serialized in the *Woman's Home Companion* and sold more than 200,000 copies in a few months, making it the year's best seller according to *Publishers Weekly*, not all critics appreciated her attack on western literature and history. One of the angriest critics was Stanley Vestal, who had made a small name for himself as a popular western historian. Ferber's unprecedented success as a first-time western writer was especially maddening. Vestal could not disparage a Pulitzer Prize–winning novelist with impunity, so he targeted her grasp of history: "She was so completely ignorant of the spirit of the pioneer days that she spoiled most of her materials in shaping them for fiction," he blustered. "The real flavour and tang of Western life in the Territory eludes her."[52] He continued snidely that it was a book only "purporting to be a historical novel," but what he and his male colleagues wrote was different:

> In our day, the West has come in for some serious study, and all the old legends are undergoing repairs and restorations. We are inclined to be very severe upon those who still prefer the old, shadowy house of myth to our brand new historical apartments. Yet it must not be forgotten that lasting literature is made of popular mythology for the most part, for the simple reason that readers prefer to be amused to being instructed. Miss Ferber's book may not be history, but it does attempt a new mythology for Oklahoma—a mythology nonetheless effective because the author regards it as gospel truth.

But Vestal's idea of authentic western history was based upon recognition of the region's "deep-seated conservatism, its reverence for racial standards." Ferber's book, with its female protagonist, mixed-race hero, and triumphant telling of the Osage's oil wealth, hardly qualified. But it was not only the novel that offended Vestal's sense of "racial standards." Ferber herself was a Jew, and therefore anathema.

It is tempting to see *Cimarron*, with its mixed-race hero, tough-minded heroine, and sustained critique of frontier expansion, as a corrective to the nativist trends in American literature during the 1920s. But as Walter Benn Michaels has pointed out, one of the tenets of modernist nativism was the tendency to cherish Native ancestors precisely because they were a vanishing race and therefore safe to assimilate within the national mythology. It is no accident that the drive for Indian citizenship coincided with the passage of staunch anti-immigration laws during the 1920s. Boasting of Native blood became part of popular culture; even cowboy humorist and native Oklahoman Will Rogers told audiences he was part Indian.[53]

But Jews were another matter entirely. The Ku Klux Klan re-formed in order to target undesirable Catholics, southeastern European immigrants, and Jews. Jewish Americans were especially visible in postwar American culture. Not only did they virtually run Hollywood, but many vaudevillians (Al Jolson, Fannie Brice), radio and stage comics (Eddie Cantor), celebrity songwriters and composers (Irving Berlin, Jerome Kern, Oscar Hammerstein,

George and Ira Gershwin), actors (Edward G. Robinson, Paul Muni), and writers (Ferber, Fannie Hurst, Dorothy Parker, Lillian Hellman) were Jewish as well. Willa Cather's *The Professor's House* (1925) and F. Scott Fitzgerald's *The Great Gatsby* (1925) were both modern westerns that illustrated the overt fear of Americanizing the Jew. Ferber's Jewishness made her critique of western history even more explosive. Her revisionist history attacked traditional masculine American narratives. Heidi Kenaga argues that Vestal's anti-Semitic review focused on Ferber's cultural incomprehension of the West, portraying her as a "racial Other."[54] This, of course, was an irony that Ferber appreciated. While critics would applaud her works' "admirable, unapologetic Americanism," her America was a multiracial and multiethnic country where women, Jews, and ethnic minorities worked and struggled against prevailing myths of masculinity and race. "America . . . seems to me to be the Jew among the nations," she affirmed in her autobiography. "It is resourceful, adaptable, maligned, envied, feared, imposed upon."[55]

The Making of American Historical Cinema

When RKO purchased the film rights of the novel, it took on both *Cimarron's* massive public appeal and its controversy. The studio paid an unprecedented $125,000 for *Cimarron*. "I assure you that the price we are paying for this novel's talking and motion picture rights is the highest price we ever paid for any piece of property of its kind, and it is our intention to put forth every effort to make the production worthy of the price we paid for the rights," wrote J. L. Schnitzer of RKO to Ferber's attorney.[56] At that time, it was the highest price paid in Hollywood for any original material. The studio executives hired Howard Estabrook, fresh from adapting Owen Wister's classic *The Virginian* (1929), to write the script, and paid him more than $30,000 dollars, a sizable sum for writers who were routinely paid less than $3,000 for a project.

RKO was a newly formed and relatively small major studio, but it spared no expense when making *Cimarron*. But some had misgivings about spending so much on a historical project. Even after the completion of Estabrook's adaptation and first script, story editor Paul Powell fretted, "Although the characters are fictitious, this is essentially a historical novel . . . historical novels have not, as a rule, proven to be good picture material, and I fear this is no exception."[57] Although *Cimarron* was a Book-of-the-Month Club selection and the number one best seller of 1930, selling hundreds of thousands of copies and proving the enduring popularity of westerns and historical novels, Powell and others feared that the history transferred to the screen would not be popular with motion-picture audiences. Successful westerns were supposed to follow the structure and narrative of *The Covered Wagon* (1923), *The Winning of Barbara Worth* (1925), *Tumbleweeds* (1925), and *The Virginian* (1929). These critically acclaimed big-box-office epics kept historical detail to a minimum and capitalized instead on silent landscapes, silent heroes, and simple tales of clashes between evil gunmen, settlers, and Indians. Ferber's *Cimarron*, with its constant referencing of historical events and figures, a powerful mixed-race hero, and an unsilent woman protagonist, did not fit this template.

Although the studios had been experimenting with new styles of historical cinema following the transition to sound, United Artists' biopic *Abraham Lincoln* (Griffith, 1930), MGM's *Billy the Kid* (1930), and Fox's historical drama *The Big Trail* (1930) did not do well at the box office. Critics were more or less scathing, even toward D. W. Griffith's first sound film, dismissing the historical discourse as traditional, conservative, and even childish.[58] RKO, formed in 1928, was a brand-new studio in comparison with Paramount, MGM, Fox, and Universal. It could not afford a big mistake. Yet in spite of these serious concerns, Estabrook refused to minimize the historical elements in favor of the fictional story; like Ferber, he did extensive research. But instead of visiting the territory and interviewing old-timers, as Ferber had done, Estabrook looked at a mix of traditional historiography, popular history, and cutting-edge perspectives on the frontier and Native Americans (Fig. 4.1).

He read the work of popular historians Walter Noble Burns and Courtney Riley Cooper and even reread Emerson Hough's fictional *The Covered Wagon*, but he did not follow their approach by patterning *Cimarron* after the triumphant chronicle of white westward expansion. Estabrook was one of the few people to read William Christie MacLeod's *The American Indian Frontier* (1928), a rare view of the white settlement of America from the Native American perspective.[59] For MacLeod, "Every frontier has two sides . . . To understand why one side advances, we must know something of why the other side retreats."[60] Rather than stressing the white westerners' heroic qualities, MacLeod portrayed the frontiersman as the scum of the East. According to MacLeod, it wasn't simply popular historians and novelists, but respected academic historians as well who shared in the guilt of romanticizing the American pioneer: "In the little red schoolhouse it is a sacrilege to intimate that the pioneers suffered from ordinary human frailties . . . But the masses were no better than the

4.1. Howard Estabrook posing with his research library, 1930 (RKO Pictures).

masses of any society."[61] MacLeod's book was unnoticed, even in academic circles (Frederick Jackson Turner refused to review it), but Estabrook was certainly influenced by the maverick historian.[62] But Estabrook also read John Collier's articles on the exploitation of Oklahoma Indians, which gave a more modern dimension to frontier skulduggery.[63]

Estabrook's major creative contribution was to invest the narrative with a distinct historical structure. Rather than simply focusing on the romantic saga of Sabra and Yancey, he retained Ferber's diverse portrait of the West, peopled with Native American men and women, mestizos, black and white Southerners, Jews, and Anglo-Saxon northeasterners. He also visualized *Cimarron*'s broader projection of history and, even more remarkably, preserved Ferber's critique of traditional western historiography.[64] Estabrook's decision was one that Warner Bros. would follow years later with *Giant* (1956), in which the perspective of Ferber's protagonist, feminist liberal Leslie Lynnton Benedict, was marginalized in favor of a broader narrative. But for 1930s Hollywood, it was an unusual step away from character-oriented narratives (*The*

Virginian) and biographies (*Billy the Kid*) and even familiar historical eulogies to westward expansion (*The Big Trail*). Estabrook and director Wesley Ruggles (*The Winchester Woman*, 1919; *The Age of Innocence*, 1924) introduced the idea of re-creating the 1889 land rush (which Ferber discussed only indirectly in her novel) and of inserting historical exposition, dates, and documents within the narrative. Estabrook planned two major text superimpositions as a text foreword, and then punctuated the fictional narrative with a series of dated historical superimpositions and smaller intertitles. Rather than reinforcing the visual narrative, as had so many silent intertitles, *Cimarron*'s "written history" was to be placed in counterpoint to the visual narrative.

At first, *Cimarron* seems to intone the traditional discourse of Frederick Jackson Turner, Theodore Roosevelt, and countless other male historians of the West: "A NATION RISING TO GREATNESS." Expansion is linked to national strength; ethnic cleansing is ignored. Following the text foreword, the film dissolves to shots of the settlers preparing for the 1889 land rush. When two Indians approach a tradesman's wagon and reach for some of his goods, the white merchant yells, "Hey, drop that, Indian, and get out!" Instead of supporting the text in the tradition of countless silent and early sound-era historical films, *Cimarron*'s opening images foreground the racism of frontier narratives. The film repeats this initial contrast between the texts' triumphant view of American history, which stresses homogenous white settlement, and the images' darker portrait of frontier expansion.[65] Later, Yancey and Sabra's newspaper will include articles on the near extinction of the buffalo and international matters, which settlers ignore in favor of local gossip. This conflict between text and image emphasizes westerners' insularity and lack of self-reflection. Curiously, *Cimarron*'s text foreword acknowledges the work of "men and women," rather than presenting a strictly white masculine frontier, as had Turner, Roosevelt, and countless *Virginian*- and Leatherstocking-inspired western films. However, while the film's revisionist historiography embraces women's work as part of national history, the images problematize the nature and impact of that work.

Much of this complexity was due to Estabrook's early instincts about the book. The screenwriter made copious notes on the book's characterizations and historical structure.[66] He was committed to keeping Ferber's frontier a masculine and feminine space. He underlined all of Yancey's paeans to the sunbonneted civilizers and paid particular attention to Ferber's description of Sabra. He also noted Sabra's parents' "prejudice against Indians" and "Sabra's indifference to Indians."[67] Although he seemed aware of Sabra's single-handed efforts for the newspaper, noting that she "maintained paper" when Yancey was off joyriding, he was sensitive to moments when her courage and drive upstaged her husband's.[68] At one point, when Sabra upbraids a group of gunfighters in front of Yancey for attempting to shoot him, Estabrook wrote, "Yancey is astounded, fearing he will be accused of hiding behind a woman's petticoats."[69] But he ignored the passage where Ferber shows Sabra's gradual awakening to male fallibility and men's exaggeration of their own importance: "Oh, my land's sakes alive! . . . Men make such a lot of work of nothing."[70] However, he seemed interested in Sabra's regeneration from unrepentant racist to political pluralist, noting that "Sabra introduces bill to permit Osages to live anywhere in US like the negro (thus perhaps unconsciously repeating the spirit of Yancey's editorial which she had criticized—see pages 281–282)."[71]

Estabrook's early thoughts about Yancey were more complex. From the beginning, he recognized Ferber's problematization of the archetypal gunfighter. He was aware of Yancey's racial hybridity, but instead of cutting this from future treatments, he determined more than once to focus on it "in dialog"—thus giving verbal weight to the many unexpressed thoughts that Ferber documented in her book.[72] In the first script, he included an exchange between Sabra's relatives about Yancey's racial status: "You'd think Yancey was an Indian! Well, some half-breeds are no darker."[73] In the margins of the script, he also noted "Yancey's partisanship for Indians": "Yancey's tales to Cim of Indians and the wrongs done to them," and underscored Yancey's Cherokee death cry when he faces an enemy. While he noted Isaiah's "grotesque imitation of Yancey" on the streets of Osage, he ignored Isaiah's mixed union with Arita Red Feather and their horrific deaths at the hands of outraged Osage Indians, who were even more emphatic about preserving racial separateness than Sabra.[74]

While Estabrook balked at including a mixed-race union between an African American man and a Native American woman, he conveyed the racial complexity of Ferber's main character. Just what does "Cimarron" mean, one character asks Sabra derisively in the course of the film. "Cimarron" was, like "mestizo," a Mexican term used in the Southwest to denote racial mixing, including combinations of Mexican, Spanish, Native American, northern European, and African heritages. Sabra is a bit uncomfortable with these questions. The film also confronts the representation of a multiracial protagonist when Isaiah, a young black boy who has stowed away from Wichita and idolizes Yancey, comes to church in Osage dressed up as a pint-sized version of his hero, right down to the heeled boots, coat, and hat. Yancey laughs when he confronts his youthful mirror image on the street, but Sabra, schooled in the post–Civil War South, does not find the implications of Yancey's double amusing (Fig. 4.2). Initially, Estabrook may have felt a bit uneasy about making Yancey a mixed-blood. At the end of the first script, he planned for Sabra to confront Yancey with the rumors about his status.[75] This was cut in the next version, preserving the film's verbal and visual "hint of Indian blood in Yancey."[76]

As Ferber had reenvisioned the western hero, so Estabrook and Ruggles challenged the prevailing critical myths and narrative structures of the Hollywood western, which overwhelmingly emphasized masculine conquest, racial exclusion, and progress.[77] Although the film opens with one of the most stunning, epic visual sequences in Hollywood history, depicting the 1889 land run, the rest of the film chronicles the day-to-day complexities of nineteenth- and twentieth-century frontier life in Oklahoma. Its images of cowboys, Indians, and gunfights are upstaged by the development of the town of Osage, the success of the *Oklahoma Wigwam*, and Sabra's struggles with Yancey. Perhaps even more unusual was the film's deliberate and multifaceted use of text, documents, and other historical devices. While many of these text inserts link the fictional, visual narrative to the more traditional, text-based historical narrative, Estabrook and Ruggles maintained the opening sequence's sense of historical irony. In the 1893 sequence, an officially worded text insert informs audiences about the opening of the Cherokee Strip to white settlement. Sabra, returning from her women's club, has just put Oklahoma's pioneer heritage in safe, historical perspective. Like historian Frederick Jackson Turner, author of the frontier thesis (1893), Sabra views the frontier as closed and proclaims a new, settled era beginning. She is therefore stunned when news of further land rushes inspires her husband first to criticize the government for its swindling of the Cherokee and then to completely undercut his convictions by running off to the strip with a group of white cronies.

This sequence not only challenges Turner's idea of a frontier that closed in 1890, by showing yet another land rush about to happen in 1893, but also proves that the lure of Yancey's expansionist rhetoric still blinds him and the nation to their own racism. Later, Sabra will act again as Oklahoma's historian, claiming, "The women of Oklahoma have helped build a prairie wilder-

4.2. Western doubles? Yancey (Richard Dix) and Isaiah (Eugene Jackson) with Sabra (Irene Dunne) in *Cimarron* (RKO, 1931).

ness into the state of today." Yet, when public officials wish to commission a statue of her as a symbol of the pioneer, she demurs, suggesting Yancey instead. The alluring images of gunfighters, Indians, and land runs are just as misleading about the history of the West as its textual historians.

Cimarron was a significant departure from Hollywood's other westerns. The theoretical structure of the western, both as a representation of the national past and as a genre, was given to documenting and celebrating rather than to critiquing the frontier. Critics have primarily viewed classical Hollywood westerns as representations of the frontier myth's simple binary conflicts—narratives that articulate the battle between red and white, good and evil, garden and wilderness.[78] In the tenets of film genre and the structure of the Hollywood western, honed for decades by film and cultural critics, there is little room to consider interracial heroes, figures who break not only racial barriers, but also the distinct categories of western myths.[79] As I argue elsewhere, these mestizos are marginal figures, overshadowed by the pure-blooded

western archetypes of cowboy and Indian, and are embarrassing remind-
ers of the consequences of racial expansion and the underside of Manifest
Destiny.[80] Films like Paramount's *Vanishing American* (1925) and *Ramona* (1928)
had Native American protagonists, but these men were pure-blooded and
doomed to extinction. Yancey (Richard Dix) is neither the white gunfighter
cleansing the frontier of redskins, nor the pure-blooded Indian condemned
to extinction in a changing environment. He even lives beyond the circumscribed boundaries of traditional frontier myths and historical periodization,
playing an active part in Oklahoma history through the state's oil boom at
the turn of the century and during the First World War.

Sabra was also a precedent for cinematic pioneer women, usually a win-
some prairie Madonna hidden behind the protecting arms of William S. Hart.
Irene Dunne's Sabra gave way to Barbara Stanwyck's Annie Oakley (1935), Jean
Arthur's bawdy Calamity Jane (*The Plainsman*, 1936) and Phoebe Titus (*Arizona*,
1940), and Gene Tierney's gun-toting Belle Starr (1941). In the 1950s, prominent
actresses like Stanwyck (*Cattle Queen of Montana*, 1953; *Forty Guns*, 1957; *Maverick
Queen*, 1958) and Joan Crawford (*Johnny Guitar*, 1954) would play independent
western mavericks, but only Irene Dunne's Sabra Cravat captured the racial
and social arrogance behind her grit, practicality, and endurance.

While both Donna Campbell and Heidi Kenaga point out the rise of the
female pioneer myth in the 1920s, the prevailing academic and popular historiography at the time focused upon the white male pioneer. Rose Wilder Lane
and Mari Sandoz would write their revisionist portraits of western women
after Ferber's book and RKO's film.[81] While Kenaga argues that the film enabled RKO to "promote itself as the 'forward-thinking' studio by acknowledg-
ing the growing influence of American women in political and civic life during the postwar era," she asserts that the publicity department and the script
attempted to regenerate western masculinity by effacing "Ferber's critique of
male Western writers' historical fictions" and "softening the more unpleasant aspects of Yancey's irresponsibility, inefficacy, and later decline."[82] This
seems untenable, given that Estabrook's script and the finished film chronicle
Sabra's life in far more detail than Yancey's. While he is away pursuing other
frontiers in Cuba, Alaska, or Europe, the film narrative remains focused on
Sabra in Osage, maintaining the newspaper and building a successful political career. Although Ferber may have seriously questioned Sabra's values and
standards of success, she eventually achieved what so many women fought
for—economic and career independence. Recall that the citizens wanted to

make her, not Yancey, the model for the Oklahoma pioneer. It is Sabra who suggests Yancey would be a better model. And possibly she is right: mythical commemoration in America so often fixates on masculine achievement. In Yancey's case, much of it is empty construction—a myth—while Sabra is the grim reality.

The Regeneration of American Film History

RKO pulled out all the stops on the publicity, but it certainly saw the relationship between Sabra and Yancey differently than Ferber and Estabrook did. All the posters show Yancey, bare-chested and brandishing a pistol, protecting Sabra or pushing her from harm. Many larger posters depict the two of them behind a team of horses—streaking to historical glory, perhaps—but it is Yancey who holds the reins and restrains Sabra in his other arm. As Heidi Kenaga argues, "This strategy reshaped the potentially subversive features of the novel into a more acceptable form for mass consumption; it confirmed patriarchal control of the historical narrative . . . while creating an acceptable space for women's supporting role in the industrial age."[83] It was not the last time that a studio publicity department tried to harness Ferber's work to traditional epic masculinity and sexuality. Either baffled or worried by the book's historical critique and female author, the studio tried to camouflage some of its feminist revisionism.

The press book capitalized on the spectacle of the run and frontier glory, proclaiming: "The Oklahoma Run: a thundering hour that shook the world. Greatest moment the screen has ever known. Fifty thousand stampeded humans sweep in a boiling, brawling mass across the line . . . crazed men . . . frenzied women . . . wild-eyed children . . . sprawling under murderous hoofs . . . careening on into a wilderness that by sundown became the maddest empire ever known" (ellipses in the original). But unusually, the studio also focused on Ferber and the film's historical value. It claimed that *Cimarron* possessed the largest readership of any modern novel and that it was "Edna Ferber's greatest—not just another novel."[84] *Cimarron* was not only a historical novel, but also a historic achievement in itself ("Millions Await New Thrill: *Cimarron* Leads to Box-office Glory as Nation Hails History Making Novel"). It continued to promote the film's significance as a frontier drama that would break new box-office frontiers in Hollywood: "Edna Ferber's great story comes through . . . Taking place with *Birth of a Nation* and *Four Horsemen* among the immortal dramas of the screen!"[85] According to the publicity department, "Edna Ferber's roaring epic" told the tale "of the men who make the empire—and the women who preserve it." It saw the frontier and Ferber's book in heroic but conventional terms. Even the studio's adaptation was promoted for its meticulous accuracy ("the screen keeps faith"). William LeBaron, the producer of the film, was quoted: "Millions have read and loved Miss Ferber's novel . . . I feel they have every right to a faithful screen version."[86] A few years later, David O. Selznick would say almost the same thing of Mitchell's *Gone with the Wind*.

It was one of the production's great ironies that Ferber's critique of oil-rich elites and their exploitation of Native Americans would be financially supported by oil companies. According to the press book, the Texas Oil Company lent thousands of dollars worth of equipment to the filmmakers. "The whole story of Texaco is told in *Cimarron*," the press book claimed. RKO got nearly fifty thousand filling stations to advertise the film for theatres. "There are sufficient Texaco dealers in every territory to make cooperative advertising worthwhile," the studio argued. "Sell them the idea . . . that Texaco is proud of the part it played in the making of *Cimarron*, greatest of all motion pictures."[87] RKO even suggested "Texaco Night at Your Theatre," when bus-loads of male Texaco employees would get free tickets to the film.

But given that Sabra winds up a successful newspaperwoman and congresswoman (Fig. 4.3), the studio also planned "Flash Stunts to Draw the Woman Fans," singling out the Daughters of the American Revolution, the Daughters of the Confederacy, and the Catholic guilds, the last of which so often voiced opposition to anything produced in Hollywood.[88] But with *Cimarron*, the studio felt that "here at last is a motion picture that will be welcomed by women's organizations."[89] To attract women, it sought the endorsement of Mrs. Tom Ferguson (Ferber's model for Sabra) and actress Irene Dunne. Fergusson approved of the film and Ferber, claiming that she "recognized the result of our talks when *Cimarron* was published." Dunne said, "I have read Miss Ferber religiously for years. For a period of seventy weeks I enacted one of her heroines in the stage play *Show Boat*. In many ways my life co-incides with the fictitious lives of Sabra and Magnolia, Ferber heroines. Like them, I'm an expatriated southerner."[90] A few years later, Dunne would reinforce her identity as a Ferber heroine when she played Magnolia in Universal's 1936 remake of *Show Boat*. However, RKO did not publish Ferber's endorsement of the film. Although later in life she would say that RKO's version of her work

4.3. Sabra as a congresswoman (*Cimarron*, RKO, 1931).

was the only one of which she totally approved,[91] she declined to give direct remarks to the publicity department.

The publicity was certainly sensitive to Ferber's status as the country's top-selling author. In addition to the numerous articles citing the film adaptation's faithfulness to the novel and its historical accuracy, the press book promoted lobby cards and billboards displaying *Cimarron*'s book cover. Posters often combined the book motif with colorized scenes from the film. The department even included biographical articles on Ferber, which competed with those of the stars: "Edna Ferber, one of America's greatest novelists of all time, whose most recent best-selling sensation, *Cimarron*, has been transferred to the screen by Radio Pictures," it proclaimed. "Miss Ferber's other successful novels include *So Big* and *Show Boat*." The article went on to quote Estabrook on the screenwriting: "Due to the popularity of the novel and the millions of Ferber readers, it was necessary to adhere closely to the original theme and plot." This cost RKO plenty. According to the press book, the studio spent $4,000 stocking its library so that star Richard Dix could prepare for his role.[92]

A $1.1 million domestic box office was impressive for 1931. But the film cost more than $1.4 million to make, and even though it was the most popular and critically acclaimed film of its year, did not recoup its costs. Heidi Kenaga argues that the film was like *The Big Trail*, an epic western failure of the early 1930s, but that *Cimarron* was possibly more handicapped by its "tainted" cultural status. RKO's attempts to market it as an authentic American epic were subverted because Ferber was a New York Jew, a historical novelist, and a woman. *Cimarron* certainly did not fit the classical Hollywood model for a western, but according to the production material and publicity, RKO intended to retain and exploit its controversial aspects. Ferber was one of them. While Kenaga sees *Cimarron*'s aberrant aspects retrospectively as costly errors for a conservative studio system bent on preserving the national heritage during a nativist era, RKO openly courted controversy.

The studio's insistence on historical accuracy was one way that it could both honor its faithfulness to Ferber's narrative and promote the film's ability to document history in ways that literature could not. *Photoplay* noted that "*Cimarron* broke many of the ironbound rules of motion picture making. Edna Ferber's great story, from which the film was made, was acclaimed as a masterpiece of literature, but was thought to be impossible for the screen. The wiseacres shook their heads when the book was bought. 'The story is too episodic,' they said. 'It covers too long a period of time. Besides—it is a costume picture—and that will never do!'"[93] At the world premiere at the Globe Theatre in New York, advertisements proclaimed its transformation of historical cinema and Hollywood history: "Tonight! Talking Pictures are born anew! . . . Tonight! Even memories of *The Birth of a Nation* and the *Four Horsemen* will be swept into oblivion!" Publicity even revealed that *Cimarron*'s filmmakers followed an unusual shooting practice. The film's program proclaimed that *Cimarron* "was filmed in exact chronological order to insure faithful adherence to the progression of the story," treating the film as if it were another historical text.

Ferber did not interfere with the production; for once, she was happy with Hollywood's adaptation of her work. She wrote to Howard Estabrook after seeing the film:

> I'll tell you how much I liked *Cimarron*, dear Mr. Estabrook. I liked it so much that I wanted to write to you long before I had this charming letter from you. For the first time in my life a man who has a sense of dialogue—a feeling

for the way people talk—and a character sense, good taste, and a rhythm sense, too, has made the motion picture version of a book of mine. I think you have done a beautiful job—you and Mr. Ruggles, and Mr. LeBaron. I saw only a preview. I haven't seen the picture at the Globe Theatre, but I shall. When I think of what you and Mr. Ruggles might have done with *Show Boat* I just excuse myself, go quietly into the next room, and cut my throat.[94]

The film would be the most critically acclaimed of Ferber's adapted works. Estabrook and Ruggles produced an American historical film that topped every major poll of the year's best films.[95] *Cimarron* would even win Academy Awards for best picture and best screenplay. The industry's recognition was even more pointed considering that *Cimarron* would be the only western to garner such accolades until the 1990s, despite the genre's accelerating popularity during the postwar era. Critics loved the film but, like many of the book reviewers, often focused on its empire-making qualities and missed the critique.[96] Mordaunt Hall of the *New York Times* saw things differently. While many assumed Yancey was the main character, Hall commented, "Cravat's nonchalance and his impulsiveness may seem more than a trifle strange at times, but he is nevertheless a person to be remembered." But it was Sabra who dominated the picture: "There is the indomitable Sabra, Cravat's Sterling wife, who sticks to the newspaper that he starts in the early days to the last. No matter how gallant Cravat may be during certain interludes, it is invariably his wife who enlists one's sympathy . . . Imagine a husband who has deserted his wife and children to go to the Cherokee Strip, returning five years later, and asking his wife whether she missed him!"[97] While Richard Watts recognized that in the adaptation of "Miss Ferber's outline of Oklahoma history," Yancey's rhetoric verged on the "bombastic," only Edwin Schallert of the *Los Angeles Times* noted the film's overt picture of a woman's West: "It portrays Sabra Cravat from the period when she is the girl-wife of the hero, until she has assumed complete sway as the publisher of her husband's newspaper, and also becomes a Congresswoman. The film is really her story."[98]

Some saw the film as a new type of history. As Elizabeth Yeaman wrote, "Like history, the picture has moments of thrilling glory and moments of repetition and daily routine. *Cimarron* does not follow the rules of story construction . . . It is, in short, a graphic interpretation of a portion of history, the history of the state of Oklahoma from the time of the first great land rush until the present."[99] But an overwhelming number of critics also noted the film as a landmark in American film history. Harrison Carroll of the *Los Angeles Herald* wrote, "Without doubt, Radio Pictures has converted Edna Ferber's novel into one of the two great film epics of the American scene. The other was *Birth of a Nation.*"[100] Robert E. Sherwood was ecstatic: "The excellence of *Cimarron* is further proof that the movie is the national art of America."[101] William Boehnel was another staunch advocate: "Those of us who have been wondering when, if ever, the talking picture would produce a Western worthy of any consideration at all, certainly had occasion to rejoice last night. For of a certainty, *Cimarron* is the best of all the Western talkies. It is more than that, it is one of the talking screen's outstanding achievements, and I am willing to wager now that when the year rolls by and it come time for the film critics to pick their list of the ten best pictures, *Cimarron* will be well up toward the top."[102]

Years later, documentary filmmaker and historian Paul Rotha would remember the film as "the American cinema's one accurate study of social history."[103] Rotha responded to both *Cimarron*'s social richness and its historical accuracy, qualities that recall the documentary tradition he helped create and historicize. Although he said nothing about the historical film's potential as a documentary mode, Rotha's rare praise raises questions about historical films' potential to chronicle and comment upon history. As film critic Thornton Delehanty concluded in 1931, "*Cimarron* has set a mark for pictures of its kind which, it is not hard to believe, may never be hit again."[104]

The Remaking of a White Western Hero

For years afterward, *Cimarron* would remain the industry's standard of excellence in historical filmmaking. There were many attempts to capitalize on *Cimarron*'s legacy. In 1939, Warner Bros. remade the Cherokee Land Rush portion of the film and mimicked the heavy use of text inserts in *The Oklahoma Kid*. A few years later, *My Darling Clementine* and *Duel in the Sun* (both 1946) experimented with prominent mixed-race female characters. Nearly ten years after making his last western, director Wesley Ruggles attempted to repeat *Cimarron*'s epic revisionism and historical seriousness with *Arizona* (1940), an early feminist western focusing on the exploits of pioneer Phoebe Titus (Jean Arthur). But RKO was too poor to remake its old masterpiece. After gambling and losing with the expensive American historical films *Abe Lincoln in Illinois* (1940), *Citizen Kane* (1941), and *The Magnificent Ambersons* (1942), the studio went into receivership. When the new management took over, *Cimarron* and many other properties were sold to MGM. MGM had a habit of gobbling up other studios' old rights and films, capitalizing on their work and reputation. When David O. Selznick ran out of money for *Gone with the Wind*, MGM provided the needed funds in exchange for a significant percentage of the profits and the rights. As soon as it could, the studio assigned writers to rewrite Estabrook's script for a remake. But nearly twenty years passed between Vincent Lawrence's first treatment and the release of Anthony Mann's version in 1960.

Lawrence's version would not have appealed to conventional western tastes any more than Estabrook's had.[105] Although Sabra's relatives do not attack Yancey as a half-breed, the writer referred to Yancey's heritage several times. At one point, when the villain, Yountis, notices the name of Yancey's paper, he remarks, "Got a little Indian blood in it, huh?" Yancey agrees.[106] Sabra's masculine qualities are enhanced. When Sabra defends Yancey from Yountis and other gunfighters, she smashes her parasol over Yountis's head! But Yancey does not get angry—he just laughs: "Hey, darling, we've got this all wrong. Here, you take the guns! I'll do the house work!"[107] After giving birth to Donna, Sabra tells Yancey she wants to start a woman's social club and "help with the paper . . . I could run a little column for the women. They buy papers too. Because this is my town now, too, and I'm eager to win my spurs, Yancey—I thought you'd like to know that, darling."[108] After Sabra makes her first public speech about Oklahoma history, one woman says, "Sabra, I think you speak equally as well as your husband!"[109] Evidently, Yancey does not like being upstaged; shortly afterward, he asks Sabra to leave with him on the next land run. She has no illusions about frontier rhetoric now: "I can't be a baby any more now, Mister! I have a family to bring up! So run along to your run—to your gamblers, drunkards, Yountises and murderers." These are the pioneers. Later, after he has returned and briefly turns politician, she urges him to run for governor. But it is her influence, she implies, that will get him elected: "I might swing it—I mean, I got the women where I want 'em—if you'll just take your coat off."[110] The film ends with her career in full swing and male colleagues urging her to run for governor.

Louis B. Mayer submitted the script to the Production Code Administration (PCA) for vetting in 1941. *Cimarron* certainly took an unusual perspective for an MGM film; the studio simply did not make films about independent women in American history. Curiously, PCA head Geoffrey Shurlock worried only that the film would project too damning a view of female pioneers. Although he advocated the social condemnation of Dixie Lee, he wrote, "This

Twentieth Century Club of women should not be picturized as hatchet-faced old busybodies, but as substantial members of the community."[111] Although strong women had remained part of the burgeoning cycle of American historical films made during the 1930s, by 1942, all the studios were cutting back on the expensive productions and channelling money into contemporary wartime dramas with the assistance of the Office of War Information. Although the studios continued to make westerns during these years, they advocated a strong, American masculinity that complemented the patriotic image of the Second World War soldier. Lawrence attacked Yancey's pioneer image even more than Ferber had. The script's overt feminism may have been a deciding factor in delaying production.

The project was shelved for sixteen years before Halsted Welles wrote another treatment. The writer cut both the feminism and the historical structure. Sabra passively follows Yancey about; she does not work on the newspaper; she never becomes a congresswoman. Yancey even has an affair with the future town madam, Dixie Lee. Although Yancey's ancestry is still open to Sabra's questioning, Welles renamed the paper the *Osage Sentinel.*[112] Welles's second version did little but enhance the tawdry affair between Dixie and Yancey and invent a couple of Indian lynchings.[113]

But Welles was dropped as screenwriter in favor of Arnold Schulman, who had a multiracial and feminist view of the narrative similar, but not identical, to Ferber's. "Essentially, this picture is to be a love story, not a 'western' or a 'cowboy' picture," he wrote. "Basically Sabra is the practical one. She comes from a wealthy, cultured background. On the surface, she seems fragile, easily offended, etc., but underneath, she is indestructible. It is the women who really settle countries, leading men like children from the impractical idealist to maturity. While the men make a great deal of noise, the women quietly go about getting things done."[114] But Schulman's main interest was in portraying a multiracial frontier: "The main subject of prejudice in our piece though will be the Indians who were pushed out of the land they rightfully owned, then branded as being inferior. Fifty years later, after what the settlers at the time considered shameful intermarriages, the ancestors of these same settlers boasted of their Indian blood." Schulman also planned to build upon Ferber's inclusion of African Americans on the Oklahoma frontier. In addition to Isaiah, Schulman had decided to make Pegler, an eighty-niner and the town's first newspaper editor, a black man: "We mentioned the possibility of showing the negro in relation to the other settlers. Many have no prejudices whatever. Many are violently prejudiced. By showing the negro being persecuted (to an extent), and then possibly venting this same sort of intolerance on an Indian, we maybe able to show how prejudice is bred and cured without making speeches about it." Undoubtedly influenced by the growing presence of African American characters in films like *Island in the Sun* (1957) and *The Defiant Ones* (1958), Schulman nonetheless added an interesting comparative dimension to American racial prejudice.

Although Schulman's first script constructs the narrative through Yancey's flashback in 1928, his memories are inspired by a political billboard reading "Re-elect Sabra Cravat, Your Fighting Congresswoman."[115] The script preserves Yancey's friendship with African American newspaperman Pegler and his sympathy for Native Americans, but without ever actually implying that Yancey is of mixed race. The script also emphasizes the contradiction between Yancey's humanism and his love of frontier adventure, echoing Lawrence's adaptation. Sabra says of Yancey's desire to make the Cherokee Strip run: "Oh sure, you love to talk about progress, just as long as we don't change anything. Leave you and the rest of you little boys alone. Let you play with your guns, sleep on the dirty ground, go duck hunting, anything, whatever you feel like, whenever you feel like. Well, what's it all supposed to lead to? . . . Stay here and accept the responsibilities of a father and a husband or else get out and stay out."[116]

Later, Schulman planned a sequence in which Yancey attempts to enlist for the First World War. He dyes his hair, but the soldiers recognize his ruse, laughing at him. But later versions of the script cut these sequences, making Sabra's protests and Yancey's bombast less extreme.[117] Eventually, the executives and writer agreed on a final script that highlights a marriage of opposites: "Adventure-loving Yancey Cravat takes his gently bred Sabra on the great Oklahoma land rush of 1889 . . . But as Sabra begins to civilize the town, his restlessness keeps taking him away from her and from their son, Cimarron. Sabra alone builds the paper into a big business. They love each other to the last, and when Yancey dies heroically, it is Sabra who suggests that Oklahoma commemorate the spirit of the pioneer with Yancey's statue."[118] Sabra, however, does not become a congresswoman, and Yancey does not die a down-on-his-luck oilman but as a soldier on the western front.

MGM went out of its way to make *Cimarron* bigger than any other contemporary western and to upstage the memory of RKO's landmark film. Postwar color and the lure of wide-screen formats may have worked in MGM's favor, but ironically, MGM avoided most of Estabrook and RKO's filmic innovations—the very qualities that drew critical praise in 1931. Anthony Mann was assigned the project, and although he had produced a trio of revisionist westerns in 1950 (*Doorway to Hell, Winchester '73, The Furies*), since then he had moved toward more conventional masculine dramas such as *The Naked Spur* (1953), *The Man From Laramie* (1955), *The Last Frontier* (1955), *The Tin Star* (1957), and *Man of the West* (1958). Despite *Cimarron's* ancestry and the significant presence of revisionist "race" westerns since the mid-1940s (*Duel in the Sun*, 1946; *Doorway to Hell*, 1950; *The Searchers*, 1956; *Giant*, 1956; *The Unforgiven*, 1960), it was repackaged as a heroic story of a great white western hero. Copying Dmitri Tiomkin and George Stevens's use of a rousing male chorale and theme song in the opening credits of *Giant* (1956), *Cimarron's* titles use giant (static) frontier vistas that are gradually populated with railroads and towns in order to mimic the narrative's "growth" in microcosm. Unlike the first *Cimarron*, these were Indian-free titles. MGM was careful to present the film as "Edna Ferber's *Cimarron*," giving Ferber her own credit shot before the title and another, more conventional one shared with writer Arnold Schulman. Even period costume designer Walter Plunkett received special, larger billing in the credits. Plunkett, who had migrated to MGM in the forties from RKO, was one of the few filmmaking links with the original.

Late in production, the filmmakers added a conventional historical foreword as a prelude to the reshot land run of 1889, which intoned the political rhetoric about the "last unsettled territories . . . given free." But unlike RKO's version, the remake did not undercut the text with scenes of Native American exploitation. Instead, the text dissolves to the elegant house of Sabra's successful, German-immigrant family, where her parents are trying to persuade her not to go west. MGM's decision to replace Ferber's southern Venables with German immigrants was based in part on the necessities of star casting. Austrian actress and MGM contract star Maria Schell was Sabra, and the filmmakers knew a southern drawl was beyond her accented English.[119] But eliminating the southern legacy in the West also removed any metaphorical connection between southern prejudice against African Americans and western prejudice against Native Americans.

Turning Sabra's family into immigrants also removed the sting of the racial comments Mrs. Venable (Sabra's mother) made in the 1930 script about Yancey's "half-breed" darkness. Later in the remake, Yancey's friend the Kid (Russ Tamblyn) addresses him as "Cimarron"—but there are no racial com-

4.4. Sabra (Maria Schell) watching Yancey (Glenn Ford) manage the paper (*Cimarron*, MGM, 1960).

ments intended here. Yancey (Glenn Ford) just smiles blandly when he hears his nickname. When the couple reaches the site of the run, cavalry officers address Yancey by his first name. MGM's decision to remove any trace of Yancey's mixed blood was even more unduly cautious given that many major male stars had played Native Americans or mixed-bloods by 1960, including Robert Taylor (*Devil's Doorway*, 1950), Victor Mature (*Chief Crazy Horse*, 1955), Burt Lancaster (*Jim Thorpe—All American*, 1950; *Apache*, 1954), and Elvis Presley (*Flaming Star*, 1960).

In another significant departure from the RKO version, the couple are childless at the beginning of the narrative. Director Anthony Mann's Sabra lacks maternal authority. When she makes her first trip west with Yancey, she is a childless, adoring young bride, unused to making domestic decisions for her home and child. In addition, Sabra lost what little authority she had as an American pioneer woman when executives cast Austrian-born, heavily accented Maria Schell as Sabra. Schell's Nordic blondness and soft manner lacked the irony of Ferber's original description or of casting Irene Dunne, whose dark hair, complexion, and fiery stubbornness linked her to the races she despised. The publicity department may have sensed some of the incongruity in casting a non-American actress as Sabra, and added an article, "*Cimarron* role taught Maria Schell about America's brave pioneer women," constructing the role as a history lesson for the outsider. But the opening sequences do not show Sabra's strength, resilience, and nerve, but reaffirm her as a passive, frightened, clinging young wife.

The narrative follows her struggle with prostitute Dixie Lee for the affections of her husband, although Sabra eventually works up enough gumption to take over the paper and order her vacillating husband out of the house. But though the film still focuses on Sabra's experiences after Yancey's departure, she is not shown running the paper, becoming a pillar of society, or standing alone without tears (Fig. 4.4). Instead, she spends the majority of her time sniffing into handkerchiefs and even commiserating with Dixie Lee! Dixie's role was built up to accommodate a standard romantic triangle and the star status of Anne Baxter. In the process, history became a sideline. Gone were RKO's intertitles, newspaper and document inserts, and ironic posturings about the destiny of Oklahoma. Even Schulman's original plan to maintain Isaiah in the cast and turn Pegler into an African American newspaperman was dismissed. There were no black people in the cast.

Needless to say, the production avoided the original Yancey's connection to African Americans and Native Americans, although as a concession to Ferber's historical beliefs, even if not in accordance with the plot of her novel, Schulman and Mann staged a scene in which a Native American family is saved from attack before the land rush. But the man is later lynched. Schulman did manage to retain the Indian reservation oil scam, and showed Yancey leaking the story to the Associated Press over Sabra's protests. But the story improbably leads the president to invite Yancey to run for governor of the territory. Again, he runs from responsibility and an invitation to political corruptness. This final decision not to be "a great American" initiates the final breakup of their marriage, but unlike the outcome in Ferber's novel and the RKO original, Sabra does not use her own political capital to take his place. When Wyatt and Sol approach her with the prospect of posing for a statue to the pioneer ("You, and a little boy, and a covered wagon") and honor her with a party, she praises her husband instead. The film ends with Sabra reading a letter from Yancey, who found a new frontier on the western front.

The studio marketed Yancey as a frontier he-man, but also attempted to update the film's frontier theme by explicitly linking the old-time pioneers with the astronauts of the 1960s. One article in the press book commented, building upon recent Kennedyesque, New Frontier rhetoric about the space program, "Today's pioneering Astronauts may seem to have little in common with their forefathers who conquered the West, but you can't convince Glenn Ford of it. 'They're cut from the same mold,' Ford declares. 'They're today's pioneers, with the same spirit that characterized the settlers of a hundred years ago.' Ford says Yancey is 'the sort of man every boy would like to grow up to be.'"[120] Casting Ford was a potentially savvy way of bridging the generation gap with westerns. Although Ford had been a major star for nearly fifteen years (*Gilda*, 1946), he represented a younger generation of viewers, and films like *Blackboard Jungle* (1955) linked Ford to teen film audiences. But he was also known as a star of solid westerns—most recently, *The Fastest Gun Alive* (1956), *3:10 to Yuma* (1957), and *Cowboy* (1958).

The studio also attempted to capture a female audience, marketing Anthony Mann's finished film as part western, part romance. They sold the sex in both the trailer and the press book. The trailer advertised the film with scenes of Ford and Schell rolling around on the grass and of Schell bathing in a convenient pond. "The story of a land. The story of a love. The story of a man," intoned the narrator. "Cimarron means wild and crazy. And that was the way love was for the beautiful Sabra . . . as she gave herself recklessly to the man she loved."[121] And yet MGM also copied RKO's publicity tactics, appealing to women's civic organizations and even Ferber's readers (who were constructed as mostly female and romantically inclined). Mercedes McCambridge, who had starred as Luz in the 1956 adaptation of *Giant*, was cast in a smaller role in *Cimarron* (as was actor Charles Watts—*Giant's* Judge Whiteside—who made another appearance as a corrupt politician). McCambridge was quoted, "'During the filming of *Giant*, [Ferber] and I became very good friends. We correspond regularly, and whenever I am in New York, I visit her. As an actress, I appreciate her ability to write such wonderful parts for women. All of her narratives, even though they are historical novels, revolve around love stories.' Miss McCambridge attributes much of the success as motion pictures of such Ferber novels as these, as well as *Show Boat*, *Saratoga Trunk* and *So Big*, to this skill at drawing feminine characterizations."[122] RKO (Dunne, *Cimarron*, 1931), Warner Bros. (Stanwyck, *So Big*, 1932), and Universal (Dunne, *Show Boat*, 1936) had all used similar strategies to link the starring actress to Ferber.

Audience-generating suggestions to exhibitors appealed to the more serious side of female viewers, advocating "the important role played by the pioneer women in America." The studio suggested: "Where an important pioneer woman, or a descendant, is available, suggest presentation of an award or trophy from the stars of *Cimarron*."[123] It even proposed involving the League of Women Voters, despite the fact that Sabra never becomes a congresswoman in the second version: "The first woman to cast a ballot was a woman of the West, eighty year-old Louisa Ann Swain. Mrs. Swain voted in Wyoming on December 10, 1869, a precedent-shattering affair. Suggest local chapters of the League of Women Voters be contacted to honor Mrs. Swain's memory in the name of all the women who have voted since that time, using this occasion to present the League with a *Cimarron* award for the part women have played in building America."[124] Even the Women's Bar Association had a potential role to play: "Suggest a special screening for Women's Bar Association or any group made up of women engaged in law enforcement capacities. At the preview a pioneer woman, Esther Morris, could be honoured. Miss Morris was the first woman Justice of the Peace, elected to this office in South Pass, Wyoming in the late 1860s. A *Cimarron* trophy should be awarded to the woman of the group most typifying the pioneer spirit in the work she is doing for the community."[125]

One of the more interesting suggestions, which appealed to both young and older female viewers, was the "Favorite Movie Heroine" contest. "In *Cimarron*, Maria Schell plays a woman who lives an exciting and rewarding life against a background of historical importance." The publicity department suggested that contestants should submit letters of up to 100 words, telling which heroine of which picture would be their choice. The studio came up with a list dominated by MGM heroines: Greer Garson in *Mrs. Miniver* (1942), Luise Rainier in *The Good Earth* (1937), Vivien Leigh in *Gone with the Wind*, and Audrey Hepburn in *The Nun's Story* (1959). These many attempts to attract female audiences represented a subtle manipulation of viewers familiar with the 1931 version and readers of women's fiction. Jan Struther (*Mrs. Miniver*), Pearl Buck (*The Good Earth*), and Margaret Mitchell were some of the most popular women writers of the previous twenty years and were responsible for some of MGM's biggest box-office grossers. Ferber, though more associated with Warner Bros. and RKO, was being carefully repackaged as an MGM author.

But the publicity department proceeded with caution, mostly because of Ferber's avid dislike of MGM. It had already purchased *Show Boat* from Universal without paying her anything for the 1951 remake. It was galling to find that

4.5. Covered wagon reenactments (*Cimarron*, MGM, 1960).

Ferber's best-known book and film were now in the hands of the studio she liked least. She wrote to Ken McCormick, making sure that the studio would not use her other books or titles as a means of promoting its film.[126] She contacted the MGM publicity department, and William R. Golden of MGM assured her that "the trailer presentation does not now contemplate the use of a montage of your various novels."[127] But still, the studio knew that one of its best chances at publicity was to use Ferber's name and her Pulitzer status. Trailers and film teasers abounded with her name, and each poster mentioned her as *Cimarron*'s author.[128]

The studio even tried to enlist Howard Estabrook's name as a means of overcoming its production difficulties. Although Estabrook had recently abandoned full-time screenwriting and producing, his name was box office in Hollywood.[129] While Arnold Schulman was struggling with the new adaptation, producers contacted Estabrook, asking if he would allow MGM to use his name as coscreenwriter. In a letter to R. Monta of MGM (dated 13 November 1959), Estabrook said that he had read the new script and would prefer not to have screen credit at all. MGM persisted, and so later in February, he was more explicit: "Naturally I have heard the trade gossip regarding the script problems on *Cimarron* and the frequent re-running of the RKO picture to try to solve the difficulties." He said that his screenplay must have been a source, and if it continued to be so, he would sue for screen credit.[130] But after looking at another, final version of Schulman's work, he realized that "this script deviates surprisingly from the book in character and intent."[131] Estabrook knew that the production was in trouble and did not want his name associated with it.

In spite of the relatively recent release of westerns sensitive to the extermination of Native Americans (*Devil's Doorway*, 1950; *Broken Arrow*, 1951; *Apache*, 1954; *The Unforgiven*, 1960), the ongoing popularity of the Western genre in the 1950s, and the casting of Glenn Ford as Yancey, critics loathed the film. *Motion Picture Daily*, noting Edmund Grainger's "slick" updated production, was nostalgic for RKO's classic: "In 1931 RKO's filmization of Edna Ferber's sweeping novel of the building of Oklahoma was one of the truly great pictures of the year, and is still considered on the lists of most motion picture experts as one of the outstanding Westerns of all time."[132] Although Bosley Crowther liked the original production, he was not impressed with this slick remake: "At this late date . . . you would think they could come up with something more impressive and illuminating in the way of an American historical saga than the present remake of Edna Ferber's *Cimarron*." After the land rush, "*Cimarron* settles down to a stereotyped and sentimental cinema saga of the taming of the frontier" (Fig. 4.5).[133]

Ferber did not have anything to do with the remake and wrote to Crowther expressing her support for his review:

> Your criticism was too mild . . . I can't do anything about this picture. I didn't even know that a second picturization of my novel *Cimarron* was being made. I receive from this second picture of my novel not one single penny in payment. I can't even do anything to stop the motion picture company from using my name in advertising so slanted that it gives the effect of my having written the picture. I am not carping because I received nothing from the profits of this picture. In 1929 writers who sold their books or plays to the motion picture companies did so under contracts which now are considered absurd . . . This is a good deal like being forced to stand by helpless while your daughter is ravished and sold into slavery.[134]

But she did have one way left to gouge MGM. She asked Crowther to reprint her letter endorsing his nasty review in his column the following week: "I do care about the form and treatment and content of this present picture entitled *Cimarron*. I do care about the publicity which conveys the false impression that I had anything to do with the writing or the presentation of this picture." He did as she asked. It was the last time that MGM made or remade any of her works.

five

Writing for Hollywood

COME AND GET IT AND
SARATOGA TRUNK, 1933–1947

lthough Ferber's next novel, *American Beauty* (1931), had sold well and received good reviews, it was not a best seller. Her portrait of cultural decay in New England was not a popular theme during the early 1930s, when so much of America was mired in a massive economic depression. The studios avoided purchasing it. While film adaptations of her series of plays coauthored with George S. Kaufman did well at Paramount (*The Royal Family of Broadway*, 1930) and MGM (*Dinner at Eight*, 1933), these modern set pieces about professional performers and social hypocrites were empty, though star-studded, dramatic exercises. Though Ferber relished her rapport with Kaufman, her relationship with Hollywood was built upon her work as an individual author. After RKO's critical success with *Cimarron* and Warner Bros.' remake of *So Big* (1932), Ferber was easily Hollywood's best-known living writer of filmable history. But Ferber knew that she could not retire on the proceeds of film remakes; by 1934, she had to write a new "cinemadaptable" property. *Come and Get It* (1935) was intended as a triumphant return to the western genre she had dominated with *Cimarron*.

During this period, Ferber's writing became more and more entwined with the demands of Hollywood filmmaking. *Come and Get It* was a popular serial in the *Woman's Home Companion* and made *Publishers Weekly's* national best-seller list, selling around 90,000 copies in its first run. Like *American Beauty*, it described the rise of new immigrant populations, but Hollywood found the Polish working-class immigrants of Wisconsin more acceptable than the new arrivals back east who capitalized on the decay of old WASP (white Anglo-Saxon Protestant) families and farmsteads. Narratives of a frontier still in transformation (Wisconsin and Michigan) possessed scenes of physical vigor, wildness, and dynamism that transferred well to the screen; stories of enervated New England lacked a sense of the forward historical movement that was essential to Hollywood. Furthermore, in *Come and Get It*, Ferber created a frontier hero as dynamic as Yancey, but turned him into a fabulously successful timber baron. Regardless of his greed, murky business ethics, and callousness, Barney Glasgow was a colorful, strong male protagonist who fit easily within the burgeoning and sometimes unconventional Hollywood biopic genre (*Abraham Lincoln*, 1930; *Billy the Kid*, 1930; *Alexander Hamilton*, 1931; *The Public Enemy*, 1931; *Scarface*, 1932; *Silver Dollar*, 1932; *I Am a Fugitive from a Chain Gang*, 1932; *The Life of Jimmy Dolan*, 1933; *The Mighty Barnum*, 1934; *Diamond Jim*, 1935).[1]

However, in *Come and Get It*, Ferber and independent producer Samuel Goldwyn attempted to revisit *Cimarron's* demystification of western history and the frontier hero. The second of Ferber's western novels was a fierce critique of the post–Civil War greed that fuelled the myth of the Gilded Age and the robber barons. Goldwyn soon discovered that Ferber's historical critiques were not always that easy to project or market to audiences. Director Howard Hawks was particularly resistant to the novel's thesis, and would attempt to salvage a brand of heroic masculinity that fascinated and revolted Ferber. Despite attempts to promote the film by invoking Hollywood's famous adaptations of *Cimarron* and *Show Boat*, the film would disappoint both Ferber and Goldwyn.

Her next novel was even more carefully tailored to Hollywood's narrative demands. Published some seven years later, *Saratoga Trunk* (1941) was devoured by readers and damned by critics for its saleable, "Hollywood" qualities. Warner Bros. purchased the rights to Ferber's book, described as a lush period romance set in late nineteenth-century New Orleans and New York, as soon as they were available. The studio paid handsomely—$175,000, advertised as the highest price paid in Hollywood for any original material.[2] But the novel, arguably, was worth it. In *Saratoga Trunk*, Ferber created two beautiful, brilliant, and unconventional protagonists—in effect, stars. But underneath the novel's period sensuality and intrigue was a cynical union between two mavericks: a Texas landowner turned double-dealing railroad magnate and a mixed-race adventuress.

Many actresses wanted to play Ferber's latest heroine, Clio Dulaine, but the studio's top star, Ingrid Bergman, got the role. She even wore a black wig for the part. Although shot and marketed as a period melodrama for women, *Saratoga Trunk* was unique in its projection of Bergman's racial ambiguity. Women's fiction was at a premium in Hollywood during the second half of the 1940s, but *Saratoga Trunk* was unique. The film, released in 1946, was the first in a postwar cycle to return to the theme explored so often in the southern period films of the 1930s—the mixed-race American heroine. Warner Bros.' ambitious racial drama owes much to *Show Boat*, but Clio Dulaine belongs to a surprisingly rich group of mixed-race heroines in pre- and postwar Hollywood. In spite of the Production Code's stringent censorship of miscegenation and other forms of racial mixing, classical Hollywood's fabrications of race, aberrant sexuality, and American history were extensive and complex, ranging from Clara Bow and Fredi Washington's modern mixed-race heroines (*Call Her Savage*, 1932; *Imitation of Life*, 1934) to Vivien Leigh's Scarlett O'Hara (*Gone with the Wind*, 1939) and Jennifer Jones's Pearl Chavez (*Duel in the Sun*, 1946).[3]

This chapter reconfronts some of the historical issues raised in Chapter Three; namely, Ferber's return to the Southern mulatta trope and the post–Civil War history of race and gender in the American South. It was no accident that Ferber named her mixed-race heroine after the muse of history. Unlike Julie in *Show Boat*, Clio is not passive or tragic, nor is she a secondary character, but an articulate, dominating protagonist intent on fracturing post–Civil War New Orleans's racial prejudices and the snobbery of white northern elites. Clio's southern femininity and "foreign" exoticism are complemented by the more traditional western masculinity of her lover and fellow swindler Clint Maroon, yet it is Clio who dominates the narrative. The second half of this chapter also explores how Warner Bros. handled Ferber's lush but potentially controversial novel. Like *Come and Get It*, the text attempted to revise the public's romantic conception of the Gilded Age, but Barney Glasgow's maverick tendencies were tame compared to Clio's. Critics and audiences, weary of stark war dramas, largely ignored the racial and feminist subtexts and instead revelled in Bergman's exoticism and the production's lavish sets, costumes, and sensual details. *Saratoga Trunk* was marketed first and foremost as a period melodrama by Edna Ferber, and this chapter explores the rhetoric of the Warner Bros. publicity department, the women's melodrama, its intersections with history in the postwar era, and the degree to which Ferber's female audiences controlled American publishing and the Hollywood box office.

The Desolation of the Frontier

In a departure from her other historical novels dominated by heroic women, *Come and Get It*'s main frontier character is a man. When she created the larger-than-life, brash adventurer and timber magnate Barney Glasgow, Ferber was in many senses following the current public taste for male-oriented historical dramas made popular by the likes of Darryl F. Zanuck (*Silver Dollar*, 1932; *The Bowery*, 1933; *The Mighty Barnum*, 1934). Back in 1931, many film critics had ignored Sabra and willfully viewed *Cimarron* as a heroic tale of frontier masculinity. In *Come and Get It*, Ferber deliberately blurred the lines between frontier eulogy and critique. While researching the Wisconsin and Michigan timber industries of the late nineteenth century enabled her to return to the sites of her midwestern girlhood, she shrugged off any lingering nostalgia. "The Grand Old Boys whose names and faces stood forth so prominently in the books on Wisconsin and Michigan pioneers and commerce turned out to be not so grand, after all," she recalled. "Cutting and slashing, grabbing and tricking, they had seized and destroyed millions of acres of forest land with never a sprig replanted; they had diverted and polluted streams and rivers; had falsely obtained right-of-way on either side of trumped-up railroads and thereby got control of untold mineral wealth as well as woodland, water and farm lands."[4] There was nothing unique about these men; they were merely greedy carbon copies of the Astors, Vanderbilts, Morgans, Fisks, Rockefellers, Goulds, Harrimans, Huntingtons, Hopkinses, and Hills of the East and West. Ferber could not understand how American Jews had become bywords of acquisitiveness when "[these] Robber Barons, ruthless, plunderers of a vast rich continent" were Gentiles to a man, and honored in libraries and museums.[5]

Ferber was not the first social crusader or historian to attack the robber barons. Ida Tarbell, author of the controversial *History of Standard Oil Company* (1904) and *The Nationalizing of Business* (1936), was one of their most eloquent critics. Tarbell's second book capitalized on the popular antagonism toward big business that had been renewed by the Great Depression. The faltering economy certainly colored historian Matthew Josephson's attitude toward the robber barons in 1934, and the persistent devastation of the Dust Bowl motivated many of Ferber's remarks about land conservation and reforestation in Come and Get It. But with these exceptions, American readers were more familiar with admiring biographies dating from the more prosperous 1920s. Even Josephson seemed as enthralled by the magnates' wealth and power as he was appalled by their greed and destruction of the environment.[6]

In spite of Ferber's instinctive loathing for these destructive American men, bred from her early admiration for the muckraking journalism and historiography of Ida Tarbell and the conservation politics of Theodore Roosevelt, Ferber found her protagonist Barney Glasgow the most dynamic, brash, and exciting character in her novel. She would later claim to be dissatisfied with the ending because, in killing off Glasgow and focusing, in the last third of the book, on the lives of the next generation of wealthy Wisconsinites, she destroyed "the most vital and engaging person in the story."[7] Goldwyn and his team of screenwriters would agree, leaving the hero battered but still alive at the end of the film. When critics and audiences saw Goldwyn's version of her novel in 1936, they too focused overwhelmingly on Edward Arnold's performance as Barney, giving only token acknowledgment to Ferber's historical critique.

Barney was self-made and selfish, and when Ferber begins her narrative, we see him in the full maturity of wealth, looking over his carved walnut furniture and French tapestry. He made his money chopping down the forests of the Midwest, and even after years of expansion, he still refuses to replant the forests: "Replanting costs money . . . I'm good and sick of paying taxes on good-for-nothing land, if you want to know. Let the gover'ment replant if it wants to."[8] According to Ferber, Barney and men like him are "like ignorant children with the power of gods."[9] The author's sympathy is with the forests. She even sees them as carriers of history, landmarks and silent witnesses to America's past that greedy men seek only to destroy. At one point, she describes in detail Barney's felling of a giant white pine: "It had seen the passing of the Indian, of the coureurs de bois and voyageurs of France, the Jesuit Fathers; of hunters and trappers and cruisers. Its rings might show the scars of arrowheads and hatchets and knives and campfires and bullets and lightning and hail. It was a living historical record of the region." But Barney's saw cuts its "flesh," and finally we hear the "first scream of anguish from the pine."[10]

Barney is healthy, rowdy, sensuous. He enjoys his food, his drink, his clothes, his house, and the company of his daughter. He worked hard as a lumberjack, but this pioneer also had the foresight to marry his boss's daughter. Though they have two children and Barney becomes ever richer, the marriage is an unhappy one. Late in life, he becomes fascinated with the grand-daughter of the woman he once loved and abandoned when he was a poor lumberjack. Lotta Lindbeck is both an inversion of the ideal of the pioneer man and a perfect complement to Barney's greed, for she is a self-made and selfish woman. Born with as few material advantages as Barney, Lotta nevertheless becomes a world traveller and socialite. Just as Barney Glasgow once destroyed thousands of acres of forests, so Lotta capitalizes on the vanity of the nearest robber baron. And it is Barney Glasgow who will help her leave the timber camps for the big cities. As she remarks to her mother, "I got ideas how I want things to be and I'm going to plan how to fix it so I can get 'em."[11] Both of Ferber's characters were pioneers, exemplifying the acquisitiveness and hardheaded drive of her title: *Come and Get It.* For Ferber, the tragedy was that Barney's generation achieved so much.

Come and Get It was widely reviewed as the new Edna Ferber best seller, but the most thorough and insightful response to the novel came from the *Jewish Advocate.* "Perhaps Miss Ferber is not as modernistic as some of our more fastidious and precious novelists," the reviewer wrote, but her real strengths lay in creating powerful historical images that no traditional historian could match. "While the more academic text-books on American history may be used in high school and colleges, [Ferber's] novels depicting segments of American history reach far larger audiences. With her latest work, *Come and Get It*, describing the development of the State of Wisconsin, Edna Ferber adds richly to the broad canvas of American life that she has been painting since she wrote *So Big, Cimarron, Show Boat,* and *American Beauty.*" Ferber was both a historian and a novelist, the review continued: "Miss Ferber is not the type of writer whose achievement can be restricted to the literary columns. Piercing deeply beneath the surface of American conventions and poses, she emerges with that which is sincere and profound in the character of her country," a vivid and often critical "picture of the American scene."[12] By 1935, critics described Ferber's fame as a historical novelist in terms of its powerful imagery and nontraditional history, qualities she shared with the major disseminator of her work—Hollywood.

The review also treated Ferber's most recent novel as part of an impressive body of historical work. Doubleday had been using this as a marketing strategy since the publication of *Cimarron*. By 1935, Ferber had covered so much historical and regional territory that the press portrayed her as something between a latter-day pioneer and a historical juggernaut: "Boxing the Compass for America," the back of the dust jacket reads.[13] *Come and Get It* dealt with the North, *Show Boat* the South, *American Beauty* the East, *Cimarron* the West, and *So Big* and *The Girls* the Midwest. "Edna Ferber's novels have always had a significance beyond the story she had to tell," claimed the press. Her historical perspective was inherently visual, stunning, vivid with "period background," and a "Panorama of America." Doubleday even portrayed her as a progressive historian whose historical narrative "binds the present to both the remembrance of the past and the imperatives of the future."

But privately, Ferber was not that happy with the book. As she wrote to Julie Ponsonby, it "isn't such a very good book . . . I tried so hard to be popular, changing so many ideas because I wanted to write something people would buy."[14] Ferber's mainstream popularity was a problem with some reviewers, particularly T. S. Matthews. In his review for the *New Republic*, he dismissed both her narrative of pioneer toil and "workmanlike" history as charmless and a repetitive exercise in modern publishing and advertising.[15] In fact, Matthews saw Ferber as less a novelist than a cultural machine, "turning out a nationally advertised product that looks as sound as this year's model always does, until next year's model comes along." He drew attention to her publisher's press campaign for the novel, in which Ferber is lauded for having "practically covered the mores of the entire United States." Matthews was snide, disliking the fanfare of mass production and consumption that always accompanied one of Ferber's novels. Was it mere sour grapes? Few of Ferber's novels ever won any praise from the *New Republic*, where reviewers often missed her historical critiques and instead pigeonholed her as a dowdy writer of patriotic potboilers. And of course, she was permanently tainted by Hollywood. One can almost detect the machinery of the motion picture industry behind Matthews's attack on Ferber's "workmanlike" productions.

But Ferber was the victim of another, more insidious attack. Polish American groups were outraged by her novel's portrait of female mill workers. The Polish National Alliance wrote to Crowell, the publisher of the *Woman's Home Companion*, complaining of Ferber's "mendacious, virulent, and scurrilous anti-Polish onslaughts. May we remind you at this time, that Miss Ferber's malignment [*sic*] of Polish and Polish-American people, and your interest in subsisting on hatred and dissension, shall not be tolerated."[16] Another reader claimed that Ferber, as a Jew, should have known better than to have made such "racial" slurs.[17] It was neither the first nor last time that anti-Semitic Americans attacked Ferber's historical perspective and authority because of her Jewish identity. However, the most notorious abuse occurred over her western novels—*Cimarron, Come and Get It,* and *Giant,* each of which critiqued the traditional notion of the pioneer westerner.

Goldwyn and Ferber: Adaptation and Independence

More than any other producer, Samuel Goldwyn built his reputation on the adaptation of classic and contemporary American and British literature, including *The Dark Angel* (1925), *The Winning of Barbara Worth* (1926), and *Raffles* (1930). Goldwyn's publicity always emphasized the producer's respect both for faithful adaptations and for writers and screenwriters. A few years after founding Goldwyn Pictures Corporation in 1916, he publicly announced the foundation of Eminent Authors, Inc., which involved popular writers like Rex Beach and Rupert Hughes adapting their own work for the screen. He also took chances on more challenging work, hiring Anzia Yezierska to oversee the adaptation of her *Hungry Hearts* (1923, screenplay by Julien Josephson), and later forming a successful partnership with playwright Lillian Hellman.[18] Goldwyn was unafraid of producing work about Jews, working women, urban poverty, and even lesbianism.

But during the early 1930s, the producer was preoccupied with adapting solid, timely prestige properties such as Sinclair Lewis's *Arrowsmith* (1931) and *Dodsworth* (1935), a critique of modern American materialism. Lewis was a contemporary of Ferber's, though not quite in the same best-selling category. He also tended to avoid historical subjects. Goldwyn, however, was reading the signs; history—particularly American—was popular with critics and audiences. His successful production of *The Barbary Coast* (1935) proved as much. *Come and Get It* may not have been set in bawdy nineteenth-century San Francisco, but Goldwyn became interested in the project after reading it in serialized form during December 1934.[19] He bought the rights to *Come and Get It* for $40,000 in 1935, and then paid Ferber an additional $10,000 for vetting the various scripts during a highly publicized visit to Hollywood (Fig. 5.1).[20] This was substantially less than she had received for *Cimarron* in 1930, and only about as much as she received from the *Woman's Home Companion* for serial-

5.1. Ferber (*third from left*) on the set of *Barbary Coast* (1935) with (*from left*) Sam Goldwyn, Miriam Hopkins, Howard Hawks, Lawrence Tibbett, and Edward G. Robinson.

ization rights. However, *Come and Get It* was not a number one best seller, and the worsening Depression had made all the studios cautious.

Screenwriter Edward Chodorov, well known for his work on historical films (*The World Changes*, 1933; *Madame Du Barry*, 1934; *The Story of Louis Pasteur*, 1935), was given the project. Although familiar with the emerging vocabulary of the historical film, he did not begin the film with a text foreword or even a superimposed date to identify the script as historical. Even more unusually, he avoided any mention of Barney's shady business dealings, his exploitation of the forests, or his son's warnings about his robber-baron tendencies.[21] Barney was merely a successful, lively man. Instead, the script focused on the more conventional theme of thwarted love—Barney's ill-fated infatuation for his friend's granddaughter Lotta, and his daughter Evvy's love for a Polish laborer, Tony. However, his first script covered the multigenerational narrative, ending with Barney's rejection by Lotta and his ensuing death from a falling tree.[22]

From the first, Chodorov resisted turning Barney's first love, Lotta Morgan, into a brazen dance-hall girl, staying close to Ferber's original characterization of a vulnerable woman who is shy from a history of physical abuse. But he also avoided Ferber's critical view of Lotta's granddaughter—the second Lotta (recast as her daughter) was portrayed as an innocent victim of Barney Glasgow's late-life lust: "The more I think of Lotta, the more certain I am that we want a combination of adorable charm, innocence and yet vitality and the kind of lush femininity that Louise [*sic*] Rainer has. We have been thinking of magnificent blondes—a hangover from the bovine purposeful Lotta of the novel entirely removed from our present conception. Rainer, more than an actress, is an acute personality. We need the very qualities she can project without trying."[23] But eventually, the twin roles of Lotta were filled by a newcomer rather than a big star. Frances Farmer's unknown qualities accentuated both women's dependence on Barney. Chodorov and Goldwyn's choice for Barney was easier and needed less justification: Edward Arnold, who had recently starred in Universal's film biography *Diamond Jim* (1935). The period piece covered the same area in American history, though backwoods Wisconsin was certainly less glitzy than New York City. Arnold would make a career as a stock historical personage, and he seemed to specialize in pioneering businessmen, playing John Sutter in *Sutter's Gold* (1936) and Jim Fisk in *High, Wide, and Handsome* (1937) after his performance in *Come and Get It*.

Chodorov's second script trimmed the multigenerational angle of the story and focused even more closely on the tangled romances. But while Chodorov abandoned much of the early frontier material, he did insert occasional rhetoric evocative of Ferber's original critique of the robber-baron generation. The writer visualized this critique as an argument between Barney and his more progressive son: "You can't keep RUINING hundreds of miles of good timber land without replanting!"[24] At the end of the film, after Lotta and his son have run off together, Barney admits his failures to his daughter: "We ruined the rest of 'em first . . . stole the land."

Evidently this was not enough for Goldwyn or Ferber. In mid-October, the producer replaced Chodorov with Jane Murfin, who had even more experience in adapting period material and seemed to specialize in women's historical pictures (*The Silver Cord*, 1933; *Ann Vickers*, 1933; *The Little Minister*, 1934; *Alice Adams*, 1935). Murfin's opening sequence is in stark contrast to Chodorov's (ellipses in the original):

Open with a Panning Shot of acres of standing timber over which the year 1878 is SUPERIMPOSED, Fading In and Out. The Screen is filled with trees as far as the eye can see, ending on a cleared spot where there is a camp. Glimpses of teams and wagons . . . lumberjacks . . . axes . . . saws . . . gigantic chains . . . all the paraphernalia of such a camp, with a background of standing timber. It is early fall. At the entrance of the cook shack a boy of fifteen appears and yells, "Come and get it!"[25]

Quite simply, in this opening sequence, Murfin identifies the film as a historical narrative. She names the period, invests it with frontier images, and places Ferber's title within the context of this history. She even planned a series of dated superimpositions (reminiscent of Estabrook's work in *Cimarron*) to document Barney Glasgow's rise from camp cook to lumber giant (1885, 1890, 1900, 1907). One of the dates was to be combined with a shot of "devastated land—a crop of stumps in f.g. [foreground]."[26] Later she would add a damning text foreword: "America . . . Land of political and religious freedom . . . land of limitless wealth, yet scarcely touched . . . Magnificent forests of pine, balsam, hemlock, beech and maple . . . All these stores of riches lay enticing and unprotected for the ambitious and violent to appropriate and ravish for private gain."[27]

Murfin was also much more interested in projecting Barney's greed than Chodorov. When Barney and Swan Bostrum (played by Walter Brennan) first meet, Murfin planned a scene in which Swan would explain just how exploitative businessmen controlled the timber industry. When Barney asks how the owner acquired so much acreage, Swan answers, "Them big fellas, they steal it. Well, not steal it . . . They make money work with the railroads and the Government." Murfin went on: "Swan explains how the Government gives away land to build railroads and Hewitt gets it and builds a bum railroad and takes miles and miles of timberland, cuts the fine pine and makes it into pulp in his paper mill in Butte des Morts with no cost to him except the logging."[28] But rather than denouncing the owner as Swan does, Barney takes it all in uncritically. He wants to be like this man, and ironically, he will literally become one of the family, marrying Hewitt's plain but rich daughter.

At one point, Murfin even planned a confrontation of sorts with trust-busting president Theodore Roosevelt. At breakfast one morning, Barney glances at the front page of his paper: "His newspaper has a cartoon of Theodore Roosevelt doing something energetic, all fists, teeth, eye-glasses and Big

Stick. He is going after Big Business. Barney's remarks are like those heard today! 'Socialists at Washington running things! Ruining things! What do any of 'em know about business.'"[29] This leads to a disagreement with his son, Bernie, who, like Ferber, shares Roosevelt's vision. When Bernie warns him that government controls are coming, Barney blusters, "Government, my foot! I'm the government when it comes to my own business. Some cheap politician tries to get solid with his gang and starts yawping about forests or railroads or waterways. I'll cut out my timber and fix my rate and ship my logs as I see fit. Always have. Always will." Bernie responds, "Yes, I know. That was fine in the old days, Every man for himself . . . but some day somebody's going to come along and ask you where you got your timberland and how you got your railroad right of way and what you pay your hands."[30] Now in a proper rage, his father accuses him of reading Roosevelt and Robert La Follette's "ranting."

But Murfin's outline and ensuing scripts also pay heed to Barney's unsuccessful attempt to court and marry his old friend Swan's daughter, Lotta, and the more suitable pairing of rich girl Evvy and poor worker Tony. But arguably, all of the characters with the exception of the younger male generation are infected with a distorted pioneering greed. In spite of the fact that the second Lotta is described as having "a quietly burning ambition, coupled with an imagination and an audacity akin to Barney's own," she is not a creator, but a spender.[31] While Barney may exploit the landscape, she exploits the exploiters, using his affection for her as a way of escaping a dull, backwoods life.

Ferber liked Murfin's adaptation, and it appears from her correspondence with Goldwyn that she may have been instrumental in demanding a new writer to replace Chodorov. She earned her $10,000 from Goldwyn, reading various script versions in New York and Hollywood during the first half of 1935. In late July 1935, she wrote to Goldwyn, "If there's anything more I can do—if you or anyone connected with the studio would care to have me do any further work on the story or synopsis in the next few days, do please call me."[32] Later in the fall the studio submitted Murfin's work to her. Producer Merritt Hurlburd wrote to Goldwyn, "I had three hours' conversation with Edna Ferber regarding Miss Murfin's treatment of *Come and Get It*. Ferber thinks that the first half of Murfin's treatment is excellent—that it gives you the background of the characters better than has been done before." However, "she rather bitterly disagrees with Miss Murfin that there are no sympathetic characters in the story. She sees Lotta as a beautiful girl with a good mind who wants to get away from her humble surroundings." Ferber also felt that "Tony should be used more to point out to us, as well as to Barney in the latter half of the story, how the changing world has passed him by; that his kind of man was right for his period but that his period is gone and the new order of things has arisen. This, Miss Ferber feels, will sustain the dignity of the story and its purpose without destroying its entertainment."[33]

But while Ferber appreciated Murfin's close adherence to her narrative, she wanted the best writers available. Hurlburd confided in Goldwyn, "Now, as to how she will work on the story, she has a great deal of faith in Miss Murfin's ability to eventually do a good job on this book. But she firmly believes, as she has from the start, that Howard Estabrook would be much better. She understands, as I do, that Estabrook is under contract to Fox and now on loan-out to Metro, but she believes that it would be worth it to make every effort to secure Estabrook and even to wait until he is free, if that be necessary. If you hire Estabrook, she would be glad to have him come on and talk to her to get her viewpoint. Since she expects to devote four or five days to this, she would expect some compensation," he reminded Goldwyn. "If you decide against Estabrook or if you cannot get him for many months, she would be glad to have Miss Murfin come on and receive the benefit of her advice and suggestions. She wants a good picture out of this as sincerely as you do, and after talking with her I am convinced that she has the proper slant on the story. Miss Ferber would appreciate some word as soon as possible as to whether you can get Estabrook and if you can, when he will be here."[34]

Although Goldwyn never managed to get Estabrook from Paramount, and he trimmed some of Murfin's historical critique by early 1936, he retained her foreword, text superimpositions, and father-son clash over Roosevelt's policies.[35] However, following Ferber's suggestion, Goldwyn asked Murfin to include some kind of eulogy to Barney, for at the end of her February 1936 script, Murfin had added Bernie's speech to his mill workers, in which the son tries to balance Barney's pioneer qualities with the new needs of big business and labor: "I think a man like my father was right for his time. He had the qualities it took to build empires . . . Your prosperity, your health, your happiness are closely interwoven with ours. Don't ever let anyone tell you our interests are separate. We stand or fall together."[36] No memos exist detailing Ferber's attitude toward this ending. Although a strong supporter of President Franklin Roosevelt, she never ended her novels with obvious plugs for the National Recovery Administration or New Deal policies. But Goldwyn, as a producer, may have seen the film as a potential prop for Roosevelt and Hollywood's troubled coalition of business and labor. After all, in the Murfin-Chodorov scripts, Barney's children both pair off with members of the working class.[37]

Once the script was ready, he hired independent director Howard Hawks. Goldwyn may have had some misgivings about hiring the maverick; although his work was currently in vogue with audiences, Hawks had a tendency of "messing with the scripts and letting actors improvise lines."[38] Goldwyn liked fidelity in his adaptations; after all, he had replaced Chodorov with the more meticulous Murfin. He may have started to worry when Hawks brought in his own screenwriter, Jules Furthman. They would work on the script for months, delaying production until the summer.

Goldwyn, though, was not in a position to monitor Hawks as closely as he would have liked. In early March 1936, he went to Europe with his wife and son for a few months' vacation. Just before they docked in New York, he became very sick. After two major operations, surgeons removed first his gall bladder and appendix and then some decayed intestines. He nearly died, and was unable to work until late May. In the meantime, Hawks had taken over the film. As Goldwyn's biographer A. Scott Berg writes, "With nobody to oppose him, Howard Hawks began to turn *Come and Get It* into something of his own."[39] The film became just another of Hawks's "buddy" pictures, with a brawling pair of men and a brazen slut who nearly wrecks their friendship. Furthman's first script, in May 1936, was certainly a departure from Murfin's. There was no critique of big business, no text foreword, nor any dated superimpositions.[40] His only nod to Ferber's historical critique was the partial preservation of Barney and Bernie's exchange over Roosevelt, in which Barney rants, "This Roosevelt and his Big Stick! What's built up this country but Big Business, I'd like to know! . . . Big Business's the backbone of this country—only the fanatics are starting in on forestry and conservation."[41]

But for a while, Goldwyn had no idea how significantly Hawks had transformed the script. He and Furthman kept to themselves, while producer Merritt Hurlburd complained to Goldwyn, "Howard Hawks now states he cannot start picture before June twelfth because he will not finish necessary script changes until June tenth . . . Professes grave doubts as to the ultimate box-office value of the story setup itself."[42] This was another of Hawks's self-serving ploys to gain more time with the script. Knowing that Goldwyn was still weak, Abraham Lehr sent wires to Mrs. Goldwyn, letting her decide how much of the bad news to mention. Although the second unit had finished the logging exteriors, Hawks still refused to begin shooting on the main sequences. "I personally consider Hawks's conduct unconscionable . . . If he goes off the picture now there are alibis he can use to save his face but last thing in world he would want to have happen is to be taken off picture after it has started," wrote Lehr.[43] Eventually, Hurlburd became so exasperated that he wrote to Goldwyn, telling him to remove his name from the credits as assistant producer because he was unable "to get Howard Hawks to change what he was doing to the picture."[44] Goldwyn realized that he was in real trouble if Hurlburd resisted having his name associated with the production.

Later that month, he viewed Hawks's footage and promptly fired him, putting his contract director, William Wyler, on the project and rehiring Murfin to fix the script through September.[45] Wyler did not want to clean up Hawks's mess, but Goldwyn allegedly threatened to ruin Wyler's career if he did not comply.[46] Goldwyn may have had another reason for putting Wyler on the project: Lillian Hellman, who had adapted her play *The Children's Hour* as *These Three* for Wyler in 1935, had a very happy working experience with Wyler, largely because the director had preserved as much as possible of Hellman's plot and characterization. They would work together again on *Dead End* (1937) and *The Little Foxes* (1941), and Goldwyn knew the key to maintaining a good relationship with his prize screenwriter. To Hellman's credit, she recognized Goldwyn's role in valuing the work of writers, and would write in November 1936, "My pleasant, affectionate feelings for you, have been said so often that I am becoming a bore. I want to write as good pictures for you as I am able to write, at any time."[47] Perhaps Goldwyn hoped Wyler would salvage his partnership with Ferber.

Wyler reshot much of Hawks's work and handled the second half of the picture. He also tried to return to the spirit of the earlier Chodorov-Murfin scripts, but it would have been too expensive to do what Goldwyn would have liked—scrap everything and start over. But Goldwyn did add a text forward targeting Barney and other "pioneers" like him: "1884 Northern Wisconsin—A cold hard country of timber and ore. The timber land—hundreds of thousands of acres of timber—went unsought until the paper mill men from New England came along. They hacked and tore and gouged and schemed and took and took and never replaced. Thousands of miles of it and no one to stop them. One of these pirates was Barney Glasgow."[48] The foreword primed audiences with Ferber's message, obscuring the fact that relatively little of it survived in the body of the narrative. But with Wyler and Murfin's help, Goldwyn managed to avert a possible disaster. Since Wyler was under contract, he did not have to be paid an exorbitant amount. Hawks's $73,000 salary was a dead loss, but even with retakes (nearly $140,000) and the cost of Furthman, the budget went over only $38,000 of the final estimated cost. At nearly $1.5 million, *Come and Get It* was an expensive film for its time, but reviews and a good first run would cover most of the expenses incurred by Hawks.[49]

In addition to budget problems, Goldwyn was worried about Ferber's reaction. They had started out on extremely good terms; they had enormous professional respect for each other. Their work ethic, devotion to family, business acumen, and shared Jewishness helped create one of her most sympathetic relationships with a filmmaker. Goldwyn had a long history of producing the work of female Jewish writers, and even Anzia Yezierska, who remembered her Hollywood experience with mixed feelings, admitted that Goldwyn's studio had given her work about Jewish immigrants in New York "prestige" treatment.[50] Goldwyn believed that cultivating relationships with writers would improve the overall cultural status of filmmaking on a number of levels. It was not just that he saw the market connection between popular literature and cinema and the importance of the script. As Yezierska recalled screenwriter Julien Josephson saying, "In our factory here we turn out stars of our own brand. But you're someone outside Hollywood, a character from the real world that makes our factory stories of success seem valid."[51] Goldwyn craved the historical status of Ferber's work and her approval in the postproduction exploitation.

When Ferber saw the finished film in October 1936, she was stunned, since it bore few traces of her suggestions. Goldwyn had gone to the additional expense of hiring Ferber to read and critique the scripts. Since Ferber had not participated in any of Hollywood's other adaptations of her work, she felt this was quite a concession to the producer. She wired Goldwyn, demanding an explanation. His letter to Ferber explains his difficulties: "I knew just exactly what your feelings were. For those were my own when I bought your book. Your attitude toward the screening of the book were set forth in my original script which I left with Howard Hawks, the director." He continued apologetically:

> But unfortunately, I was taken very ill . . . when I returned to the studio I
> found that Hawks had filmed a completely different story from what you

had written. After I saw what he had filmed, I suffered a relapse for a full two weeks, it upset me so. I then proceeded to complete my original purpose when I bought your book. I decided to try to get as much of your story onto the screen as I possibly could, under the conditions. I threw away most of what Hawks had photographed, put William Wyler onto the picture and spent a good two months rephotographing it, trying to get what I thought would come as near to your book as possible.[52]

He tried to console her, letting her know that the film was doing well critically and at the box office. "I do hope that on your next book you will give me an opportunity to do more justice to it," he wrote.

Ferber responded on 28 October 1936:

I know that you have had a difficult and costly time of it with *Come and Get It*. You see that book is not only a story of a man's rise and fall, it is primarily a story of the rape of America. It is a story of the destruction of forests and rivers by the wholesale robber barons of that day. On the front page of every newspaper today you will read that story for now we know that the droughts and flood and dust storms of our time are the result of the rapacity of the Barney Glasgows of fifty years ago.

It was a timely historical narrative, and in Ferber's view Goldwyn had not gone far enough in exploiting the contemporary resonances. The producer had asked for her endorsement of the film, but in light of the way the production had evolved, she felt this was impossible. "Please don't think me thankless or graceless when I say that I cannot take part in that end of the picture's presentation. I never have."[53]

And she never would publicly endorse any of Hollywood's adaptations of her work—even when she was a coproducer years later. *Come and Get It* taught her not to expect too much from Hollywood, even when filmmakers seemed eager to transfer her historical vision to the screen. Yet Goldwyn's decision to fire a major director, his screenwriter, and scrap weeks of expensive shooting indicates Hollywood's unusual regard for Edna Ferber and her narratives. Ferber-oriented posters and lobby cards also dominated Goldwyn's publicity for the film (Fig. 5.2). Goldwyn's respect for her work did mollify Ferber somewhat. In 1939, she would work briefly for him on the adaptation of her modern New York story "Nobody's in Town." It was not produced.[54]

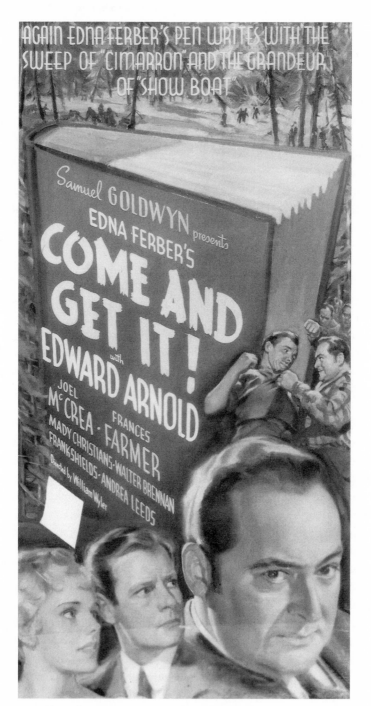

5.2. Publicity for *Come and Get It* (United Artists, 1936).

5.3. Edward Arnold as tycoon Barney Glasgow (*Come and Get It*, United Artists, 1936).

Critics seemed to appreciate the film marginally more than audiences, and they highlighted both its historical portrait of a flawed hero and Goldwyn's prestigious adaptation of Ferber's work. Goldwyn was always a favorite with the critics, but even the film periodicals emphasized that it was a "Ferber production." Ferber's name was key to the film's prestige and box-office potential. The *New York American* began portentously: "Unfamiliar as I am with Edna Ferber's *Come and Get It*, [it is] a novel the ballyhoo boys assure me takes rank with *Cimarron* the immortal and *Show Boat* the unforgettable."[55] The *Hollywood Reporter* wrote: "In bringing the Edna Ferber novel, *Come and Get It*, to the screen, Samuel Goldwyn has contributed a completely worthy companion piece to his *Dodsworth*. Though radically different in subject, both dramas are American to the core, are authentic and moving studies of character, and have a wide range of appeal."[56] But the trade paper predicted that Ferber's work would have broader appeal than Sinclair Lewis's *Dodsworth* because of its historical background. *Time* concurred and related the film to the emerging American historical cycle. Many of the more recent films had starred Edward Arnold, who played Barney (Fig. 5.3): "*Come and Get It* gives Edward Arnold, recently seen as Diamond Jim Brady and General John Sutter, another subject for his full-length screen portraiture of hearty, colorful US types. Lifted this time from Edna Ferber fiction instead of history, the subject is Bernard Glasgow, Wisconsin millionaire."[57]

Frank Nugent of the *New York Times*, another fan of Goldwyn and Ferber, saw the film as a merger between two superior entertainers who were not afraid of demystifying American myths. Goldwyn, he wrote, was "one of the few producers in Hollywood who refuses to be content with mediocrity . . . You won't find *Come and Get It* a thoroughly Ferber work, but enough of her has been retained and enough good Goldwyn added to make it a genuinely satisfying picture."[58] The *Motion Picture Herald* also focused on the film's historical critique: "The story concerns an ambitious lumberjack who violates every principle of business ethics and every tenet in the moral code in a ruthless drive for power and might."[59] While other papers stressed the film's American theme, many agreed that it was hardly a celebratory portrait of the frontier spirit.[60]

William Boehnel was one of the few who disliked the film, but blamed Goldwyn's adaptation rather than Ferber's original material: "Since the story on the screen is a distorted version of the original, the fault cannot be laid at the feet of Miss Ferber. Instead, it must be charged against the adapters, Jules Furthman and Jane Murfin, or against the directors, Howard Hawks and William Wyler."[61] The *New York Sun* agreed that the filmmakers had cut the theme of the book: "Barney's idealistic son, Richard, does talk, at occasionally painful length of reforestation and business reforms. The picture, however, never shows what ruthless ambition and thoughtlessness has done to the once wooded lands of the West. It is concerned only with that love story of two generations, of Barney, the two Lotties and young Richard."[62] But *Variety* found Ferber's tale of a "great man's" decline depressing. The trade paper argued that it was Goldwyn's preservation of Ferber's critique that handicapped the film as entertainment.[63]

Variety may have been on to something. *Come and Get It* was an expensive, million-dollar production and needed to do well to recover its costs. While there are indications that it played moderately well in key cities, Goldwyn's box-office records show that it always underperformed next to *Dodsworth*. United Artists reported that in key-city first runs (New York not included), *Dodsworth* netted $326,690, while *Come and Get It* netted $279,210. This was 15 percent lower. Prestige had a price. Yet the film stood out in the New York Film Critics and *Film Daily*'s annual lists of the most important productions. Although box office was a part of the critics' decision, they were more influenced by elusive qualities of prestige, intellectual depth, and human interest. Historical films routinely made the *Film Daily* lists during the 1930s, as did adaptations of Ferber's work. But often, critical portraits of the national past, even those backed by best-seller figures and literary reputations, did not thrive like the uncritical, action-packed, empire-building eulogies produced by Cecil B. De-Mille (*The Plainsman*, 1936) and Darryl Zanuck (*In Old Chicago*, 1937).[64]

Saratoga Trunk and the Triumphant Mulatta

Despite the risks associated with producing historical films like *Come and Get It*, they remained popular investments until the Second World War altered production in 1942.[65] More than the work of any other writer of her generation, Ferber's historical fiction was closely linked to Hollywood and its production trends. But while Hollywood had previously adapted itself to her critical interventions, flawed protagonists, feminism, and satire, *Saratoga Trunk* was written *for* Hollywood. Bluntly, the novel makes use of a tempestuous, racially ambiguous southern heroine, a mysterious western adventurer with southern roots, and Gilded Age gilt. All of these qualities drove the sound-era American historical cycle in its first decade. *So Red the Rose* (1935), *Jezebel* (1938), *Gone with the Wind* (1939), *The Plainsman* (1936), *The Prisoner of Shark Island* (1936), *Wells Fargo* (1937), *Jesse James* (1939), *Diamond Jim* (1935), *Come and Get It* (1936), *High, Wide, and Handsome* (1937), *Lillian Russell* (1940), and *The Rose of Washington Square* (1940), to name only a few, capitalized on these narrative strategies. *Saratoga Trunk* was constructed with particular astuteness, because it capitalized on the public's appetite for historical westerns (*Wells Fargo*, 1937; *Jesse James*, *Stagecoach*, and *Union Pacific*, all 1939; *The Westerner*, 1940), southern belles (*Gone with the Wind*), and stars—all key components of Hollywood's top box-office films in 1939 and 1940, when Ferber was finishing the book.

Saratoga Trunk begins in modern New York. A group of newspapermen are eager to interview Clint and Clio Maroon, fabulously wealthy Gilded Age relics and personalities. But Ferber and Clint do not view the post–Civil War generation as a national asset: "I've robbed my country for sixty years. My father, he ran the town of San Antonio back in 1840 before the damn Yankees came along and stole his land for a railroad."[66] His father, he says, was a real hero and fought at the Alamo. The Maroons are giving away their fortune as a means of making up for their past robber-baron misdeeds and double-dealing. Clint rages, "They called us financiers. Financiers, Hell! We were a gang of racketeers that would make the apes today look like kids stealing turnips out of a garden patch. We stole a whole country—land, woods, rivers, metal. They've got our pictures in museums. We ought to be in the rogues' gallery."[67] But the reporters do not want their quaint pioneer idols toppled. They merely laugh at him, ironically calling his controversial exposé "movie stuff." Clio says nothing throughout this exchange; she realizes that Americans would prefer to believe in myths rather than the more disappointing truth about their past. She escapes the crush of reporters and fans, and remembers. Then the narrative flows chronologically from her perspective, and although we see Clio as a vengeful adventuress and Clint as an opportunistic swindler, they are still glamorous, romantic figures. Again, Ferber focuses on the woman as the true vehicle and interpreter of American history. Clint may try to change the traditional public perspective on the post–Civil War past via the conventional means of reporters and "fact finders." But while his audience will not hear him, Ferber and Clio's historical perspective, constructed through personal memory, is given in all its detail.

While Clint seems like an old-style Texas cowboy, an American icon, there is something exotic, even foreign, about Clio. Although she was over seventy, "even the least perceptive among those present must have felt something exotic and quickening about her . . . Her white hair was still so strongly mixed with black that the effect was steel-grey. In certain lights it had a bluish tinge."[68] Years before, racial purists hunting for mulatto or mixed African American and white blood saw bluish tints in fingernails or skin as evidence of mixed blood.[69] Ferber soon confirms this. The flashback focuses on the life of Clio Dulaine, the natural daughter of a Creole aristocrat and a New Orleans placée (mixed-race common-law wife). Clio's mother, Rita Dulaine, was "queen of that half-world peopled by women of doubtful blood."[70] Clio's ancestors had come to New Orleans from Haiti; her grandmother was a free woman of color.[71] Although Clio keeps insisting on her white Creole blood, her mixed-race maid, Angelique, reminds her of her other lineage. Clio too seems to embrace her racial mixture; although in the course of the narrative she will perform the roles of great southern lady and French aristocrat, at home she sings African American spirituals while she cleans the house.

Clio's mixed ancestry is not the outlandish fantasy of a historical novelist. New Orleans had the largest community of free blacks and mixed-race African Americans in the United States before the Civil War. Many were extremely wealthy and influential, and as Judith Berzon writes, many young quadroons, or pale, mixed-race women, would be trained to become the mistresses of powerful white men.[72] The "matches" were arranged at the New Orleans quadroon balls. Novelist George Washington Cable wrote extensively about these communities during the 1880s and early 1890s, and in "Madame Delphine," a short story in Cable's *Old Creole Days* (1879), he depicted a retired quadroon mistress saving her daughter from a similar fate by denying her parentage.[73] In "'Tite Poulette," another story in *Old Creole Days*, a mixed-race mother and daughter face a similar situation. Ferber drew upon Cable's body of work; like Cable's young heroines, Clio and her mother live in genteel poverty. But during Clio's youth, they live in France. They are forced to leave New Orleans after her mother accidentally shoots her white "husband." Instead of continuing to escape racial prejudice in Europe, Clio returns to New Orleans to avenge her mother, confronting both the Creole family and New Orleans's racial double standards.

Clio's life is based on a series of cultural, gendered, and racial performances. To take revenge on the white Dulaine family that persecuted her mother years before, she pretends to be a French countess. She goes to a famous local restaurant, knowing her presence and Dulaine face will embarrass her relatives. But Ferber's description of her preparation for this excursion into wealthy white society is telling: "Indeed the naturally creamy skin was dead white with the French liquid powder she used, so that her eyes seemed darker and more enormous; sadder too, and the wide mouth wider. Almost a clown's mask, except for its beauty."[74] Clio makes up in whiteface. As film historians Michael Rogin and Richard Dyer point out, these attempts to visually accentuate a performer's white skin ironically emphasize the performer's lack of perfect whiteness.[75] Clio's excess of white, or white mask, serves only to make her mixed blood more apparent. Clint Maroon, meeting Clio for the first time at Begue's, recognizes her disguise. When she remarks on how odd his western clothes look in fashionable New Orleans, he replies, "Far's that goes, you look kind of funny yourself, Ma'am, with all that white stuff on your face."[76]

As Judith Berzon points out, the "most frequently encountered stereotype in mulatto fiction" is the tragic mulatta.[77] In many nineteenth-century American novels, mulattas return to racist America from egalitarian Europe, leading to their tragic downfalls. Passive, virtuous, and imposed upon, they eventually commit suicide when their relationships with white men fail. In 1937, African American poet and critic Sterling Brown dismissed the presence of all mixed-race African Americans in American literature as mere "tragic mulattos." Brown's opinion dominated the critical discussion of mixed-race characters for many years. According to him, mulattos were tragic because they were nearly white. They were brave, beautiful, and intelligent men and women, yet they were condemned to bondage, making their condition more unfortunate that that of pure African Americans. According to Brown, this melodramatic stereotype of a "withering woman" or a "rebellious man" was devoid of social critique and was nothing more than the racist escapism of white novelists and readers who "could only sympathize with white heroes and heroines."[78] Although in 1937, African American writer Zora Neale Hurston wrote against the tragic tradition (*Their Eyes Were Watching God*, 1937), creating a mixed-race heroine who used her heritage as a site of empowerment, she was in a minority.[79] As Cassandra Jackson writes, "More critical attention has been paid to those who used 'the tragic mulatto,' black or white writers, than to a more fundamental question of whether or not this configuration is in fact the dominant mode of mixed-race fiction."[80]

Ferber, however, created a heroine even more formidable than Hurston's. Clio is arguably the first unabashedly successful mulatta. It is not simply that *Saratoga Trunk* was purchased by Warner Bros. and went on to become one of the biggest grossers of 1945-1946. Clio is not interested in racial solidarity— white or black—or in categorizing herself and therefore limiting her experience. Clio's is a success story. Her relatives pay her an enormous sum of money to leave New Orleans before the scandal about her and her mother becomes public knowledge. The money enables her to travel to a wealthy spa in Saratoga Springs, New York, where she can exploit the robber barons. As Clio uses her mixed racial status to triumphant advantage in the South, so she plans to use her feminine performance to unsettle the world of northern-based masculine business. Her femininity is just as much a performance as her whiteness. While Ferber often describes Clio's "dark" hair, eyes, and imitations of maid-companion Angelique as contrasting with her "white" skin and public voice, she describes Clio as signing her name in a "bold, almost masculine hand" and smoking in public with men at the fashionable New York resort.[81] She fools everyone, and even enlists the help of a social-climbing precursor to Elsa Maxwell to authenticate her French aristocratic title.

It is difficult not to see Margaret Mitchell's Scarlett O'Hara (*Gone with the Wind*, 1936) in Clio. Like Scarlett, Clio is resented by other women because she plays the feminine role so convincingly.[82] She shares Scarlett's display of excessive femininity (lowest-cut dress, tiniest waist), but that excess hides a grim, mathematically precise realist unafraid of stealing, cheating, or killing to defend her home. But like Scarlett, Clio is both sexually and racially transgressive. While Mitchell tellingly describes a "darkened" Scarlett working in the fields in 1864–1865 Georgia, sunburned, frizzle haired, wearing hoopless dresses and Mammy's sunbonnet, Ferber's Clio conceals her darkness behind a coating of white powder in post–Civil War New Orleans. While she is campaigning for the hand of a wealthy businessman in Saratoga, jealous rumors circulate, inferring that as a Creole, Clio is of mixed race. Gossip says she has "got a touch of the tar-brush."[83] But rather than being annoyed by this, Clio confronts their racism with yet another performance. At the hotel's glamorous costume ball, she appears not as a powdered, white-gowned, eighteenth-century aristocrat, but as a poor black street seller.[84] She covers herself in black greasepaint and pads her figure, challenging their stereotyped images of black femininity.

Clio's ironic series of performances in socially conscious Saratoga Springs operates against the nouveau riche aspirations of the businessmen and their wives. To a certain extent, Clint also uses his guileless, homespun western image as a means of securing the trust of other businessmen. Clint and Clio, born of old southern families, call Jay Gould and his colleagues "white trash." Clio's flouting of social and racial conventions proves how little she cares for the post–Civil War hypocrisies of the new elites. By the end of the novel, she and Clint have managed to swindle a railroad out of them, capitalizing on their social vulnerability. The robber barons have been outplayed by two masters of disguise.

Even though the newspapers interview Clint, it is Clio's perspective that constitutes the historical narrative.[85] Again, Ferber gives historical credibility to another one of America's misfits. Clio is perhaps the first-ever wealthy and powerful mulatta in American literature. But is she merely clever at "passing," at raising herself up the white economic ladder? Hardly. Ferber's heroine is not afraid of racial exposure; in fact, she openly courts it in New Orleans and at the Saratoga costume ball. Clio knows the intricacies of racial and gender roles, but she plays by her own rules. She is completely self-made and exploits the American fascination with glamor, excess, and performance. But Ferber also named her heroine after the muse of history. Her perspective on the past not only functions as an exposure of modern complacency and myths about the Gilded Age, but also proves how much of modern American history is about performance and the exploitation of racial and gender stereotypes.

Yet, like so many great female performers and mulattas, Clio has no children to survive her. Like Ferber's other mulatta, Julie Laverne, Clio does not reproduce. This is one of the more disturbing elements of Ferber's America. While in *Cimarron, Giant*, and *Ice Palace*, major characters are either born mixed Native American and white and have children or marry and raise families with Mexican American and Native American partners, mixed African American and white unions do not help populate the next generation of Ferber's America. But this does not necessarily suggest Ferber's reluctance to embrace a mixed African American and white nation. Instead, many of Ferber's novels suggest that the heroic, predominantly female qualities most prized in the nation's past (Selina's spiritual vision, Julie and Magnolia's musical heritage, and Clio's steely courage and sense of survival) are not transferable by blood. If Ferber's novels are guilty of any nostalgia, it is that the legacy of so many women has been lost. In this sense, Ferber was never completely committed to a progressive historical view of America.

Adapting to a Mixed-Race Heroine: Warner Bros. and Ingrid Bergman

Evidence suggests that Warner Bros. contacted Ferber in advance of the novel's serialization, and for once she allowed it access to the story before publication.[86] The studio's offer may have swayed her: $175,000 was the highest price yet paid for a Ferber work. It was a triple coup for Ferber. With the assistance of top agent Leland Hayward, she demanded and received payments in instalments over a nearly two-year period in order to reduce the income tax she would owe; she got complete copyright reversion after eight years; and she retained dramatic, musical, television, and radio rights.[87] Although Warner Bros. may not have foreseen it, Ferber knew that television was potentially as lucrative as film. By 1958, she alone had the right to sell the film to the television studios, something that galled Warner Bros.[88] Her contract also had tough screen-credit clauses that demanded her name appear in type larger than any screenwriter's, alone on a separate title card.

But Ferber's demand for screen-rights reversion after eight years cost Warner Bros. more than it bargained for. Irritated when delays in production and in the postwar release threatened to take her work out of the Hollywood spotlight, she fumed to agent Leland Hayward: "If they want more time I expect them to pay for it and they expect to pay for it . . . Your letter stated that Warners were making a large expensive and well-cast picture." "That's fine," she continued tartly. "They're not doing this because they are crazy about my big brown eyes."[89] Ferber persuaded the studio to renegotiate and pay an additional $25,000 for an extension on the rights. In 1949, long after the film had secured a top box-office position, Warner Bros. paid $25,000 for another extension so that it could enjoy the rerelease dividends and maintain an option on future remakes.[90]

Saratoga Trunk would be a landmark Hollywood business deal for other filmmakers. Star Gary Cooper played Clint Maroon without an acting fee, instead demanding 10 percent of the film's domestic and worldwide gross in exchange for $100,000 of production money.[91] Cooper would eventually sell his share in the film negative for more than $531,000 in 1946.[92] Cooper was not the first star to trade a high fee for a percentage of the gross, but the move made sense. As an article in the *Washington Evening Star* noted in 1943, actors could be taxed for up to two-thirds of any large salary ($50,000–$100,000), but if they formed their own stock companies and treated their services as stock traded to the studios, they would be subject to only around 25 percent in capital gains. Cooper's method was designed "to take the sting out of the Government's salary restrictions," and it soon became the gold standard for star salaries in the postwar era.[93] While Cooper owned 10 percent, Warner Bros. did not want to give director Hal Wallis a similar deal. In fact, the legal department was so stunned by the money given to Cooper that it did its best to convince Wallis to take only 5 percent.[94] *Saratoga Trunk* would be Hal Wallis's final film before leaving Warner Bros. to become an independent producer. Perhaps Cooper's independent business acumen finally cured Wallis of accepting studio salaries.

Saratoga Trunk would cost the studio more than $1.75 million, and regardless of how Wallis felt about Warner Bros., he spared no expense on the production. The studio's top screenwriter, Casey Robinson, was assigned to the project. Robinson specialized in adapting highly successful "women's pictures," often starring Bette Davis (*Now, Voyager*, 1942). Initially, Warner Bros. seemed leery of Clio's mixed-blood status, though it had produced films with racially ambiguous, even masculine heroines in the past (*Jezebel*, 1938). While Harriet Hinsdale's initial story report cautiously mentioned Clio's "dusky" complexion, she said nothing of her mixed ancestry.[95] The original outline also did its best to dull Ferber's sharp sense of history: "Specifically and particularly no character depicted or talked about is to be connected in any way with any of the following names: Gould, Vanderbilt, Morgan, Whitney, Crocker, Stanford, Keen, Huntington, Hopkins, Rhinelander."[96] But Robinson's first treatment begins like Ferber's novel and includes Clint's denunciation of America's crass past: "In my day you could get away with wholesale robbery, bribery in high places, and murder—and brag about it. They're famous names—with towns and libraries and universities named after us."[97]

Robinson built up Clint's reassuring western background as a corrective to Clio's lush southern femininity and suspiciously dark features. But this western hero does not dominate the southern heroine. In Robinson's script of 17 October 1941, it is Clio's reminiscence that triggers the film's flashback. His initial description of Clio does not mention skin color but does note her "big, black, soft eyes. She can be young and gay or driving and hard. Usually she is the actress. But even when she is not acting, she is still a paradox: gay and gentle, or fiery; brazenly unconventional, absurdly correct; tender, hard; generous, ruthless." Robinson uses inference rather than overt dialogue to convey her mixed status. When the reporters are awaiting the pair in their hotel room, one woman remarks, "What a pair! Rich, powerful and respectable for sixty years. And color? The word was made up to describe them."[98] While Robinson uses the restaurant sequence in which Clint and Clio meet, he does not include Ferber's mischievous exchange about the white powder on her face. However, occasionally Robinson draws subtle attention to Clio's background. In one of the early sequences, Clio is described while cleaning her house, "her hair wound around with a turban almost like Kaka's [Angelique]."[99]

Although executives could do little about any visual manipulation of Clio's racial status, they attempted to limit potentially explosive sequences among the three foreign, marked characters: Clio, Angelique, and Cupidon. Executive Roy Obringer wrote to Jack Warner in March 1943, arguing that several key early scenes were a problem because of race issues: "Briefly, the scene depicts 'Clio' with her negro maid, 'Angelique' and the dwarf 'Cupidon' in the fashionable and widely known 'Begue' restaurant in New Orleans. The research department advises that there is in fact a Begue restaurant in New Orleans today."[100] He went on:

In the state of California and other states, we have a Civil Rights law in that you can not generally exclude negroes. I have not checked as to whether such law exists in New Orleans, but in any event it is a well established fact that there is a definite and marked limit to the negro's rights and privileges in the Southern state and their association with white people . . . While it is true that the script does not show the dwarf or negro maid at the table, nevertheless, they are in the restaurant. People of the Southern states may very strongly resent the inference that colored people are permitted to co-mingle with white people in restaurants and public places, and, above all, it is not unlikely that the proprietors of the Begue restaurant will attempt some claim of libel based on the argument that the reputation of the restaurant and their business is materially damaged and held in disrepute.

Obringer's sensitivity to potential lawsuits made him an asset to Warner, but he knew very little about the actual legal basis for the Jim Crow laws. Warner and Wallis also wanted clarity, and he reported to them with surprise, "In checking, I also find that the state of Louisiana does have a civil rights law which restricts discrimination on account of race or color but I also find that the practice of the state is contrary to the law."[101] Obringer did not want to offend social convention, and neither did many of his colleagues. But to Jack Warner's credit, the scene remained in the film, showing the three of them within the white restaurant (though Clio is the only one to sit down and eat).

Later, Robinson and director Sam Wood added several other touches emphasizing Clio's (Ingrid Bergman) mixed racial status—elements that did not appear in the preliminary and final scripts sent to the censors for comment. The film begins with a shot of Bergman, veiled, all in black. We do not even see her face for the first few minutes. Her hair is covered by a black hat and scarf, so that when she finally removes it, her lustrous black hair is a shock. Robinson enhanced the racial undertones in several scenes. The first shot of Clio's face is not in a standard star close-up or medium shot, but a two-shot with the mulatta Angelique (Flora Robson) slightly in the background (Fig. 5.4). In another key sequence, Clio argues with Angelique over her conduct in New Orleans. While Angelique scolds, Clio cleans the family chandelier with a rag covering her hair (Fig. 5.5). During the argument, Angelique reminds Clio that Clio's mother was a placée and her "grandma was a—" The words are unspoken, but those familiar with Ferber's novel knew that Angelique re-

above: 5.4. Ingrid Bergman as the dark Clio, with Flora Robson as Angelique (*Saratoga Trunk*, Warner Bros., 1945). *below:* 5.5. Clio, in a headscarf, helping clean her family home (*Saratoga Trunk*, Warner Bros., 1945).

vealed she was a "free woman of color." Clio cuts her off in anger, raging, "Then remember no matter what I say I am, that I am. I don't want any more of this telling me who am and what I am to do. Do as I say."

The early scripts did not include any of Angelique's comments about the mixed-race status of Clio's mother and her grandmother's Afro-Caribbean roots. Robinson's screenplay merely included some rather oblique comments of Clio's regarding her identity: "No more treating me like a baby. No more telling me who I am or what I am to do. I shall do what I choose and I shall be what it suits me to be."[102] Robinson's and director Sam Wood's faithfulness to Ferber's novel in this sequence is striking. It actually chronicles the heroine's racial ancestry over several generations, affirming her mixed-race status. The scene also parallels Sidney Howard and Victor Fleming's exchange between Scarlett and Mammy in *Gone with the Wind*. Like Mammy, Angelique is concerned that Clio will pass as a proper white lady. Both films focus upon transgressive female protagonists who never behave like proper white belles.

When Clint (Gary Cooper) first meets Clio, in the New Orleans restaurant, he tries to put Clio in one category, asking her bluntly, "Where I come from, women are two kinds—good or bad. Which one are you?" Naturally, she equivocates, and the question, meant to define her moral background, also has implications for her race. For Clio is neither black nor white. But most unusually, Wood ignored the script and included Ferber's exchange between Clint and Clio over the color of her skin. In this sequence, Bergman wears white, which darkens the tone of her skin. But Clint notices her overuse of white powder and remarks, "You look kind of funny yourself with all that white stuff on your face." They laugh with shared understanding. This exchange was not included in the final revisions submitted to the PCA from February through June 1943—and for good reason.[103] Like the earlier exchange between Clio and Angelique, it reveals the basis of Clio's racial performance.

Saratoga Trunk was Ferber's first novel in nearly seven years, and competition was hot for the plum role of Clio. *Cosmopolitan*, which had serialized the novel before publication from April to October 1941, held a contest in 1941 to see whom readers would nominate for the roles of Clio and Clint. Top star and recent Academy Award–winner Gary Cooper, well known as a lanky cowboy (*The Cowboy and the Lady*, 1938; *The Westerner*, 1940), got the most votes for Clint (441); however, many readers evidently saw Ferber's novel as a potential replay of *Gone with the Wind*. Clark Gable was runner-up, with 213 votes. Their choice for Clio was telling—Vivien Leigh with 374. The next choices had only 70 votes, but one of them, Paulette Goddard, had been Selznick's choice for Scarlett before meeting Leigh in 1939.[104] Reviewers noted the similarities too. *Motion Picture Daily* remarked, "*Saratoga Trunk*, in a way, reminds of certain aspects of *Gone with the Wind*."[105] The poll was taken only a year after *Gone with the Wind* was circulating in national theatres. Ingrid Bergman, who eventually played Clio, was a more or less unknown Warner Bros. contract star. At the time, Warner Bros. might have thought the property ideal for Bette Davis, since Casey Robinson, who wrote Davis's last picture, *Now, Voyager*, had been hired to write the script. Davis had won an Oscar, her second, for playing another tempestuous, transgressive southern belle in *Jezebel* (1938). But production on *Saratoga Trunk* was delayed for a year. By that time, Bergman had become a major box-office star (*Casablanca*, 1942; *For Whom the Bell Tolls*, 1943).

Bergman's director on *For Whom the Bell Tolls* (which also costarred Gary Cooper) was Sam Wood. He did not get along well with the Warner Bros. production system. He knew he had been hired to duplicate his recent success with the same two lead actors. He also knew that Warner Bros. liked to operate under a tight time schedule, and that *Saratoga Trunk* was a prestige film. Wood evidently did not like the script that the studio gave him, and his changes to the script, particularly regarding Clio's racial status, give weight to his position. Production began on 23 February, and soon executives were complaining bitterly about the small amount of film he shot each day. Eric Stacey wrote to T. C. Wright: "As I have told you, on many occasions, he is very vague about how he is going to stage scenes, and after he has done a scene, goes home and sleeps on it, gets another idea and does it over again the next day."[106] An exasperated Jack Warner pestered Wallis, "It is appalling to note the small amount of film Sam Wood is getting every day. You can tell him I said so and I am very discouraged to think a man with his ability, a script that is complete, a great acting cast composed of professional people with whom he has only two or three to work with at a time, that he should be virtually three weeks behind on a sixty-day schedule."[107] Production closed on 25 June 1943, a whopping forty-three days behind schedule. But, ironically, Wood's instincts about revising the script brought it closer to Ferber's original text and gave the Clio-Clint relationship a depth it had lacked in Robinson's censored material.

The Women's Market

Warner Bros. held onto the film for two years before releasing it in the fall of 1945. In fact, most audiences did not see it until the following spring. The decision to hold it back originated from the studio's fear of marketing period melodramas during a war. Although Twentieth Century-Fox had spent lavishly to adapt several period musicals, *Saratoga Trunk* was a straight historical drama. It represented a type of film that all studios had eschewed since 1942. Recall that Jack Warner kept Jerry Wald's plans to remake *So Big* at bay and that MGM abandoned its plan to remake *Cimarron* in 1944. Biopics had not performed well (Warner Bros.' ill-fated *Adventures of Mark Twain*, 1944, for example) unless they were grafted onto an obvious Second World War "message," like *Jack London* (1943) or *Captain Eddie* (1945). Even Paramount's hugely successful *For Whom the Bell Tolls* was a war story.

But by 1945, the studios learned that period melodramas were no longer out of step with production trends. The conflict was drawing to a close; by August, the war in the Pacific was over. Bette Davis made an early transition with *Mr. Skeffington* (1944) and *The Corn Is Green* (1945). But with soldiers returning home and reentering the domestic economy, the studios looked to the women's market as the center of film production and reception. As Steve Neale points out, producers believed, sometimes in the absence of any market research, that "women constituted an important, even dominant sector of the viewing population."[108] Filmmakers undoubtedly courted female viewers with Ferber's historical prestige, but as M. Alison Kibler admits, women brought cultural respectability at a price: "Critics throughout the twentieth century have used femininity to symbolize the passivity and decay they identify in mass culture."[109] Beneath much of the critical respect for prestigious women's pictures was an undercurrent of highbrow derision. Even an Edna Ferber property was not immune to such jibes.

The studio publicity focused on Ferber as a means of preparing audiences for the return of the historical melodrama. Posters and advertisements all bore Ferber's name above the title, and others advertised the film with a giant copy of her book, a technique that had been used since the release of *So Big* and *Cimarron*. Ferber was in her own right a Hollywood star—her name had made the industry millions. But for several years, her work had been absent from theatres. The last Ferber film was the 1937 adaptation of Kaufman and Ferber's *Stage Door*. The press book for *Saratoga Trunk* gushed, "Edna Ferber, winner of the Pulitzer Prize, has earned for herself an unquestioned place as one of America's greatest novelists." Rather than dwelling on her great female characters, though, the article mentioned a trio of her less-than-impressive "heroes": "Recognized as a great story-teller, she has gained her greatest fame, however, as creator of such unforgettable characters as Yancey Cravat, Barney Glasgow and Gaylord Ravenal. In *Saratoga Trunk* she creates two of her most dynamic characters, Clio Dulaine and Clint Maroon."[110]

Clint Maroon was undoubtedly Ferber's most unabashedly heroic male protagonist, and Cooper was perfect for the part. For over twenty years, Gary Cooper was arguably Hollywood's most versatile male star—popular in comedies, romances, war films, and westerns. Warner Bros. had no difficulties marketing him as a Texas adventurer and gambler in nineteenth-century New Orleans and Saratoga. But publicizing the industry's new "Norse goddess" as a dark, exotic Creole belle was dicier. The last prominent New Orleans belle in Hollywood's historical genre had been Bette Davis (*Jezebel*, 1938), famous for her pallor and blond hair. Even though her character, Julie Marsden, was consciously linked with African Americans through her conduct, dialogue, staging, costume, and lighting, Davis's physical looks never directly enhanced her supposed mixed-race status.[111] For *Saratoga Trunk*, the studio decided to use Bergman's dark hair and Scarlett O'Hara–esque role as novelty assets. Posters, lobby cards, and magazine advertisements frequently showed Cooper in white Stetson and white suit opposite black-haired and black-gowned Bergman (Fig. 5.6). The bold decision on the part of Wallis and Warner Bros. foregrounded not only her exoticism but also her "color" in contrast to the pure white Cooper.

Their acting styles could not have been more different in the film. Although Cooper maintains his almost-silent laid-back persona, honed through years of westerns, Bergman rages and storms, strikes attitudes, and dominates the film. Although it is possible to view her emotive performance as a means of defining her sexual and racial difference from Cooper, Bergman and her character are neither sexually nor racially subservient. Clio motivates camera movement and the narrative structure; her decisions drive them from New Orleans to Saratoga; her dialogue clarifies the plot. Cooper merely follows, half amused, half irritated, in her wake.

Although many critics of classical Hollywood cinema dismiss studio films as racist reinforcements of dominant racial stereotypes and historical attitudes, supporting the fear of racial mixing and mixed-race characters, Bergman's role belongs to a surprisingly large genre of classical Hollywood films with mixed-race protagonists, many of them adapted from works by historical novelists. Clio's precursors were Bette Davis's Julie and, of course, Vivien Leigh's indomitable Scarlett O'Hara. But *Saratoga Trunk* was the first of several postwar films with mixed-race American protagonists, including Selznick's *Duel in the Sun* (1946), starring Jennifer Jones, and Twentieth Century-Fox's *Pinky* (1949), with postwar star Jeanne Crain in the title role. In 1947, Twentieth Century-Fox released its production of Frank Yerby's *The Foxes of Harrow*, a historical novel set within the mulatto community of New Orleans. However, John Stahl's film avoided much of Yerby's material about interracial romance—surprising, given Stahl's work on *Imitation of Life* (1934).

Critics were divided in their reactions to the film; Bergman's performance was especially controversial. Jack Grant of the *Hollywood Reporter* was one of *Saratoga Trunk*'s few unabashed admirers: "All of you admirers of Ingrid Bergman—and you are legion—can prepare for a rich treat. Her performance of Clio Dulaine in the Edna Ferber story, ST, surpasses in brilliance, fascination and tempestuousness any other work in a screen career that always has been admirable. She is literally a sensation in projecting a fire never previously displayed, a vitality and vividness that meets and conquers each requirement of one of the most exacting roles ever filmed."[112] But many reviewers found Bergman's dark hair disturbing. Kate Cameron wrote, "Ingrid Bergman plays the fascinating and revengeful heroine of the Ferber story as though she didn't quite know what to make of the passionate New Orleans beauty, Clio Dulaine . . . neither star nor director have been able to turn a Norse goddess into a lusty, fiery-tempered, shady Southern lady, in spite of a dusky wig . . . It is Miss Bergman's picture, rather than Gary Cooper's, as the feminine half of the starring team is in almost every foot of film."[113] Cameron also noted that while the studio had obviously spent a great deal on the film in an effort to make it a prestige vehicle, the story's "slightly trashy tinge" showed through. The critic's language is reminiscent of writings about mulattas; like a mixed-race heroine trying to pass in a white world, *Saratoga Trunk* showed too much "color" for some reviewers.

But the press steered clear of mentioning Bergman's mixed status, instead identifying Flora Robson as the "evil mulatto" character.[114] Warner Bros.' press book drew upon many of the more common racial stereotypes about the savage mulatto. Press releases noted that for the role, Robson "wears a dark-face makeup and her eyes are weirdly slanted to give her an uncommonly sinister appearance."[115] However, Robson was uniformly commended for her performance as a disapproving half-caste "mammy" and was even nominated for an Academy Award—though, unlike Hattie McDaniel (*Gone with the Wind*, 1939), the blackface British actress did not win.

The studio marketed the lavish sets and lively re-creation of postwar New Orleans almost as heavily as it did Bergman's star quality, accentuating the connection between Ferber's historical novels, female audiences, and prestige filmmaking. *Look: America's Family Magazine* did a special issue on *Saratoga Trunk*: "The American scene forcefully comes to life in the novels of Edna Ferber . . . Considered by many critics the most brilliant and colorful of all her American novels, *Saratoga Trunk*, which has now become one of the season's most important motion pictures, sweeps in all its grandeur from the old French quarter of New Orleans to the swank piazza of the elegant Saratoga Springs Hotel."[116] The studio publicity emphasized the film's historical accuracy, linking it to past prestige productions: "To create authentic replicas of New Orleans's old French Market and the lavish interior of an aristocratic Creole's home, Warner Bros. set designers produced exact reproductions of some of the city's most famous landmarks. The set dressers and property men took 11,385 different articles out of the studio's storerooms and arranged them on one of the street sets."[117] Eileen Creelman of the *New York Sun* responded to the marketing strategy, "The picture, again like the book, has open, unashamed enjoyment in everything luscious to behold, delicious to eat, wonderful to smell, delightful to hear." But she felt that "it has no message. It has no purpose, except to divert."[118] Rose Pelswick highlighted it as a "Ferber Film at Hollywood" and said it was "flashy" box office.[119] But Bosley Crowther dismissed it as "gaudy junk": "The Warners have taken the novel which Edna Ferber wrote—a novel of high romantic polish and maddening emptiness underneath—and have given it a visualization in the grand, flashy, empty Hollywood style."[120]

Interestingly, a few critics blamed Ferber for *Saratoga Trunk*'s gaudy but empty plot, and attributed its virtues to Casey Robinson. The *Hollywood Review* commented, "Edna Ferber's *Saratoga Trunk*, a lush but by no means great shakes as a novel, was all Casey Robinson needed for a story basis that gives literacy in his screenplay."[121] *Daily Variety* agreed: "The script is a confusion about three basic stories. It meanders—possibly following the Edna Ferber book—from France to New Orleans to Saratoga, with a glimpse of Texas in the background."[122] Lowell Redellings of the *Hollywood Citizen-News* wrote, "Not all of Edna Ferber's romantic novel of New Orleans and Saratoga of the 1870s is included in the Warner Bros. film version (thank goodness) but with a lot of familiar Hollywood hocus pocus there's enough emotional claptrap to please the most famished for this sort of thing."[123] But all agreed with Louella Parsons that Ferber's novel had become a moneymaking "woman's film."[124] In a highly competitive year, *Saratoga Trunk* was among the top ten domestic grossers, making an impressive $4.25 million. But the reception of Ferber's work was in transition. The Hollywood studios had long valued her tendency to write about American women, attract female readers and filmgoers, and appeal to male audiences with historical interests. While the masculine drama of *Come and Get It* garnered more modest profits and admiring reviews, *Saratoga Trunk*'s gendered reception indicates a critical dismissal of women's literature, cinema, and their perceived historical romanticism. This tension between women's history and cinema, profits, and critical regard would continue through

Warner Bros.' remake of *So Big* in 1953 and even affect the reception of *Giant* and *Ice Palace* on-screen.

Nevertheless, Ferber recognized *Saratoga Trunk's* moneymaking potential beyond Warner Bros. and did her best to maximize it. She saw *Saratoga Trunk* as a way of recouping the money she had lost when she sold *Show Boat* and its musical rights for more modest sums years before. In 1954, she explored the possibility of producing the book as a musical. While film critics in 1945 had avoided recognizing Clio's color as a mixed-race woman, Ferber tried to bring these issues out in the planned musical. At one point, Lena Horne, the African American actress-singer who had been rejected by MGM for the role of tragic mulatta Julie in the 1951 version of *Show Boat*, was a serious contender for the musical role of Clio. Director Robert Lewis (*Brigadoon*, Broadway, 1947) wrote to Ferber, addressing the unusual black-white casting for a Broadway show: "I know that there was some question before as to the advisability of this kind of casting, but I feel that Miss Horne's appearance in *Jamaica* puts a different light on the matter now," he assured her. "I refer not only to the natural acceptance of her playing with Ricardo Montalban as her leading man but to the fact that her performance itself has been so enthusiastically received by critics and the audience . . . Lena could be magnificent now in *Saratoga Trunk* . . . You have my assurance that Miss Horne will be thrilled also to work in this project with me."[125]

But unfortunately, Lewis's plans for the production, which would have confronted racial mixing on several levels, fizzled. For several years, musical teams, including Alan Jay Lerner and Frederick Loewe, refused the job. Eventually Johnny Mercer and Harold Arlen were hired to write the music and lyrics in 1959. Starring Howard Keel and Carol Lawrence, a white actress, in the role of Clio, the musical finally tried out in Philadelphia in the summer of 1959 and opened on 7 December 1959 at the Winter Garden Theatre in New York. It was a disaster and closed within ten weeks. Although *Saratoga Trunk's* issues of race, sexuality, and history were visible on screen, *Saratoga Trunk* was not destined to become another *Show Boat* on Broadway.

six

Jim Crow, Jett Rink, and James Dean

RECONSTRUCTING GIANT, 1952–1957

n December 1954, Edna Ferber wrote to director George Stevens, emphasizing her continued interest in his production of her latest book, *Giant*. She believed that *Giant*'s value lay in its exposure of racial prejudice against Mexican Americans in Texas, and that its racial themes had become "more vital, more prevalent today in the United States than ... when I began to write the novel."[1] Ferber hoped that one day Anglo oil millionaires like Bick Benedict and Jett Rink, the originators and perpetuators of these inequalities in the economic and social hierarchies of America's new West, would be "anachronisms like the dear old covered wagons and the California gold-rush boys." Later, in May 1955, when shooting first began on the film, Ferber wrote to Henry Ginsberg, producer and cofounder of the independent film company Giant Productions, "I don't quite know why the motion picture presentation of *Giant* interests and fascinates me much more than the screen career of any of my other novels or plays. That goes for *Show Boat*, *So Big*, *Cimarron*, and many others. Perhaps it is because behind the characters and events in *Giant* there stands a definite meaning, a purpose."[2]

Although Ferber had considered writing a historical novel about Texas as early as 1939, she allegedly shied away from the project because it was "a man's job."[3] Ferber knew from her experience with *Cimarron* and the misogyny of historians like Stanley Vestal that any female writer who dared to challenge America's frontier myths was in for a rough time. When she wrote *Cimarron*, back in 1929, there were few female historians of the West, and things had not changed more than twenty years later. Constance Lindsay Skinner, Angie Debo, and Mari Sandoz were, in their different ways, marginalized by mainstream western historians and would only achieve recognition after their deaths.[4] Arguably, Texas had more male mythmakers than any other western state. The wartime and postwar publishing boom for books about Texas, ranging from George Sessions Perry's admiring portrait, *Texas: A World in Itself* (1942), to Carey McWilliams's study of Mexican Americans, *North From Mexico: The Spanish-Speaking People of the United States* (1949), was still dominated by men. But Ferber, intrigued by Texas's persistent hold on the American imagination, started researching the topic seriously. Perry's admiration of Texans' wealth, success, and boundless financial frontiers was representative of a more general, crass American materialism that sickened her.[5] The new America was dominated by unabashed greed, garishness, and waste; as Ferber saw it, the nation had reverted to its Gilded Age–robber baron past, an era that she had critiqued decades ago in her first two novels of the American frontier, *Cimarron* and *Come and Get It*, and in the more recent *Saratoga Trunk*.

McWilliams's book helped her link Texas's greed with its history of exploitation of Mexican Americans. She wrote to McWilliams in early 1949, telling him of her plans, and he, familiar with her critical appraisals of western history and national myths, responded: "Needless to say I was delighted to receive your letter with its most kind and generous praise of my book. You have, of course, my permission to use the book for factual material and background. I shall look forward to reading your novel with the keenest anticipation."[6] As the book took shape, America's "most popular woman writer" became, in her words, "An Angry Old Woman."[7] Once again, critics would compare her to Harriet Beecher Stowe—and not all of the comparisons were complimentary.[8] *Giant* was the result, a chronicle of three generations of the cattle- and oil-rich Benedicts viewed from the perspective of the family matriarch, Leslie Lynnton Benedict. As both an educated woman and an eastern-born outsider, Leslie functions as Ferber's constant critical voice.

In a recent study of American best sellers from the 1950s, Jane Hendler argues that "Ferber's Bick [Benedict] is as anachronistic in postwar America as a claw-footed Victorian bathtub in a Levittown home."[9] While Ferber's novel, via the perspective of her heroine, Leslie, attacks the mythology of the traditional masculine, western narrative, Hendler and others have claimed that director George Stevens's film adaptation made some effort to rehabilitate Bick's racism and bolster the patriarchy (thus making it more acceptable to Texas and national viewers).[10] Although Hendler's contrasting readings of the novel and film are persuasive, she ignores two of Ferber's most fundamental themes: the woman in the West as narrator and critic of history, and the protagonist as a racial and gender hybrid. Like *Cimarron*'s Sabra Cravat and especially Ferber herself, Leslie comes to question the male-dominated frontier. But more than Sabra, Leslie is interested in the intersections of race and gender in this masculine space. An outsider, she is strangely drawn to another Texas hybrid who first alerts her to the racial injustice on Reata, the poor white cowhand Jett Rink.

George Stevens would also pursue the film's gender and racial issues, most memorably in showing Leslie (Elizabeth Taylor) actively bettering the living conditions for Mexican Americans on Reata and in visualizing the racial otherness of Jett Rink (James Dean). Yet Stevens's deployment of Ferber's critique was in the end more palatable to Texas and national audiences. It was not simply that the film softens Ferber's muckraking criticism, in particular by eliminating many of her overt connections between African American and Mexican American Jim Crow laws. Leslie's introspective character and her critical perspective on Texas racism and chauvinism are marginalized by the epic icons of more traditional western cinema—boots and saddles, lone cowboys, cattle, expansive empires, wealth, and sheer bigness.[11] These images dominate the screen and even Leslie's critical voice.

But Stevens's and Ferber's examinations of the twin historical themes of American wealth and racism intersect in another character, Jett Rink, the poor white ranch hand who ends up as Texas's most oil-rich citizen. In Stevens's adaptation, Jett becomes the most magnetic of the three main protagonists, mainly because of James Dean's performance.[12] In the years since *Giant*'s release, the legend of James Dean as one of America's preeminent cultural icons has eclipsed the film's complex portrait of Texas and Ferber's ironic construction of the persistence of the masculine frontier myth in the twentieth century. Ferber's reputation as one of America's most successful novelists, her critique of Texas racism and postwar masculinity, the critics' reaction to a woman's view of the West and its iconic heroes, Stevens's and Ferber's competing visions for the film, censorship battles, and the film's resonance with contemporaneous racial incidents have all been lost in Dean's epic shadow. But ironically, Jett Rink and Dean's magnetism are crucial for understanding Ferber's and Stevens's confrontation with the darker side of America's frontier myths and *Giant*'s enduring racial legacy.

America's "Angry Old Woman" and the Unmaking of Texas

In a note to her publisher shortly before publication, Ferber said of *Giant*, "Leslie does not become a listening and respectful wife. But her fine mind and her love don't make a dent on Bick or on anyone else in that Texas crowd, really. I never intended they should. That's the point of the book. If that isn't clear the book is a failure. Do you really think that I imagine a Leslie could make a dent on the hard hide of Texas! She wins—or will in the end win—through her son and daughter."[13] Leslie, unlike her husband Bick, is capable of analyzing and interpreting the past without becoming part of its frontier legacy. She inhabits the present, speaks (although does not act) in the interests of the Mexican Americans at Reata, helps bring up her children, and is one of the few people aware of a new history for Texas. But like most historians, she thinks, talks, and even writes—but does not act.

In her first encounter with Bick in the mid-1920s, people are talking about the Scopes trial and are reading Theodore Dreiser's *American Tragedy*. Bick has only the vaguest notion of the trial and has never heard of Dreiser or his book.[14] He is out of the cultural loop of modern America, and certainly looks like a frontier relic, with his boots and Stetson. Ironically, he is first attracted to Leslie during the annual Hunt Ball, when she is dressed in an anachronistic sidesaddle hunting costume. He tries to interest Leslie by telling her that in Texas, "No one there tells you what to do and how you have to do it" (certainly a case of modern false advertising!).[15] He associates the state with frontier freedom, and yet he has a very rigid idea of Texas history, one that will brook no questioning or interrogation from Leslie, particularly when she reminds him, "We really stole Texas, didn't we? I mean, away from Mexico." When Bick tries to convince her that Texas is "history" and "a world in itself," closed off, finished, impossible to question, she responds, "There isn't a world in itself."[16] According to Leslie, everything is subject to questioning; nothing is sealed off in untouchable perfection. It is Leslie's constant questioning of Texas, her reading of history and own articulated conclusions, that forms the basis for Ferber's critique.

Giant is Ferber's third major historical novel about the American West. Both *Cimarron* and *Come and Get It* are revisionist westerns that contrasted and connected the old-style nineteenth-century frontier to twentieth-century civilization. *Giant* is set completely within post–First World War America, roughly from 1925 to 1950, but this modern generation of Texans still remains prisoners of their past. In her research, Ferber came across more than one article that noted, "Today the allure of the past is almost an obsession in the minds of many Texans . . . Texans looking backwards see only what they want to see in the 'never, never land' of the early West."[17] As Texan Vashti Hake complains to Leslie in the novel, "Easterners always yapping about Bunker Hill and Valley Forge and places like that, you'd think the Alamo and San Jacinto were some little fracas happened in Europe or someplace."[18] Vashti's historical comparison highlights Texans' belief that not only was the Mexican War a fight for freedom from foreign oppression, but also that Texans still have to defend their historical and present interests against the assumption that they too are foreign—still tinged with the taint of Mexico and Mexicans.

For Ferber, one of the greatest ironies about elite white Texans was that they would freely quote Crockett, Houston, and Bowie and mention the Alamo to justify their national importance, but they never mentioned that Texans' main complaint against Mexico before the formation of the republic was that the Mexican government had outlawed slavery in 1821.[19] For white Texans, "freedom" was only ever for the few. Although Ferber's main attack on twentieth-century Texas concerns the white treatment of Mexican Americans, she invests Leslie's understanding of Texas history with its tradition of a slave culture and its continuing Jim Crow legacy. After looking at the Mexican shanties, Leslie calls her husband Bick "Simon Legree" (of *Uncle Tom's Cabin*). When Bick tries to defend himself by criticizing the South, he argues, "I noticed your nigger cabins in the dear old South weren't so sumptuous,"[20] forgetting that Texas is part of both the South and West and therefore contains Jim Crow laws for Mexican Americans as well as African Americans. As historian Neil Foley points out: "While longhorns, Stetson hats, and the romance of ranching have replaced cotton, mules, and overalls in the historical imagination of Anglo Texans today, the fact remains that most Anglo Texans were descended from transplanted Southerners who had fought hard to maintain the 'color line' in Texas and to extend its barriers to Mexicans."[21] *Giant* is one of the few western novels to confront the mythic legacy of the free frontier via its multiracial Jim Crow history.

Ferber's earlier revisionist westerns had strong women protagonists, and Leslie Lynnton Benedict is no exception. Her thoughts and attitudes toward Texas structure the novel. But while Leslie locates the racial continuities in the hierarchies of the South and West throughout the book's several hundred pages, it is Jett Rink, a relatively minor character, who initially has to translate things for her. On her first visit to the Benedict workers' shantytown, he has to explain why Mrs. Obregon and her new son, Angel, have no doctor to care for them and why the other Mexican workers live in such poverty. Later on, when Bick's excuses for such inequities have dampened her crusading outrage, it is Jett who has to remind Leslie of the racial and historical realities of Texas society and how the white elites acquired the land: "Bought it—hell! Took it off a ignorant bunch of Mexicans didn't have the brains or guts to hang onto it. Lawyers come in and finagled around and lawsuits lasted a hundred years and by the time they got through the Americans had the land and the greasers was out on their ears . . . You asked me and I told you straight out. If you didn't want to know you got no call to ask me. You want everything prettified up, that's what's the matter with you."[22]

As a landless, wage-earning, poor white Texan, Jett is on the same economic level as Reata's Mexican American vaqueros and servants, and is looked down upon by wealthy landed whites. But though he shares their economic status, Jett is arguably more anti-Mexican than Bick. In a state where "not all whites . . . were equally white," he has to work harder to assert his whiteness and inherent superiority to the Mexican Americans at Reata.[23] Neil Foley has written about the Texas poor whites' hybrid status in the racial and economic hierarchies of the state's cotton culture, and those same rules still applied at the Reata cattle ranch during the 1920s. It was the same era that saw both the publication of Lothrop Stoddard's *The Rising Tide of Color against White World-Wide Supremacy* (1920) and a popular eugenics movement that classified those whites considered biologically inferior.[24] Because poor whites shared economic and living conditions with Mexican Americans and African Americans, they were socially darkened, class and racial hybrids who undermined the socially constructed borders between black, white, and brown.

Although at the conclusion of the novel, the proprietor of a diner mistakes Leslie for a Mexican American, Ferber codes Jett as black, using him as a symbol of the rest of Texas's racial prejudice.[25] It is not merely his name, which is another color for dark or black. As Ferber describes him after he struck oil and ran in triumph to the Benedict house: "His face was grotesque with smears of dark grease and his damp bacchanalian locks hung in tendrils over his forehead . . . He came on, he opened the door of the screened veranda, he stood before the company in his dirt and grease, his eyes shining wildly . . . The man stood, his legs wide apart as though braced against the world. The black calloused hands with the fingers curiously widespread as they hung, his teeth white in the grotesquely smeared face."[26] Ferber's language, emphasizing Jett's degenerate, "grotesque" physicality and sexuality, is heavy with the ironies of traditional racial stereotyping of black masculinity. In emphasizing Jett's visual as well as economic continuities with Mexican Americans and African Americans via the greasy blackness of his skin, Ferber deconstructs the racial borders marking Texas society. The man who would attempt to preserve Jim Crow color lines in post-Second World War Texas (by having separate lavatories for Mexicans and Anglos and publicly calling Jordan Benedict III's Mexican American wife Juana a "squaw") was not pure white himself.

Critics and Controversy

Giant was a major success for Ferber. She was once again on the best-seller list and selected for the Book-of-the-Month Club. Detractors who had harped on the relative failure of *Great Son* in 1945 were silenced. After seven years, Ferber again proved that she was capable of a major generational historical novel with a female protagonist. As she predicted, her portrayal of white Texans' prejudice against Mexican Americans was controversial. War hero and activist Dr. Hector Garcia, who helped Ferber with research contacts and served as a model for Angel Obregon, congratulated her and continued: "The majority of the people who have read your novel find it very interesting and very true to life."[27] While Mexican American readers may have enjoyed the book, white Texas natives were abusive. Since Ferber's work was first serialized in the *Ladies' Home Journal* before publication, many of the angry readers were women. Nannie D. Tomlinson complained in a seven-page letter: "I thought I had heard every misconception of Texas and its people and every form of ridicule possible to small minds, but you have left me speechless with astonishment—such colossal ignorance I have ever encountered."[28] Marilyn Glass of Hooks, Texas, denied there was any racism in Texas, but then continued: "If any Texas cowhand, be he the owner's son or anyone else's made the mistake of marrying a Mexican, she certainly would not be entertained in the living room with the honoured guests, especially in Texas!"[29] Others, like Frances McKelvey, said she should have written about Sam Houston or Jim Bowie, and that in focusing on the Benedicts, she misrepresented Texas history.[30]

One writer was especially vociferous in her justification of segregation:

> Aside from your misrepresentation of a fine group of people, I note that you are also trying to weave in the race prejudice you northerners, especially Jews, are always raving about. You mention such an inappropriate item, if even true, as that at the hotel there were signs "Ladies" and "Colored Women." I know such things as toilets so designated do not exist in hotels in Texas for the simple reason that colored people do not go to the best hotels, as they are not permitted at the best hotels in New York or anywhere else. You northerners are always preaching about segregation when there is more flagrant segregation in the north than in the south. We have separate schools, yes; the Negroes want this as much as we do. By giving them equal opportunity in schools of their own, we give them a challenge to take pride in their race, to try to achieve higher standards as a race. Since we have so many Negroes in the South is [sic] would not be practical for all to attend the same schools, therefore, we provide equal but separate schools.[31]

It was unlikely Ferber ever read a more fervent defense of modern racial segregation.

Although some non-Texas American reviewers carped dismissively about "women's literature" and Hollywood novels, reviews were largely positive outside of Texas. In Chattanooga, Christine Noble Govan wrote, "Texas won't like this picture of themselves, but Miss Ferber is too practiced an observer, too good a craftsman to have built it all from thin air."[32] John Barkham of the *New York Times* also endorsed it, focusing in particular on her picture of racism. Leslie was Ferber's mouthpiece, he wrote: "Most of all she resents the treatment of the Mexican-American in his native Texas. To the monolithic men in cream-colored Stetsons and tooled boots whose daughters cost heifer a day to keep in Swiss finishing schools, the Mexican is a sub-human to be used as a vaquero or a ranch-hand but out of public places meant to white folks."[33] Eleanor Howard, in her syndicated California column, wrote in the

Malibu Times, "W. Somerset Maugham, never one to flatter generously, once wrote of Edna Ferber that her stories would live long after most of her contemporary authors had been forgotten. Everyone who was read Miss Ferber's novels will undoubtedly agree, for even her earliest short stories still rank with the best."[34] *Giant* was no exception.

But Texas interests could sometimes impact the reception of her book at major journals. The *Saturday Review* hired a Texas native, William Kittrell, to attack the book, even though he had no literary or historical status. Ferber was shocked that the magazine would hire an amateur to defame her book. Then she discovered that major Texas figures bankrolled the magazine. In a hard-hitting letter to the editor, Henry S. Canby, Ferber wrote, "Beneath the article on page 15 of that issue your magazine has stated the qualifications for book reviewing possessed by a William Kittrell. He is, one is told, a Texan of pre-Revolutionary stock. I assume that this refers to the Texas Revolution." She continued nastily, "To a few people outside Texas the term pre-Revolutionary may sometimes refer to the American Revolution. Mr. Kittrell is further equipped for literary criticism though being the operator of a Texas Press Clipping Bureau, a peanut farm, and a peach orchard." "This list of occupations," she wrote, "is not one which ordinarily would be considered sufficiently literary in its background to fit one for book reviewing . . . Your reasons given for the choice of this particular reviewer are an affront to you and your editorial staff and to your subscribers and to your readers and to me." She wondered why her work had to suffer from incompetent reviews when Hemingway's and Steinbeck's did not. "Why did you not choose . . . a Cuban sugar planter for Hemingway's short story? Or a Salinas California lettuce grower for Steinbeck's novel? Can the choice of Mr. William Kittrell have any connection with the fact that Mr. E. DeGolyer, whose financial relation to your magazine is so well known, and who is Chairman of your Board of Directors, also happens to be a wealthy Texas oil man?" When the *Saturday Review* refused to print the reference to DeGolyer, Ferber sent a stinging reply and dropped the matter.[35]

But in Texas, reviewers were more than abusive, and while they did not list Jett's black-Mexican-Anglo hybridity as one of her offenses, their abuse was close to a verbal lynching. Ferber literally became the deviant outsider, the woman infringing upon the masculine territory of the West, the New York Jewish despoiler of the pure Texas myth. In the *San Angelo Standard-Times,* Jack Allard wrote, "Many Texans . . . are calling for a burning at the stake of

Miss Ferber. Instead of faggots, they would pitch copies of *Giant* on the fire."
He offered to hold the match.[36] In Houston, columnist Carl Victor Little attacked her gender and the genre of women's fiction, dismissing her research
as "steeped in backstairs gossip and what girl novelists call local color."[37] In
yet another article, he said she should be lynched.[38] Lon Tinkle, in Dallas,
maligned her as "berserk," an author who had "never written a really serious or significant work in her life," and warned her, "You aren't writing *Uncle
Tom's Cabin*."[39] Margaret Cousins, the managing editor of *Good Housekeeping*,
explained much of this vicious, misogynistic criticism to Ferber: "If Texans
had been able to be objective about this book, your whole thesis would have
been belied. To an extent, their foaming at the mouth about it simply bore
out what you had to say about them. They are still in the middle of frontier
growing pains of which chauvinism is so much a part, but I cannot but be
amused by the fierceness and passion of their reactions."[40]

But Ferber was not prepared to laugh off all the abuse. In a letter to her
publisher, Ferber wrote, "If a resentful Texan reviews my book it will be a bad
business. Much of the published comment I have seen (Texan) is real Nazi
stuff. For that matter, it has just occurred to me that the set-up down there
reminds me more of the Nazi ideology and behavior than any community
I've ever encountered."[41] The reviews were motivated not only by anti-Semitism, but also by misogyny. While most attacked her gender and attempted to
dismiss her as a poor novelist and inept historian, one Texan did offer some
unusual insight into the book in relation to Ferber's other work. The reader,
one Sam Nugent, fumed:

> By this time the warped thinking of Miss Ferber on the feebleness of the male
> animal should be obvious. Her books retread the same ground to a degree
> that even a casual reader can predict the outcome in advance. In *Show Boat*
> the gambler Ravenal was glamorous and weak and sneaked out on his wife
> when the going got rugged. In *Cimarron* Yancey Cravat was also glamorous—
> and unstable; he also disappeared and it was the wife who became congress-
> woman (if I remember aright). In *So Big*, not only did the heroine, Selina,
> carry on after her loutish and unprogressive farmer husband died, but her
> son is left, at the book's close, a sophisticated failure. Only the women are
> worth their salt! It is obvious that Miss Ferber's contention is that men may
> be attractive, but only in the sense that children are attractive. She seems
> to feel men are only excess baggage in her tidy little feministic world. Thus

in her books, without exception, women are the builders, men are picturesque—but really useless.[42]

In effect, Ferber's work challenged the basic principle of traditional American
history—that men were the doers and women the decoration. Ferber may
have been writing about racial issues, but in reviews of the book, rabid critics
took the greatest exception to her gender and strong heroines. These same
sorts of questions would impact the film adaptation between 1954 and 1956.

Giant Productions

George Stevens first tried to obtain the galleys in early 1952, but without success. Ferber was famous for keeping prying studio eyes away from her novel
until it was actually on the shelves. *Daily Variety* gloated in mid-May, "Edna
Ferber denies film studios peek at her new novel," and mentioned that "there's
considerably less interest in the new Ernest Hemingway yarn, *The Old Man
and Sea*"; the public and the studios cared more about Ferber's work. "Effort
and intrigue to lay hands on a manuscript or galley proofs of the Ferber novel
arises out of the writer's reputation for turning out profitable film fare," continued the journal, citing Ferber's huge successes with *Cimarron*, *So Big*, and
Show Boat. The journal noted: "She's always been tough, however, in deals
for screen rights. She's insisted on leasing her properties, rather than selling
them, and has collected fabulous payments for yarns to which she has retained basic ownership."[43]

Stevens read *Giant* with thousands of others when it was first serialized in
the June 1952 issue of the *Ladies' Home Journal*. As his secretary summarized the
first instalment: "It is hard to say whether or not it will turn out worthwhile."
She noted blandly that the novel was "based on Texas, Texans and their great
wealth and superiority (?) and sophistication." The first instalment merely
introduced the main characters and "will be based on character sketches of
these 'giants'—their intrigues—great wealth—race hatred for the Mexicans—
and one central character called Jett Rink—who is more fabulously wealthy
than all others."[44]

Stevens appreciated Ferber's attack on Texas racism. He also shared Fer-
ber's commitment to creating unusual perspectives on the American past
(*Annie Oakley*, 1935; *I Remember Mama*, 1948; *A Place in the Sun*, 1951; *Shane*, 1953).
His independent film company bought the rights in the summer of 1952, and

then convinced Warner Bros. to put up the money for the production and distribution.[45] Production chief Roy Obringer finally confirmed *Giant's* director and budget with Jack Warner in December 1953. Fred Guiol and Ivan Moffat, longtime associates of Stevens, were hired to adapt and write the screenplay with Stevens's help. The director had already made extensive notes on his copy, highlighting the scenes of racial prejudice against Mexican Americans, including the near ejection of a Latin American ambassador from Jett's hotel (later cut), Leslie's comparisons between the Mexican shantytowns and those for African Americans in the South (never used by the screenwriters), Angel's emerging *pachuco* (Mexican American youth) identity (also cut), and Leslie's inflammatory comment to Jett that the Mexican Americans at Reata were "more American than you [and her husband] are."[46] But Stevens was also in love with the West and the western hero; his last film, *Shane* (1953), proved as much. His desire to condemn racism and enshrine the old-style toughness of the western hero would result in a deeply conflicted western.

Ferber may have suspected that Stevens would not adopt all her book's incisive critique. When MGM remade *Show Boat*, it excised much of her original attack on southern racism and antimiscegenation laws.[47] So she kept an eye on Stevens. When she sold the film rights in 1952, Ferber retained her usual copyright reversion and television rights, but also acquired a percentage in Giant Productions. She, Stevens, and producer Henry Ginsberg were the three heads of Giant Productions. It was almost unprecedented for a writer, even a historical novelist of Ferber's national stature, to acquire this kind of power-sharing deal in a film production. As *Variety* noted, "The G-S-F setup will also embrace future filming of previous Ferber works, including remakes of some of her past film successes, rights to which have reverted [to her]."[48] But Ferber wanted more than executive privileges and a percentage of the profits. Preserving *Giant's* critique of frontier racism was important, and she wanted to help construct the screenplay, particularly after she saw Moffat and Guiol's first draft. "I want to work as an unsalaried writer," she wrote to Ginsberg.[49]

All told, she spent eleven weeks in Hollywood working on the script, advising on technical issues, and meeting with the cast and crew in Texas. While recognizing Stevens's gifts as a director, Ferber disliked the way the writers cheapened Leslie's dialogue, cut the character dimensions of her daughter, Luz, and embellished Bick's role at the expense of Leslie.[50] As the filmmakers strove to build up Bick's unpleasant character, Leslie's critical vision diminished in importance. Ferber argued, "I feel that Leslie has to quite a degree, faded into a somewhat pale character as the two leading male characters have taken on additional stature . . . When Bick takes that flag off the wall and drapes it around the casket of Angel, I reject that act. It is a thing Leslie might do; Bick would not. Not yet, at least. It is a tear-jerker, but it is not the truth."[51] Although Elizabeth Taylor's star power added strength to Leslie's characterization, many film critics like Hollis Alpert would focus on the film's characterization of Bick (Rock Hudson). Even with the magnetic James Dean as Jett on the front cover of the *Saturday Review*, Alpert wrote, "Perhaps the strongest [point] involves the slow education of Bick Benedict to the nature of prejudice. He learns the hard way as he fights for the right of a Mexican family (and his own daughter-in-law) to eat in a roadside luncheonette."[52]

In spite of her status as coproducer, most of Ferber's script comments were ignored. It was not an experience she liked. As she later wrote to her editor at Doubleday, "I got myself into something really grisly when, in my youth and innocence, I came out here to write the *Giant* dialogue . . . The script dialogue was beyond belief at that time. I never would have permitted it to be used. For eight weeks, at exactly nothing a week, I've been working with a young man named Ivan Moffett [*sic*]." Of Moffat's and Hollywood's taste in writers in general, she was scathing: "He is 36, charming, talented, sensitive; he has taste, a feeling for words; he can't write worth a damn, he is indolent and can't do a real day's work. He knows as much about Texas as I know about Iran. Less." She continued, "If I get out of this town without killing him it will be the greatest known triumph of restraint against honest impulse."[53]

Scripting Contemporary History

Ferber's worries were somewhat exaggerated. Stevens was committed to projecting a critique of contemporary Texas racism. He took Ferber's advice and consulted Mexican American civil rights activist Dr. Hector Garcia during production.[54] The first treatment, dated 24 March 1954, does roughly follow the outline of Ferber's book.[55] Leslie's early comments about Texas being stolen from Mexico were preserved and even enhanced. In Stevens's annotated copy of the treatment, the director penciled additional dialogue in the margin: "After all, it's in the history books, isn't it?"[56] Most crucially, though, Leslie's abortive attempts in the novel to improve the living and working conditions of the Mexican Americans attached to the Reata ranch economy were actually made realities in the script. It is Leslie who first works with

Dr. Guerra on the Nopal settlements, not her son, Jordy.[57] Whereas Ferber's Leslie was thwarted at every turn, Stevens invested her with more traditional frontier ingenuity and success. However, as a result, the few Mexican American characters appear far more powerless and victimized than in Ferber's novel. In *Giant*, Ferber briefly discusses the rise of LULAC (League of United Latin American Citizens) and postwar–Latin American activism and chronicles the friendship between Jordy and Angel Obregon. However, Stevens made the white Leslie the instigator of social change.[58]

Stevens also improved Leslie's relationship with Jett Rink, creating sympathy between the two characters that had not existed in Ferber's novel. In Stevens's annotated copy of the "Ferber script," dated the summer of 1954, Stevens paid particular attention to Jett and Leslie's tour of the Reata slums. When Leslie first expresses her horror, he blames Bick: "It's part of Reata, like all the rest of it. The ranch people live here." Then he talks about her "neighbors" the Obregons and Mrs. Obregon's illness. Stevens penciled in the margin, "More from Jett here as he shows her the slums. Leslie has been exclaiming that everything is beautiful, oh so beautiful. The plainest thing is beautiful and Jett is bored with this—He shows her the slums so that she can exclaim that this is beautiful too."[59] Jett becomes Leslie's educator in Texas social hierarchies.

But the writers also edited Ferber's racial history of Texas and references to the state's entwined Mexican American and African American Jim Crow culture. Although the first treatment opens with a montage of Texas scenes and close-ups of Mexican American and Anglo children, emphasizing the state's ethnic populations, the sequence features no African American children or adults. Leslie's frequent comments to Jordan in which she explicitly links white Texas elites' treatment of Mexican American migrant workers to white southerners' Jim Crow laws were never integrated in the script.[60] While Ferber was all too ready to see the connections between southern and western racism, the filmmakers may have balked at attacking the 1950s' biggest social problem.

The Supreme Court announced the decision to end segregation in the public schools, *Brown v. Board of Education of Topeka*, in mid-May 1954, and public debates over the issue continued throughout 1954 and 1955, when the process of implementation began.[61] Was it too hot a contemporary issue to discuss openly within an already controversial adaptation? Arguably, Stevens and his writers skilfully referenced some aspects of Jim Crow culture without visualizing the segregation of African Americans in the South. In the 22 October 1954 script, Moffat and Guiol, with Ferber's input, included a scene in which Leslie and the other Texas cattle barons' wives discuss their husbands' fixing of the Mexican American vote in local elections. Fidel Gomez, the Benedict henchman, has been forcing the Mexican Americans living around Reata to vote according to Benedict interests. Shortly after Luz Benedict's funeral, Gomez is shown meeting with the men. Leslie does not understand the import of his conversation, and the others must explain Texas election "laws" to her. Adarene tells her, "Gomez's vote is important," and Leslie responds innocently, "Anybody's vote is important." Vashti, characterized as the shyest and least intelligent of the women, explains the facts of Texas life to Leslie as though she were a child, "It's important that they vote right, honey. There's taxes going up to worry about and all . . . "[62]

This scene would be totally reworked in the final script, dated 4 April 1955, and in the film.[63] In the final script, Judge Whiteside tells Gomez, "Now you get with it, Gomez! Get your people out! I don't want anybody sitting on their honkers come election day." Gomez replies obsequiously, "Everything will be bueno, Senor. It will be the same—good. Adios—buenas noches, Senores." After he leaves, Leslie makes her famous attempt to enter the political discussion with her husbands' friends. The women do not comment on and explain the election bending. Instead, they show absolutely no interest in Gomez, and even Leslie ignores him and fails to comprehend or question the situation.[64]

Why was this scene made more oblique for the audience and for Leslie? The Texas women obviously appear more stupid and passive than their novelistic counterparts; the emphasis in the Hollywood adaptation is on male action and control, not on women's commentary and critique. But perhaps even more crucial for the filmmakers, scenes representing election tampering and the forcing of ethnic or racial groups to vote in a certain way illustrated the tenets of the southern Jim Crow "laws." Showing Bick's complicity in this system demonstrated in a very obvious way that he was part of this racist system, a system that left the eastern outsider, Leslie, and much of the audience, dumbfounded. But ironically, the filmmakers tweaked the scene to avoid legal trouble from Texas families that were still embroiled in these corrupt policies. During the 1950s, the Klebergs of the King Ranch and Glenn McCarthy were probably the most notorious cattle and oil elites, and the possible connections obsessed the Warner Bros. legal department.

Legal Troubles?

If Ferber was proud of her intense historical research on a topic, she was much more cautious about her characters' biographical antecedents—particularly if the models were still living and capable of suing her for libel. If the Klebergs were her models for the Benedicts and the King Ranch was Reata, she did nothing to endorse such an attitude, even in her research practices. She never interviewed the Klebergs or asked them for assistance when researching *Giant*. But the Warner Bros. legal department was hypersensitive to even the most tenuous case of libel and went about collecting everything it could on the family and their ranching empire. As Carl Milliken wrote to Henry Ginsberg in December 1954, "Since Warner Bros. Pictures, Inc. will be a co-defendant in any action brought against an independent producer releasing through Warner Bros., it is our custom to examine the scripts for independent production in the same way that we would our own."[65] He wanted an integrated system of checking between the research department and the legal department. As he noted to Ginsberg: "Edna Ferber's *Giant* is a specially worrisome property because it has been accepted, to a large extent, in the public mind as a true document not only of life in Texas but also specifically of the lives of the Kleberg family, which owns and operates the King Ranch, and of Glenn McCarthy, the much publicized Texas oil millionaire."

Milliken's paranoia was not entirely unfounded. The King Ranch was renowned as "the birthplace of the American ranching industry," and by the 1950s was a sprawling multinational business.[66] Sometimes its power seemed almost sinister. In May 1938, a *Reader's Digest* feature article on the ranch and the Klebergs noted: "Rumors persist that 'armed riders with Winchesters patrol the fences and that in the last two years four men crossing the fence to hunt have not returned.'"[67] This story was eerily like Jett Rink's revelation about his father's mysterious death at the hands of the Benedict overlords. Obviously, this connection between the Benedicts and the Klebergs, which suggested that elite Texas families regularly "lynched" trespassers or squatters, could not go in the script, and therefore Jett, when asked, merely says that his folks "weren't so foxy [as the Benedicts]."[68]

In addition, Texas papers had emphasized these connections in hopes of getting Ferber embroiled in a legal suit, but Milliken even quoted the *Saturday Review* as evidence of the widespread assumption that Jett was Glenn McCarthy and the Benedicts the Klebergs: "'Despite the disclaimer in the front of the book, the characters in *Giant* will strike many Texans as bearing a remarkable resemblance to actual persons.' It is about as difficult to identify the characters and places in *Giant* as it would be to recognize the Washington Monument if it were painted purple," Milliken gloomed.[69] He continued that if the Klebergs could prove a connection between themselves and the Benedicts, Warner Bros. could be sued: "The Benedict family is shown, in the main, as a sort of feudal structure which is arrogant in its relationships with other people, contemptuous of Mexican Americans ('wetbacks' and 'pachucos,' as they are called), and as accustomed to riding roughshod over the rights of lesser people." Although Milliken liked the way the script showed Bick "undergoing a regeneration which is not apparent in the novel," he wanted even more careful handling of the race issue. Jett Rink's resemblance to Glenn McCarthy was simply too much: "We portray Rink as a thoroughly obnoxious character, one who is licentious, habitually drunk, and dedicated to the false principles of racial discrimination."

But Milliken's fears were largely self-created. If the Klebergs and McCarthy had not already sued Ferber, how could Warner Bros. undergo such an ordeal, since its only credited source was Ferber? Curiously, the rest of the *Saturday Review* article he initially quoted to Ginsberg actually challenged the view that *Giant* was a secret exposé of real-life Texans:

> Some will think that this is actually the story of the King Ranch and Bob Kleberg, and of the Shamrock Hotel and Glenn McCarthy, but on closer examination they are wrong. Very carefully but casually, Miss Ferber brings Bob and Glenn and the Shamrock into her narrative, this proving beyond a peradventure of a doubt that Glenn McCarthy is Glenn McCarthy himself, not Jett Rink, Bick Benedict is not Bob Kleberg after all, and the little old King Ranch of only a million or so acres is definitely not the giant Reata spread of which Miss Ferber speaks . . . Miss Ferber has done a lot of homework on this book and there is some meat in it . . . Her dislike of the treatment of the wetback and of the discrimination against Latin-Americans is shared by many of us.[70]

But Milliken was so worried that he had researchers mine the lives of Bob and Helen Kleberg and Glenn McCarthy.[71] Research files noted that like Ferber's heroine, Mrs. Kleberg was from Virginia, so Stevens was forced to change Leslie's origin to Maryland. Researchers worried over the parallels between the Klebergs' seventeen-day courtship and Leslie and Bick's quick romance. Uncle Bawley's management of distant Benedict domains resembled the life of Bob's cousin Caesar, so no scenes of Uncle Bawley's ranch were allowed.[72] They took note of the similarities between Jett's Conquistador Hotel and McCarthy's famed Shamrock in Houston. They read *Life on the King Ranch*, by Frank Goodwyn; *Time*'s article on McCarthy, "King of the Wildcatters"; another expose of the Klebergs, "America's Forbidden Kingdom," in *Reader's Digest*; and cover articles in *Fortune* on McCarthy's unbelievable wealth.[73] They even contacted the Klebergs, hoping to stall any potential lawsuits by assuring them that Warner Bros. would not photograph their ranch or any members of their family. In fact, the studio's mediator "was quite sure that Warner Bros. would be in a favourable position to acquire the rights of the new book about the King Ranch to produce a picture based thereon, which new book would give a true, correct and factual history of the King Ranch."[74] Whether Warner Bros. executives would actually have done such a thing is debatable, but in their efforts to forestall any potential lawsuits, they revealed a lack of any political or social commitment to Ferber's material. The studio was not stupid enough to hand a copy of the script over to the Klebergs for their final approval, realizing that "sending them a script would only result in a lot of arguments, differences, re-writings, delays, etc.," but it was not adverse to promising a pro-Texas, all-white western.

Not surprisingly, however, the studio was less concerned about the possible prototypes for the Mexican American characters and incidents of discrimination. Researchers turned up a possible connection between Angel Obregon and Sergeant John R. Rice, a Native American soldier killed in Korea. Cemetery officials in Sioux City, Iowa, refused to bury him in the town plot "on the grounds it violated a clause in all lot-purchase contracts prohibiting the internment of any others except the white race."[75] President Truman ordered the army to bury him at Arlington, Virginia, "after learning that a grave had been denied the Winnebago Indian and that his body had remained at the grave site five hours yesterday after the ceremonies were halted."[76] Not all racists lived in Texas, it seemed.

Racial and Gender Profiles

Despite Stevens's preoccupation with Texas prejudice against Mexican Americans, he did not invest the Mexican American characters with any active roles in the narrative. Angel Obregon was Ferber's rebellious pachuco and Medal of Honor war hero, an articulate young man aware of his Latin American (not Mexican or U.S.) identity.[77] But Stevens transformed him into a silent victim of the Second World War and cast the tiny, wide-eyed, vulnerable Sal Mineo in the role. Contemporaries Jordy (Dennis Hopper) and Bob (Earl Holliman) tower over him, and, significantly, Mineo's was not a speaking role. Stevens also diluted Juana's character (Elsa Cardeñas), but one exhibitor argued that "it is this weakness of her character which sells the racial problem to an even greater degree than if she had been a strong character like Katy Jurado."[78] This comment raises the possibility that Stevens deliberately reworked the Mexican characters to be passive victims in order to garner mainstream support for Mexican American civil rights.

Another minority character, Leslie, does resist passivity and victimization in the patriarchal ranch system. Yet *Giant* is not a feminist western; Stevens and Warner Bros.' sympathies were not entirely with Leslie, despite the fact that she is the only one of the three white protagonists to combat prejudice against Mexican Americans. *Giant* may represent what Peter Biskind calls "the decay of patriarchy," but Leslie's feminism and egalitarian values do not win the West.[79] In the Warner Bros. character profiles written in the spring of 1954, the filmmakers said that Leslie could be irritating: "There was a strong element of the dilettante in her constant harping upon the conditions of the Mexican servants . . . There was a self-indulgent quality in her compassion." And later: "Leslie romanticised truth, without necessarily understanding it."[80] In these early profiles, Stevens's writers undercut Leslie's seriousness and commitment to change at Reata and dismissed her humanism as a pose. In contrast, they tried to justify Texas racism: "The trouble with anything of this sort on Leslie's part was not so much that conditions in Texas were worse than in other places, but the Texans were exceptional in their unwillingness to admit that their State stood short of perfection."[81]

Stevens seemed most drawn to Jett Rink of all Ferber's characters. In his original notes on the novel, the director quoted Jett's angry comment on the Benedicts: "Nobody's king in this country—no matter what they think." "Memorable line," he mused. "Should register on some people later on."[82] In both Ferber's novel and Stevens's adaptation, Jett introduces Leslie to the evils of the Benedicts' ranch system and their treatment of Mexican Americans. He instigates Leslie's desire for change in Texas. Stevens even toned down Jett's unrepentant racism and made the character more central to the narrative. Although he occasionally bridles at Leslie's comments linking him and his lifestyle with that of the Mexican Americans ("You mean that bunch of wet-backs? Don't you get me mixed up with them. I'm just as much Texas as Bick Benedict is. I'm no wetback."), Stevens softens Jett's character while retaining many of Ferber's initial devices to link the lives of poor whites with those of Mexican Americans and even African Americans.[83] In the process, Jett—rather than Leslie—becomes the dominant racial crossover character in the film. Through Jett's combination of racism and hybridity, Stevens undermines the racial assumptions structuring Jim Crow prejudice in Texas.

The character profile on Jett touches carefully on these issues and makes him even more sympathetic by emphasizing his classic self-made-man qualities: "At the lower depths of a great nation there sweeps an undertow of the human tide, a restless flux that is forever in motion, thrust forward and drawn backward by the pull of the economic and social seasons, and peopled by the marginal, the unskilled, the migratory and the anonymous . . . Jett had many reasons, as a young man, to be angry. First, he was a drifter in a world where he found himself one of the few under-privileged and yet non-Mexican employees of a young man of great wealth."[84] The profile emphasizes his marginality and his individuality, his closeness with Mexican Americans and other underprivileged groups in Texas, and his separateness. The profile returns to this issue, rewriting Jett's attitude toward Mexican Americans: "Jett did not dislike the Mexicans. He knew, more than most, that they were getting a raw deal. But his only interest in life was to get into the same position as those who were giving the Mexicans that same raw deal."

Stevens made Jett's hybridity even more explicit through the film medium. When Jett (James Dean) strikes it rich, the camera lingers on him as he becomes increasingly black with oil—clothes, hands, and face (Fig. 6.1). And when his truck zigzags over the immaculate lawn of the big house at Reata, it is as though an Okie or a black southern sharecropper had strayed onto the white plantation. A few minutes later, a blackened Jett faces the white-skinned, white-bloused Leslie on the front steps in an explosive two-shot (Fig. 6.2). As he reaches out to touch her (a sexual action that will literally cover her in oil and his blackness, figuratively profaning her white racial purity), Bick strikes him. In this sequence, Stevens recontextualizes D. W. Griffith's seminal film *The Birth of a Nation* (1915), in which Gus, a mulatto, or mixed-race, African American, pursues the white hero's younger sister.[85] Like the actor who played Gus, James Dean is painted black to overemphasize his transgressive, mixed status.

above: 6.1. Jett (James Dean) blackened with oil (*Giant,* Warner Bros., 1956); *below:* 6.2. *The Birth of a Nation* revisited: Jett confronting Leslie (Elizabeth Taylor) in *Giant* (Warner Bros., 1956).

But as both Michael Rogin and Richard Dyer have pointed out, Hollywood filmmakers' eagerness to differentiate blacks and whites and to blacken mulatto characters with excessive makeup, lighting, and binary characterization has often undercut the social and visual construction of racial categories.[86] If "color" has to be painted on in order to represent racial difference, then what lies beneath is dangerously ambiguous and even indistinguishable. While Griffith's racism is well documented, Stevens's reworking of *The Birth of a Nation* on both a narrative and visual level is ironic. The script preserves Ferber's original, highly charged, racialized language linking the poor-white hero with other "colored" minorities. Uncle Bawley (Chill Wills), who has observed everything, even suggests that lynching Jett might have solved all their problems. Leslie responds, "Yes, that's what you would have done in the old days. Thank heaven these days are different."[87] While Gus is lynched by the Ku Klux Klan, Jett escapes and even delivers the final blow to Bick. Although Jett's black "paint," or "grease," connects him to both African Americans and Mexican Americans (pejoratively known as "greasers") in Texas, it also enables this dangerous racial hybrid to cross both class and racial barriers in Texas.[88] Oil makes Jett the richest man in Texas.

The Gender of Authorship and Publicity Clashes

Shooting began in May 1955 and continued through mid-October. The film's budget, originally set at a modest $1.5 million, eventually ballooned to $3.2 million.[89] Although Ferber occasionally suggested big names like Burt Lancaster for Bick, Audrey Hepburn or Grace Kelly for Leslie, and Robert Mitchum for Jett, Stevens settled on the dark-haired Elizabeth Taylor (star of Stevens's *A Place in the Sun*, 1951), whose Latin-like beauty echoed Ferber's original, racialized description of Leslie ("her eyes were large, dark, and warmly lustrous"[90]), and two younger male stars, Rock Hudson (Bick) and James Dean (Jett). Giant Productions migrated to Marfa, Texas, for principal on-location shooting.

As production continued and the studio publicity machine kicked into gear, Leslie was not the only woman upstaged by powerful men. Ferber was pushed more and more to the side as *Giant*'s controversial author. The film was no longer a woman's western with an outsider's critical perspective. After all, George Stevens's last film was the archetypal *Shane*, one of Hollywood's most lyrical defenses of frontier masculinity.[91] Stevens's deployment of Ferber's critique was in the end more palatable to Texas and national audiences. The film does not merely soften Ferber's muckraking criticism by eliminating many of the connections between African American and Mexican American Jim Crow laws. Leslie's character and her critical perspective on Texas racism and chauvinism are marginalized, and as Jane Hendler argues, when Stevens humanizes Bick at the end of the film by having him fight for Mexican Americans' right to eat at a "white" diner, the traditional patriarchy is saved and rehabilitated.[92] Although Leslie is shown achieving a certain amount of progress for the Mexican Americans on Reata, the film never employs her critical historical voice as a voice-over. Instead, as one Stevens biographer wrote recently, *Giant* became "a luscious, colourful, exuberant kind of national epic [that] looked enthusiastically to the future."[93] Independent filmmaker or not, Stevens was caught up in the Hollywood of the 1950s and its own kind of fascination with size and wealth. The scope of wide-screen filmmaking and the lushness of Warnercolor were celebrated, and the Texas elites emerged more or less unscathed. Stevens's first shot of Bick Benedict is telling—a close-up of his elegant heeled boots and branded gear—the icons of the cowboy. In the film's final shot, Bick has become the battered but happy head of a multiracial family.

Another film released in 1956 and distributed by Warner Bros., John Ford's *The Searchers*, also examines the racism motivating traditional frontier history. Set in nineteenth-century Texas, *The Searchers* focuses on the quest of Ethan Edwards (John Wayne) for his niece Debbie, who was abducted by Comanches following the murder of her family. It becomes evident that Ethan's lengthy search is less a rescue than a planned racial execution, since he assumes—correctly, as it turns out—that the captive Debbie has crossed sexual and racial boundaries in her gradual integration into the tribe. Many film scholars point out that Ford's portrayal of Ethan's excessive and violent racism forces a reconsideration of racial mixing and segregation in western history and in contemporary American society.[94] Yet the differences between Ford's and Stevens's work are striking. *Giant*'s feminine literary antecedents and protagonist, racially ambiguous antihero, and portrayal of a successful mixed-race union contrast with Ford's white, masculine-driven narrative, which repeatedly marginalizes and victimizes women and Native Americans. However, Stevens's more positive outlook for racial integration, as Bick drives his new American family back to Reata in the final shots, ironically represents a public relations whitewashing of Ferber's harsher racial critique.

During production, the studio carefully released news blurbs emphasizing George Stevens's and Warner Bros.' less inflammatory attitude toward

Texas's overblown masculinity, crass wealth, and racism. Actress Jane Withers (Vashti Hake), herself a native Texan, reportedly "had only one condition . . . that the script not treat Texans as harshly as the Edna Ferber best-selling book about the nation's largest state."[95] Whether Stevens listened to Withers is open to question, but Warner Bros. certainly put pressure on the director to modify some of Ferber's more pointed prose. As film critic Kate Cameron remarked upon seeing the film, "Although Stevens hasn't eliminated the sharp, bitter criticism of the people of Texas that was part of the book, he has blunted the point so that some of its propagandistic scenes do not strike the beholder as unfairly biased."[96]

As far as most reviewers were concerned, this whitewashing benefited the film. Long uneasy about Ferber's controversial critique of Texas oil elites, the press repackaged her novel as the ravings of an eastern virago. As one *Time* reviewer wrote, "Indeed, the best-selling 1952 novel by Edna Ferber, on which this picture is based, bellowed from the bookstalls that Texas in modern times is a microcosm of materialism, a noisome social compost of everything that is crass and sick and cruel in American life."[97] Ferber's attack on the entrenched Jim Crow status quo for Mexican Americans living in Texas was seen as an extremist's polemic rather than a serious, well-supported argument about modern Texas history and American race relations. While critics increasingly dismissed Ferber as just a writer of potboilers, Stevens was hailed as a mature screen artist: "In the hand of a master moviemaker, *Giant* has been transformed from a flashy bestseller into a monumental piece of social realism."[98]

In contrast, many critics accepted Stevens's scenes about racial prejudice and implied that he had enhanced Ferber's weak material. Was *Giant*'s view of Texas more palatable to the American public when projected by a man, one known for the spare, masculine western *Shane*? Although female reviewers like Rose Pelswick praised Ferber's original work and actually claimed that the film, although good, was an expurgated version in which "the satire of the Ferber novel [is] almost entirely toned down," these views were a minority.[99] Far more prevalent were pronouncements like that of Philip K. Scheuer of the *Los Angeles Times*: "It is, I suspect, much more Stevens's movie than Edna Ferber's novel—the work of a distinctive and distinguished cinema stylist and creative artist."[100] The rhetoric of Texas reviewers like John Bustin of the *Austin Statesman* was even more explicit: "The Edna Ferber novel, *Giant*, told a harsh, often inaccurate and always bitter story about Texas and Texans during a trying period of change, and Texans were doubtless justified in finding it a vitriolic and frequently unfounded caricature of a small segment of their state," he complained. "In bringing Miss Ferber's story to the screen, though, Stevens has given it not only more accuracy and more point, but more real, life-sized human qualities than were even hinted at in the original novel."[101] According to this perspective, Ferber's historical fiction is inaccurate and therefore invalid. However, Stevens, using her material, is a competent man to tell the story of Texas. Alton Cook said something similar: "Stevens found a much more solid and compact drama than was given to the readers of the Edna Ferber novel on which the film is based. His conflict is keener and the issues are more clearly defined."[102] There is not anything specific that Cook uses to justify such criticism. Stevens is just a more acceptable source. But it seems that Ferber could never win. For Bustin, her "grasp of the issues" was too taut and unrelenting; for Cook, she was less focused on the social problem of prejudice than Stevens.

The *Hollywood Reporter*'s favoritism was easier to understand. When its reviewer wrote "The screenplay by Fred Guiol and Ivan Moffat seems superior to Edna Ferber's novel," the magazine was merely hyping the medium that put it in business. But the *Reporter* also paid tribute to Ferber's ability to create "unusual characterization" and praised her as a historical novelist.[103] After all, she too had been responsible for making films successful since the 1920s. In July 1956, the production team's publicity department planned a "*Giant* Pre-Release Campaign" that emphasized Ferber's unusual investment in the project—her ten weeks of script and production work in Hollywood—and her close relationship with cast and crew. Publicity man Tom Carl even planned a "George Stevens Byline on Edna Ferber," in which the director would discuss her integrity as a person and as a writer as he experienced both during their work together on the preparation of *Giant*. The piece "should make a strong Sunday section story for the newspapers" and "might possibly be a good plant with one of the better women's magazines with whom Ferber is a well-known personality in her own right."[104] Carl knew how to capitalize on Ferber's reputation for the benefit of the film.

Other publicity ideas also focused on Ferber: "Try for book editor stories on Edna Ferber, her fabulous success in motion pictures and of course her latest *Giant*."[105] The 1956 press book and program contain several articles on Ferber, her best-selling reputation, and her long-standing relationship with Hollywood, but a great deal of attention was paid to her close working partnership with Stevens. Her endorsement of the film added to its historical accuracy and cachet: "Miss Ferber held lengthy consultation with George Stevens and Henry Ginsberg. And she worked with Fred Guiol and Ivan Moffat, the screen writers, for three months on the screenplay for the film," bragged the publicity machine. But while Ferber's name was on every poster and advertisement, press-book articles about her were wedged toward the back of the booklet, overwhelmed by the publicity on Stevens, Taylor, Hudson, Dean, and the other stars.[106]

Later on, however, the publicity department nearly destroyed Ferber's partnership with Ginsberg and Stevens. *Giant*'s publicity team, with the consent of producer Ginsberg and possibly even Stevens, engaged in some front-page competition with the author. Although Ferber had astutely insisted in her contract that any film publicity carry her name with the film's title, the production company occasionally managed to undermine her authority as *Giant*'s originator and one of the most respected novelists in America. In a letter to Ginsberg dated 17 August 1956, Ferber wrote that the *New York Evening Post* had carried an article by Sidney Skolsky on 16 August, claiming that "Edna Ferber, after seeing *Giant*, told George Stevens, 'Thanks—that's the story I wanted to write.'"[107] Ferber was justifiably outraged by the publicity, since, as she reasoned, it could have originated only "in an organization devoted to the George Stevens publicity campaign in connection with *Giant*." Not only had she not even seen *Giant*, but she also would "not stand for this sort of publicity which is beneficial to some one else while it breaks me down." Ferber demanded a retraction and said that if it were not made soon, she would take action that "will work against the picture's career." An author's endorsement still mattered to the Hollywood studios, and Warner Bros. valued the money her works brought in, particularly in the 1950s, when a huge film attendance could be won only by big stars, big expense, and big literary properties with broad readerships. Ferber knew this: "I wrote the novel *Giant*. I wrote it as I wanted to write it." But Ferber went further than this, not only distancing herself from Hollywood but also denying her relationship with it: "It was not written with the idea of a motion picture sale in mind. I never have written with the idea of a motion picture sale in mind. A statement such as the one quoted at the beginning of this letter amounts to madness on the part of its instigator."

Was it really madness? Certainly Ferber had never been publicly enthusiastic about Hollywood's adaptations of her work. Only RKO's *Cimarron* won her approval, since it maintained her critique of the frontier as well as her attention to historical detail. But to say that she had "never written with the idea of a motion picture sale in mind" is a bit disingenuous. Ferber's career as a best-selling novelist was well documented, but her reputation and continued sales could not have been maintained for so long were it not for Hollywood's almost constant work on a Ferber project.

But if Ferber and Hollywood capitalized on each other, it was especially hard for Ferber to maintain her independent reputation. She had no vast publicity machine or corporate organization behind her—only her secretary, lawyer, and contacts at Doubleday. And this wasn't the first time that the studio had attempted to put words into Ferber's mouth in order to promote the film at the novel's expense. A year before, Ferber had written to Ginsberg about an "alleged" interview with Joe Hyams of the *New York Herald Tribune*. The interview, which had never taken place, was composed of doctored dialogue. Ferber fumed, "Henry, I can't and won't have this sort of thing. You must remember that my position is not that of a Hollywood writer or actor. No studio owns me. No one has the authority to send out an interview in my name without my permission . . . I am as keenly concerned as you are in the possible success of *Giant* . . . But I won't be used as a piece of studio property because that I am not, never have been, and never shall be."[108]

Ferber knew how Hollywood usually treated its writers; she spent more than thirty years making sure that her experience would be different. Her vigilance included maintaining her name as the author on every piece of publicity released for public consumption, monitoring her alleged remarks about the films in newspapers and journals, and policing the implications of Hollywood's rhetoric about her and her status as a serious historical novelist.

Reception and Race

Relations may have been strained between Ferber and her film partners, Henry Ginsberg and George Stevens, but Hollywood critics saw the film as a major triumph for Warner Bros. and the film industry as a whole. American audiences went to see *Giant* in large numbers; according to the records published in *Variety*, in 1956 it made $12 million in domestic rentals and was the third-biggest grosser behind DeMille's *Ten Commandments* and Mike Todd's *Around the World in Eighty Days* (Fig. 6.3). Critics and audiences tended to focus on two major elements of the film: the film's history of racial discrimination in Texas and James Dean's magnificent performance as Jett Rink. Ironically, in spite of

the popularity of westerns with audiences in the 1950s, reviewers tended to downplay *Giant*'s connections with the genre and instead bolstered its reputation as a prestige picture by emphasizing its historical content and the very quality of bigness that Ferber had denounced in her novel. As critic Judith Crist wrote in October 1956: "But in spite of its locale, [*Giant*,] George Stevens, the film's producer-director notes, is not a 'Western,' but rather a panorama of the American scene."[109] The studio may have planted the publicity blurb precisely because it feared that a major western would not perform at the box office. In a wire to George Stevens a month before, publicist Albert E. Sidelinger worried: "All evidence shows that to sell or suggest in any way that *Giant* is a western will hold gross index down to 16.50 which would cost 4 to 5 million in film rental. Infrequent movie-goers who now make up 75 percent of adult population just won't buy westerns—they say they see westerns on television." The interviews revealed that the "overwhelming reason why respondents who do not want to see *Giant* is because 'it looks like just another western.'"[110]

6.3. *Giant* premiere, 1956.

Giant's historical seriousness was linked to its presentation of Texas racial issues. *Newsweek* joined the chorus of critics who praised the film's tackling of a serious social issue: "For a movie of its kind, *Giant* has an odd distinction; expensive productions like this usually stand clear of controversy; *Giant*'s racial-segregation theme (involving Mexicans) will rile many a Texan and many another."[111] *Variety*'s review praised Ferber for "an unflattering vivid portrayal" of Texas racism and also Stevens and the screenwriters, who "did not flinch [from] the discrimination angle."[112] For *Variety*, *Giant* was "a powerful indictment of the Texas superiority complex. Not since Darryl F. Zanuck found the courage to make *Pinky* [1949] and *Gentleman's Agreement* [1947] has the screen spoken out with such a clear voice against group snobbery."

Other critics connected it with different milestones in Hollywood's production history. In a review for *Motion Picture Daily*, James D. Ivers compared the film's enormous scope and historical perspective to *Gone with the Wind* (1939).[113] Written by another key female American historical novelist, Margaret Mitchell, *Gone with the Wind*, though less concerned than *Giant* with right-ing racial wrongs, did focus on the unconventional perspective of a woman who was an outsider, a nonconformist, and, because of her Irishness, a racial crossover character. Although Ivers did not point out the feminist continu-ities between the books and films, he did stress the historical content as a way, ironically, of drawing attention away from a narrow "feminine perspective." Because *Giant* "covers a huge slice of that American phenomenon known as Texas from the early 20s until today," it "plants this production firmly as a landmark in motion picture history." One of Stevens's more significant marks on the adaptation was allegedly to have moved from the personal perspective of Leslie, which dominated the novel, to "the very much wider perspective made possible by the mobility of the camera." The *Hollywood Reporter* saw this widening of scope in terms of the film's social realism, arguing that *Giant* faced Texas's past and present racism and "in a very genuine way has the drumbeat of contemporary history."[114] Ferber's female protagonist and feminist history lacked mainstream credibility.

Preview audiences also responded to the film's presentation of Jim Crow laws in Texas and their effects on Mexican Americans, but were slightly more ambivalent. Surviving comment cards give a fairly complete picture of the ways in which many California audiences (who were familiar with racial clashes between white Okie and Mexican American groups during the recent Depression) responded to the film.[115] Over a period of several months (May through September 1956), filmgoers in San Diego, El Cajon, Riverside, Long Beach, Encino, and Bakersfield had a chance to make suggestions. Over 80 percent of the 300-plus viewers at each screening gave the film top ratings. In San Diego at the Preferred Theatre screening on 22 May, one of the 302 viewers wrote: "About the segregation problem—it is a good point brought out that people realise it is no good when it hits 'at home.'" An 18–30-year-old man identified the "true theme of the picture—Mexicans disliked in Texas, altho Texas did belong to Mexico." However, several men did not like the overemphasis on the segregation issues—also called "the racial stuff" and "the lecture on wetbacks." Another viewer, identified only as a Texan, disliked "the emphasis on the anti-Mexican part." Still another, who had lived in Texas at one point, said that the real segregation issue in Texas was African American discrimination.

At the Fox Theatre in Riverside, men generally disliked the racial issues, while one female viewer actually came out in favor of their treatment. Two men who were "over 45" were especially adverse to the interracial marriage of Jordan Jr. and Juana, and they also identified Mexican Americans as "wetbacks." Although previews in Encino and Long Beach in late September also generated enormously positive responses, it was the discrimination issue that got people writing their comment cards. One "over 31 year-old woman" wrote that Stevens had concentrated on the Mexican American question at the expense of Ferber's other critiques of Texas: "Not enough ridicule of Texas as in the book—wetback problem became the dominant one," she complained.

Curiously, one of the youngest viewers, a 12–17-year-old girl from San Diego, commented, "I don't think this is a picture to be shown abroad." Warner Bros. executives may have taken this comment a bit too seriously, or have had their own worries on the impact of the film abroad. The studio was obviously concerned about incurring lawsuits from the Klebergs and angering other Texas elites, but in an unusual and controversial move, studio executives acted over the heads of George Stevens's production team and edited the film version to be shown in Mexico and other Latin American countries. The *Hollywood Citizen-News* reported on 27 August 1957: "Mexico City newspapers are running angry front page stories protesting the censorship of *Giant*. The film (called *Gigante* south of the border) has had more than half an hour chopped out of it, including all references to anti-Mexican discrimination. The Edna Ferber novel enjoyed a good sale down there. Mexican critics seem agreed that there was no point to cutting the defamatory sections since a pro-Mexican moral wins out in the film. They know all about the American (uncensored) version from translated American periodicals in general circulation in Mexico."[116]

Stevens wrote at once to his and Ferber's counsel, Morris Ernst, and asked what could be done. He believed that a certain executive at Warner Bros., Benjamin Kalmenson, might have been responsible for the action. "We know that Kalmenson wanted to do this with the film for America, and also consulted with me at another time about cutting the film for England," he wrote. "I suppose this comes about due to the fact that they think they can get away with it because our interest has had no management since the first of May this year."[117]

When Stevens sent this clipping to Ferber with a note asking for her thoughts, Ferber responded that she had known about the Mexican situation for months.[118] "As I had read of this months ago, I naturally thought that you knew about the picture-cuts for Mexico," she responded. "I was appalled at the time. Also, I read that these cuts are to be made (or have been made) for all Spanish-speaking countries, including, of course, the South American Spanish-speaking countries whose audience potential is very large."[119] Ferber had her own theories about why the studio had ordered the cuts behind Stevens's back: "When I read of this the first thought I had was Texas. This, I thought, was due to Texas pressure because of the Mexican-Texas labor situation. I don't know if you have seen Texas (Mexican labor) work camps. Down around the Brownsville border I visited a ranch which was paying 25 cents an hour for Mexican labor. Texas could bring a lot of pressure to bear on Warner for a cut in the Mexican showing. I don't know what their interest would be in South America." Ferber had a point, but the real pressure may have come from oil interests offended by her portrayal of Jett Rink's racism. As early as 1948, Carey McWilliams had documented the oil elites' growing investments in Hollywood.[120]

As a Coventry, England, film review indicates, Warner Bros. did not cut the film's scenes depicting prejudice against Mexican Americans for European audiences: "The story reflects the greatness and the weakness of Texans— their drive, sturdiness, hospitality, and their rawness, obstinacy and prejudice toward the Mexican 'wetbacks' who are their economic slaves."[121] But Frank Z. Clemente translated the September 1957 issue of the Mexican periodical *Cine Universal* for the studios, and a review of *Giant* stated that Mexicans were disappointed in the film because the cutters had excised all the incidents showing white racial prejudice against Mexicans in order to avoid possible negative publicity from Mexico: "We understand that this is due to the merciless 'cutting' so as not to injure the sensibilities of the Mexicans."[122] The film was cut from twenty-two reels to nineteen reels, losing seventeen minutes of screen time. Warner Bros.' clumsy attempt at public relations backfired: "Since *Giant* was amputated of all that 'smelled' like racial discrimination, the picture remains 'cut-off,' confusing, very long and without detail in that which refers to the Benedict family. It is a shame that this happened."[123]

Stevens initially seemed interested in legally pursuing the studio's tampering with his work. However, correspondence with Morris Ernst on the subject faltered after late September 1957. By that time, the director was already at work on another project, *The Diary of Anne Frank*, and his fame from making *Giant* was ensured. Censorship issues may have seemed less important than before. But the issue was crucial enough for Warner executives to have interfered in the project. While Ferber's suspicions of Machiavellian Texas oil interests seem valid, considering the legal department's outsized worries about lawsuits from the Klebergs and McCarthy, equally important were recent public incidents of Texas prejudice with international implications. Only two years before, Texas airport officials subjected the Indian ambassador to the United States to their Jim Crow laws. The United States government had to apologize to the Indian government when Gaganvihari Lallubhai Mehta was forced to leave a dining room at Houston International Airport because, as the *New York Times* reported, "he was mistaken for a Negro."[124] This was an especially ill-timed incident for the Eisenhower government, since relations between India's prime minister Nehru and the United States had been under strain because of the premier's neutral stance toward communist governments in Asia. As the *Times* reported, "It was feared that Communist and non-Communist critics of the United States would exploit the incident to aggravate relations with India and to discredit the United States throughout Asia."

Did Juana's expulsion from the hotel beauty parlor at the end of *Giant* touch a raw nerve with some officials? Although Texas-based LULAC distanced itself from radical politics and denounced communism, other Mexican American civil rights groups, like ANMA (Asociacion Nacional Mexico-Americana), were frequently accused of communist leanings during the 1950s. In highlighting America's racial and class inequities, they problematized democratic propaganda.[125] In 1952, Ferber's public critics had excoriated her for challenging the myth of free white Texas, but they stopped short of calling her a communist. Nevertheless, Ferber's support of Mexican American civil rights caused one angry reader to sneer, "I am sure the boys in the Kremlin will be very happy about both the serialization and the book."[126] Whatever the case, studio censors eradicated all scenes of racial discrimination in the film, both the modern incidents and the ones from sequences set from 1925 through the Second World War.

The Legend of Jett Rink–James Dean

The studio may have been anxious about the number of scenes depicting Mexican American exploitation and discrimination, but it could not get enough of James Dean. For the studios, Dean represented Hollywood exploitation at its best. Since he was a studio contract star, his salary on the picture cost Warner Bros. only a pittance—$18,500, compared to Elizabeth Taylor's mammoth $177,430 and Rock Hudson's $101,667.[127] But toward the end of production, Dean's *East of Eden* and *Rebel Without a Cause* (both 1955) were released to massive acclaim, and he became a star. That September, before Stevens began postproduction and dubbing, Dean was killed in a car accident in California. Almost immediately, he was on his way to becoming one of Hollywood's greatest legends. Ferber appreciated Dean long before his untimely death. She thought Dean was "magnificent" in his role as Jett Rink, conveying the modern Texas icon's mystery, simmering menace, and unexpected humor. The two of them had met on Ferber's trips to Los Angeles and Texas and, with Dean's friend and costar Mercedes McCambridge, spent a lot of time talking and laughing on the set (Fig. 6.4).

Curiously, it seems that Warner Bros. was uncertain about how to market Dean on the picture after his death. In a letter to friends, Ferber mused, "Poor Jimmy Dean! They are now trying to play him down in the publicity. He has grown into a kind of dreadful cult."[128] Eventually, glowing reviews that spoke of his "legend" and acting genius made Warner Bros. reconsider its treatment of the dead star, and his image began to dominate publicity.[129] In 1957, Sidelinger & Co., the publicists for Stevens's production company, prepared an "ad analysis" on the film, noting that the previous April, 8.75 million people had heard of *Giant*: "At the time, the great interest was attributed to the enthusiasm for the late James Dean and the furore which had been created by the Edna Ferber novel from which Mr. Stevens made the picture."[130] Although Ferber's name continued to be associated with the picture, it was largely through the legal enforcement of her contract, which specified that her name as author appear with any advertising for the film. But the studio saw the profit in promoting Dean's contribution, and in rerelease press books in 1963 and 1970, stories on Dean easily outnumber those on Stevens, Hudson, Taylor, and Ferber. Dean's famous lounging pose in the Benedict automobile, legs stretched out and casually crossed, battered hat pulled down over his eyes, became the key selling icon for the film.

Those same California preview audiences that had argued about the number and length of *Giant*'s antisegregation scenes all agreed on one thing: James Dean was the best element in the picture. But was it just Dean's magnetic personality that made him the only thing worth looking at on the screen, or was it also Jett Rink? One of the film's most memorable sequences involves Jett marking the boundaries of his new piece of land, a bequest from Luz Benedict (McCambridge). He strides up hills, accompanied only by the score, silhouetted against the horizon, black against the light (Fig. 6.5). When

6.4. Edna Ferber (*left*) on the set of *Giant* with (*clockwise from top*)
James Dean, Victor Milan, and Mercedes McCambridge, 1955.

he finally climbs up the battered windmill and dangles his booted legs over the sides, Stevens conveys Jett's dauntless individualism and ties to former pioneers. After all, he is the only character we see reenacting the settlement and development of his land. He is the frontier hero—a man without a past, but with a future.

Jett's working-class iconoclasm, his distaste for the Benedicts and other ruling elites in Texas, his understanding of anti-Mexican prejudice and his own racism, his drive and determination, his poverty, and his success all added to his appeal to 1950s Americans. In the October 1956 edition of *Movie Secrets*, the editors did an extensive spread of James Dean images and devoted a chunk to his yet-unseen performance in *Giant*. It may have been more than a year since his death, but the Dean legend was already powerful: "Again Jimmy Dean plays a rebel . . . As Jett Rink, Jimmy portrays a man with bitter hatreds towards his 'betters' always smouldering beneath a surface that manages to be arrogant even while being polite."[131] The Horatio Alger tale has always been popular with Americans, and when the self-made man is rebellious, assertive, and slightly mysterious, he has even greater appeal. But in Ferber's novel, Jett Rink is a violent man, abusing both women and ethnic minorities. Although as a poor, landless white man, Jett is marked as neither black, brown, nor white in Texas culture, and therefore understands racial otherness, his racism is as rigid as Bick Benedict's. Stevens may have covered him with oil and reenacted the southern racial clash during the scene between him and Leslie on the white veranda of Reata, but viewers showed little awareness of these visual ambiguities. In fact, many of the California viewers who focused on Jett as the picture's highlight shared his racial outlook. Some, while claiming to abhor the Texas hypocrisy and double standards, then pointed out that they were not Mexicans and not black. As one viewer in El Cajon said of the film, there were "too many reference[s] to wetback[s]. May I add that I am not a Mexican—never met any I have cared anything about." This was the audience Ferber and Stevens had to conquer.

But what is slightly disturbing about Dean's enduring hold on the picture's memory in popular culture is that he played the unredeemed racist and the great capitalist success. If Bick Benedict learns something about the history of Texas racism at the end of the film, Jett does not. And what of Leslie, Ferber's original outsider-protagonist and vehicle for Ferber's own discussions of race and gender hierarchies? Stevens and Giant Productions believed from the beginning that a woman could not dominate and narrate a history of mod-

6.5. The iconic western hero: Jett (Dean) surveying his new homestead (*Giant*, Warner Bros., 1956).

ern Texas; Ferber's great expectations for *Giant* were never realized. Stevens bolstered Leslie's racial activism and complicated Jett's racial makeup, but censorship dulled the novel's racial and gender issues for both national and international releases. Ferber's ego as a major American writer and popular historian was also bruised. As the filmmakers shifted the focus to Jett and even to Bick and away from Leslie as the protagonist, so studio publicity and reviews lionized Stevens for the racial crusade that Ferber had truly authored. As she wrote to her editor at Doubleday in August 1957, "The thing eventually will turn out to be enormously profitable, I suppose, but it never will be worth the annoyance and irritation and time and precious energy it has cost me. I wish I could walk away from the whole thing right now and never hear of it again."[132]

But Ferber liked money and would soon regret her words. Late that year, she entered into an agreement with Warner Bros., finally executed in March 1959, in which the studio paid her $650,000 for her one-third interest in the film negative (via her partnership in Giant Productions).[133] In April 1958, much to Stevens's chagrin, the studio paid Ferber 11 percent of the film's gross from all sources over $18,750,000 for granting it the television rights. As with all of

Ferber's studio deals, Warner Bros. was legally bound to print her name with any mention of the film's title. Stevens may well have feared that control of *Giant* was slipping from his grasp. Ferber knew that in shifting her allegiance to Warner Bros., she guaranteed her continued association with the film and a lucrative income. Where *Giant* was concerned, Ferber was determined to retain and exert power. It was one of the last times that she got the better of the Hollywood system.

seven

The New Nationalism:

ICE PALACE, 1954–1960

ven as her unofficial tenure ended as *Giant*'s script vetter and production assistant, Edna Ferber was in the midst of two more frontier dramas. *Cimarron* was nearly thirty years old, and MGM was remaking RKO's masterpiece. Ferber had nothing but contempt for MGM, but realizing that she could do nothing to stop the latest remake of her work, she simply ignored the studio's letters asking for her endorsement of the script. Her health was failing, and Ferber needed all her resources to finish her final novel, *Ice Palace*. *Ice Palace* grew out of Ferber's research for *Giant* and reflected the author's predilection for historical critique and examinations of race and gender on the twentieth-century frontier.[1] But *Giant* had been a somewhat unpleasant experience for Ferber; she was determined to enjoy the process of creating *Ice Palace*.

During the production of *Giant*, Ferber planned several trips to Alaska, using them as a means of evading Hollywood and Giant Productions' publicity events.[2] After her first visit, in November 1954, she returned to New York exhilarated, and some of her excitement was transferred to her editor at

Doubleday. "I can't tell you how happy I am to hear that you are on fire again about a book," Ken McCormick wrote to her. "Something happens to your voice and your whole manner when you begin to become interested in writing."[3] But Ferber wasn't just on a pleasure trip; her new novel about Alaska mixed the legacy of nineteenth-century frontier history with current controversial political issues about economic exploitation, race relations, and statehood. For years, wealthy Alaskans, along with corporate executives based in Seattle and Washington, D.C., successfully fought working- and middle-class Alaskans' demands for a territorial legislature, regulation of the fisheries, and, later, statehood. But since the end of the Second World War, the statehood movement and proponents of racial equality (the other major long-term controversy in Alaska) had gained power.[4] Ferber always loved a battle—particularly a historical fight for political and personal freedom. From the beginning of her research, she consulted the foremost pro-statehood, antisegregation political advocate in the state, Governor (later Senator) Ernest Gruening. Gruening also doubled as the territory's most popular historian (*The State of Alaska*, 1954), and Ferber's relationship with him would anchor the political discourse of her own narrative.[5]

Ice Palace represented a return to many of Ferber's old historical themes: generational conflict, environmental and racial exploitation, the problematic masculine frontier ideology, and the new generation of mixed-race American women. But many literary critics would attack the book for its apparent enthusiasm for some of those old-style frontier values while ignoring the racial arguments driving her story of mixed-blood Christine Storm. However, Ferber's instinct to publish the book shortly before Congress voted on Alaska's admission as the forty-ninth state not only guaranteed her best-seller status, but also made her a major American social and political figure. It also helped her negotiate another fantastic contract with Warner Bros.

Narratives about Alaska had been a niche market of the western genre since the 1920s. Between Charlie Chaplin (*The Gold Rush*, 1925) and Rex Beach (*The Spoilers*, 1914, 1923, 1930, 1942, 1955), American filmmakers projected a successful image of gold rushes, dance-hall girls, Eskimos, whiskey brawls, and ice. Possibly Jack Warner thought this was what he was getting when he bought *Ice Palace*'s screen rights without reading the book. Some hearts sank when they read the female-centered political and racial drama. But initially, scriptwriters were less interested in the current political drama than in *Ice Palace*'s potential as a racial drama. If it was not another *Spoilers*, it could be the

next *Giant*. But after one of the most labored and expensive script developments in Hollywood history, Warner Bros. obscured many of the interracial
and feminist issues and instead exploited the book as a two-fisted, masculine frontier melodrama. Although it lacked the historical clichés of the gold
rush made familiar to audiences through countless remakes of *The Spoilers*,
the modern battles of statehood and race were less important than the exotic
scenery and "last frontier" masculinity, which were well known from other
Alaska-set westerns, including *Alaska* (Monogram, 1944), *Alaska Seas* (Paramount, 1954), *Alaska Passage* (1959, Associated Producers), and *The Far Country*
(MGM, 1954).

While Ferber saw Alaska as America's last and greatest western landscape,
she avoided the gold-dust travelogue legacy of Rex Beach and Jack London so
popular with Hollywood. Ferber's challenge to the racial and gender dimensions of America's frontier legacy were unchanged, even enhanced, since the
writing of *Giant* and *Cimarron*. However, following the releases of *Ice Palace* and
Cimarron in 1960, film and literary critics reconfigured her reputation. Edna
Ferber became an old-fashioned writer of American epics; her interests in
narrative and history were dismissed as literary flaws in an author who had
never focused on characterization beyond its broader resonance with historical events and ideologies. Her fascination with political, sexual, and personal
freedom was first trivialized and then ignored. This popular view of Ferber
has persisted since her death, even as critics have forgotten *Ice Palace*'s unique
multiracial protagonist and Ferber's lifelong fascination with multiracial
American women. Mixed-race women figure prominently in Edna Ferber's
fiction, but only in her last novel, *Ice Palace*, does Ferber return to *Cimarron*'s
questions about the frontier, race, and the persistence of Native America in
the twentieth-century West. Although literary historian Donna Campbell
cites Ferber's interest in mixed-race marriages, her study ignored Yancey's ancestry and failed to mention *Ice Palace*.[6] Ferber's last historical novel, an epic
of twentieth-century Alaska, was doomed, like its subject, to be "an unheeded
stepchild . . . neglected."[7]

But from the moment Ferber announced her post-*Giant* plans, Ken Mc-
Cormick and Doubleday were enthusiastic. The publisher gave her a $10,000
advance and a 15 percent royalty on the retail price. McCormick, who worried
that the temperamental Ferber would not be impressed by the terms, wrote to
her: "Against your ultimate earnings of this book, this is modest indeed, but it
is tangible evidence of our interest."[8] Ferber agreed to the contract, but as her

research and writing progressed, kept a wary eye on the publishing market about Alaska. When in May 1955, an article appeared in *Fortune* about Alaska, she worried to McCormick that other writers would claim-jump her subject. He soothed her: "I certainly wouldn't worry . . . I know you're uneasy that this might be a tip to other authors to do a quickie about Alaska, but the fact remains that no one's quickie, or anybody else's novel for that matter, would be the book that you will write."[9] As she communicated more of her ideas for the novel, Ken McCormick responded enthusiastically: "This isn't going to be just any book by Edna Ferber; this is one of the most challenging books you've ever come to grips with."[10] Alaska was several times larger than Texas, and shared many of the problems that plagued that state: racism, segregation, environmental exploitation, and a sentimental, jealously guarded investment in the myth of the "last frontier." Ferber planned that this book, perhaps her last, would have a proportionally bigger impact.

Frontier Exploitation

Nearly twenty years after the U.S. government purchased Alaska from Russia, H. H. Bancroft published the first detailed history of the territory, *The History of Alaska, 1730-1885*.[11] Popular novelists such as Jack London and Rex Beach then wrote Alaska into the American imaginary. Popular historians also stressed the continuities between the frontier experience in the American West and in Alaska in the 1890s, and increasingly in the twentieth century, they called Alaska the nation's "last frontier." However, Alaska did not enjoy equal status with the rest of the West within American frontier mythology. Surprisingly, in 1893, when Frederick Jackson Turner wrote his synopsis of frontier development, he failed to mention the territory. Mary Lee Davis summarized Turner's attitude and his legacy when she titled her popular history *Uncle Sam's Attic*. Davis laughed at those who argued that "the Frontier has departed": "The American Frontier is not closed to our generation, for Alaska is still gloriously open to us."[12] But the U.S. government treated Alaska somewhat differently from other territories that had grown into states through democratic political demand. For decades, Congress and the president had helped thwart the established course of frontier development.

Between 1867 and 1897, the U.S. government showed little or no interest in the territory. In 1897, news of the Klondike gold rush temporarily altered the national attitude toward Alaska, but most Americans viewed the territory as something rich to exploit, not to develop. Native Alaskans and permanent residents could neither regulate nor tax the massive fishing and mining corporations that annually carried off millions of dollars in revenue—and put nothing into the coffers of the territorial government. Often, even jobs at the canneries were difficult for native Alaskans to obtain, since outside CEOs routinely hired cheap itinerant Asian labor for the canning season. Congress turned a blind eye to these lucrative dealings. Even the Department of the Interior ignored Alaska; its *Statistic of Indian Tribes, Indians Agencies and Indian Schools of Every Character* (1899) listed over three hundred tribes in the states and territories, but completely ignored those in Alaska. As historian and governor Ernest Gruening noted, "The complete omission and ignoring of the existence of the Alaska aborigines in this official publication was symptomatic of the department's attitude toward those particular Alaskan charges . . . In that respect, however, it did not differ materially from the federal attitude toward Alaskans in general."[13] It wasn't until 1926 that Turner formally recognized Alaska as America's "last frontier." "The opening of the Alaska wilds," he wrote, "furnished a new frontier and frontier spirit to the Pacific Northwest as well as to the nation."[14]

Although the national exploitation of Alaska continued, a group of Alaska natives intent on self-determination, a limited number of Washington politicians, and popular historians stressed both its frontier spirit and the U.S. government's colonization and economic exploitation of the territory. The impact of the Second World War pushed many who were formerly ambivalent about Alaska statehood to give their support. A population boom driven by veterans returning to take advantage of Alaska's 160-acre homestead and veteran acts, a troubled salmon industry, and awareness of Alaska's proximity to Russia convinced Americans that the territory needed to become a state.[15]

In planning *Ice Palace*, Ferber was most influenced by a history written in this tradition, Gruening's *The State of Alaska* (1954). In the fall of 1954, she wrote to Gruening, asking about the status of his forthcoming book. He replied with enthusiasm, guessing that the book "will give you a great deal of the background which you will probably want . . . Now I am elated at the thought that you are thinking of Alaska and may write a novel about that wonderful part of America."[16] Gruening had read *Giant* and knew how well Ferber could cut Texas elites down to size. Just as Carey McWilliams had once endorsed Ferber's perspective on Mexican Americans and their exploitation by Anglo elites, Gruening eagerly anticipated an exposé of Alaska's economic and political parasites in Seattle and Washington, D.C. He introduced Ferber to other prominent Alaskans, and they too looked forward to what she would do in the book. Real estate and farming businessman Roger Hurlock wrote to her: "If Texas needed a good 'debunking' (and it did!), Alaska needs one even more. I am certainly not an authority on the Territory, having been a resident here for only six years; but I am just Johnny-come-lately enough to take a hard-bitten and detached—and somewhat dim—view of some of the shenanigans here."[17] Gruening also anticipated that the book would duplicate the triumph of *Giant* and benefit from the sort of publicity Ferber was capable of generating: "I hope it will be as successful as *Giant*, and in every way have a similarly brilliant run on the screen."[18] The politician could not have asked for a better public advocate for Alaska statehood.

Gruening's awareness of Alaska's frontier ties was tempered by a sense of its status as a colonized and exploited territory. However much an independent pioneer spirit helped build modern Alaska, as he and many others saw it, the territory was still controlled by absentee landlords in Washington. He had always been a staunch supporter of statehood, and in the late 1950s, more Alaskans came to share his political commitment. In early 1956, following the Alaska Constitutional Convention, he wrote to Ferber: "For the first time the label of colonialism has been pinned squarely on Uncle Sam where, in the case of Alaska, I regret to say, it properly belongs—and has for some time. If 'ideas are weapons,' I am hopeful that this may prove to be an implement to help pry us loose from the Federal embrace."[19]

However, in the government's almost total neglect of the territory and refusal to allow traditional squatters' rights and homesteading, Gruening felt that Native Americans had some advantages: "For the first seventeen years of United States rule over Alaska, the aboriginal inhabitants . . . were as devoid of attention, or even mention, as was the population as a whole." As he reasoned in 1954, "They became, by virtue of the organic act of 1884, in one respect at least, a mildly privileged or at least less disadvantaged, group, as compared with subsequently arriving Americans." For the act provided "that the Indians or other persons . . . shall not be disturbed in the possession of any lands actually in their use or occupation or now claimed by them."[20] The natives' right of occupation was, in other words, reaffirmed, while all later settlers had to wait decades for land laws that would guarantee possession. However, Gruening continued, "The Indians and other aborigines were not disturbed in the possession of any lands actually in their use, nor indeed have they been since. But they were gravely disturbed in what to them was more vital than land—the supply of the marine and terrestrial wild-life upon which they subsisted."[21]

White settlers, Eskimos, Inuit, and other Native Alaskans were all under threat by cannery monopolies, whaling industries, overtrapping, and a lack of federal spending on education and transportation. But in his 1954 history, Gruening highlights the unique racial amalgamation in Alaska as a happy distinction from the ethic strife that troubled other American frontiers (and from the ongoing problems in the American South, where controversies like school desegregation and antimiscegenation laws still persisted and made headlines in national papers). Trappers, fisherman, and prospectors had all intermarried with native women since the nineteenth century, and there was a significant mixed-blood population in the territory. Gruening points out that by the 1920s native men were participating in local government (like William and Louis Paul), and by the 1940s, Alaska elected the first (nonvoting) Native American senators.[22] In 1945, the Alaska legislature passed its first antidiscrimination law. Governor Gruening was one of its staunchest supporters.

But all these racial gains did not come without a struggle, and Gruening's characterization of Alaska multiculturalism, targeted at a national audience in order to point out Alaska's social maturity and readiness for statehood, was a bit exaggerated. Racism among white Alaskans was rampant in the twentieth century and also targeted mixed-bloods, who, like their full-blooded Native counterparts, were educated in separate schools, forced to sit in separate seats at theatres, refused admission in some restaurants, and denied access to USO clubs during the Second World War. It was the particularly harsh treatment of Alaskan natives by military officials like General Simon Bolivar Buckner, Jr., and the forced removal and internment of the Aleuts in 1942 that finally forced Gruening and others to take political action.

Though much credit was due to Gruening in getting the 1945 antidiscrimination law passed, native-rights advocates (and mixed-blood Creoles) Elizabeth and Roy Peratrovich were equally influential. But it was the experience of Alberta Schenck, a half Eskimo teenager from Nome, Alaska, that generated the final public support for the bill. Schenck was thrown out of a theatre for sitting in the "whites only" section, and had the foresight to send a telegram to Gruening when she was in jail.[23] Though the bill was hailed as a major breakthrough by native-rights advocates, racism persisted in Alaska.

As Roger Hurlock pointed out to Ferber, the myth of racial equality and multiculturalism in Alaska persisted into the 1950s, and was just a myth: "It is said Alaskans tend to take an unusually liberal attitude on racial questions and the rights of minorities . . . Only today I heard a respected citizen of Juneau, and one who should know better, refer contemptuously to 'those dirty Indians' in asking one of his own play-begrimed children if that boy wanted to be just like them."[24]

Ice Palace, Race, and Frontier Myths

Ferber incorporated much of Gruening's historical perspective within *Ice Palace*. As she remembered in her 1963 autobiography, "Here, then, was this Alaska, paradoxical, almost unknown generally; a prize, a treasure potentially for almost any country in the world other than wasteful careless over-fat North America . . . vital, handsome, rugged, containing who knew what treasure; hardworking ambitious, resourceful."[25] She used her four main protagonists as historical shorthand for Alaska's post-gold-rush history: "Perhaps if all historical data of the past half century in the Alaska Territory had been lost, swept from memory and from record, leaving Thor Storm, Czar Kennedy, Christine Storm, and this Bridie Ballantyne only, there might still have emerged from these informal records a fairly comprehensive history of the manners and mores and events of the time and place."[26]

Alaska was an anomaly: a frontier territory with its nineteenth-century rough-and-ready spirit persisting well into the twentieth century. One *Ice Palace* character, iconic westerner Bridie Ballantyne, compares more-traditional American frontiers with Alaska: "We're . . . two times the size of that bitty Texas they're always yawping about."[27] Alaskans may not have the press and political lobby of other classic frontier environments, Bridie argues, but their qualities of resilience, independence, and courage were not merely manufactured for the tourist industry or the movies. At one point, Ferber describes old-timers watching Texas-based western films on television: "They regarded these melodramas as a tolerant but undeceived parent views the capering of the children playing cops and robbers."[28] This kind of frontier was a mere dead myth, but the "wilderness" and its challenging climate still existed in modern Alaska. Although Ferber perceived the continuities between the classic and new frontiers, she believed that Alaska must become a new kind of western territory—it must make up for the ravages of the nineteenth-century frontiers. As Thor Storm, trapper, newspaperman, and grandfather of the mixed-blood Christine, remarks, Alaska must be different: "Not like the history of other parts of the United States in the old days. They grabbed and schemed and kept it for themselves—the land and the metals and the forests and the streams. This time, the last of the free land, it must be for the good of the people. All of them."[29]

However fascinating she found the twentieth-century frontier paradox, Ferber was arguably more occupied with questions of race and cultural integration in Alaska. Although Gruening had been instrumental in getting the first antidiscrimination laws passed in 1945, he saw the native Alaskans' history since 1867 within the same framework of national neglect that dominated the history of white settlement in the territory. Ferber appropriates Gruening's theme of economic and political exploitation, but rather than equating the "conquered" territory with an equally noble but helpless Native American hero, she maps Alaska's struggle onto the body of mixed-blood Christine Storm: "Visitors often mistook her for something purely ornamental like the scenery. They were completely wrong. They were wrong about the scenery too. Hidden in those fabulous peaks and creeks and torrents were copper and gold and uranium and platinum and cobalt and tin and tungsten and nickel and lead; in the tundra and flatlands coal and oil; in the vast streams and inlets and seas millions of finned and furred creatures from salmon to seals to whales. But they were not for the casual passer-by".[30] She, like Yancey Cravat, is no doomed vanishing American or passive mixed-race Ramona, but one whose mixed native blood will prepare Alaska for its twentieth-century frontier struggle for statehood and self-determination. As Christine Storm remarks to her grandfather Thor, he cannot tell the difference between her and Alaska.[31] In fact, Ferber explicitly makes Christine, the mixed-blood Eskimo and Scandinavian American, the modern protagonist of *Ice Palace*. Christine's unique racial and cultural background (at college, she studies modern history and "race studies") gets as much text as Alaska's fight for statehood.

The first time Ferber describes Christine, she brings out her visual ambiguity and startling beauty: "But then, even the girl's appearance had a tinge of incredulity. Her eyes were black, her hair golden. Baffled by the unusual combination, strangers assumed that the yellow hair was tinted. The eyes were long, narrow, and ever so slightly pinched at the outer corners. The skin was warmly golden, but this, too, was complicated by a faintly pink touch on the rather high cheekbones like the flush on the cheek of a good English peach."[32]

Everyone ponders Christine's appearance, from puzzled but admiring white pilots to her mixed-blood romantic counterpart, Ross, to her Scandinavian grandfather who married a native woman. Christine is proud of her mixed status, and she treats Seattle outsiders to an Alaska history lesson when she tells them of her mixed identity.[33]

Ferber highlights the unique history of racial amalgamation in Alaska, from the descendants of Russian-Eskimo Creoles to the children of white air force pilots and Eskimo women, but this multiracial frontier also has its traces of prejudice. However, Ferber attributes these to part of the old, outside frontier legacy. Zeb "Czar" Kennedy, a twentieth-century robber baron, fears the mixed-blood Ross as a possible suitor for Christine and calls all Eskimos "mongrels" and, with a touch of southern social Darwinism, "monkeys."[34] Mainstream Alaska society has a more inclusive and multicultural perspective on people like Christine: "Real streak of Eskimo in her, too . . . Nothing surprises us, nothing mixes us up . . . Maybe we're more civilized than they are Outside."[35] Ferber is perhaps too gentle with white Alaskans' prejudice; she makes Czar, the symbol for "outside" exploitation of Alaska, the main source of racism in Baranof.

Outsiders lack Alaskans' pride in pluralism: "We're people—all kinds of people—just like you in the States," Christine explains to an outsider. "We're white and black and brown."[36] When an outsider meets Ross in Alaska, he asks his nationality, evidently believing one of mixed Eskimo blood must be "foreign," Eskimo, and therefore not part of America. Ross, like Christine, challenges this traditional, racist view of the Native American: "My folks live in a frame house in Oogruk . . . they have a radio and a phonograph and an outboard motor and a sewing machine and they eat steaks when they can afford them and the girls wear silk stocking and read *Life* and the movie magazines, and they go to the movies."[37] Outsiders' views of Native Alaskans are as dated as the perceptions of tourists who come to Alaska in 1958 and expect to prospect for gold and drink in a saloon. For years, Alaska's Eskimo and Inuit populations have adapted what they chose from white cultures, just as Natives and European settlers have intermarried to form a new kind of "native" American.

In Christine, Ferber created one of her most intriguing and complex characters. To a certain extent, she seems overwhelmed by the wealth and power of Czar, the rhetoric of Thor, and the teachings of Bridie. Although Bridie tolerates some of Christine's rebelliousness, both men seem to resent her questioning of their statements about Alaska's future; even Thor dismisses her own judgments with "I brought you here to see, not to talk. You can do your talking later, perhaps five years from now."[38] While Thor tries to shape her attitude toward statehood, and Zeb tries to engineer a politically expedient marriage for her, Christine has other ideas, preferring to go to college and plan a career as a congresswoman or future governor of Alaska.[39] Thor, Czar, and Bridie (nurse, mother figure, chamber of commerce, and memoirist) have a stronger appeal in some sense precisely because they represent Alaska's past, and Ferber was a historical novelist. Christine embodied Alaska's history of racial mixing, but she was the future, and still an unknown quantity.

In spite of Ferber's preoccupation with a new generation of mixed-blooded Americans, Doubleday's publicity department ignored the racial angle and instead combined the legacy of the old pioneer opposites, Zeb Kennedy and Thor Storm, with the struggle for statehood. The back cover claims: "More than a personal struggle of wills, this decades-long conflict between Thor Storm and Czar Kennedy is in fact Alaska's long-fought struggle toward statehood." But Doubleday was even more invested in pushing Ferber as America's premier historical novelist and adding a new, angry, political dimension to her profile: "Edna Ferber has summoned up all her vast natural resources as a superior novelist to depict today's Alaska in *Ice Palace* . . . This is an angry novel, telling of the fifty-year battle between two titans trying to dominate Alaska's future. And this is the story of their lovely young granddaughter, Christine Storm, who had to choose between two younger titans—a choice that stood, in a way, for Alaska's future." Doubleday claimed she was "America's most famous woman novelist" and mapped her literary territory: "The whole panorama of America—the Midwest of *So Big*, the Oklahoma of *Cimarron*, the Wisconsin of *Come and Get It*, the Seattle of *Great Son*, the Louisiana and New York of *Saratoga Trunk*, the Mississippi of *Show Boat*, and the Texas of *Giant*. *Ice Palace*, with its heroic theme, its powerfully conceived characters, and its life-loving vigor, is in the matchless Ferber manner." Ferber's literary progress strangely paralleled the westward obsession of American expansion, and Doubleday, like America, seemed caught by the aura of national size. It was not the historical content that drove Ferber's publicity on the dust jacket, but the sprawl of her settings and the physical territory she claimed in American literature.

The Harriet Beecher Stowe of Statehood

The publication of *Ice Palace* was beautifully timed, and Ferber had worked hard to get the manuscript in before Congress voted on the statehood bill in mid-1958. Her editor at Doubleday liked the publicity angle involved, but worried that she was hurrying. "I agree with you that if the book could come out before Statehood it would be that much more in its favor," he wrote. "I simply didn't mean that you should get involved in a political race while creating a piece of literature."[40] But Ferber responded, "Though you thought that Statehood would make no difference in the book's timeliness, I feel that it should come out before that possible event."[41] Wanting this to be a timely work of literature and contemporary history, she sent nearly all the manuscript to McCormick by September. Soon Hollywood heard about the impending publication of *Ice Palace*, and Charles Vidor, a representative from Columbia named Albert Johnson, and agents representing United Artists contacted her in the autumn of 1957 about producing the film.[42] Did they hope *Ice Palace* would outgross *Giant*, even as Alaska geographically dwarfed Texas?

Ferber let Gruening know how close she was to finishing and revealed her title. His response was mixed. Although he looked forward to reading it, "Alaskans are—and will be—unhappy about the title. For ninety years they have battled against the misconception that Alaska is a land of snow and ice, an arctic waste hardly fit for human (white!) habitation. That belief—widespread outside of Alaska—has handicapped the stepchild. They would have been delighted with the title 'Great Land' which is what A-la-as-ka in the Aleut language signified. Can't you change it?"[43] But Ferber remembered her less-than-successful novel about Seattle, *Great Son*, and didn't want to jinx her work with too much self-conscious bigness. Also, Gruening missed Ferber's irony; as *Giant* had demystified the bigness of Texas and Texas men, so *Ice Palace* would reveal the fallacies about America's free "last frontier." As one Petersburg, Alaska, paper wrote a few months later, "*Ice Palace* Melts Igloo Myth."[44]

In spite of Gruening's initial worry about the title, many Americans found that reading Ferber's book helped clarify the national debates over statehood. It was also the first time that she would receive political recognition for her work. In March 1958, Gruening wrote to her: "You will be delighted to know that *Ice Palace*, even in advance of publication, is materially helping the Statehood cause."[45] He drew her attention to a *Denver Post* article published earlier in the month in which Alaska statehood got two huge sources of support:

the case was covered on television by Edward Murrow and in Ferber's latest novel:

> Later this month, statehood for Alaska will get another powerful boost from an unexpected source when Edna Ferber's first novel in five years, *Ice Palace*, is issued. Miss Ferber, whose books automatically become best-sellers over night, has written this time about Alaska and Alaskans. Her most sympathetic characters are ones, who, in the contemporary scene, are all plugging for Alaska's acceptance as a state. Contrasted with them are the "exploiters," who take what they can get from Alaska but who would keep the territory in an indefinite state of vassalage. Alaskans reading the book may well recall the political effectiveness of a former American lady novelist, Harriet Beecher Stowe, whose *Uncle Tom's Cabin* made history.

Yet again Ferber was compared to Stowe. Her friends Dan and Linda Melnick of ABC sent her a playful wire: "Congratulations Dear Harriet Beecher Hawaii Next."[46] Ferber's reputation as a twentieth-century Stowe, dating back to her creation of tragic mulatta Julie Laverne, persisted in the public mind. Several years after Alaska achieved statehood, Gruening compiled an Alaska reader for the Appleton-Century Press, which included Ferber's work. The editor of the press wrote that Gruening "reminds the reader that the newspaper reviewers called your book the *Uncle Tom's Cabin* of the crusade for statehood."[47]

By then, Ferber may have been used to the comparison, but unlike the circumstances surrounding *Giant's* reception, Ferber's recognized connection with Stowe and politically conscious literature bore significant political results. With *Ice Palace*, her political impact was too formidable to ignore, particularly where American women were concerned. As the *Denver Post* story put it: "Congressmen dallying with the statehood bills, especially the one pertaining to Alaska, will return home next summer to find a great number of their lady constituents have just read *Ice Palace*, and that they have suddenly become tremendously interested in the book's locale. They are apt to have greater faith, too, in Miss Ferber's report than in any alibi a congressman can invent. And right when the November election comes up, *Ice Palace* will doubtless be at the peak of the best seller lists. A shrewd politician will not underestimate the power of a lady novelist."[48] This awareness of Ferber's power was directly connected to her impact on female readers and voters;

like Hollywood critics, political newspapermen realized the extent of women's cultural and political control.

Ice Palace was even mentioned in the *Congressional Record*—"Edna Ferber's New Novel Emphasizes Case for Alaskan Statehood," the headline read. On 8 May 1958, the Honorable Richard L. Neuberger of Oregon addressed the Senate: "There is also extant in the nation today a new novel by the gifted American writer, Edna Ferber, entitled *Ice Palace*. Several years ago Mrs. Neuberger and I had the privilege of entertaining Miss Ferber at luncheon in the Senate dining room when she was visiting Washington with that illustrious advocate of Alaskan statehood, Delegate E. L. 'Bob' Bartlett. As a result of her visit to Alaska under the auspices of Delegate and Mrs. Bartlett, Edna Ferber has written a novel which will bring to millions of readers the case for Alaskan statehood in dramatic and vivid form."[49] Neuberger went on to cite a prominent Oregon news editorial that drew parallels between Texas (*Giant*) and Alaska (*Ice Palace*) in her last two novels: "She could poke fun at Texas, but she is deadly serious about Alaska." The editorial was one of the few to mention that Leslie Lynnton "raged against the exclusiveness of the male talk of booted Texans" and that "the heroine of *Ice Palace* does the same when Alaskan males huddle." Neuberger concluded: "The outside will be hearing much of Miss Ferber's case for Alaskan statehood. The book is already among the best sellers, and motion-picture rights have been sold for more than a half-million dollars. Congress has just a few months to meet the challenge of statehood. If it fails to do so, as it has failed in the past, it can properly be cast among the villains in *Ice Palace*."

When the book was published in the early spring of 1958, the Alaskan response fractured along statehood persuasions. George Sundborg of the *Fairbanks Daily News-Miner* told Ferber that he loved it and claimed that the *Anchorage Daily News* had given it a bad review because of its editor's antistatehood stance. "Interestingly enough," he wrote, "the paper was started by, or at least with the help of the money of, the man who I think served as a model for 'Czar' Kennedy" (He was thinking of cannery magnate Austin Eugene "Cap" Lathrop).[50] Doubleday's April 1958 press release, entitled "*Ice Palace* Generates Heat," quoted Alaskan papers like the *Petersburg Press*: "This book won't make the Seattle Chamber of Commerce too happy as it indicates how the stateside groups are bleeding Alaska and oppose statehood for the territory. The Seattle Chamber of Commerce's refusal to endorse statehood sort of bears out novelist Ferber's contention."[51] Just before Alaska finally won statehood on

7 July 1958, Alaskan Henry Vidal wrote to thank her: "Alaska statehood in a great measure has been due to your magnificent book *Ice Palace*."[52]

Many critics across the nation were caught by the way Ferber's novel enhanced the cause for statehood. The novel was too powerful to ignore. Many reviewers mentioned the Stowe connection. The *Christian Science Monitor* commented: "With statehood for Alaska still in the offing, *Ice Palace* may be the most formidable example of fiction as propaganda since *Uncle Tom's Cabin*."[53] Others focused upon Ferber's reputation as a nationally known historical novelist. The *San Francisco Chronicle* reported: "Miss Ferber needs no words of introduction. Her latest novel ranks high on the best seller lists throughout the country." The *Charlotte Observer* wrote: "She has once more turned her facility for ridicule upon governmental high brass, upon even the halls of Congress itself; upon racial prejudice, upon social hypocrisy, upon all the things she has fought all these years."[54] Alice Dixon Bond of the *Boston Globe* added that Ferber's novels "have illumined for us many facets of our American history, customs and civilization."[55]

Still others made the connection between Ferber's identity as a powerful female historical novelist and her huge contingent of thinking American women readers. An advertisement in the *Ladies' Home Journal*, Ferber's frequent choice for the serialization of her work, proclaimed: "Never Underestimate the Power of a Woman!" The ad depicted one woman reading *Ice Palace*, then lots of women reading the book, and then finally headlines of the *New York Star* with the announcement of Alaska statehood in headlines. "Not the power of the women's magazine whose editorial ideas spur more women to *action* than any other magazine in the United States—from Point Barrow to Scarsdale," the advertisement read.[56]

It was Christine Storm whom reviewers paid attention to. The *San Francisco Chronicle* also made a connection between Alaska's history and Ferber's female protagonist: "If you haven't yet read this romantic, fiery story of a young girl caught in the conflict that surrounds America's relationship with Alaska today, you're missing one of the most timely and forceful novels of the year."[57] Ferber's strong female protagonist also caught the eye of Walter Havighurst of the *Saturday Review*: "Her heroine . . . here is the difference between Miss Ferber and the 'modern' novelists, and a reason for the multitude of her readers. She still sees people in large dimensions, strong enough to be actors rather than to be acted upon. This novel contains a whole gallery of them, with Christine Storm in the center."[58] Havighurst even mentioned

Christine's mixed blood, something that only a handful of critics mentioned directly. Harrison Smith's article in the *Saturday Review* also mentioned that Ferber's heroine was a mixed-blood: "A large number of Texans expressed their profound dislike of Miss Ferber's *Giant*, and the elder citizens who find a copy of *Ice Palace* in a Nome bookstore may be equally disturbed. She appears to be as familiar with the life of the Eskimos as she is with the Americans who have found a strange delight in the excitement and danger of the long polar nights."[59] The *Cleveland Plain Dealer*, *Charlotte Observer*, and the *Vermont Catholic Tribune* all mentioned Ferber's attack on racism in Alaska and her mixed-race heroine.[60] Curiously, Ernest Gruening, who wrote the review for the *New York Herald Tribune*, avoided discussing Christine's interracial heritage, obliquely calling the book "the first all-Alaskan novel."[61]

Cold War in Alaska?

Ferber also tied the controversies surrounding Alaska statehood and racism to the ongoing Cold War. Many critics acknowledged Alaska's successful bid for statehood as a reflection of the Eisenhower government's heightened awareness of the state's proximity to the Soviet Union, especially after the Aleutian campaigns and the U.S. plans to invade Japan via Alaska in the Second World War. Ferber made many historical connections between Russia's economic expansion in Alaska in the eighteenth and nineteenth centuries and America's more recent occupation of the territory. But she was no cold warrior; she did not endorse statehood as a means of checkmating the USSR's ambitions in the Pacific. However, her attitude toward the Soviet Union was difficult to gauge. On the one hand, the robber baron and statehood opponent Zeb Kennedy is nicknamed "Czar" by his archrival, Thor.[62] Kennedy's ambitions to dominate the Alaskan economy and stamp out its political activism are likened to those of the Russian dictators.

But Ferber complicates this critique of Russia. Czar attempts to demonize Christine's plans to study modern history and race relations as those of "a long-faced Commie."[63] Russia may have sold the territory to the United States in 1867, but its frontier legacy persists. On Christine's first major tour of northwest Alaska, she meets and admires many Creoles, the descendants of Russian traders and native women, and sees traces of the old Russian Orthodox Church in Sitka. Ferber even named Christine's fictional hometown and the center of the narrative Baranof, after the famous Russian explorer and trader Aleksandr Baranov. And Christine is made to feel the physical proximity of the other empire. As they pass between Big Diomede (Soviet) and Little Diomede (U.S.), Thor explains how natives of the Soviet-held island deride the western "freedoms" of the United States: "We have been told about you, we know you are slaves, all the people of Alaska are slaves, they cannot even say who shall be their President. But rest, be patient, one day we will come and free you."[64]

This was what many former statehood opponents in Washington were afraid of. Toward the end of the Second World War, popular historian Daniel Henderson compared the frontier ambitions of the two allies in *From the Volga to the Yukon: The Story of the Russian March to Alaska and California, Paralleling Our Own Westward Trek* (1944). Henderson believed that studying the Russians "when they were occupying American territory" would have future value for readers, who could decide "whether Russian ambitions and marches under the Czars, were different from what they will be under the Soviet Union."[65] Henderson's story of exploration, trade, exploitation, ethnic cleansing, and racial mixing put American expansion in perspective. Ferber also argues, against Turner, that the frontier experience was not uniquely American and, in *Ice Palace*, refuses to endorse either Russian or American frontier practices. Both were simply part of Native Alaska's greater history. As mixed-blood Ross Guildenstern remarks to one white tourist, "Eskimos don't need civilization. Your kind, I mean . . . And maybe in another two thousand years we'd still be here, cosy as anything, waiting for a new white race to come along and discover us."[66]

In the Pacific edition of the *Wall Street Journal*, Doubleday placed an advertisement for the book targeted to a West Coast audience: "If you care about the issues involved in Alaska statehood . . . or if you want an accurate cross-section of public opinion on big business in the Northwest, you should read this best-selling novel." Roger O'Mara of the *New York Star* wrote: "The author preaches to some degree in her evident desire for statehood for Alaska, but it is not to an annoying degree. Its closeness to Russia is emphasized and international politics enters as the men from Siberia jibe at the Alaskans as slaves who cannot vote for their President."[67] In April, *Herald Tribune* reporter Emma Bugbee noted that both Ferber and John Gunther were honored at a Waldorf-Astoria lunch given by the paper and the American Booksellers Association. Gunther had written a recent best seller about modern Russia (*Inside Russia Today*, 1958), which was not a condemnation. After statehood, Roscoe Drummond of the *New York Herald Tribune* wrote an article entitled "Alaska—Next to Russia, Yet So Far," in which he mentioned that now that Alaska was a state, Russia was thwarted in its designs to recover the territory.[68]

Although reviewers praised Ferber's grasp of contemporary political issues and history, they attacked her ability and national reputation as a novelist. Charles Poore of the *New York Times* wrote: "Her story is too repetitious and disorderly to win a prize in the world of literature. But I shouldn't be surprised at all to hear it had helped measurably to win statehood for Alaska." Kathleen Graham was more explicit: "Considered as a survey of Alaska; its history, geography, industry, people, hopes and ambitions *Ice Palace* is good. Considered as a novel it is terrible . . . As I read this it became increasingly obvious to me that Miss Ferber ought to have written a non-fiction book about Alaska and its unique problems . . . But the novel is the wrong medium of expression."[69] Were novels incompatible with serious ideas and issues?

Most credited her with shrewd business acumen in selling the movie rights to Hollywood even before publication, whatever her gifts as a novelist. In the *Wichita Falls (TX) Times*, a reviewer reasoned: "Perhaps this characteristic—Ferber's ability to get the feel, smell, atmosphere, excitement, legends, traditions, prejudices, hopes and frustrations of a community down on paper—makes characterization secondary and aids in the success of adaptation to celluloid. For Edna Ferber has done right well—an understatement—in selling movie rights."[70] In Anchorage, one paper compared the somewhat repetitive structure of the novel to Alaska's own pattern of historical development: "They need not blame Miss Ferber if the story seems repetitious. That is the history of Alaska—repetition ad infinitum, of the same old problems from generation to generation. The story of Alaska is repetitious and anyone who tells it must be guilty of the same."[71] But George Sundborg was a bit more caustic: "There doesn't seem to this reviewer to be much of a plot and Hollywood is going to have to start practically from scratch to produce a movie from it. Alaska is the book's hero, drawn often with dazzling accuracy, but seldom doing anything which will look like much before the cameras."[72] The novel certainly would pose problems for Warner Bros.' screenwriters.

Warner Bros. and Ferber's Last Frontier

Sadly, despite Hollywood's history of tackling interracial women's issues in both historical and contemporary films (*Duel in the Sun*, 1946; *Pinky*, 1949; *Imi-*

tation of Life, 1934, 1959), the Warner Bros. production of *Ice Palace* did not retain Ferber's emphasis on Native Alaska or the female protagonist, Christine
Storm. But the studio's early enthusiasm for the book was almost comical.
Jack Warner bought the property before it was even published and before
he or anyone else had read it. Harold Hecht of Hecht-Hill-Lancaster had
wanted the property for his production company, and was especially miffed
with Ferber, since he had "not had an opportunity to at least read your new
novel."[73] Ferber's agent in Hollywood, Irving "Swifty" Lazar, lived up to his
name with this business deal. Warner Bros. bought the novel for $350,000
and 15 percent of the net profits. Lazar was gleeful. As he wrote to Ferber in
January 1958, a couple of months after the deal was announced: "I think it
gives you the same opportunity to get all the breaks that could go with a big
hit movie, as in *Giant*, at the same time the guarantee lest the movie is not a
success. It may seem incredible to you, but there are movies which do not
make money."[74] Lazar may not have been so sure that the book would make
money, so his deal for Ferber was something of a coup. Typical of the critical response to Ferber's work in the late fifties was that of Dick Williams of
the *Los Angeles Mirror-News*: "At 72 Edna Ferber is enjoying a new vogue. Her
books are best sellers and more of them are being made into screen and stage
plays." But Williams admits he was never a fan, since, like Fanny Hurst, Ferber is a "specialist in schmaltz."[75] This undercurrent of resentment that targeted Ferber's gender, success with the public and the film industry, and her
allegedly kitschy, sentimental, female-focused literature hadn't changed in
twenty years.

Ironically, though, Warner Bros.' adaptation of *Ice Palace* would diminish
the importance of the two female protagonists, Christine and Bridie, instead
focusing on the historical and ideological conflicts between the two old pioneer grandfathers, Thor (crusading Norse newspaperman and proponent of
racial equality) and "Czar" (the ruthless industrial magnate). Producer Walter
MacEwen promoted the perspective of screenwriter John Twist: "In spite of
the number of characters, he sees it as a simple story of two men who, although in constant conflict with each other, have a deep underlying respect
and affection."[76] This does follow Ferber's lifelong preoccupation with history, "the American Dream and the American nightmare," as she called it.
However, Christine loses her central position in the narrative. One fan, in-
censed with the studio's decision to focus on the older generation of classic
white male pioneers, eventually raged to the studio, "Why is it necessary to

change the author's work? . . . Christine Storm was the character that tied the whole story together. Your movie did not have this tie."[77]

Warner Bros. gave the job of writing, producing, and directing to two newcomers, husband and wife Art and Jo Napoleon. Why Warner would spend so much money on the rights, only to throw it away on a couple of inexperienced filmmakers, is a mystery. Although the Napoleons gave Walter MacEwen the impression they were eager and grateful ("They seem to be impressed with the potential of the subject," MacEwen reported), they also confessed that they felt "Miss Ferber left a great deal to the imagination which will have to be developed and dramatized."[78] The Napoleons must have sensed the importance of the project (*Giant* had been a top grosser and won the studio several Academy Awards in 1956), but they took a high-handed and dismissive attitude toward Ferber's work from the first. "Not only is Ferber's research colorless," they complained to producer Steve Trilling, "but even a superficial cross-check reveals that much of it is outdated as well."[79] But their idea of research was to "discover" that the Ice Palace (Baranof's prime hotel) was no longer "the only tall building in town." Baranof was a fictional town, though. What could they have meant? In spite of the fact that Warner Bros.' research library was one of the most impressive in California, they complained about the "very little useful research material available." What the Napoleons really were angling for was a trip to Alaska, but they tried to justify it by arguing that if they went to Alaska, they would have a chance "to find more interesting and exciting sequences to play the characters against than those Ferber used in the book."

Although they got their trip to Alaska, the Napoleons did not add anything that Ferber had not already discussed in her novel. They seemed most interested in the interracial components of the story and the characters of Christine and Ross, but curiously they did not give Ferber credit for introducing their interracial romance or the elements of multiracialism and Alaska prejudice. The Napoleons' biggest contribution to the new script was to add more heavily sexualized scenes between Ross and Christine, which would emphasize his racial primitivism and virility. The Napoleons wanted to show that Ross was not really integrated, but was still "a savage at heart." They disliked the scene Ferber described in which Ross tries to introduce Christine to the self-sufficient Eskimo economies of the far north, where whaling and seal skinning are a way of life.

Not only would this scene be distasteful on the screen but—even worse—dull. What we'd rather do is use a vignette we recall about a hunt in which all the men of the village, armed only with spears, go after a giant polar bear to prove their manhood. We would use this idea for a sequence in which Guildenstern, the professionally smooth and civilized TWA Captain, gets carried away by the almost religious fervor of the hunt and, as Christine watches, reverts to his primitive heritage with passion and virility. We think it's a good scene and we would probably follow it up with a love scene in a fur lined Eskimo hut and then top that with the revelation that Guildenstern has a son.[80]

Compared to this, Ferber's material is certainly "pallid," but their sexed-up ethnographic scene reverted to many of the racial clichés Ferber attempted to undermine with dual images of the persistence and transformation of native Alaskan cultures.

In May, Jo and Art Napoleon wrote to Trilling that they planned to focus on "modern Alaska" and wanted to avoid the epic historical angle. They criticized the book as "a rambling, plotless social tract with cut-out characters." Although they said that they could make it "a 'saga,'" they emphasized that "without any doubt at all we feel that by far the most dynamic and successful picture is the one based on modern Alaska . . . Despite the fact that we will soft pedal the political; a modern story best takes advantage of the reasons Alaska is and will be increasingly in the news—the growing clamor for statehood and its strategic proximity to Russia . . . to dilute the picture with a prologue of old history would be to rob it of its vitality."[81] The modern political narrative and the romance between Ross and Christine were the most interesting components precisely because Hollywood had not done this kind of story before. But *Ice Palace*'s potential visualization of political controversy and Cold War politics was far less titillating than the interracial romance.

They wrote with enthusiasm to Trilling, saying that they had developed "a strong personal story for him [Ross] and Christine," but they admitted that their focus on race and romance would not take advantage of the larger statehood issues ("The problem of involving a half-Eskimo airplane pilot with the destiny of Alaska is something else again.").[82] However, they may have thought that the statehood issue would be more or less moot by the time the film was released. On 20 June, Gruening wrote to Art Napoleon, inviting him to come to Washington to watch the statehood bill being passed. But as Art and Jo wrote to Trilling three days later, they would prefer not to: "As things stand now our approach barely deals with Statehood at all, but whether we intensify or eliminate the issue in the final script has no real bearing on whether we should or should not go to Washington to see Gruening."[83] They would explain to Gruening that "controversial films are too much of a commercial risk; it is more important to have a strong personal story motivating a picture than a political issue, etc."[84] However, the writers recognized that Alaska statehood was "becoming less and less controversial each day." Almost everyone favored it, and *Ice Palace* would look silly not to even mention the issue.

But if the Napoleons wanted to avoid political controversy, they also were invested in maintaining Hollywood's masculine-centered narratives. Despite their evident interest in race, their screenplays replaced Christine with Ross as the dominant mixed-race protagonist. In June 1958, they wanted to focus "the story to take better advantage of the character of Ross Guildenstern, the virile, smart half Eskimo . . . We feel he is the one genuinely interesting and exciting character in the book, and can be built into a very unique and fascinating lead for a motion picture, far different form anything that has been seen on the screen for some time."[85] Christine's intellectual and emotional development, which drove the later stages of Ferber's historical narrative, did not interest them. Christine mattered only insofar as she romantically affected Ross. In their 19 September story outline, the Napoleons' narrative describes Christine meeting Ross by accident when the boom of her sailboat hits her on the head and knocks her into the freezing Alaskan waters. He is asleep in swim trunks when it happens, "the perfect picture of the noble savage in the primeval forest were it not for the stack of college text books beside him."[86] Rather than maintaining his original identity as a wartime pilot, veteran, mixed-race Alaskan, and an urban man, Ross is placed back in nature as a young Indian "stream guard." The whole treatment focuses on the love story between the two of them (she the helpless little rich girl caught between two powerful guardians, and he the man of action), but there is no sense that Christine has a mind of her own or is part Eskimo—instead, Ross is the only racially marked character. They emphasized her blondeness and richness while obscuring his white ancestry.

To varying degrees, these stereotyped racial and sexual polarizations had been the basis for dozens of Hollywood films about interracial romance (*The Birth of a Nation*, 1915; *Broken Blossoms*, 1919; *The Vanishing American*, 1925; *The*

Cisco Kid, 1929; *So Red the Rose*, 1935; *Gone with the Wind*, 1939; *Duel in the Sun*, 1946; *My Darling Clementine*, 1946; *Pinky*, 1949; *Devil's Doorway*, 1950; *Show Boat*, 1951; *Oklahoma!* 1955; *The Searchers*, 1956; *South Pacific*, 1958). By ignoring Ferber's own construction of two mixed-race Alaskans and making them pure Indian and pure white, the Napoleons perpetuated racial and cultural separateness and fears of integration and amalgamation.

The Studio Takeover

But the Napoleons were eventually supplanted by Harry Kleiner and John Twist, who had worked on *So Big*'s script seven years earlier. Twist authored twenty-one *Ice Palace* script versions and Harry Kleiner would write thirty-five. Warner Bros. executives were frustrated by the Napoleons' slow pace, and Kleiner and Twist, two studio writers, must have seemed like better risks. Twist worked on the script from September 1958 to early March 1959, and Kleiner continued to tweak it for the next eight weeks.[87] From the first, the two screenwriters structured the script as a generational battle between Thor Storm and Zeb Kennedy. Although Ferber had parenthetically alluded to Christine's two grandfather's long-standing feud over their family and the future of Alaska, that conflict did not absorb the setting or focus of the novel, which remained on Christine and her gradual understanding of Alaska's history and future. But Twist and Kleiner wanted to emphasize the personal histories of two major male public figures in the territory. Women, always the focus of Ferber's work, had little or no place in Hollywood's version of *Ice Palace*.

Walter MacEwen wrote to Steve Trilling in late September 1958, giving him John Twist's reaction to the book:

> He feels that the book has the makings of a great picture, in spite of the fact that as it now stands it is a conversation piece, and a travelogue. Essentially, he believes it must be made in the tradition of the other great Ferber sagas, and cannot be restricted entirely to a present day setting. In spite of the number of characters, he sees it as a simple story of two men who, although in constant conflict with each other, have a deep underlying respect and affection (e.g., Gable and Tracy in *Boomtown* [1940]). Although the men would go from youth to age, it would in effect be a one generation story, with the interest maintained as the men aged.[88]

Twist cited the precedent of RKO's *Cimarron*, in which Richard Dix had gone from his thirties to age seventy, but with most of the action centered in his prime. MacEwen continued: "Cinematically, he sees the picture open in the present, with Bridie Ballantyne, now an old lady, preparing to sew a 49th star on to the Stars and Stripes. From this the camera would go . . . back to the year 1901, when she first arrived in Baranof . . . We would see Baranof grow as did the town in *Cimarron*."

At first, Twist maintained some marginal interest in Christine as the future generation of Alaska. According to MacEwen, Twist believed that "her two suitors [Bay and Ross] represent the two directions of Alaska's development."[89] But Twist also suggested that if Warner Bros. did not like the idea of aging the two male leads, Christine could be Czar Kennedy's daughter and Ross, Thor's son. They would then marry, and their child would become "the symbol of new Alaska—of pioneers who conquered hardships and threw off the yolk of selfish exploitation."[90] But gradually, even Christine's place as a convenient antiaging tool for the two male leads dissolved, as did her symbolic role as Alaska's future. As Twist continued with the script through January 1959, he suggested to producer Henry Blanke that Christine's parentage be in contention. Czar could seduce Christine's mother, but Thor would marry her and take her north. This odd romantic triangle would be amplified for months.[91]

Although two serious political figures allegedly dominated the script, it was not national issues like monopolies, Seattle businessmen's control of Alaskan industries, debates over segregation and integration, and the destruction of the environment that interested Twist and Kleiner. The big issues were Thor and Zeb's shared romantic interest in Bridie Ballantyne and an almost prurient focus on the parentage of Christine's mother. Twist wrote to Blanke that although he was "not trying to upset the status quo of the Ferber novel," he planned to sex up the whole connection between Thor and Zeb through the "uncertainty of parenthood" of Christine.[92] There would be no Eskimo angle at all. "We would not in this version carry Chris beyond adolescence," he wrote, since they did not want any "juvenile and ingénue romances"; "Thor and Czar and Bridie would be the whole adult story." Twist confessed that he did not like Ferber's "two rather sexless politicians of the novel" and concluded, "The story would end LONG before the coming of Alaskan statehood, but it would be apparent that Thor was the crusading pioneer who brought it about—who, through his death, even converted Czar to his side. Politics, a subject with a poor box office record, would merely underscore the personal drama of this sort of treatment." Even with Alaska statehood no longer a controversial issue in 1959, Twist wanted to avoid all controversy. He wanted a masculine, personal saga, and removed Ferber's historical context, political and racial questions, and female focus from the equation.

Kleiner's work merely streamlined some of Twist's ideas. His script formalized the structure by dividing the narrative into three chronological periods—1958, 1927–1937, and 1958—but by July, Kleiner had eliminated the flashback structure and instead began the script in 1919, with Zeb Kennedy's return to Seattle after serving in the First World War (something he does not do in the novel).[93] The First World War had long been used as historical shorthand for any twentieth-century historical drama, and at Warner Bros., flawed American heroes were often partially explained by the psychological impact of serving in the trenches and returning to find their jobs taken (*The Public Enemy*, 1931; *The Roaring Twenties*, 1939). Twist and Kleiner's idea for an elaborate love triangle between Bridie, Thor, and Czar remained, but while Thor and Czar were major public figures (Thor rising politically, like Gruening, in the Roosevelt era, and Czar paralleling the career of Cap Lathrop, cannery and newspaper mogul), Bridie was strangely disempowered. In Ferber's book, she is a fiercely independent woman, and by the early 1950s, an Alaska institution, but in the final script and film, Bridie (Carolyn Jones) is first seen scrubbing the floors of her father's hotel in Baranof. She is a dutiful daughter and drudge, not the salty woman who would write her memoirs and become famous. Jones's star status also resonated with Bridie's lack of authority. Although she began her career in 1952, Jones was known mostly as a supporting player, and in *Ice Palace* she was easily upstaged by costars Robert Ryan (*The Set-Up*, 1949; *The Naked Spur*, 1953; *Alaska Seas*, 1954) and Richard Burton (*The Robe*, 1953; *Alexander the Great*, 1956).

Kleiner kept some of the Alaska-exploitation rhetoric that had dominated Ferber's novel. Thor was the mouthpiece for this position. As he explains to the young Czar Kennedy, "Oh, yes, we're citizens, but we have no rights. We pay taxes but we have no vote. For over fifty years, ever since Alaska was bought from the Russians, it's been treated like an orphan. What we need and what we want no one pays any attention to."[94] But rather than questioning the tradition of frontier expansion, exploitation, and racism, and planning a new frontier for Alaska, Thor uses the same rhetorical tools as dozens of nineteenth-century expansionists. He calls opponents of statehood and his political enemies "enemies of progress." The only new aspect of Thor's frontier conflict is its Cold War context, in which the Russians are recast in the traditional savage role formerly given to the native Alaskans and other Native Americans in western films. In one political speech, he claims that "a cold war whose temperature can be instantly changed by the press of a button" makes statehood imperative. He continues thunderously: "And our northernmost bastion of defense is Alaska . . . There we face a common enemy. A police state, whose geographical juxtaposition is an ever-lasting threat. So it is not only of Statehood I speak, but of national safety . . . Ask yourselves this self-evident question: if the United States does not consider Alaska important enough to make it a part of its body politic, why should this calculating enemy treat it with any greater respect, *and not attempt some day to occupy it!*" He wraps up with a call to action: "Therefore, I charge you to prevent such a tragedy from ever befalling this nation! And I know of no better way in which Alaska can become a bulwark of the Western World—not merely of arms—but a shining demonstration of our deep and abiding faith in democracy—than to make it the forty-ninth state!"[95] This anti-Russian bombast was quite different from Ferber's original curiosity about the persistence of Creole (Russian-Eskimo) culture in certain regions of Alaska, but it provided a necessary political context for Alaska's past quest for statehood and continued relevance in 1959–1960.

By mid-July, when Kleiner finally finished what the front office would approve as the final script, Warner Bros. had paid for over forty script versions. The chaos and contradictory narratives showed a production system with little understanding of Ferber's story or the expense already accrued. Warner Bros.' publicity tried to explain the confusion by sending out blurbs blaming any screenwriting delays on the shapelessness of Ferber's novel. Ivan Spears of *Box Office* argued:

> Because of the stratospheric popularity of *Giant*, also adapted from a Ferber tome, the trade and the public will expect great things from *Ice Palace* . . . Those who have read the book will be quick to agree that therein is not the dramatic core that made so mighty a photoplay of *Giant* or, for that matter, *Cimarron, Showboat, Saratoga Trunk* and other Ferber works from which memorable motion pictures stemmed. In its original form, *Ice Palace* is little more than a wide-eyed, *Alice in Wonderland* Cook's tour account of contemporary Alaska, verbose, repetitious, and comparatively plotless. Some of its characterisations are extreme and unbelievable, its dialog childish in places.[96]

7.1. Romantic realignments: *Ice Palace* couples Richard Burton (Zeb Kennedy) and Martha Hyer (Dorothy Wendt Kennedy), and Carolyn Jones (Bridie Ballantyne) and Robert Ryan (Thor Storm) (Warner Bros., 1960).

He concluded: "*Ice Palace* will need considerable shrewd scripting, impressive casting and interpolation of plot before it can become the feature that the public and exhibitors expect from the studio and novelist that gave them *Giant*."

Warner Bros. attempted to duplicate *Giant's* star appeal by casting frequent western film star Robert Ryan as Thor. Ryan was already part of the Alaska western genre, having appeared in *Alaska Seas* a few years earlier. The emphasis in the script and the publicity was on the great dramatic personal story linking Thor, Czar, and Bridie together—another variation on *The Spoilers's* classic melodrama (Fig. 7.1). The trailer mentions Warner Bros.' similar production of Ferber's *Giant* and described the story as "a romance . . . a saga . . . a clash of passions."[97] Ads emphasized the raw sexual passion between

above: 7.2. Thor Storm (Robert Ryan) with his future wife, Una (Dorcas Brower), and mother-in-law (*Ice Palace*, Warner Bros., 1960). *below:* 7.3. Miscegenation? Robert Ryan and Dorcas Brower in *Ice Palace* (Warner Bros., 1960)

7.4. Christine's father (Sheridan Comerate) shortly
before his death (*Ice Palace*, Warner Bros., 1960).

Czar and Bridie: "It had to be this night, this way, with Thor only a room
away."[98] However, the publicity department did not touch the potential titil-
lation of interracial unions, despite the film's inclusion of several racy scenes
involving nude native women and pregnancy. In one scene, two nude Eskimo
women warm the half-frozen Thor with warmth from their bodies (Fig. 7.2).
Later, one of these women will become Thor's wife, and one sequence depicts
her solitary childbirth and presentation of son Christopher to Thor (Fig. 7.3).
Curiously, the Production Code administrators paid absolutely no attention
to the racial component of these sequences. Geoffrey Shurlock only showed
perfunctory concern about the native women being "adequately covered"
during the healing and pregnancy sequences.[99]

The next generation's interracial union between Christopher (Thor's half-
Eskimo son) and Grace (Czar's daughter) is less visually physical, but still oc-
cupies a large discursive part of the racial narrative. Of course, the union between Chris and Grace is doomed. While Chris dies in a primitive battle with
a ravenous bear (Fig. 7.4), she conveniently dies in childbirth. The script and
film highlight Zeb's racism through his slurs about Thor's mixed-race son

and Christine's father ("that half-breed kid of yours") and later an incredible remark he makes to Christine on her ability to "pass" as white because of her blonde hair. Transposing southern prejudices to the Alaskan frontier, Kennedy grumbles, "Thank Heavens with your skin and your complexion, you can pass."[100] Curiously, he seems to be the only one in the film with any dislike of Eskimos, Inuit, or mixed-bloods.

But Christine is still a marginal and disempowered figure, not appearing in the script until page 101.[101] She also seems totally unaware of the statehood and exploitation debates, and is stymied when she discovers (through Bridie) that Kennedy engineered her engagement to Bay Husack as a ploy to take political control from Thor. She is dwarfed by her grandfathers, and the screenwriters predictably cut any reference to her plans of becoming governor herself, rather than a governor's wife. And although they did not remove all references to Christine's mixed parentage, Kleiner was against the theme of racial mixing where she was concerned, and wrote to the front office: "The scene between Ross and Christine has been completely rewritten, so that it isn't on a 'date' basis which made it similar to her scene with Bay."[102] In the final script, they planned an exchange between Ross and Christine in which she tells him of her mixed blood, but this was cut from the film.[103]

Christine's role was further eroded by casting Diane McBain as Christine (Troy Donohue's frequent costar in the 1950s and 1960s), whitening Ferber's heroine so that her mixed status leaves no trace (Fig. 7.5). However, the filmmakers managed to capitalize on Christine-McBain's appearance of whiteness to attack the idea of racial separation. Studio publicity also highlighted McBain's appearance and contrasted it with the alleged racial reality. One publicity blurb noted the actress's blond, blue-eyed appearance but added, "She proudly admits she has American Indian blood in her heritage too. Her great great grandmother was captured by the Colorados when crossing the Great Divide in the middle of the nineteenth century and subsequently married one of the braves in an Indian marriage ceremony. The only trace of this union visible in Diane is her rather high cheekbones."[104] Although censorship records noted Christine's mixed ancestry ("quarter-breed Eskimo") and the screenwriters did not ignore her parents' and grandparents' interracial unions, reviewers would not comment on its racial components.

Studio publicity also tried to make something of Dorcas Brower, the young University of Alaska student and Miss Alaska who was chosen to play Una, Thor's native wife. She was touted as the first Eskimo to play a featured

7.5. Blond, blue-eyed Diane McBain as Christine, with
Carolyn Jones (*Ice Palace*, Warner Bros., 1960).

role in a motion picture, but her career did not last long. After making the
film, she returned to work as an Alaska Airlines stewardess.[105] Publicity man
Charles Cohen wrote to Bill Hendricks in the studio's Distributing Corporation in April 1960, telling him of their plans to hype Dorcas Brower with a
visit to New York. He also noted that "any Eskimos who appear in the film
. . . would make excellent guests on TV shows looking for unusual personalities."[106] Ernest Gruening also sensed the importance of making the most of
Brower, and asked Ferber to go to the lunch the studio had planned for her in
New York in June 1960.[107] Gruening had been more involved than Ferber in
the production. In 1958 his son Hunt had shown studio people around Alaska, and later Gruening gave them permission to use his name in the script.[108]
He also tried unsuccessfully to keep Republican Mike Stepovich out of Thor's
list of great Alaskans.[109] Stepovich had changed his stance on statehood only

after it became politically expedient, and both Ferber and Gruening were un-interested in eulogizing him. But Stepovich remained in the script and final film as a concession to pleasing all political parties in the new Alaska.

Cool Critical Response

Film critics nationwide commented on the saga's lack of historical form and completely ignored the studio's halfhearted attempt to convey white Alas-kans' racial prejudice. After Alaska's adoption as the forty-ninth state in 1959, statehood became a moot political issue, and the filmmakers' emphasis on the contentious road to statehood, nation making, and old-fashioned mascu-line values in an era of Cold War frontiers (screenwriters Art and Jo Napoleon were the first filmmakers involved in the project to comment upon Alaska's "strategic proximity to Russia") failed to capture Americans' historical imagi-nation.[110] *Variety* was cutting, but blamed Warner Bros. rather than Ferber's novel: "The end cinematic result, being neither historically nor dramatically gratifying, places the film's box-office prospects in the doubtful category. In chiselling away at Miss Ferber's attempt to correlate some historical signifi-cance into the romantic haggling of a handful of Alaska's more emotional residents, scenarist Harry Kleiner has constructed an old-fashioned soap opera that moves, under Vincent Sherman's direction, with glacial hesitation to a telegraphed conclusion."[111] Paul V. Beckley of the *New York Herald Tribune* commented similarly: "There are some hints of social content that no doubt were enlarged and more sharply defined in Miss Ferber's original novel before Harry Kleiner (*The Garment Jungle*) turned it into a screenplay. In the opening sequences Burton comes home from World War I to find that his job as a can-nery foreman has been taken by another man. During the latter portion of the film he becomes the most powerful man in Alaska and opposed statehood in order to protect his financial interests. But these elements are swallowed up in the general melee of romantic melodrama."[112]

Bosley Crowther, reviewing the film for the *New York Times*, was blistering: "They say that several of the characters in Edna Ferber's *Ice Palace* were drawn from life and that the story of the development of Alaska is based on things that occurred. If so, you would not suspect it from the film that has been made from the book. It is as false and synthetic a screen saga as has rolled out of a color camera in years," he complained. "The characters are about as real as the clotheshorses in a sporting-goods shop . . . Finally the picture of Alaska and Alaskan problems you get in this film is the bit you may glimpse in the background between the heads of the people mentioned above. And that is no more authentic than cornstarch snow on a studio set."[113]

However, a significant number of critics attacked Ferber as viciously as they did Warner Bros. *Motion Picture Daily* dwelled on the elaborate plot of romance and counterromance, but blamed Ferber rather than the filmmakers: "Sound complicated? You bet it is, but Edna Ferber is a skilful (if superficial) story-teller who knows how to keep a plot spinning through numerous strands and intricacies. . . . This is a 'woman's picture'—if ever there was one."[114] How she must have fumed at this! Others dismissed both Ferber and *Ice Palace* as creators of a turgid "woman's picture." *Time* commented: "*Ice Palace* is the sort of film that will be described by misogynists as a good women's picture. The tearful vapidity of Edna Ferber's outsize novel about Alaska is faithfully reflected."[115]

Fifteen years earlier, Hollywood reviewers had respect for the box office that Ferber and female audiences could generate, but things had changed. There are a number of possible explanations. There is a certain misogyny in many of these reviews, and a growing critical fear of Ferber's reputation. The *Saturday Review*, actively hostile to Ferber since the publication of *Giant*, reflected many of these attitudes:

> Ever since *So Big* and *Show Boat* hit pay dirt, Edna Ferber has been finding ways to tell essentially the same story against different backgrounds . . . Whatever the background, Miss Ferber has managed to discover there a strong, suffering woman who looks on while two or three generations squabble and hate, and ultimately, through her wise, patient intervention, achieve reconciliation just as the territory achieves statehood . . . Needless to say, this mingling of history and bittersweet romance, successful enough in book form, has proven irresistible to the movie companies. Her tear-drenched pages hold all the ingredients for what the industry calls, quite respectfully, a "woman's picture."[116]

The *Saturday Review* did not share the industry's respect, but this canted attack went beyond normal criticism of her work. Ferber's writing was never "tear-drenched," only two of her novels deal even peripherally with statehood, and although many of her historical novels are generational, there is very little "squabbling." Yet the critic was determined to cast her as a cheap author of "weepies," and derided her use of national history. Although it seems unlikely that he ever read any of her work, the reviewer does reveal an obvious fear of Ferber's strong heroines as historical protagonists. For Ferber and many filmmakers, a women's picture, or a women's novel, had a female protagonist who acted rather than was acted upon. Although *Ice Palace* certainly failed in this regard, Ferber's thirty-year reputation in Hollywood proved otherwise— and rankled with many who liked women to stay on the sidelines of American history.

But Ferber was also associated with old Hollywood, and in the late 1950s, both she and the studios were under assault. The latter had been slowly loosing their grip on national entertainment since earlier in the decade. Other media were stealing audiences, and deprived of the income from their theatre holdings while being beset by rising costs, the growing number of independent production companies, and union difficulties, the industry could not compete. Realism was replacing romance. Although Ferber had authored her share of historical critiques, 1950s Hollywood was increasingly unable to cope with these nuances. The obsession with bigness that *Giant* dramatized so well was deadening the industry's sense of the past. Bigness, wide-screen lenses, Warnercolor, exotic location shooting, and high-magnitude stars had all been ways of emphasizing the importance of an Edna Ferber film, but at a certain point, they upstaged and overwhelmed the original vitality of her work.

Ferber was also to blame: beginning in the mid-1930s, she tailored her historical novels to the filmmaking demands of the historical genre. Heroic, fascinating protagonists replaced the flawed but complex and changing characters of *So Big, Show Boat*, and *Cimarron*. With *Giant*, Ferber attempted a return to many of the racial and sexual themes of these earlier novels. Many critics reacted violently to this twentieth-century Harriet Beecher Stowe. But as she covered more and more American territory, Ferber seemed to become like one of the frontier explorers she admired and hated.

Around the time of the release of *Ice Palace*, she decided to cut her losses and prevent future editions of her historical novel from being contaminated by the film's failure. Ken McCormick had asked Ferber to approve a new cover for the book, which connected it to the film (he had proposed accompanying the title with "Now an epic Warner Bros Motion Pic in Technicolor"). She responded: "I hereby refuse to permit Bantam Books or Doubleday to use the jacket of the novel *Ice Palace* as an advertising medium for Warner Brothers

Motion Pictures . . . I refuse to advertise Richard Burton, Robert Ryan, Carolyn Jones, Martha Hyer, in the manner you and Bantam propose."[117]

Ferber was tired of Warner Bros. making the most of her. She found the finished film appalling. Studio ads mentioning the film's steamy romance and drama also used Ferber as a promotional tool. "Edna Ferber now gives us another *Giant*!" screamed one. "In *Giant* you saw Edna Ferber's unforgettable people of modern Texas. And now, as only she can, Edna Ferber excitingly brings you the story of people in a land in the turmoil of creation—Alaska today—its lavish splendour, its stripped passions, its tremendous personal drama."[118] After totally altering her narrative and shearing it of most of its historical and social commentary, the publicity department used Ferber's name to push what it undoubtedly feared would be a dreary, turgid historical epic. The theatrical program began: "*Ice Palace* is a Technicolor version of Edna Ferber's novel of the taming of Alaska and the struggle of this great northern wilderness to become America's 49th State. Following its serialization in the *Ladies' Home Journal* in 1959, it stayed on best-seller lists for 22 weeks to further enhance Miss Ferber's reputation as the world's most popular living woman novelist." But with or without Ferber, the film became one of Warner Bros.' biggest disasters of 1960. The film made only $1.55 million in gross domestic rentals, according to *Variety*. It made only $2,199,865.01 total worldwide ($1,480,219.20 in the United States; $62,307.81 in Canada; $657,338.00 in other countries), but even without accounting for publicity and overhead, the production had cost $3,436,028.18. The forty scripts had ended up costing the studio $2,806,594.49.[119]

Ferber would later admit that *Giant* was a better novel than *Ice Palace* because she loved Alaska and was not fuelled by a sense of injustice when writing about it: "I think in order to write really well and convincingly one must be somewhat poisoned by emotion. Dislike, displeasure, resentment, fault-finding, indignation, passionate remonstrance, a sense of injustice, are perhaps corrosive to the container but they make fine fuel."[120] In spite of white Alaskans' past mistreatment of native Alaskans, she believed things were never as bad as they had been for the Mexican Americans in Texas. Alaska was still attractive to her because it maintained some of the old-fashioned frontier qualities that she thought had disappeared by 1950.

Hollywood's interest in Ferber's Alaska novel is more difficult to assess. Warner Bros. bought it sight unseen, and there seems to have been a discrepancy between what filmmakers expected of Ferber (a masculine drama along

the lines of *The Spoilers*) and what she actually wrote (women-centered historical novels with racial and political contexts). Perhaps Warner Bros. thought
that any Ferber novel could be reshaped to fit the *Giant* template of two men
clashing over a huge wealthy territory. But even screenwriters as contemptuous of Ferber's work as the Napoleons reproduced some of her racial concerns.
In the last stages of adaptation, Twist and Kleiner tried to negotiate her frontiers of gender and race, but reviewers ignored the film's racial components
and instead pointed out the turgid, old-fashioned plot—something more to
be expected in a review of a *Spoilers* remake. But without the political controversies and mixed-race heroine, this is precisely what *Ice Palace* resembled.

Ice Palace and, later, MGM's remake of *Cimarron* ended Ferber's relationship
with Hollywood. The studios still tried to win her endorsement for other motion pictures—some based on Texas characters resembling those in *Giant*—
but Ferber angrily refused.[121] She had never publicly endorsed the adaptations
of her own books. After finishing *Ice Palace*, she tried to begin the research for
a modern novel with a Native American female protagonist.[122] The work of
historian Mari Sandoz arguably influenced her on a number of levels. Her biography of *Crazy Horse* (1942) and story of the Trail of Tears in *Cheyenne Autumn*
(1953) were important critiques of mainstream western history. The writers
also shared a Hollywood connection, although Sandoz did not fare well with
the studios. She always believed that Twentieth Century-Fox had stolen much
of her material for the 1955 Victor Mature vehicle *Chief Crazy Horse*, and when
Warner Bros. purchased the screen rights to *Cheyenne Autumn* (1964), it only
paid $1,000.[123]

Historians and critics attacked both Sandoz's imaginative style and lack
of historical "consistency" because she chose to write in a style reliant upon
oral history, fragmented memories, and imagined dialogue. Ferber too had
suffered for combining the attributes of novelist, social critic, and historian.
But Ferber may also have been attracted to Sandoz's belief, expressed in
Crazy Horse, that the white destruction of Native American culture fostered
a "domestic form of Nazism" that would undermine the best of American
values.[124] Sandoz's views sharpened in *Cheyenne Autumn*, and Suzanne Clark
argues that "her representation of genocide in *Cheyenne Autumn* takes on
resonance with the Holocaust."[125] Many writers have noted the relationship
between the annihilation of Native American tribes and anti-Semitism, and
reading *Cheyenne Autumn* may have inspired Ferber to write a darker narrative
of America's "legacy of conquest" and its connection with twentieth-century

ethnic cleansing. While *Ice Palace* and even *Cimarron* created a place for racial mixing and a multicultural future for American men and women, notes on her last project focus on the poverty and sense of hopelessness experienced by contemporary Native Americans. Though critics had recently attacked Ferber for her old-fashioned historical tales, even at the end of her life the writer anticipated Hollywood's contemporary social-protest films and revisionist westerns (*Tell Them Willie Boy Is Here*, 1969; *Little Big Man*, 1970; *Soldier Blue*, 1970; *Chato's Land*, 1972).

Unfortunately, she never got beyond the early stages of research in the Southwest. The author was in very poor health, and had suffered for years from trigeminal neuralgia, a condition that paralyzed the muscles of her face and caused enormous pain, and later developed cancer. She continued to travel to reservations in Arizona and New Mexico, filling notebooks with observations and research, but eventually, the cancer in her body became too painful. After publishing the second part of her autobiography in 1963, she remained in her longtime home of New York. She died in 1968.

It has been fifty years since Hollywood adapted or remade an Edna Ferber property. Although contemporary filmmakers continue to make and remake western biopics and narratives (*The Assassination of Jesse James by the Coward Robert Ford*, 2007; *3:10 to Yuma*, 2007) and adapt the work of American novelists like Patricia Highsmith (*The Talented Mr. Ripley*, 2000) and Upton Sinclair (*There Will Be Blood*, 2007), Ferber is largely forgotten. This may appear surprising, given her interest in women, minorities, historical critiques, and social issues, but contemporary American historical cinema is arguably more conservative and driven by traditional masculinity than it was two generations ago when *Giant* was dominating national theatres. Historical films about influential women are rare, and though racial and ethnic minorities occasionally get historical treatment, these are patterned after the standard "great man" biopics popular a century ago (*Malcolm X*, 1992; *Ray*, 2005).

Over a fifty-year career, Ferber envisioned many people and many stories within her historical framework of the United States, and Hollywood's preoccupation with her work should not be discounted. Ferber was proud of being a Jew, an American, and a woman. Her "outsider" status gave her a different and perhaps greater insight into American history than other historians, historical novelists, and filmmakers. In Edna Ferber's America, women, mixed-race Americans, and cultural outsiders all shape the conflicts and course of national history, regardless of region. Some saw only the color of historical romance in her work. But many Hollywood filmmakers, also branded with a kind of cultural exclusion, looked beneath the context and image of "colorful historical romances" and projected the visual untenability of racial difference, the grim, unromantic heroism of ordinary women, and the vitality of a multicultural America. For over thirty years, studio-era Hollywood shared part of Edna Ferber's vision, and made women's pictures *national* pictures.

Notes

CHAPTER ONE

1. Ferber, *A Peculiar Treasure* (Literary Guild of America, 1939), 54.

2. It was produced in 1921, retitled *No Woman Knows*.

3. Ferber, *Peculiar Treasure*, 262.

4. Ibid., 260.

5. Ibid., 262–263.

6. White to Ferber, 17 September 1920, box 1, folder 1, Edna Ferber Papers, U.S. MSS 98AN, State Historical Society, Madison, Wisconsin (hereafter cited as Ferber Papers).

7. Howard Teichmann, *George S. Kaufman* (Angus and Robertson, 1972), 89–90.

8. *Variety*, 25 October 1932, lists Kaufman first in its review of *Dinner at Eight*, as did reviews by Brooks Atkinson, "Sinister New York," *New York Times*, 6 November 1932; Walter Winchell, *New York Daily Mirror*, 24 October 1932; and Robert Garland, *New York World-Telegram*, 24 October 1932; box 21, folder 9, Ferber Papers.

9. *The Land Is Bright*, playbill, 20 October 1941, George S. Kaufman papers, box 1, folder 10, U.S. MSS 12AN, State Historical Society, Madison.

10. Review of *The Royal Family of Broadway*, directed by George Cukor and Cyril Gardner, *Film Daily*, 28 December 1930; *Variety*, 24 December 1930; *Stage Door* one-sheet posters, press book, Academy of Motion Picture Arts and Sciences, Margaret Herrick Library, Beverly Hills, California (hereafter AMPAS Core Collection).

11. Ferber, *Peculiar Treasure*, 387.

12. Kaufman cowrote *A Night at the Opera* (MGM, 1935) with Morrie Ryskind.

13. White to Ferber, 17 January 1944, box 1, folder 4, Ferber Papers.

14. "*Giant* Renews Ferber Influence," *Los Angeles Times*, 2 August 1953, Ferber Clipping File, AMPAS Core Collection.

15. *Weekly Variety*, 24 April 1968, Ferber Clipping File, AMPAS Core Collection.

16. Ferber "outfilms" even the likes of Mark Twain and Ernest Hemingway.

17. See J. E. Smyth, *Reconstructing American Historical Cinema from "Cimarron" to "Citizen Kane"* (Univ. Press of Kentucky, 2006), 6–10, 28–29.

18. Tino Balio, *Grand Design: Hollywood as a Modern Business Enterprise, 1930–1939* (Univ. of California Press, 1996), 1, 179–211.

19. "Trouble in Paradise," *New Republic*, 24 February 1947, 41; Thomas Schatz, *Boom and Bust: American Cinema in the 1940s* (Univ. of California Press, 1997).

20. *Saratoga Trunk* (1945) earned $4.25 million domestically, making it the thirteenth most-seen film of 1946, when *Variety* first began recording domestic box-office returns; *Show Boat* (1951) took in $5.2 million, making it the second most-seen film of 1951. *Giant* (1956) was the third-highest domestic grosser in its year ($12 million).

21. Mary Rose Shaughnessy, *Women and Success in American Society in the Works of Edna Ferber* (Gordon Press, 1977). Christopher Wilson, *White Collar Fictions: Class and Social Representation in American Literature, 1885–1925* (Univ. of Georgia Press, 1992), looks only at the author's early short stories and nonhistorical work.

22. Julie Goldsmith Gilbert, *Edna Ferber and Her Circle* (Applause, 1978); Marion Meade, *Bobbed Hair and Bathtub Gin: Writers Running Wild in the Twenties* (Doubleday, 2004).

23. Miles Kreuger, *"Show Boat": The Story of a Classic American Musical* (Oxford Univ. Press, 1977); Lauren Berlant, "Pax Americana: The Case of *Show Boat*," in *Cultural Institutions of the Novel*, ed. Deirdre Lynch and William B. Warner, 399–422 (Duke Univ. Press, 1996); Linda Williams, *Playing the Race Card: Melodramas of Black and White from Uncle Tom to O. J. Simpson* (Princeton Univ. Press, 2001).

24. For more in-depth studies, see Donna Campbell, "'Written with a Hard and Ruthless Purpose,'" in *Middlebrow Moderns: Popular American Women Writers of the 1920s*, ed. Lisa Botschon and Meredith Goldsmith, 25–44 (Northeastern Univ. Press, 2003); Heidi Kenaga, "Edna Ferber's *Cimarron*, Cultural Authority, and 1920s Western Historical Narratives," in *Middlebrow Moderns*, 167–201; Smyth, *American Historical Cinema*. Christine Geraghty, *Now a Major Motion Picture: Film Adaptations of Literature and Drama* (Rowman and Littlefield, 2007), provides a more general film summary.

25. Joan Shelley Rubin, *The Making of Middlebrow Culture* (Univ. of North Carolina Press, 1992).

26. Fitzgerald to Perkins, 1 June 1925, in *A Life in Letters: F. Scott Fitzgerald*, ed. Matthew J. Bruccoli (Scribner's, 1994), 118–119.

27. Ferber to McCormick, 28 January 1951, box 1, folder 5, Ferber Papers.

28. Stanley Vestal, "Oklahoma Is Setting of Edna Ferber's New Book," *Dallas Morning News*, 30 March 1930.

29. Lon Tinkle, "Ferber Goes Both Native and Berserk: Parody, Not Portrait, of Texas," *Dallas Morning News*, 1952; box 12, folder 7, Ferber Papers.

30. Stowe's *Uncle Tom's Cabin* was first published in 1852, a century before *Giant*.

31. Sam Nugent, "Some Think This Giant Not So Big," *Dallas Morning News* [1952], box 12, folder 7, Ferber Papers.

32. Margaret Lawrence, *The School of Femininity* (Stokes, 1936); Shaughnessy, *Women and Success*; Diane Lichtenstein, *Writing Their Nations: The Tradition of Nineteenth-Century American Jewish Women Writers* (Indiana Univ. Press, 1992).

33. Shaughnessy, *Women and Success*, 9.

34. Edna Ferber, *Come and Get It* (Doubleday Doran, 1935), dust jacket, and *Ice Palace* (Doubleday, 1958), dust jacket.

35. William R. Parker, "A Stranger's Story of Edna Ferber," *English Journal* 19, no. 6 (June 1930): 447–449.

36. William Allen White, "A Friend's Story of Edna Ferber," *English Journal* 19, no. 2 (February 1930), 101–106.

37. Walter Johnson, *William Allen White's America* (Holt, 1947); Edward Gale Argran, *Too Good a Town: William Allen White, Community, and the Emerging Rhetoric of Middle America* (Univ. of Arkansas Press, 1998); Sally Foreman Griffith, *Home Town News: William Allen White and the "Emporia Gazette"* (Oxford Univ. Press, 1989).

38. White, "Friend's Story," 105.

39. Dorothy Van Doren, "A Pioneer Fairy Story," *Nation*, 23 April 1930, 494.

40. Review of *Great Son*, by Edna Ferber, *Time*, 5 February 1945, 94, 96.

41. William Uricchio and Roberta E. Pearson, *Reframing Culture: The Case of the Vitagraph Quality Films* (Princeton Univ. Press, 1993); David Eldridge, *Hollywood's History Films* (Tauris, 2006); Smyth, *American Historical Cinema*.

42. Martin Jackson and John E. O'Connor, eds., *American History/American Film: Interpreting the Hollywood Image* (Ungar, 1979); George F. Custen, *Bio/Pics: How Hollywood Constructed Public History* (Rutgers Univ. Press, 1992); Robert Brent Toplin, *History by Hollywood: The Use and Abuse of the American Past* (Univ. of Illinois Press, 1996). See also Dixon Wecter, *The Hero in America* (C. Scribner's Sons, 1941).

43. Gilbert, *Ferber and Her Circle*, 12.

44. Nanette Kutner, "Edna Ferber Today," *Everywoman's Family Circle*, February 1959, 30–31, 57, 59.

45. Mary V. Dearborn, *Pocahontas's Daughters: Gender and Ethnicity in American Culture* (Oxford Univ. Press, 1986), 128–130; Smyth, "New Frontiers in American Interracial History: Edna Ferber and the Indian Mixed-Blood," *European Journal of Native American Studies* 20, no. 1 (2006): 39–45.

46. Daniel Bernardi, ed., *Classic Hollywood, Classic Whiteness* (Univ. of Minnesota Press, 2001); Williams, *Race Card*; Susan Courtney, *Hollywood Fantasies of Miscegenation* (Princeton Univ. Press, 2005); Richard Dyer, *White* (BFI, 1997); Gwendolyn Audrey Foster, *Performing Whiteness: Postmodern Reconstructions in the Cinema* (State Univ. of New York Press, 2003).

47. R. Barton Palmer, ed., *Twentieth-Century American Fiction on Screen* (Cambridge Univ. Press, 2007) contains essays on Faulkner's *Intruder in the Dust* and Fitzgerald's *Last Tycoon*. See also Joseph P. Millichap, *Steinbeck and Film* (Ungar, 1983); Gene D. Phillips, *Fiction, Film, and Faulkner: The Art of Adaptation* (Univ. of Tennessee Press, 2001); Regina K. Fadiman, *Faulkner's "Intruder in the Dust": Novel into Film* (Univ. of Tennessee Press, 1978);

Aaron Latham, *Crazy Sundays: F. Scott Fitzgerald in Hollywood* (Secker and Warburg, 1972); Tom Dardis, *Some Time in the Sun: The Hollywood Years of Fitzgerald, Faulkner, Nathanael West, Aldous Huxley, and James Agee* (Deutsch, 1976).

48. Julie Des Jardins, *Women and the Historical Enterprise in America* (Univ. of North Carolina Press, 2003).

49. Cari Beauchamp, *Without Lying Down: Frances Marion and the Powerful Women of Early Hollywood* (Scribner's, 1997).

50. Anzia Yezierska, *Hungry Hearts* (Houghton Mifflin, 1920), *Children of Loneliness* (Funk and Wagnalls, 1923), and *Red Ribbon on a White Horse* (Virago, 1987); L. L. Henriksen, *Anzia Yezierska: A Writer's Life* (Rutgers Univ. Press, 1988); Delia Caporoso Konsett, *Ethnic Modernisms: Anzia Yezierska, Zora Neale Hurston, Jean Rhys, and the Aesthetics of Dislocation* (Palgrave, 2003).

51. Lillian Hellman, *Scoundrel Time* (Little, Brown, 1976); Joan Mellen, *Hellman and Hammett* (HarperCollins, 1996); Bernard F. Dick, *Hellman in Hollywood* (Fairleigh Dickinson Univ. Press, 1983).

52. Robert and Helen Merrell Lynd, *Middletown: A Study in Modern American Culture* (Harcourt, Brace, 1929), 231.

53. Ibid., 239.

54. Ibid., 230–234.

55. Note from Beatrice Blackmar Gould (*Ladies' Home Journal*) to Ferber, reporting that the *Giant* issue sold 4.7 million copies, 3 September 1952, box 9, folder 7, Ferber Papers.

56. While both Tino Balio (1996; 235) and Steve Neale (2000; 194) note that Hollywood producers were preoccupied with female audiences, they assert that this occurred in the absence of market research. The Lynds' small-scale research in that area in 1929 may have influenced Hollywood perceptions.

57. Rick Miller, *Photoplay Edition: A Collector's Guide* (McFarland, 2002); Moe Wadle, *The Movie Tie-In Book* (Nostalgia Books, 1994).

58. "Making the Movies Sell Books," *Publishers Weekly*, 17 September 1932, 1027–1030.

59. See Ferber to secretary Harriet Pilpel, 28 April 1960, box 10, folder 1, Ferber Papers, in which she complains about "The Giant of Marathon" (an ad in *Variety*, 20 April 1960, 6).

60. Ferber to Hayward, 8 November 1942, box 1, folder 4, Ferber Papers.

61. Alice Payne Hackett and James Henry Burke, *Eighty Years of Best Sellers, 1895–1975* (Bowker, 1977), 3–5.

62. Ibid., 3.

63. Fannie Hurst's *Back Street* (Cosmopolitan Book, 1931) and *Imitation of Life* (Harper and Bros., 1933) were both filmed twice. For more on Hurst and melodrama, see Barbara Klinger, *Melodrama and Meaning: History, Culture, and the Films of Douglas Sirk* (Indiana Univ. Press, 1994); Brooke Kroeger, *Fannie: The Talent for Success of Fannie Hurst* (Times Books, 1999); Stephanie Lewis Thompson, *Influencing America's Tastes: Realism in the Works of Wharton, Cather, and Hurst* (Univ. Press of Florida, 2002).

64. Edward Wagenknecht, *Cavalcade of the American Novel from the Birth of the Nation to the Middle of the Twentieth Century* (Holt, Rinehart and Winston, 1952), 425.

65. Ibid., 476–477.

66. Clement Greenberg, "Avant-Garde and Kitsch," *Partisan Review* 6, no. 5 (1939): 34–49; Dwight MacDonald, "Masscult and Midcult" (1960), in *Against the American Grain*, 3–75 (Random House, 1962).

67. Gilbert Seldes, *The Seven Lively Arts* (1924; repr., Sagamore Press, 1957); Michael G. Kammen, *The Lively Arts: Gilbert Seldes and the Transformation of Cultural Criticism in the United States* (Oxford Univ. Press, 1996).

68. Paul Skenazy, *The New Wild West: Urban Mysteries of Dashiell Hammett and Raymond Chandler* (Boise State Univ. Press, 1980); William Luhr, *Raymond Chandler and Film* (Florida State Univ. Press, 1991); R. Barton Palmer, *Perspectives on Film Noir* (Hall, 1996).

69. Rubin, *Middlebrow Culture*, xv.

70. Rubin, *Middlebrow Culture*, xi; Margaret Widdemer, "Message and Middlebrow," *Saturday Review of Literature*, 18 February 1933, 433–434.

71. Steve Neale, *Genre and Hollywood* (Routledge, 2000), 193–194; Jackie Stacey, *Stargazing: Hollywood Cinema and Female Spectatorship* (Routledge, 1994).

72. Ferber's semiautobiographical novel *Fannie Herself* focused on the life of a female Jewish protagonist, but was not recognizably historical like her subsequent works. See Lichtenstein, *Writing Their Nations*; Janet Burstein, *Writing Mothers, Writing Daughters: Tracing the Maternal in Stories By American Jewish Women* (Univ. of Illinois Press, 1996).

73. Lichtenstein, *Writing Their Nations*; Joyce Antler, *America and I: Short Stories by American Jewish Women Writers* (Beacon, 1990).

74. Edna Ferber, *A Kind of Magic* (Doubleday, 1963), 286.

75. Vincent Starrett, "The Best Loved Books," *New York Herald Tribune*, 23 May 1954, box 24, folder 11, Ferber Papers.

76. Nina Baym, *Women's Fiction: A Guide to Novels by and about Women in America, 1829–1870* (Cornell Univ. Press, 1978), 277.

77. Ibid., 11–12, 277.

78. Ann Douglas, *The Feminization of American Culture* (Doubleday, 1988), 62.

79. Ferber's Emma McChesney stories were first serialized in *Cosmopolitan* and *American* before being published by Stokes in *Roast Beef, Medium* (1913), *Personality Plus* (1914), and *Emma McChesney & Co.* (1915).

80. Ann Douglas, *Feminization of Culture*, 65.

81. Hayward to Gerber, 28 January 1944, box 1, folder 4, Ferber Papers.

82. Charles Edward Stowe, *Harriet Beecher Stowe: The Story of Her Life* (Houghton Mifflin, 1911), 203.

83. Theodore Purdy, editor of Appleton Century Press, to Ferber, 21 December 1965, box 13, folder 5, Ferber Papers.

84. Bonnie Smith, *The Gender of History: Men, Women, and Historical Practice* (Harvard Univ. Press, 1998), 7.

85. Des Jardins, *Women and the Historical Enterprise*, 1–30.

86. Ann Douglas, *Feminization of Culture*, 184.

87. Ibid.

88. Des Jardins, *Women and the Historical Enterprise*, 7–8.

89. Ibid., 71.

90. Angie Debo, *The Rise and Fall of the Choctaw Republic* (Univ. of Oklahoma Press, 1934) and *And Still the Waters Run: The Betrayal of the Five Civilized Tribes* (Princeton Univ. Press, 1940); Mari Sandoz, *Crazy Horse* (Knopf, 1942); Mary Beard, *On Understanding Women* (Grosset and Dunlap, 1931), *Woman as Force in History: A Study in Tradition and Realities* (Macmillan, 1946), and, as editor, *America through Women's Eyes* (Macmillan, 1933).

91. Suzanne Clark, *Cold Warriors: Manliness on Trial in the Rhetoric of the West* (Southern Illinois Univ. Press, 2000), 133.

92. After completing *Ice Palace*, she researched a book on the lives of contemporary Native Americans (see box 18, folder 5, and box 19, folders 4–5, Ferber Papers).

93. *Reveille in Washington, 1860–1865* (Harper and Bros., 1941) and *In the Days of McKinley* (Harper and Bros., 1959) received the award. Edna Ferber to Margaret Leech, letters, 1940–1967, Houghton Memorial Library, Harvard University, Cambridge, Mass.

94. Ferber, *Peculiar Treasure*, 10.

95. Palmer, *Fiction on Screen*, 2–7; Robert Stam, "Beyond Fidelity: The Dialogics of Adaptation," in *Film Adaptation*, ed. James Naremore, 54–78 (Rutgers Univ. Press, 2000).

96. Reyher to Ferber, 8 July 1957, box 1, folder 6, Ferber Papers.

CHAPTER TWO

1. Ferber, *Peculiar Treasure*, 276.

2. Quoted in ibid., 280.

3. Ferber in the *New York Evening Post Literary Review*, 1 August 1925, box 4, folder 8, Ferber Papers.

4. Doubleday to Ferber, 4 September 1923 and 15 August 1924, box 1, folder, 1, Ferber Papers.

5. Lynn Dumenil, *The Modern Temper: American Culture and Society in the 1920s* (Hill and Wang, 1995).

6. Robert Lynd and Helen Lynd, *Middletown*, 500.

7. Stanley Coben, *Rebellion against Victorianism: The Impetus for Cultural Change in 1920s America* (Oxford Univ. Press, 1991), 35.

8. Rubin, *Middlebrow Culture*, xi–xvii.

9. Edna Ferber, *Kind of Magic*, 118, 122–123.

10. Ida Tarbell, *The Early Life of Abraham Lincoln* (McClure, 1896), *In the Footsteps of the Lincolns* (Harper and Brothers, 1924), and *Life of Abraham Lincoln* (Macmillan, 1917).

11. Ferber to Norman Cousins, 2 December 1953, box 1, folder 5, Ferber Papers.

12. Des Jardins, *Women and the Historical Enterprise*, 84–85. See also Jane Addams, *The Long Road of Woman's Memory* (Macmillan, 1916).

13. Ferber to Russell Doubleday, 9 September 1923, box 1, folder 1, Ferber Papers.

14. Edna Ferber, *So Big* (Grosset and Dunlap, 1924), 43.

15. Walter Benn Michaels, *Our America: Nativism, Modernism, and Pluralism* (Duke Univ. Press, 1994).

16. Michaels, *Our America*, 13; Campbell, "'A Hard and Ruthless Purpose,'" 25.

17. Campbell, "'A Hard and Ruthless Purpose,'" 25–44, 33.

18. Ferber, *So Big*, 47.

19. Ibid., 125.

20. Ibid., 2.

21. Annette Kolodny, *The Land before Her: Fantasy and Experience of the American Frontiers, 1630–1860* (Univ. of North Carolina Press, 1984), and Brigitte Georgi-Findlay, *The Frontiers of Women's Writing: Women's Narratives and the Rhetoric of Westward Expansion* (Univ. of Arizona Press, 1996), 29–30.

22. Ferber, *So Big*, 139.

23. Georgi-Findlay, *Frontiers of Women's Writing*, 29–30.

24. Ferber, *So Big*, 121.

25. John Higham, *Strangers in the Land: Patterns of American Nativism, 1860–1925* (Atheneum, 1989), 312–324.

26. William R. Handley, *Marriage, Violence, and the Nation in the American Literary West* (Cambridge Univ. Press, 2002), 138.

27. Ibid.

28. Ferber, *So Big*, 204.

29. Ibid., 208.

30. See Nancy Cott, *The Grounding of Modern Feminism* (Yale Univ. Press, 1987).

31. See J. Stanley Lemons, *The Woman Citizen: Social Feminism in the 1920s* (Univ. Press of Virginia, 1990).

32. Ibid., 153–180.

33. Ferber, *So Big*, 285.

34. Ibid., 289.

35. Fanny Butcher, "Edna Ferber Full Length Character Picture in Latest Novel: *So Big*," *Chicago Daily Tribune*, 23 February 1924. See also the review of *So Big*, "So Big the Diminishing Son," *New York Sun and the Globe*, 1 March 1924; and "TP," "Book of the Week: The Woman behind the Plough," *TP's and Cassell's Weekly of London*, 5 April 1924, both in box 4, folder 8, Ferber Papers.

36. Lena Morrow Lewis, "A Big Story," *New Leader*, 8 March 1924, box 4, folder 8, Ferber Papers.

37. Betsy Greenebaum, "For Better or for Worse," *Chicago Evening Post Literary Review*, 22 February 1924, box 4, folder 8, Ferber Papers.

38. Review of *So Big*, by Edna Ferber, *New York Evening Post*, 20 February 1924.

39. Laurence Stallings, unmarked press clipping, 22 February 1924, box 4, folder 8, Ferber Papers.

40. Margaret Lawrence, *The School of Femininity* (Stokes, 1936).

41. Quoted in Harold Bloom, ed., *Jewish Women Fiction Writers* (Chelsea House, 1998), 24–26.

42. Russell Doubleday to H. V. Koerner, 29 January 1925; Sales Book for Book Sellers, Doubleday, both in box 4, folder 7, Ferber Papers.

43. Greenebaum, "For Better or for Worse," 6.

44. Ferber, *Peculiar Treasure*, 7.

45. William Allen White to Frank Doubleday, 27 January 1925, and White to Frank D. Fackenthal, 2 February 1925, box 4, folder 7, Ferber Papers.

46. Doubleday to Koerner, 29 January 1925, box 4, folder 7, Ferber Papers.

47. White to O. W. Firkins, 7 March 1925, box 4, folder 7, Ferber Papers.

48. Carl Becker, "Kansas," in *Everyman His Own Historian: Essays on History and Politics* (Chicago: Quadrangle Books, 1935), 2.

49. Jefferson B. Fletcher to the Pulitzer committee, 3 April 1925, box 4, folder 7, Ferber Papers.

50. Ibid.

51. White to Fletcher, 9 March 1925, box 4, folder 7, Ferber Papers.

52. White to Fackenthal, 7 April 1925, box 4, folder 7, Ferber Papers.

53. White to Ferber, 28 April 1925, box 4, folder 7, Ferber Papers.

54. Rubin, *Middlebrow Culture*, 133.

55. Ibid., 143.

56. White, introduction to "Cheerful by Request," reprinted in *So Big*, ed. Rogers Dickinson (Grosset and Dunlap), 367.

57. Hannah Sintow to Ferber, 6 April 1925, box 4, folder 7, Ferber Papers.

58. Saimi Fassett to Ferber, 25 April 1925, box 4, folder 7, Ferber Papers.

59. Frank D. Fackenthal, 21 April 1925, box 4, folder 7, Ferber Papers.

60. White to Ferber, 25 August 1925, box 4, folder 8, Ferber Papers.

61. Received-check note, Greenbaum, Wolff and Ernst, 10 December 1931, United Artists Collection, U.S. MSS 99AN, record group 1, series 1.7, Warner Bros. contracts and copyright file, box 65, A355, State Historical Society of Wisconsin, Wisconsin Center for Film and Theatre Research, Madison (hereafter cited as United Artists Collection).

62. Warner Bros., legal file 12727, first contract dated 27 March 1924, Warner Bros. Archive, University of Southern California, Los Angeles (hereafter cited as WB Archive).

63. Greenbaum, Wolff and Ernst to Morris Ebenstein, 5 December 1931, box 65, A355, United Artists Collection.

64. Memo from Ebenstein to Jacob Wilk, 17 October 1938, box 65, A355, United Artists Collection.

65. Colleen Moore, *Silent Star* (Doubleday, 1968), 157.

66. Adelaide Heilbron, *So Big* [1924], 182 pp., AMPAS Core Collection.

67. Des Jardins, *Women and the Historical Enterprise*, 5–8, 93.

68. Ibid., 3–6.

69. Ibid., 20.

70. Mordaunt Hall, "Solid Folk," *New York Times*, n.d., box 24, Ferber Papers.

71. Mildred Spain, "See Colleen as Selina," *New York Daily News*, 5 January 1925, box 24, Ferber Papers.

72. Moore, *Silent Star*, 158.

73. Miriam Hansen, *Babel and Babylon: Spectatorship in American Silent Film* (Harvard Univ. Press, 1991).

74. See Smyth, *American Historical Cinema*.

75. J. H. Hazen to S. E. Morris, 9 May 1930, series 1.7, box 65, folder 046, United Artists Collection.

76. Jacob Wilk to Morris Ebenstein, 20 November 1931, series 1.7, box 65, folder A355, United Artists Collection.

77. *So Big* short file, 29 April 1930, WB Archive.

78. Memo from Brian Foy to Vic Vance et al., 11 April 1930, WB Archive.

79. Smyth, *American Historical Cinema*, 27–55.

80. J. Grubb Alexander, *So Big*, cutter's script, 22 December 1931, 1–3, WB Archive.

81. Alexander, *So Big*, 22 December 1931, 129–130, series 1.2, box 363, folder 7, United Artists Collection.

82. *So Big*, picture file, studio memo, 7 December 1931, WB Archive.

83. By 1932, *Show Boat* and *Cimarron* had been adapted for the screen.

84. Stills exist showing Selina (Stanwyck) selling her vegetables on the streets of Chicago after male buyers refuse to buy her produce in the Haymarket. Others show a policeman accosting her shortly before her reunion with wealthy friend Julie Hempel (AMPAS Core Collection).

85. Alexander, final script, 22 December 1931, 85–86, series 1.2, box 363, United Artists Collection.

86. Zanuck cut footage from the final script (pages 82–92).

87. *Thirty-sixth Annual Report of the Illinois Farmers' Institute*, 30 June 1931; *So Big* research file, WB Archive.

88. The screenwriters were thinking of the 1893 financial panic, which hurt business and farmers alike.

89. *So Big* (1932), dialogue transcript, undated, box 67, 3, reel 7, United Artists Collection. See also Alexander, final script, 22 December 1931, 110, series 1.2, box 363, United Artists Collection.

90. *So Big*, notes on 1932 version in AMPAS fiche (release date 30 April 1932); review in the *Motion Picture Herald*, 19 March 1932.

91. Press book, 5, series 1.4, Warner Bros. press books, United Artists Collection.

92. Dumenil, *Modern Temper*, 178–181.

93. Jo Pagano to Jerry Wald, 12 October 1943, *So Big* (1953) story file, WB Archive.

94. The last two publicity campaigns had stressed the studio's faithfulness to Ferber's novel (press book, Madison).

95. Ibid.

96. Jerry Wald, script, 11 February 1944, 152 pp., WB Archive.

97. Note especially Wald's work with Mark Hellinger on *The Roaring Twenties* (Warner Bros., 1939).

98. Wald to Jack Warner, 12 November 1943, mentions "School Teacher Story," WB Archive.

99. Wald to Warner, 17 July 1945, WB Archive.

100. Pagano to Wald, 19 July 1945, title suggestions for *So Big: Selina Peake*, WB Archive.

101. Schatz, *The Genius of the System* (Pantheon, 1988), 413.

102. Wald to Steve Trilling, 3 November 1945, WB Archive.

103. Wald to Trilling, 3 January 1948, states that three years earlier he had completed a first draft of *So Big* and would now like to go forward with the project with Massey and Neal in the roles; WB Archive.

104. Wald to Warner, 29 March 1948, WB Archive.

105. Ibid., with Warner's penciled annotation, "Advised to Wald will take up later," Jack Warner Papers, University of Southern California, Los Angeles (hereafter Jack Warner Collection).

106. Transcript, CBS, 30 December 1947, adapted by Addie Richton and Lynn Stone, directed and produced by Fletcher Markle, WB Archive.

107. Edith Sommer to Carl Milliken, 4 August 1950; see also the research log, WB Archive.

108. The film's research log indicates that Sommer worked on script though 1950, when production was stopped for another year.

109. Ebenstein to Roy Obringer, 23 April 1952, Warner Bros. legal file 12727, WB Archive.

110. Script, 20 June 1952, 98 pp.; estimating script, 9 September 1952, 113 pp.; revised final script, 13 February 1953, 119 pp., WB Archive.

111. Revised final script, 13 February 1953, WB Archive. The voice was female, but not Selina's.

112. Walter MacEwen to Henry Blanke, 29 January 1953, WB Archive.

113. Jane Hendler, *Best-Sellers and Their Film Adaptations in Postwar America* (Lang, 2001), 115–152.

114. John Murchy to studio, 4 January 1953; Murley Severtson to studio, 8 January 1954; Mrs. Robert Iott to studio, 30 October 1953, memos and correspondence file, WB Archive.

115. Schatz, *Hollywood Genres* (Random House, 1981), 226; Jackie Byars, *All That Hollywood Allows: Rereading Gender in 1950s Melodrama* (Univ. of North Carolina Press, 1991); Joan Meyerowitz, *Not June Cleaver: Women and Gender in Postwar America, 1945–1960* (Tem-

ple Univ. Press, 1994); Susan Douglas, *Where the Girls Are: Growing Up Female with the Mass Media* (Three Rivers Press, 1995).

116. Olive Higgins Prouty's *Stella Dallas* (1925) and Alexandre Bisson's *Madame X* (1910) also focus on narratives of personal loneliness and romantic and maternal tragedy.

117. Byars, *All That Hollywood Allows*, does not cover this aspect of women's cinema in the 1950s.

118. Roy Obringer to Steve Trilling, 15 December 1952, *So Big* picture file, WB Archive.

119. *So Big* advertisement, *New York Post*, 20 October 1953.

120. *So Big*, 1932 press book, 11, 14–15, series 1.4, Warner Bros. press books, WB Archive.

121. *So Big*, 1953 press book, WB Archive.

122. Review of *So Big*, directed by Robert Wise, "So Big Mild, But Wyman Strong in Female Lead," *Los Angeles Daily News*, 4 November 1953; Lowell E. Redellings, "*So Big* an Inspiring Film Version of Pulitzer Prize Novel," *Hollywood Citizen News*, 4 November 1953.

123. Review of *So Big*, directed by Robert Wise, *Cue*, 24 October 1953, clipping file, WB Archive.

124. Review of *So Big*, directed by Robert Wise, *Newsweek*, 9 November 1953, 18.

125. Review of *So Big*, directed by Robert Wise, *Variety*, 30 September 1953.

126. Nat Kahn, "Edna Ferber Story Too Old-Fashioned," *Hollywood Reporter*, 30 September 1953, 3.

127. R. J. Obringer to Morris Ebenstein, 11 December 1952, series 1.7, box 65, folder A355, United Artists Collection.

128. Ferber to Bosley Crowther (*New York Times*) and Otis Guernsey (*New York Herald Tribune*), October 1953, box 1, folder 5, Ferber Papers.

129. Ibid., and Guernsey to Ferber, 27 October 1953, box 1, folder 5, Ferber Papers.

130. A. Dwye Evans to Ferber, 11 February 1954, box 4, folder 7, Ferber Papers. Her lawyer would not allow publication of a film book for less than a 7.5 percent royalty.

131. Robert Fryer to Ferber, 5 June 1953, box 4, folder 7, Ferber Papers. See also L. Arnold Weissberger to Harry Mayer, 19 March 1952, series 1.7, box 65, folder A355, United Artists Collection.

132. Morris Ebenstein to Harry Mayer, 3 April 1952, series 1.7, box 65, folder A355, United Artists Collection.

133. Heywood Broun, "It Seems to Me," *New York World*, 7 March 1924.

CHAPTER THREE

1. Kreuger, Berlant, and Williams give the most sustained examinations of *Show Boat*, but all tend to focus on the stage and film versions of the musical.

2. Teresa C. Zackodnik, *The Mulatta and the Politics of Race* (Univ. Press of Mississippi, 2004); Eve Allegra Raimos, *The "Tragic Mulatta" Revisited: Race and Nationalism in Nineteenth-Century Anti-Slavery Fiction* (Rutgers Univ. Press, 2004).

3. Margaret Mitchell, *Gone with the Wind* (Macmillan, 1936).

4. Smyth, *American Historical Cinema*, 141–165; Williams, *Race Card*; Tara McPherson, *Reconstructing Dixie: Race, Gender, and Nostalgia in the Imagined South* (Duke Univ. Press, 2003).

5. Williams, *Race Card*, 160–162.

6. Berlant, "Pax Americana," 403.

7. Ferber, *Peculiar Treasure*, 287–288.

8. Martin Ridge, prologue to Billy Bryant, *Children of Ol' Man River: The Life and Times of a Showboat Trouper* (Donnelley and Sons, 1988), xxv–lxix, xxvii. See also Philip Graham, *Showboats: The History of an American Institution* (Univ. of Texas Press, 1951).

9. For more on the careers of Augustus and Callie French (and their striking similarities to those of Captain Andy and Parthenia Hawks), see Philip Graham, *Showboats*, 40–77.

10. Ferber, *Peculiar Treasure*, 289.

11. Ibid., 291. Ferber's novel and the subsequent films would spur popular and academic articles on the showboat (see Graham, *Showboats*, 204–210), but only a few memoirs and isolated articles discuss the phenomenon before 1925; see Carl Holliday, "American Showboats," *Theatre Magazine* 25 (May 1917): 246.

12. Ferber, *Peculiar Treasure*, 289.

13. Ibid., 287.

14. Philip Graham, *Showboats*, 14.

15. Ibid., 23.

16. Ferber would remember this detail, using the image of a powdered mixed-race woman in *Saratoga Trunk* (1941).

17. Charles M. Hunter to Ferber, 20 October 1925, box 4, folder 10, Ferber Papers.

18. Ferber to Bernard Sobel, 25 January 1928, box 1, folder 1, Ferber Papers.

19. Edna Ferber, *Show Boat* (Doubleday, 1926), 85–88.

20. Ibid., 103.

21. Harry Joe Brown, *Injun Joe's Ghost: The Indian Mixed-Blood in American Writing* (Univ. of Missouri Press, 2004), 20; Judith R. Berzon, *Neither Black nor White: The Mulatto Character in American Fiction* (New York Univ. Press, 1978), 54.

22. Suzanne Bost, *Mulattas and Mestizas: Representing Mixed Identities in the Americas, 1850–2000* (Univ. of Georgia Press), 2.

23. Cassandra Jackson, *Barriers between Us: Interracial Sex in Nineteenth-Century American Literature* (Indiana Univ. Press, 2004), 9–29.

24. Ferber, *Show Boat*, 2, 4.

25. Ibid., 28.

26. Ibid., 41.

27. James Fenimore Cooper, *The Last of the Mohicans: A Narrative of 1757* (1826; repr., Viking Penguin, 1986), 19.

28. Ferber, *Show Boat*, 68.

29. Ibid., 69.

30. Ibid., 69 (Julie), 86 (Magnolia).

31. Ibid., 88.

32. Ibid., 102–107.

33. Ibid., 111–112.

34. Ibid., 115.

35. Berlant, "Pax Americana," 409–410.

36. Ibid., 400, 402, 410; Williams, *Race Card*, 161.

37. Ferber, *Show Boat*, 92.

38. Ibid.

39. Magnolia's career is similar to Caroline Chapman's; see Philip Graham, *Showboats*, 17.

40. Ferber, *Show Boat*, 136–138.

41. Ibid., 132.

42. Ibid., 155–156.

43. Ibid., 142.

44. Ibid., 106, 142.

45. Ibid., 184. Ferber mentions the 1888 murder of Simeon Peake in Chicago and describes Selina's bereft condition, tying the historical context of her novels together.

46. Ibid., 209, 227.

47. With the exception of Christine Storm, Ferber's heroines all age and show their power and grit with roughened hands, lined faces, and grey hair.

48. Ferber, *Show Boat*, 274–275.

49. M. Alison Kibler, *Rank Ladies: Gender and Cultural Hierarchy in American Vaudeville* (Univ. of North Carolina Press, 1999), 118.

50. Ibid., 113.

51. Ibid., 117–121.

52. Ferber, *Show Boat*, 295.

53. Ibid., 296, 298.

54. For a contemporaneous exception, see Grant Overton, "The Social Critic in Edna Ferber," *Bookman*, October 1926, 139–143.

55. Louis Kronenberger, "*Show Boat* Is High Romance," *New York Times Book Review*, August 1926, in *Jewish Women Fiction Writers*, ed. Harold Bloom, 20–22 (Chelsea House, 1998).

56. Ferber, *Kind of Magic*, 112; Kreuger, *Classic American Musical*, 17; Shaughnessy, *Women and Success*, 166.

57. Berlant, "Pax Americana," 400.

58. Ibid., 401.

59. Ibid., 403.

60. R. B. Willis, *Show Boat*, 7 August 1926, MGM Script Collection, box 2876, folder 1061, AMPAS.

61. This studio employee's suggestion anticipated Hammerstein's libretto (in which this reconciliation takes place) by several months.

62. Ferber, *Peculiar Treasure*, 304.

63. Kreuger, *Classic American Musical*, 18.

64. Ferber, *Show Boat*, 79.

65. Rick Altman, *The American Film Musical* (Indiana Univ. Press, 1989), 115; Jane Feuer, *The Hollywood Musical* (Macmillan, 1982), 52.

66. Berlant, "Pax Americana," 401–402.

67. Kreuger, *Classic American Musical*, 32.

68. Charles Kenyon, *Show Boat*, adaptation and continuity, 19 April 1928, 149 pp., MGM Script Collection, box 2876, folder 1063.

69. Ibid., 15.

70. Ibid., 106.

71. La Plante was dubbed by Eva Olivotti (Kreuger, *Classic American Musical*, 81).

72. Kreuger, *Classic American Musical*, 83.

73. Ferber's character Jo was renamed "Joe" in the musical and film versions for unexplained reasons.

74. Kenyon, *Show Boat*, adaptation and continuity, 11–12, MGM Script Collection, box 2876, folder 1063.

75. Creighton Peet, review of *Show Boat*, directed by Harry Pollard, *New York Evening Post*, April 1929.

76. Quoted in Kreuger, *Classic American Musical*, 85.

77. Richard Watts, *New York Herald Tribune*, quoted in Kreuger, *Classic American Musical*, 85.

78. Sime Silverman, review of *Show Boat*, directed by Harry Pollard, *Weekly Variety*, 24 April 1929.

79. See Smyth, *American Historical Cinema*.

80. For more on West's films and their mixed racial backgrounds, see Jill Watts, *Mae West: An Icon in Black and White* (Oxford Univ. Press, 2001).

81. Oscar Hammerstein, *Show Boat*, 3 August 1927, copied 25 September 1933, recopied 12 August 1938, and recopied 2 August 1944, 122 and 116 pp., script II, 43, MGM Script Collection, box 2876, folder 1062. This exchange was part of a longer sequence cut from Hammerstein's 1928 libretto (Kreuger, *Classic American Musical*, 27).

82. Oscar Hammerstein, *Show Boat*, temporary complete script, 23 November 1935, copied 9 November 1950, 255 pp., MGM Script Collection, folder 1064.

83. Ibid., 90.

84. Oscar Hammerstein, *Show Boat*, final continuity, 1936, 228 pp., MGM Script Collection, box 2877, folder 1065. Note that credits read: "Carl Laemmle presents Edna Ferber's *Show Boat* . . . Stage play, screen play, and lyrics by Oscar Hammerstein II," reel 1, 6.

85. Ibid., reel 3, 3–4, 9.

86. See Alan Trachtenberg, *The Incorporation of America* (Hill and Wang, 1982), on Daniel Burnham's white-plastered neoclassical city and its impact on the black population of Chicago.

87. Wes D. Gehring, *Irene Dunne* (McFarland, 2003), 64.

88. *Chicago Tribune*, 2 October 1929; *Cleveland Plain Dealer*, 11 February 1929; Leon Surmleian, "It's the Irish in Her," *Motion Picture Story Magazine*, July 1936, 68.

89. Dunne-RKO contract, 10 April 1930, box 1, RKO folder, Irene Dunne Papers, Cinema-Television Library, University of Southern California, Los Angeles.

90. Gehring, *Irene Dunne*, 27, notes the connection to Ferber.

91. Ibid., 66.

92. Kreuger, *Classic American Musical*, 117.

93. *Picture Play* and *Modern Screen*, July 1936, Irene Dunne scrapbooks, Constance Mc-Cormick Collection, USC Cinema-Television Library, Los Angeles.

94. Michael Rogin, *Blackface, White Noise: Jewish Immigrants in the Hollywood Melting Pot* (Univ. of California Press, 1996), 115. See also Eric Lott, *Love and Theft: Blackface Minstrelsy and the American Working Class* (Oxford Univ. Press, 1993).

95. Kibler, *Rank Ladies*, 115.

96. Williams, *Race Card*, 140.

97. Ibid., 174-176.

98. Hammerstein's father was a successful vaudeville theatre owner and often commissioned minstrel acts (Kibler, *Rank Ladies*, 134).

99. Tracy C. Davis, *Actresses as Working Women: Their Social Identity in Victorian Culture* (Routledge, 1991).

100. Andreas Huyssen, "Mass Culture as Woman: Modernism's Other," in *After the Great Divide: Modernism, Mass Culture, and Postmodernism*, 44-64 (Indiana Univ. Press, 1986); Ann Douglas, *Feminization of American Culture*.

101. Berlant, "Pax Americana," 417.

102. *Motion Picture Herald*, 18 April 1936, 16.

103. See Harrison Carroll, "Irene Dunne Dons Blackface to Play Scene in *Showboat*," *Motion Picture Herald*, 10 March 1936; "No Cloud in the Sky," *Picture Play*, August 1936; "The New Dunne," *Detroit News*, 31 May 1936, also pays attention to Dunne's first shuffle and has a photo of her doing a blackface dance without any greasepaint.

104. Richard Dyer, *Heavenly Bodies: Film Stars and Society* (St. Martin's, 1986), 87, 105-106; Williams, *Race Card*, 166-171.

105. Smyth, *American Historical Cinema*; Custen, *Bio/Pics*.

106. Albert Auster, *Actresses and Suffragists: Women in the American Theater, 1880-1920* (Praeger, 1984).

107. Sam Goldwyn's production of *Come and Get It* was also released in 1936.

108. Review of *Show Boat*, directed by James Whale, *Variety*, 20 May 1936.

109. John McManus, "Magnolia of the Movies," *New York Times*, 1 May 1936.

110. Douglas Gilbert, "Song and Sentiment Pageant in *Show Boat* at Music Hall," *New York World-Telegram*, 15 May 1936.

111. Frank Nugent, review of *Show Boat*, directed by James Whale, *New York Times*, 15 May 1936.

112. *Show Boat* legal file, WB Archive. Note that on 29 April 1938, Universal sold *Show Boat* to Loew's.

113. As Thomas Schatz points out, MGM produced over half of all musicals from 1946 to 1955 (*Hollywood Genres*, 447); see also Drew Casper, *Postwar Hollywood* (Blackwell, 2005), 271–282.

114. George Wills, *Show Boat*, temporary complete script, 3 October 1944 through 24 October 1944, 112 pp., 2, MGM Script Collection, folder 1068.

115. Ibid., 107–108.

116. John Lee Mahin, *Show Boat*, temporary complete script, 8 September 1949 though 16 December 1949, 170 pp. See changes, 10 September 1949—later changed to an exchange with Pete during which he calls her "zebra gal"—10 October 1949, 8–8a, MGM Script Collection, folder 1070.

117. Ibid, 8, 11.

118. Berlant, "Pax Americana," 415.

119. Mahin, *Show Boat*, temporary complete script, 31.

120. "Why Was I Born?" was an old song from Kern's repertoire.

121. Mahin, *Show Boat*, temporary complete script, changes, 28 September 1949.

122. John Dunning, editor, *Show Boat*, continuity, 19 June 1951, 97 pp., MGM Script Collection, folder 1085. Julie's song after the miscegenation incident is gone.

123. Mahin, *Show Boat*, 1 August 1950, 87, box 26, folder 262, Agnes Moorehead Collection, U.S. MSS 161 AN, State Historical Society of Wisconsin, Wisconsin Center for Film and Theatre Research, Madison (hereafter cited as Moorehead Papers).

124. Sean Griffin, "The Gang's All Here: Generic versus Racial Integration in the 1940s Musical," *Cinema Journal* 42, no. 1 (Fall 2002): 28.

125. Ibid., 40.

126. George Sidney, research notes, 19 August 1950, 26 pp., MGM Script Collection, folder 1077. There are only quoted excerpts from the book with descriptive passages. He does not quote the miscegenation incident.

127. Mahin, *Show Boat*, 1 August 1950, 28, box 26, folder 262, Moorehead Papers.

128. Preview audience comment cards, George Sidney Papers, Cinema-Television Library, University of Southern California, Los Angeles.

129. Review of *Show Boat*, directed by George Sidney, *New Yorker*, 28 July 1951, clipping files, AMPAS Core Collection.

130. Ferber to Ken McCormick, 28 January 1951, box 1, folder 5, Ferber Papers.

131. *Show Boat*, press book, AMPAS Core Collection.

132. Ibid., 3.

133. *David and Bathsheba* was number one (*Variety*).

134. Review of *Show Boat*, directed by George Sidney, *Hollywood Reporter*, 5 June 1951.

135. Reviews of *Show Boat*, directed by George Sidney, *Hollywood Citizen-News*, 24 July 1951, and *Weekly Variety*, 6 June 1951.

136. Kreuger, *Classic American Musical*, 184, 177.

137. Ibid., 190–191.

138. Berlant, "Pax Americana," 415.

139. Ibid., 416.

140. Ibid., 418.

141. W. G. Rogers, "In Moonlight and Magnolia the Protest Was Lost," *New York Times Book Review*, 8 September 1963, box 24, folder 11, Ferber Papers.

CHAPTER FOUR

1. Ferber, *Peculiar Treasure*, 172.

2. Ibid.

3. See chapter 1 of Smyth, *American Historical Cinema*.

4. Ferber, *Peculiar Treasure*, 325.

5. Ibid.

6. Ibid., 326.

7. Des Jardins, *Women and the Historical Enterprise*, 102–103. Elizabeth Ellet, *Pioneer Women of the West* (Porter and Coates, 1852), was one of the few exceptions.

8. Ferber, *Peculiar Treasure*, 327.

9. Ferber to the Foxes, 15 May 1928, box 1, folder 1, Ferber Papers.

10. Ferber to the Foxes, 19 May 1928, box 1, folder 1, Ferber Papers.

11. Ferber to the Foxes, May 1928, box 1 folder 1, Ferber Papers.

12. Ferber to the Foxes, 26 May 1928, box 1, folder 1, Ferber Papers. See Linda Williams Reese, *Women of Oklahoma, 1890–1920* (Univ. of Oklahoma Press, 1997).

13. Ferber to the Foxes, 26 May 1928.

14. Ferber to Mary Austin, 17 November 1931, AU 2372, Mary Austin Collection, Huntington Library, San Marino, California.

15. Susan Armitage and Elizabeth Jameson, eds., *The Women's West* (Univ. of Oklahoma Press, 1987); Ava F. Kahn, ed., *Jewish Life in the American West: Perspectives on Migration, Settlement, and Community* (Heyday Books, 2002).

16. Richard Slotkin, *The Fatal Environment* (Univ. of Oklahoma Press, 1985) and *Gunfighter Nation* (Univ. of Oklahoma Press, 1992).

17. Slotkin, *Gunfighter Nation*.

18. Leslie Fiedler, *The Return of the Vanishing American* (Stein and Day, 1968), 50.

19. Georgi-Findlay, *Frontiers of Women's Writing*, 8.

20. Edna Ferber, *Cimarron* (Doubleday, 1929), 166.

21. Ferber, *Peculiar Treasure*, 339.

22. William Lyon Phelps, "On American Books of 1931," McClure Newspaper Syndicate, for release 29 November 1931, box 24, folder 10, Ferber Papers.

23. Quoted in Julie Goldsmith Gilbert, *Ferber and Her Circle*, 42.

24. Donna Campbell, "'A Hard and Ruthless Purpose,'" 30.

25. Ibid.

26. Campbell and Kenaga both cite William Henry Dethlef Koerner's *Saturday Evening Post* illustration of Molly and E. C. Marland's plans, begun in 1925, for a statue of a female Oklahoma pioneer (Kenaga, "Ferber's *Cimarron*," 173–174).

27. Campbell, "'A Hard and Ruthless Purpose,'" 30.

28. Constance Lindsay Skinner, *Becky Landers, Frontier Warrior* (Macmillan, 1926). An enormously popular book geared to young female readers, it went through twenty-seven editions in forty years.

29. Georgi-Findlay, *Frontiers of Women's Writing*, 29–30.

30. Ferber, *Cimarron*, 172.

31. Ferber, *Peculiar Treasure*, 129.

32. Ferber, *Cimarron*, 2.

33. Kenaga, "Ferber's *Cimarron*," 179.

34. Donna Campbell, "'A Hard and Ruthless Purpose,'" 32.

35. Kenaga, "Ferber's *Cimarron*," 179.

36. Georgi-Findlay, *Frontiers of Women's Writing*, xii and passim.

37. Cooper, *Last of the Mohicans*, 35.

38. Ferber, *Cimarron*, 11.

39. Harry Brown, *Injun Joe's Ghost*, 7.

40. William Scheick, *The Half-Blood: A Cultural Symbol in Nineteenth-Century American Fiction* (Univ. Press of Kentucky, 1979), quoted in Harry Brown, *Injun Joe's Ghost*, 13.

41. Helen Hunt Jackson, *Ramona* (Roberts Bros., 1884).

42. Dearborn, *Pocahontas's Daughters*, 130.

43. Ferber, *Cimarron*, 9–10.

44. Ibid., 84.

45. Georgi-Findlay, *Frontiers of Women's Writing*, xv.

46. Ferber, *Cimarron*, 106–107.

47. E. F. Edgett, review of *Cimarron*, by Edna Ferber, *Boston Transcript*, 29 March 1930.

48. Review of *Cimarron*, by Edna Ferber, *New York World*, 20 March 1930, box 24, folder 10, Ferber Papers.

49. Harvey Fergusson, review of *Cimarron*, by Edna Ferber, *Books*, 23 March 1930, 7, box 24, folder 10, Ferber Papers.

50. Dorothy Van Doren, "A Pioneer Fairy Story," review of *Cimarron*, by Edna Ferber, *Nation*, 23 April 1930, 494.

51. "Miss Ferber's Vivid Tales of Oklahoma's Setting," review of *Cimarron*, by Edna Ferber, *New York Times Book Review*, 23 March 1930.

52. Stanley Vestal, "Oklahoma Is Setting of Edna Ferber's New Book," review of *Cimarron*, *Dallas Morning News*, 30 March 1930.

53. Betty Rogers, *Will Rogers* (Garden City, 1941), 33.

54. Kenaga, "Ferber's *Cimarron*," 183.

55. Ferber, *Peculiar Treasure*, 10.

56. J. L. Schnitzer to Morris Ernst, 7 March 1930, box 1, folder 13, Ferber Papers.

57. Paul Powell, "Story treatment and critique," 28 June 1930, 5, *Cimarron* script collection, RKO Script Collection, Arts Special Arts Collections, University of California, Los Angeles.

58. Harry Alan Potamkin, "*Storm Over Asia* and *Abraham Lincoln*," *New Masses*, October 1930, 16.

59. William Christie MacLeod, *The American Indian Frontier* (Knopf, 1928); Howard Estabrook, *Cimarron* research, Estabrook Papers, AMPAS (hereafter cited as Estabrook Papers).

60. MacLeod, *American Indian Frontier*, vii.

61. Ibid., 366.

62. Kerwin Lee Klein, *Frontiers of the Historical Imagination: Narrating the European Conquest of Native America, 1890–1990* (Univ. of California Press, 1997), 146–147.

63. John Collier, "The Red Slaves of Oklahoma," *Sunset*, March 1924 (Estabrook placed an asterisk next to this entry); Collier, "The Rich Case of the Poor Indian," *Survey* 3 (June 1916), box 1, folder 16, Estabrook Papers. The research bibliography lists thirty-eight magazine entries.

64. See Smyth, *American Historical Cinema*, 32–55.

65. Early drafts of the script and notes confirm that Estabrook conceived this structural practice from the beginning.

66. Ferber, *Cimarron* (Estabrook's personal copy), box 1, folder 13, Estabrook Papers.

67. Ibid., 19, 41, 45.

68. Ibid., 338.

69. Ibid., 92.

70. Ferber, *Cimarron*, 106–107.

71. Ibid., 378.

72. Ibid., 11.

73. Estabrook, *Cimarron*, adaptation and structure of screenplay, 22 May 1930, 20, folder 17, Estabrook Papers.

74. Ferber, *Cimarron* (Estabrook's personal copy), 59, 125, 136, 239–246.

75. Estabrook, adaptation and script, 112.

76. Estabrook, *Cimarron*, estimating script, 15 July 1930, 368 pp., sequence A, folder 18, Estabrook Papers.

77. John G. Cawelti, *The Six-Gun Mystique* (Bowling Green University Popular Press, 1971); Andre Bazin, "The Evolution of the Western," in *What Is Cinema?* 2:149–157 (Univ. of California Press, 1972); Jack Nachbar, ed., *Focus on the Western* (Prentice-Hall, 1974); Will Wright, *Sixguns and Society: A Structural Study of the Western* (Univ. of California Press, 1975); Jim Hitt, *The American West from Fiction (1823–1986) into Film (1909–1986)* (McFarland, 1990); Edward Buscombe, *Stagecoach* (BFI, 1992); Slotkin, *Gunfighter Nation*; Ian Cameron and Douglas Pye, eds., *The Book of the Western* (Continuum, 1996); Peter Stanfield, *Hollywood, Westerns, and the 1930s: The Lost Trail* (Univ. of Exeter Press, 2001).

78. Henry Nash Smith, *Virgin Land: The American West as Symbol and Myth* (Viking, 1950); see also Cawelti, *Six-Gun Mystique*; Wright, *Sixguns and Society*; and Slotkin, *Gunfighter Nation*.

79. More recent criticism by Laura Mulvey on Pearl Chavez and *Duel in the Sun* ("Afterthoughts on Visual Pleasure and Narrative Cinema," in *Visual and Other Pleasures* [Indiana Univ. Press, 1989]) and by Charles Ramirez Berg on the multicultural aspects of John Ford's westerns ("The Margin as Center: The Multicultural Dynamics of John Ford's Westerns," in *John Ford Made Westerns*, ed. Gaylyn Studlar and Matthew Bernstein, 75–101 [Indiana Univ. Press, 2001]) reconsiders the racial and sexual transgressions of Hollywood cinema and genre.

80. Smyth, "Classical Hollywood and the Filmic Writing of Interracial Women's History, 1931–1939," in *Mixed Race Hollywood*, ed. Mary Beltrán and Camilla Fojas, 23–44 (New York Univ. Press, 2008).

81. Rose Wilder Lane, *Free Land* (1938; repr., Univ. of Nebraska Press, 1998); Sandoz, *Crazy Horse*; Sandoz, *Cheyenne Autumn* (McGraw-Hill, 1953).

82. Kenaga, "Ferber's *Cimarron*," 186.

83. Ibid.

84. *Cimarron*, press book, 4, AMPAS Core Collection.

85. Ibid., 5.

86. Ibid., 13.

87. Ibid., 9.

88. Ibid., 9, 11.

89. Ibid., 11.

90. Ibid., "Irene Dunne in Second Mighty Role as Sabra," 15.

91. Ferber, *Peculiar Treasure*, 339.

92. *Cimarron*, press book, 16.

93. *Photoplay* [1931], 66–67, 111.

94. Ferber to Estabrook, 14 February 1931, Estabrook Papers.

95. Jack Alicoate, ed., *The 1932 "Film Daily" Year Book of Motion Pictures* (Film Daily, 1932).

96. Regina Crewe, "*Cimarron* Mighty in Cinema Achievement," *New York American*, 27 January 1931.

97. Mordaunt Hall, "Oklahoma Then and Now," review of *Cimarron*, directed by Wesley Ruggles, *New York Times*, 7 February 1931.

98. Reviews of *Cimarron*, directed by Wesley Ruggles: Richard Watts, unmarked press clipping, AMPAS Core Collection; and Edwin Schallert, "Pioneer Days Well Depicted," *Los Angeles Times*, 7 February 1931.

99. Elizabeth Yeaman, "*Cimarron* Proves Thrilling Epic of Early Days," *Hollywood Daily Citizen*, 7 February 1931.

100. Harrison Carroll, "*Cimarron* Epochal Smash Hit," *Los Angeles Herald*, 7 February 1931.

101. Robert Sherwood, "The Moving Picture Album," review of *Cimarron*, directed by Wesley Ruggles, *Hollywood Reporter*, 7 February 1931.

102. William Boehnel, "*Cimarron*, Beautiful Picturization of Southwest, Hails as Best of All Its Kind," *New York Telegram*, 27 January 1931.

103. Paul Rotha, *The Film Till Now*, rev. ed. (Spring Books, 1967), 447–448.

104. Thornton Delehanty, "The New Films," review of *Cimarron*, directed by Wesley Ruggles, *New York Evening Post*, 27 January 1931.

105. Vincent Lawrence, *Cimarron*, temporary complete script, 5 June 1941, MGM Script Collection.

106. Ibid., 57–58.

107. Ibid., 49.

108. Ibid., 79–80.

109. Ibid., 85.

110. Ibid., 93, 123.

111. Geoffrey Shurlock to Louis Mayer, 3 October 1941, *Cimarron* (1960), Production Code Administration Files, AMPAS (hereafter cited as PCA Files).

112. Halsted Welles, *Cimarron* continuity, 18 April 1958, MGM Script Collection.

113. Welles, *Cimarron*, 17 December 1958, MGM Script Collection.

114. Arnold Schulman to Sol Siegel and E. Grainger, notes on *Cimarron*, 16 February 1959, 2 pp., MGM Script Collection.

115. Schulman, *Cimarron*, temporary complete script, 2 June 1959, 1, MGM Script Collection. The script opens in 1928 with an oil-derrick landscape.

116. Ibid., 153.

117. Schulman, *Cimarron*, annotated final script, 13 August 1959, 202 pp., MGM Script Collection. On page 153, red-penciled "146," the screenwriter has crossed out Sabra's speech deriding Yancey as an immature failure.

118. Thumbnail, Synopsis of OK Script, 13 November 1959, 1, MGM Script Collection, AMPAS.

119. In a letter to Bosley Crowther, Ferber wrote that she was appalled at MGM's "selection of a foreign-born actress with a slight foreign accent to play the part of the American-born bride" (26 February 1961, box 24, folder 6, Ferber Papers).

120. *Cimarron*, press book, 2.

121. Trailer dialogue and cutting continuity, 30 December 1960, MGM Script Collection.

122. *Cimarron*, press book, 6.

123. Ibid., 14.

124. Ibid.

125. Ibid.

126. Ken McCormick to Ferber, 14 October 1960, box 24, folder 6, Ferber Papers.

127. William R. Golden to Ferber, 3 November 1960, box 24, folder 6, Ferber Papers.

128. *Cimarron*, trailer dialogue and cutting continuity, 30 December 1960: "Cimarron: from the Pulitzer Prize Novelist Edna Ferber," MGM Script Collection.

129. *The Big Fisherman* (1959, directed by Frank Borzage) was Estabrook's last adaptation.

130. Estabrook to R. Monta, 27 January 1960, box 1, folder 19, Estabrook Papers.

131. Estabrook to R. Monta, 11 February 1960, folder 18, Estabrook Papers.

132. Review of *Cimarron, Motion Picture Daily*, 6 December 1960.

133. Bosley Crowther, "Who Won the West," review of *Cimarron*, directed by Anthony Mann, *New York Times*, 26 February 1961, box 24, folder 6, Ferber Papers.

134. Ferber to Crowther, 26 February 1961, box 24, folder 6, Ferber Papers; reprinted in the *New York Times*, 4 March 1961.

CHAPTER FIVE

1. Though George Custen (in *Bio/Pics*) is right in claiming that Hollywood honored a large share of conventional political heroes and wealthy magnates, it also put prize-fighters, gangsters, unknown war veterans, and mavericks in its biopic canon.

2. "Ferber Novel Brings $175,000 in Films," *New York Times*, undated [1941] press clipping, box 19, folder 10, Ferber Papers.

3. Courtney, *Fantasies of Miscegenation*; Williams, *Race Card*; Smyth, *American Historical Cinema* and "Filmic Writing"; Mulvey, *Visual and Other Pleasures*; Tania Modleski, "A Woman's Gotta Do. . . What a Man's Gotta Do? Cross Dressing in the Western," *Signs* 22, no. 3 (Spring 1997): 519–544.

4. Ferber, *Peculiar Treasure*, 371.

5. Ibid.

6. Ida Tarbell, *History of the Standard Oil Company* (McClure, Phillips, 1904) and *The Nationalizing of Business, 1878–1898* (Macmillan, 1936); Arthur D. Howden-Smith, *Commodore Vanderbilt: An Epic of American Achievement* (McBride, 1927); John K. Winkler, *Morgan the Magnificent, the Life of J. Pierpont Morgan* (Garden City, 1930); Matthew Josephson, *The Robber Barons: The Great American Capitalists, 1861–1901* (Harcourt, Brace, 1934).

7. Ferber, *Peculiar Treasure*, 372.

8. Edna Ferber, *Come and Get It* (Doubleday, Doran, 1935), 187–188.

9. Ibid., 66.

10. Ibid., 98.

11. Ibid., 177.

12. Alexander Brin, "Great American Historian," review of *Come and Get It*, by Edna Ferber, *Jewish Advocate*, 8 March 1935, box 24, folder 11, Ferber Papers.

13. Ferber, *Come and Get It*, dust jacket of the first edition.

14. Ferber to Julie Ponsonby, 28 March 1937, box 1, folder 3, Ferber Papers.

15. T. S. Matthews, "Novels by Weight," review of *Come and Get It*, by Edna Ferber, *New Republic*, March 1935, quoted in Bloom, *Jewish Women Fiction Writers*, 23–24.

16. W. Doligalski and M. Malinowski, Polish National Alliance, to Crowell Publishing, 3 October 1934, box 1 folder 2, Ferber Papers.

17. H. J. Kubiack to Ferber, n.d., box 6, folder 2, Ferber Papers.

18. Rights Notes for *Hungry Hearts*, ca. 1921, "Story—GPC 2, #5003," Samuel Goldwyn Papers, AMPAS (hereafter cited as Goldwyn Papers); see also letters from Lillian Hellman to Goldwyn: *These Three*, folder 2375, production memoranda; *The Little Foxes*, L177, production memoranda; *Dead End*, production memoranda (all Goldwyn Papers).

19. Goldwyn to Freddy Kohlmar, 13 December 1934, folder 314, Goldwyn Papers.

20. While Berg claims that Goldwyn paid $100,000 for the rights, Goldwyn's budget says otherwise (A. Scott Berg, *Goldwyn: A Biography* [Knopf, 1989], 275); see folder 311 (Budget), *Come and Get It* files, Goldwyn Papers. For more on Ferber's trip to Hollywood, see Louella Parsons, "Edna Ferber in a New Role: Substitutes Talking for Writing," *Los Angeles Examiner*, 21 July 1935; photo, *Los Angeles Sunday Times*, 11 August 1935; Evelyn Wells, "Author pays San Francisco a Visit," *San Francisco Call-Bulletin*, 8 August 1935.

21. Edward Chodorov, *Come and Get It*, revised script, part I, 13 September 1935 (M. Hurlburd's copy), 114 pp., box 41, folder 284, Goldwyn Papers.

22. Chodorov, *Come and Get It*, revised script, part II, 21 September 1935, 115–154, folder 285, Goldwyn Papers.

23. Chodorov, *Come and Get It*, revised script, 27 September 1935, 166 pp., cast notes, box 41, folder 286, Goldwyn Papers.

24. Ibid., 20.

25. Jane Murfin, *Come and Get It*, suggested treatment, 28 October 1935, 35 pp., box 41, folder 288, Goldwyn Papers.

26. Ibid., 6.

27. Murfin, *Come and Get It*, script, 6 December 1935, 228 pp., 4, box 41, folder 289, Goldwyn Papers.

28. Murfin, *Come and Get It*, suggested treatment, 28 October 1935, 35 pp., 2, box 41, folder 288, Goldwyn Papers.

29. Murfin, *Come and Get It*, script, 6 December 1935, 8.

30. Ibid.

31. Ibid., opening character analysis.

32. Ferber to Goldwyn, 29 July 1935, folder 314, Goldwyn Papers.

33. Merritt Hurlburd to Goldwyn, 6 November 1935, folder 314, Goldwyn Papers.

34. Ibid.

35. Murfin, *Come and Get It*, script, 11 February 1936, 211 pp., 1, box 42, folder 293, Goldwyn Papers, has foreword and the date 1871, but lacks Swan's initial description of the robber barons.

36. Ibid., 209.

37. Daughter Evvy marries Polish American mill hand Tony Schwerke. This was a departure from Ferber's book, in which both Evvy (caught in a loveless marriage with a wealthy man) and Barney die in a freak accident.

38. Berg, *Goldwyn*, 275.

39. Ibid., 280.

40. Jules Furthman, *Come and Get It*, first revised script, 7 May 1936, 167 pp., folder 295, Goldwyn Papers.

41. Furthman, *Come and Get It*, final script, 16 June 1936, 151 pp., 71, box 42, folder 297, Goldwyn Papers.

42. Hurlburd to Goldwyn, 5 June 1936, Goldwyn Papers.

43. Abraham Lehr to Mrs. Goldwyn, 8 June 1936, folder 314, Goldwyn Papers.

44. Hurlburd to Goldwyn, 30 September 1936, folder 314, Goldwyn Papers.

45. Murfin, *Come and Get It*, revised final script, 12 August 1936, 53 pp., box 43, folder 301; Murfin's script, 95 pp., with revisions, box 43, folder 302; Murfin, revisions, 1 September 1936, 40 pp., folder 304, Goldwyn Papers.

46. Berg, *Goldwyn*, 283.

47. Hellman to Goldwyn, 5 November 1936, Goldwyn Papers.

48. *Come and Get It*, cutting continuity, folder 209, Goldwyn Papers.

49. The film was finished on 19 September 1936. Comparison of estimate and cost, 19 September 1936: estimated cost to 8 August: $938,352.00; estimated cost of retakes: $171,848; estimated final cost: $1,111,200.00; net over final estimated cost: minus $38,377.96, folder 310, box 44, Goldwyn Papers.

50. Yezierska, *Red Ribbon on a White Horse*, 41–70.

51. Ibid., 55.

52. Goldwyn to Ferber, undated typed letter, Goldwyn Papers.

53. Ferber to Goldwyn, 28 October 1936, Goldwyn Papers.

54. Goldwyn bought the rights in 1938, and Ferber wrote the first adaptation, but because of Lillian Hellman's heavy schedule, Goldwyn delayed the project (Ferber to Frances Manson, 3 June 1938; Leland Hayward to Ferber, 23 August 1938; both in box 1, folder 3, Ferber Papers). Sidney Howard was to complete the screenplay, but the project was abandoned following his death, in 1939 (folder 316, Goldwyn Papers).

55. Review of *Come and Get It*, directed by William Wyler, *New York American*; clipping in *Come and Get It* distribution material, "*Hollywood Reporter* Critical Reviews" booklet, folder 312, Goldwyn Papers.

56. Review of *Come and Get It*, directed by William Wyler, *Hollywood Reporter*, 27 October 1936.

57. Review of *Come and Get It*, directed by William Wyler, *Time*, 16 November 1936.

58. Frank Nugent, review of *Come and Get It*, directed by William Wyler, *New York Times*, 12 November 1936.

59. Review of *Come and Get It*, directed by William Wyler, *Motion Picture Herald*, 7 November 1936.

60. Review of *Come and Get It*, directed by William Wyler, *Daily Variety*, 27 October 1936.

61. William Boehnel, review of *Come and Get It*, directed by William Wyler, *New York World-Telegram*, 12 November 1936.

62. Review of *Come and Get It*, directed by William Wyler, *New York Sun*; clipping in *Come and Get It* distribution material, "*Hollywood Reporter* Critical Reviews" booklet, folder 312, Goldwyn Papers.

63. Bige, review of *Come and Get It*, directed by William Wyler, *Variety*, 18 November 1936. ("Bige" was a pen name of a *Variety* editor.)

64. *The Plainsman* grossed more than $2 million domestically (Robert S. Birchard, *Cecil B. DeMille's Hollywood* [Univ. Press of Kentucky, 2004], 293); Smyth, *American Historical Cinema*, 131–133, 388.

65. See Smyth, *American Historical Cinema*, 337–338.

66. Edna Ferber, *Saratoga Trunk* (Doubleday, Doran, 1941), 9.

67. Ibid., 10.

68. Ibid., 6.

69. Bost, *Mulattas and Mestizas.*

70. Ferber, *Saratoga Trunk*, 16.

71. Ibid., 21, 25.

72. Berzon, *Neither White nor Black*, 105–106.

73. George Washington Cable, *Old Creole Days* (Scribner's Sons, 1879).

74. Ferber, *Saratoga Trunk*, 64–65.

75. Michael Rogin, "'The Sword Became a Flashing Vision': D. W. Griffith's *The Birth of a Nation*," in *The Birth of a Nation*, ed. Robert Lang, 250–293 (Rutgers Univ. Press, 1994); Dyer, *White.*

76. Ferber, *Saratoga Trunk*, 72.

77. Berzon, *Neither White nor Black*, 99.

78. Quoted in Cassandra Jackson, *Barriers between Us*, 2.

79. Bost, *Mulattas and Mestizas*, 69; Berzon, *Neither White nor Black*, 75–76; Zora Neale Hurston, *Their Eyes Were Watching God* (Lippincott, 1937).

80. Cassandra Jackson, *Barriers between Us*, 2.

81. Ferber, *Saratoga Trunk*, 100, 172, 141, 213.

82. Darden Asbury Pyron, ed., *Recasting: "Gone with the Wind" in American Culture* (Univ. Presses of Florida, 1983); Williams, *Race Card*; Tara McPherson, *Reconstructing Dixie: Race, Gender, and Nostalgia in the Imagined South* (Duke Univ. Press, 2003); Smyth, *American Historical Cinema.*

83. Ferber, *Saratoga Trunk*, 278.

84. Ibid., 306–307.

85. Shaughnessy, *Women and Success*, 244.

86. Harriet Hinsdale's story report is dated March 1941 (WB Archive); the novel was first serialized from April to October 1941 in *Cosmopolitan.*

87. Edna Ferber contract, 22 April 1941, 5–7, *Saratoga Trunk* contact file, series 1.7, box 60, folder 044, United Artists Collection.

88. Ebenstein to Carlisle, 21 April 1941, legal file, *Saratoga Trunk*, WB Archive. See also Vivienne Nearing to Benjamin Kalmenson, 29 August 1966, WB Archive.

89. Ferber to Leland Hayward, [1944], box 1, folder 4, Ferber Papers.

90. Ferber contract, 15 January 1946 (extension of rights to 22 April 1950) and contract dated 29 August 1949, to extend rights to 22 April 1954; *Saratoga Trunk* contact file, series 1.7, box 60, folder 044, United Artists Collection. The rights would then terminate in 1958.

91. Cooper contract, 23 February 1943, *Saratoga Trunk* contact file, series 1.7, box 60, folder 044, United Artists Collection.

92. Agreement between WB and Arnold Grant, 4 December 1946; *Saratoga Trunk* contact file, series 1.7, box 60, folder 044, United Artists Collection. Cooper had conveyed the rights to Grant earlier that year.

93. "Scheme to Escape High Taxes Studied by Movie Celebrities," *Washington Evening Star*, 1 March 1943; *Saratoga Trunk* contact file, series 1.7, box 60, folder 044, United Artists Collection.

94. Herbert Freston to Stanleigh Friedman of WB, New York, 10 March 1943, *Saratoga Trunk* contact file, series 1.7, box 60, folder 044, United Artists Collection.

95. Harriet Hinsdale, reader's report on *Saratoga Trunk*, 19 March 1941, story file, WB Archive.

96. Casey Robinson, *Saratoga Trunk* outline, n.d., story material, WB Archive.

97. Robinson, *Saratoga Trunk* outline, n.d. [1941], 53 pp., story file, WB Archive.

98. Robinson, *Saratoga Trunk*, temporary script, 17 October 1941, 8, WB Archive.

99. Ibid., 46.

100. Roy Obringer to Jack Warner, 19 March 1943, story file, WB Archive.

101. Obringer to Hal Wallis, 9 April 1945, research file, WB Archive.

102. Robinson, *Saratoga Trunk*, temporary script, 17 October 1941, 49, WB Archive.

103. Typed revisions for 4 February script, p. 9–b, revised 23 February 1943, WB Archive. There are no references to white paint here or in the revised final script of 10 May 1943.

104. *Saratoga Trunk* story file, WB Archive.

105. *Motion Picture Daily*, 21 November 1945.

106. Eric Stacey to T. C. Wright, 9 April 1943, *Saratoga Trunk* production files, WB Archive.

107. Jack Warner to Hal Wallis, 12 April 1943, *Saratoga Trunk* story file, WB Archive.

108. Neale, *Genre and Hollywood*, 194.

109. Kibler, *Rank Ladies*, 12.

110. *Saratoga Trunk* press book, WB Archive, n.p.

111. Smyth, *American Historical Cinema* and "Filmic Writing."

112. Jack Grant, review of *Saratoga Trunk*, directed by Sam Wood, *Hollywood Reporter*, 21 November 1945.

113. Kate Cameron, "Bergman's the Show in *Saratoga Trunk*," *New York Daily News*, 22 November 1945, picture file, WB Archive.

114. Reviews of *Saratoga Trunk*, directed by Sam Wood: *Variety*, 21 November 1945; *Hollywood Reporter*, 21 November 1945.

115. "Opposing Love Is Strictly Business to Flora Robson," *Saratoga Trunk*, press book, 18, AMPAS Core Collection.

116. *Look*, n.d. [1945], *Saratoga Trunk* publicity file, WB Archive.

117. Ibid.

118. Eileen Creelman, review of *Saratoga Trunk*, directed by Sam Wood, *New York Sun*, 23 November 1945.

119. Rose Pelswick, review of *Saratoga Trunk*, directed by Sam Wood, *New York Journal-American*, 23 November 1945.

120. Bosley Crowther, review of *Saratoga Trunk*, directed by Sam Wood, *New York Times*, 22 November 1945.

121. Review of *Saratoga Trunk*, directed by Sam Wood, *Hollywood Review*, 3 December 1945.

122. Review of *Saratoga Trunk*, directed by Sam Wood, *Daily Variety*, 20 November 1945.

123. Lowell E. Redellings, "*Saratoga Trunk* a Slow Photoplay but Charming," *Hollywood Citizen-News*, 9 March 1946.

124. Louella Parsons, "Saratoga a Woman's Film," *Los Angeles Examiner*, 9 March 1946.

125. Robert Lewis to Ferber, 30 January 1958, box 22, folder 7, Ferber Papers.

CHAPTER SIX

1. Ferber to George Stevens, 7 December 1954, box 51, folder 614, George Stevens Papers, AMPAS (hereafter cited as Stevens Papers).

2. Ferber to Henry Ginsberg and George Stevens, 17 May 1955, box 51, folder 614, Stevens Papers.

3. Julie Goldsmith Gilbert, *Ferber and Her Circle*, 176.

4. For studies of Debo and Sandoz, see Shirley A. Leckie, *Angie Debo: Pioneer Historian* (Univ. of Oklahoma Press, 2000), and Helen Stauffer, *Mari Sandoz, Story Catcher of the Plains* (Univ. of Nebraska Press, 1982); on female historians generally, see Des Jardins, *Women and the Historical Enterprise*, 1–51, 101–117.

5. George Sessions Perry, *Texas: A World in Itself* (McGraw-Hill, 1942) and Carey McWilliams, *North From Mexico: The Spanish-Speaking People of the United States* (1949; repr., Greenwood, 1968); on consumerism, see Shelley Nickles, "More is Better: Mass Consumption, Gender, and Class Identity in Postwar America," *American Quarterly* 54, no. 4 (December 2002): 588.

6. Carey McWilliams to Ferber, 9 February 1949, box 1, folder 4, Ferber Papers. Ferber also consulted the *LULAC News* for contemporary views; see box 10, folder 2 for her copies.

7. Shaughnessy, *Women and Success*, 283.

8. I. M. Kravsow, "A Gigantic Prejudice," review of *Giant*, by Edna Ferber, *Hartford Courant* [1952]: "Essentially, this book is a woman's book. I doubt whether many men will find it up to the calibre of a Pulitzer Prize–winning author. . . . Miss Ferber is trying to make *Giant* into another *Uncle Tom's Cabin*."

9. Hendler, *Best-Sellers*, 152.

10. Byars, *All That Hollywood Allows*, 228.

11. Marilyn Ann Moss attributes the racial critique and strong female protagonist to Stevens rather than Ferber (*Giant: George Stevens, a Life on Film* [Univ. of Wisconsin Press, 2004], 223–224).

12. Hendler, *Best-Sellers*, 119; Hollis Alpert, "It's Dean, Dean, Dean," review of *Giant*, directed by George Stevens, *Saturday Review*, 13 October 1956, 28–29. Over forty biographies of James Dean were published between 1974 and 2006; there have been no major studies of *Giant*.

13. Ferber to Ken McCormick, 3 February 1952, box 9, folder 6, Ferber Papers.

14. Edna Ferber, *Giant* (Doubleday, 1952), 82.

15. Ibid., 94.

16. Ibid., 89–90, 110.

17. "Frontier Myth and Texas Politics," *Texas Spectator* 3, no. 33 (24 May 1948): 3, box 10, folder 2, Ferber Papers.

18. Ferber, *Giant*, 284.

19. For discussions of Texans, memory, and slavery, see Gregg Cantrell and Elizabeth Turner, eds., *Lone Star Pasts: Memory and History in Texas* (Texas A&M Univ. Press, 2007); Randolph B. Campbell, *An Empire for Slavery: The Peculiar Institution in Texas, 1821–1865* (Louisiana State Univ. Press, 1989).

20. Ferber, *Giant*, 268–270, 259.

21. Neil Foley, *The White Scourge: Mexicans, Blacks, and Poor Whites in Texas Cotton Culture* (Univ. of California Press, 1997), 2; see also Matthew Frye Jacobson, *Whiteness of a Different Color: European Immigrants and the Alchemy of Race* (Harvard Univ. Press, 1998); David Roediger, *The Wages of Whiteness: Race and the Making of the American Working Class* (Verso, 1999).

22. Ferber, *Giant*, 215, 216.

23. Foley, *White Scourge*, 5; David Montejano, *Anglos and Mexicans in the Making of Texas, 1836–1986* (Univ. of Texas Press, 1987).

24. Foley, *White Scourge*, 6; see also 163–182.

25. Ferber, *Giant*, 439–440.

26. Ibid., 364. Ferber's creation of a class-race hybrid was not unique in American literature; see Smyth, "Filmic Writing."

27. Dr. Hector Garcia to Ferber, 12 June 1952, Box 9, folder 7, Ferber Papers. For more on Garcia, see Ignacio M. Garcia, *Hector Garcia: In Relentless Pursuit of Justice* (Arte Publico, 2001).

28. Nannie Tomlinson to Ferber, 30 May 1952, box 9, folder 6, Ferber Papers.

29. Marilyn Glass to Ferber, 8 June 1952, box 9, folder 6, Ferber Papers.

30. Frances McKelvey to Ferber, 3 June 1952, box 9, folder 6, Ferber Papers.

31. Alice Lee Fischer to Ferber, 3 June and 28 August 1952, box 9, folder 7, Ferber Papers.

32. Christine Noble Govan, "Cattle-Rich Texas Family Poses Problems for Bride," review of *Giant*, by Edna Ferber, *Chattanooga Times*, 5 October 1952.

33. John Barkham, "Where It's the Biggest and Bestest," review of *Giant*, by Edna Ferber, *New York Times Book Review*, 28 September 1952.

34. Eleanor Howard, review of *Giant*, by Edna Ferber, *Malibu Times*, 10 October 1952.

35. Ferber to Henry Seidel Canby, 28 September 1952, folder 7, Ferber Papers. Morris Ernst, in a letter to Ferber dated 25 September 1952, let her know about DeGolyer. On 30 September, Norman Cousins, editor in chief of the *Saturday Review*, said no to publishing Ferber's reference to DeGolyer. She replied on 3 October—all or nothing.

36. Jack Allard, "Ferber's Big Book on Texas Overdoes Even Zealot's Role," review of *Giant*, by Edna Ferber, *San Angelo Standard-Times*, 28 September 1952.

37. Carl Victor Little, "Ferber's Big Bust: She Fills Texas Air with Private 4-Engine Jobs," *Houston Press*, 20 June 1952.

38. Carl Victor Little, "By-the-way discusses Ferber's New Book, Midget," *Houston Press*, 13 September 1952: "We have generously offered to furnish the rope if someone else furnishes the martinis."

39. Tinkle, "Ferber Goes Native."

40. Margaret Cousins to Ferber, 24 November 1952, box 9, folder 8, Ferber Papers.

41. Ferber to Ken McCormick, 25 August 1952, folder 7, Ferber Papers.

42. Sam Nugent, "Some Think This Giant Not So Big," *Dallas Morning News* [1952], box 12, folder 7, Ferber Papers; quoted in Gilbert, *Ferber and Her Circle*, 190.

43. *Daily Variety*, 21 May 1952.

44. Julie [no surname given] to George Stevens, 28 May 1952, folder 707, story file 1952–1954, Stevens Papers.

45. Roy Obringer to Jack Warner, 21 December 1953, Jack Warner Collection.

46. George Stevens, annotated copy of Ferber's novel, box 35, folder 456, Stevens Papers. See especially 55–56, 89–90, 218, 259, 355, 384, 411–415, which are heavily underlined and bracketed by the director.

47. Berlant, "Pax Americana."

48. *Variety*, 13 May 1953.

49. Ferber to Henry Ginsberg and George Stevens, 12 June 1954, box 51, folder 614, Stevens Papers.

50. Ferber to Ginsberg, 4 May 1954, 27 May 1955, folder 614, Stevens Papers.

51. Ferber to Ginsberg, 27 May 1955, box 51, folder 614, Stevens Papers.

52. Alpert, "It's Dean, Dean, Dean."

53. Ferber to Ken McCormick, 15 August 1954, box 9, folder 7, Ferber Papers.

54. Ferber to George Stevens, 13 September 1954, folder 614, Stevens Papers. Garcia became part of Stevens's cast as Dr. Garcia.

55. Treatment for screenplay, 366 pp., no date through 24 March 1954, box 35, folder 461, Stevens Papers.

56. *Giant*, treatment annotated by Stevens, 28, box 36, folder 462, Stevens Papers.

57. *Giant*, estimating script, 22 October 1954, 94–95, 104, story file, WB Archive.

58. Ferber, *Giant*, 384–385, 424–425.

59. Stevens's copy of white script by Ferber, dated 28 June 1954–23 August 1954, 285 pp., 85, box 39, folder 472, Stevens Papers.

60. See Ferber, *Giant*, 157, 209, 259, 268–270, 355.

61. For the background of the Court's decision, see James T. Patterson, *"Brown v. Board of Education": A Civil Rights Milestone and Its Troubled Legacy* (Oxford Univ. Press, 2002); and Richard Kluger, *Simple Justice: The History of "Brown v. Board of Education" and Black America's Struggle for Equality* (Knopf, 1976).

62. *Giant*, estimating script, 22 October 1954, 81–85, WB Archive.

63. *Giant*, final screenplay, 4 April 1955, 178 pp., box 39, folder 482, Stevens Papers.

64. Ibid., 62–65.

65. Carl Milliken, Jr., to Ginsberg, 14 December 1954, 8 pp., folder 622, legal file, Stevens Papers.

66. See Frank Goodwyn, *Life on the King Ranch* (1951; repr., Texas A&M Univ. Press, 1993).

67. *Reader's Digest*, May 1938, 11; article preserved in Stevens Papers, box 56, folder 699.

68. For more on the lynching of Mexican Americans, see Laura Gomez, *Manifest Destinies: The Making of the Mexican American Race* (New York Univ. Press, 2007).

69. Milliken to Ginsberg, 14 December 1954.

70. William Kittrell, review of *Giant*, by Edna Ferber, *Saturday Review*, 27 September 1952, 15.

71. *Giant* research file, WB Archive; see also Carl Milliken, Jr., to Ginsberg, 14 December 1953, *Giant* legal file 2954, Stevens Papers.

72. Carl Milliken, Jr., to Roy Obringer, 12 April 1955, folder 622, Stevens Papers.

73. The research bibliography (research file, WB Archive) lists Goodwyn, *Life on the King Ranch*; "King of the Wildcatters," *Time*, 13 February 1950, 18–21; Hubert Kelly, "America's Forbidden Kingdom," *Reader's Digest*, May 1938, 11–14; "The King Ranch," *Fortune*, December 1933, 48–109; "Big Time in Houston," *Fortune*, May 1949, 80–82.

74. Roy Obringer to Warner, 15 April 1955, 2 pp. and cc'd to Ginsberg, folder 622, legal file, Stevens Papers.

75. *Los Angeles Times*, 30 August 1951.

76. Ibid.

77. For studies of Mexican Americans in the Second World War, see Maggie Rivas-Rodriguez, *Mexican Americans and World War II* (Univ. of Texas Press, 2005); and Richard Griswold del Castillo, ed., *World War II and Mexican American Civil Rights* (Univ. of Texas Press, 2008).

78. Chuck Cochard to George Stevens, 29 June 1956, 2, Riverside and Bakersfield previews, folder 662, Stevens Papers.

79. Peter Biskind, *Seeing Is Believing: How Hollywood Taught Us to Stop Worrying and Love the Fifties* (Pluto Press, 1983), 285.

80. Bick Benedict profile, 4, and Leslie profile, 4, 30 June 1954, *Giant* story file, WB Archive.

81. Ibid.

82. George Stevens notes, 1, folder 485, Stevens Papers.

83. *Giant*, final screenplay, 4 April 1955, 79, box 39, folder 482, Stevens Papers.

84. Jett Rink profile, 3–4, 30 June 1954, *Giant* story file, WB Archive.

85. For more on *The Birth of a Nation*, see Rogin, "'Sword Became a Vision'"; Courtney, *Fantasies of Miscegenation*; Sterling Brown, *The Negro in American Fiction* (Association of Negro Folk Education, 1937); Cassandra Jackson, *Barriers between Us*; Williams, *Race Card*; Donald Bogle, *Toms, Coons, Mulattoes, Mammies, and Bucks: An Interpretive History of Blacks in American Films* (1973; repr., Continuum, 2003); Thomas Cripps, *Slow Fade to Black: The Negro in American Film, 1900–1942* (Oxford Univ. Press, 1977).

86. Rogin, "'Sword Became a Vision,'" 256–293; Dyer, *White*, 82–144.

87. *Giant*, treatment for screenplay, 366 pp., through 24 March 1954, 222, box 35, folder 461, Stevens Papers.

88. David Roediger, *Working toward Whiteness: How America's Immigrants Became White* (Basic Books, 2006).

89. *Giant* production budget, 19 May 1955, WB Archive.

90. Ferber, *Giant*, 66.

91. See Edward Countryman and Evonne von Heussen-Countryman, *Shane* (BFI, 1999).

92. Hendler, *Best-Sellers*, 152. Hendler ignores the book and film's problematization of race via Jett.

93. Moss, *George Stevens*, 203, 206.

94. See, for example, Brian Henderson, "*The Searchers*: An American Dilemma," in *"The Searchers": Essays and Reflections on John Ford's Classic Western*, ed. Arthur Ekstein and Peter Lehman, 47–73 (Wayne State Univ. Press, 2004); Charles Ramirez Berg, "Margin as Center," 75–101.

95. Clippings, March–April 1955, *Yuma (AZ) Sun and Sentinel*, 15 March 1955; *Hollywood Citizen-News*, 14 March 1955, box 54, folder 679, Stevens Papers.

96. Kate Cameron, "Ferber's *Giant* a Giant Film," review of *Giant*, directed by George Stevens, *New York Daily News*, 11 October 1956, box 56, folder 700, Stevens Papers.

97. Review of *Giant*, directed by George Stevens, *Time*, 22 October 1956, 108, 110, 112.

98. Ibid.

99. Rose Pelswick, "Film Lives Up to Its Name in Everything," *New York Journal-American*, n.d., box 24, folder 2, box 56, folder 700, Stevens Papers; also Ferber Papers, box 24, folder 2.

100. Philip K. Scheuer, "*Giant* Looms as Towering Saga of Texas Boom Years," review of *Giant*, directed by George Stevens, *Los Angeles Times*, 7 October 1956.

101. John Bustin, "Show World," review of *Giant*, directed by George Stevens, *Austin Statesman*, 9 November 1956.

102. Alton Cook, unmarked press clipping, box 56, folder 700, Stevens Papers.

103. Review of *Giant*, directed by George Stevens, *Hollywood Reporter*, 10 October 1956.

104. "Giant Pre-Release Campaign," Tom Carl to Bill Rice, 12 July 1956, book 3, box 3, Stevens Papers.

105. "Campaign ideas on *Giant*," n.d., 3, box 2, Stevens Papers.

106. *Giant* press book, 27, 32, AMPAS Core Collection.

107. Ferber to Ginsberg, 17 August 1956, box 9, Ferber Papers.

108. Ferber to Ginsberg, 17 August 1955, folder 614, Stevens Papers.

109. Judith Crist, "George Stevens' *Giant* a Panorama of Texas," unmarked press clipping, 7 October 1956, box 56, folder 700, Stevens Papers.

110. Albert E. Sidelinger to George Stevens, 21 September 1956, 2, box 57, folder 703, Stevens Papers.

111. Review of *Giant*, directed by George Stevens, *Newsweek*, 22 October 1956, 112, 114.

112. Review of *Giant*, directed by George Stevens, *Variety*, 10 October 1956.

113. James Ivers, review of *Giant*, directed by George Stevens, *Motion Picture Daily*, 10 October 1956.

114. Review of *Giant*, directed by George Stevens, *Hollywood Reporter*, 10 October 1956.

115. Folders 661–663, Stevens Papers; also see James Gregory, *American Exodus* (Oxford Univ. Press, 1989).

116. *Hollywood Citizen-News*, 27 August 1957; also in folder 610, Stevens Papers.

117. George Stevens to Morris Ernst, 18 September 1957, folder 610, Stevens Papers.

118. George Stevens to Ferber, 18 September 1957, folder 610, Stevens Papers.

119. Ferber to George Stevens, 22 September 1957, Stevens Papers.

120. Carey McWilliams, "Oilmen Invade Hollywood," *Nation*, 16 October 1948, 429.

121. Review of *Giant*, directed by George Stevens, *Coventry (UK) Evening Telegraph*, 26 February 1956.

122. Review of *Giant*, directed by George Stevens, *Ciné Universal* (Mexico), September 1957, translated by Frank Z. Clemente of West Hollywood, 15 November 1957, box 56, folder 700, George Stevens Papers; see also the *Hollywood Citizen-News*, 27 August 1957.

123. Ibid.

124. "Envoy Is Victim of Segregation," *New York Times*, 24 August 1955. The story was also carried in the *New York Evening Post*, 23 August 1955. Ferber sent both articles to Stevens (folder 614, Stevens Papers).

125. See Mario T. Garcia, *Mexican Americans: Leadership, Ideology, and Identity, 1930–1960* (Yale Univ. Press, 1989).

126. L. P. Teas to Curtis Publishing Co. (*Ladies' Home Journal*), 17 November 1952, box 9, folder 8, Ferber Papers.

127. *Giant* production budget, 19 May 1955, WB Archive.

128. Ferber to David and Eliza [no surname given], 26 August 1956, box 1, folder 6, Ferber Papers.

129. See Alpert, "It's Dean, Dean, Dean"; George Scullin, "James Dean: The Legend and the Facts," *Look*, October 1956, 120–124; Daniel Yergin, "Young Dean's Legacy," *Newsweek*, 22 October 1956, 112, 116.

130. Ad analysis of *Giant* by Sidelinger & Co., prepared for Warner Bros., 1 March 1957, 6 pp., 2, box 57, folder 703, Stevens Papers.

131. "James Dean: As You Will See Him," *Movie Secrets*, October 1956, 26–27.

132. Ferber to Ken McCormick, 23 August 1957, box 9, folder 11, Ferber Papers.

133. Unsigned letter detailing deals, 1 April 1970, folder 696, Stevens Papers.

CHAPTER SEVEN

1. Her publisher and others suggested that she write "a muckraking novel" about Joseph McCarthy in 1953 (Ken McCormick to Ferber, 20 March 1953, box 1, folder 5, Ferber Papers).

2. First trip, 11 November 1954 (box 13, folder 4, Ferber Papers). She stayed in the Baranof Hotel in Juneau, which inspired the Ice Palace Hotel in the fictional Baranof.

3. Ken McCormick to Ferber, 24 February 1955, box 13, folder 4, Ferber Papers.

4. John S. Whitehead, *Completing the Nation: The Alaska and Hawaii Statehood Movements* (1986; repr., Univ. of New Mexico Press, 2004), 201–236.

5. Ferber and Gruening began to correspond in the fall of 1954.

6. Donna Campbell, "'A Hard and Ruthless Purpose,'" 33.

7. Ferber, *Kind of Magic*, 279.

8. Ken McCormick to Ferber, 5 May 1955, box 1, folder 6, Ferber Papers.

9. McCormick to Ferber, 11 May 1955, box 1, folder 6, Ferber Papers.

10. McCormick to Ferber, 20 May 1955, box 1, folder 6, Ferber Papers.

11. H. H. Bancroft, *The History of Alaska, 1730–1885* (Bancroft, 1886).

12. Mary Lee Davis, *Uncle Sam's Attic: The Intimate Story of Alaska* (Wilde, 1930), 4–5.

13. Ernest Gruening, *The State of Alaska* (Random House, 1954), 355–357.

14. Frederick Jackson Turner, "The West—1876 and 1926: Its Progress in a Half-Century," *World's Work* 52 (July 1926): 327, quoted in Melody Webb, *The Last Frontier* (Univ. of New Mexico Press, 1985), 2.

15. Whitehead, *Completing the Nation*, 205–212; see also Evangeline Atwood, *Anchorage: All American City* (Binford and Mort, 1957); Ernest Gruening, *The Battle for Alaska Statehood* (Univ. of Alaska Press, 1967).

16. Ernest Gruening to Ferber, 29 October 1954, box 13, folder 4, Ferber Papers.

17. Roger W. Hurlock to Ferber, 20 June 1956, box 13, folder 4, Ferber Papers.

18. Gruening to Ferber, 5 June 1957, box 13, folder 4, Ferber Papers.

19. Gruening to Ferber, 23 January 1956, box 13, folder 4, Ferber Papers.

20. Gruening, *State of Alaska*, 355.

21. Ibid.

22. Ibid., 363.

23. Terrence M. Cole, "Jim Crow in Alaska: The Passage of the Alaska Equal Rights Act of 1945," *Western Historical Quarterly* 23 (November 1992): 429–449.

24. Roger Hurlock, "Some Caustic Comments on Alaska Mores," 5 pp., 2, box 13, folder 10, Ferber Papers.

25. Ferber, *Kind of Magic*, 279.

26. Ferber, *Ice Palace* (Doubleday, Doran, 1958), 113.

27. Ibid., 18.

28. Ibid., 29.

29. Ibid., 128.

30. Ibid., 13.

31. Ibid., 219.

32. Ibid., 16.

33. Ibid., 370.

34. Ibid., 178–179.

35. Ibid., 143.

36. Ibid., 14.

37. Ibid., 58–59.

38. Ibid., 225.

39. Ibid., 281, 390.

40. Ken McCormick to Ferber, 31 July 1957, box 13, folder 4, Ferber Papers.

41. Ferber to McCormick, 28 July 1957, box 1, folder 6, Ferber Papers.

42. Charles Vidor to Ferber, wire, 27 October 1957; Albert Johnson to Ferber, 6 November 1957; United Artists (Barbara Tolnai) to Ferber, 18 November 1957; all in box 13, folder 4, Ferber Papers.

43. Gruening to Ferber, 18 November 1957, box 13, folder 4, Ferber Papers.

44. *Petersburg (AK) Press*, editorial, 14 March 1958.

45. Gruening to Ferber, 18 March 1958, and *Denver Post* article, 5 March 1958, box 13, folder 5, Ferber Papers.

46. Dan Melnick to Ferber, wire, 2 July 1958, box 13, folder 5, Ferber Papers.

47. Theodore Purdy, editor of Appleton-Century Press, to Ferber, 21 December 1965, box 13, folder 5, Ferber Papers.

48. *Denver Post* article, 5 March 1958, box 13, folder 5, Ferber Papers.

49. *Ice Palace*, story file, WB Archive; speech by Senator Richard L. Neuberger, 85th Cong., 2nd sess., *Congressional Record* 104 (8 May 1958): Appendix, A4282.

50. George Sundborg to Ferber, 27 March 1958, box 13, folder 5, Ferber Papers. Actually, the *Fairbanks Daily News-Miner* panned it, while the Anchorage paper gave her fair coverage of the statehood issue.

51. Doubleday press release, April 1958, box 13, folder 5, Ferber Papers.

52. Henry Vidal to Ferber, 1 July 1958, box 13, folder 5, Ferber Papers. President Eisenhower signed the Alaska statehood bill on 7 July 1958; Alaska officially became the forty-ninth state on 3 January 1959.

53. Ruth Chapin Blackman, "Miss Ferber's Alaska," review of *Ice Palace*, by Edna Ferber, *Christian Science Monitor*, 27 May 1958.

54. Review of *Ice Palace*, by Edna Ferber, *San Francisco Chronicle*, 15 June 1958; Jack McLarn, "A Literary Legend: Edna Ferber Scores Again," review of *Ice Palace*, by Edna Ferber, *Charlotte Observer*, 30 April 1958.

55. Alice Dixon Bond, "The Case for Books; Edna Ferber Pleads Eloquently for Alaska in her *Ice Palace*," review of *Ice Palace*, by Edna Ferber, *Boston Globe*, 4 June 1958.

56. Advertisement for *Ice Palace*, *Ladies' Home Journal*, 2 August 1958, 41.

57. Review of *Ice Palace*, by Edna Ferber, *San Francisco Chronicle*, 15 June 1958, box 13, folder 5, Ferber Papers.

58. Walter Havighurst, "Big A," *Saturday Review*, 29 March 1958.

59. Harrison Smith, review of *Ice Palace*, by Edna Ferber, *Saturday Review*, 29 March 1958.

60. Robert I. Snyder, "Ferber's Alaska Novel Lashes 'Robber Barons,'" review of *Ice Palace*, by Edna Ferber, *Cleveland Plain Dealer*, 30 March 1958; McLarn, "Literary Legend,"

Charlotte Observer, 30 April 1958; Ellen McGinley, review of *Ice Palace*, by Edna Ferber, *Vermont Catholic Tribune*, 18 April 1958.

61. Ernest Gruening, "Edna Ferber's Novel of Alaska Dreams and Drama," review of *Ice Palace*, by Edna Ferber, *New York Herald Tribune*, 20 March 1958.

62. Ferber, *Ice Palace*, 25–26.

63. Ibid., 177.

64. Ibid., 314.

65. Daniel Henderson, *From the Volga to the Yukon: The Story of the Russian March to Alaska and California, Paralleling Our Own Westward Trek* (Hastings House, 1944), ix.

66. Ferber, *Ice Palace*, 65.

67. Advertisement for *Ice Palace*, by Edna Ferber, *Wall Street Journal*, 18 May 1958; Roger O'Mara, "Edna Ferber Limns Alaska in Paean of Praise," review of *Ice Palace*, by Edna Ferber, *New York Star*, 13 April 1958.

68. Emma Bugbee, *New York Herald Tribune*, 15 April 1958; Roscoe Drummond, "Alaska—Next to Russia, Yet So Far," *New York Herald Tribune*, 6 July 1958.

69. Charles Poore, review of *Ice Palace*, by Edna Ferber, *New York Times*, 27 March 1958; Kathleen Graham, review of *Ice Palace*, by Edna Ferber, *Toronto Leader-Post*, 12 April 1958.

70. Press clipping, review of *Ice Palace*, by Edna Ferber, *Wichita Falls (TX) Times*, 30 March 1958, Box 13, folder 5, Ferber Papers.

71. "Ferber dramatizes Alaska's Sad Story," editorial, *Anchorage Daily News*, 3 April 1958.

72. George Sundborg, "*Ice Palace* Should Insure Early Breakup for Alaska," review of *Ice Palace*, by Edna Ferber, *Fairbanks News-Miner*, 27 March 1958, box 13, folder 5, Ferber Papers.

73. Harold Hecht to Ferber, 12 December 1957, box 13, folder 4, Ferber Papers.

74. Irving Paul Lazar to Ferber, 21 January 1958, box 24, folder 4, Ferber Papers.

75. Dick Williams, *Los Angeles Mirror-News*, 4 November 1959, clipping file, AMPAS Core Collection.

76. Walter MacEwen to Steve Trilling, 24 September 1958, *Ice Palace* story files, WB Archive.

77. Harry L. Spencer, Jr. to Warner Bros., 3 August 1960, *Ice Palace* legal files, WB Archive.

78. MacEwen to Trilling, 12 March 1958, *Ice Palace* story file, folder 4, WB Archive.

79. Art and Jo Napoleon to Trilling, 21 March 1958, *Ice Palace* story file, folder 4, WB Archive.

80. Ibid.

81. Art and Jo Napoleon to Steve Trilling, 23 May 1958, 2, *Ice Palace* story file, WB Archive.

82. Art and Jo Napoleon to Steve Trilling, 23 May 1958 and 9 June 1958, *Ice Palace* story file, WB Archive.

83. Gruening to Art Napoleon, 20 June 1958; Art and Jo Napoleon to Trilling, 23 June 1958; both in *Ice Palace* story file, folder 4, WB Archive.

84. Art and Jo Napoleon to Trilling, 23 June 1958.

85. Art and Jo Napoleon to Steve Trilling, 23 May, 9 June, and 14 June 1958, *Ice Palace* story files, WB Archive.

86. Napoleons, *Ice Palace* story outline, 19 September 1958, 87 pp., WB Archive.

87. MacEwen to Roy Obringer, 9 March 1959, and MacEwen to Obringer, memo, 27 February 1959, *Ice Palace* story file, folder 2, WB Archive.

88. MacEwen to Trilling, 24 September 1958, *Ice Palace* story file, folder 3, WB Archive.

89. John Twist to MacEwen, 24 September 1958, *Ice Palace* story file, folder 3, WB Archive.

90. Ibid.

91. John Twist to Henry Blanke, 19 January 1959, *Ice Palace* story file, folder 3, WB Archive.

92. Ibid.

93. Harry Kleiner, *Ice Palace*, first draft, 19 May 1959, WB Archive.

94. Harry Kleiner, *Ice Palace*, final script, 16 July 1959, 16, story file, WB Archive.

95. Harry Kleiner, *Ice Palace*, final script, 16 July 1959, 103, Carolyn Jones Collection, Special Arts Collections, UCLA (hereafter cited as Jones Collection).

96. Ivan Spears, *Box Office*, 20 July 1959.

97. Trailer transcript, 20 June 1960, WB Archive.

98. Advertisements in the *New York World-Telegram* and *New York Sun*, 28 June 1960.

99. Geoffrey Shurlock to Jack Warner, 9 July 1959, PCA Files.

100. Kleiner, *Ice Palace*, final script, 109.

101. Ibid., 101.

102. Kleiner to Steve Trilling, 16 October 1959, *Ice Palace* story file, correspondence, file 1, WB Archive.

103. *Ice Palace*, Carolyn Jones's personal copy of shooting script, dated 16 July 1959, 150 pp., 129, Jones Collection.

104. *Ice Palace* publicity notes, 2, WB Archive.

105. *Ice Palace* program, production notes, WB Archive.

106. Charles Cohen to Bill Hendricks, 5 April 1960, *Ice Palace* publicity file, WB Archive.

107. Gruening to Ferber, 3 June 1960, box 13, folder 5, Ferber Papers.

108. Gruening to Ferber, 7 April 1959, box 13, folder 5, Ferber Papers.

109. P. Knecht to Henry Blanke, 8 September 1959, *Ice Palace* research file, WB Archive.

110. Art and Jo Napoleon to Trilling, 23 May 1958, *Ice Palace* story files, WB Archive.

111. Review of *Ice Palace*, directed by Vincent Sherman, *Variety*, 17 June 1960.

112. Paul V. Beckley, review of *Ice Palace*, directed by Vincent Sherman, *New York Herald Tribune*, 30 June 1960.

113. Bosley Crowther, review of *Ice Palace*, directed by Vincent Sherman, *New York Times*, 30 June 1960.

114. Richard Gertner, review of *Ice Palace*, directed by Vincent Sherman, *Motion Picture Daily*, 15 June 1960.

115. Review of *Ice Palace*, directed by Vincent Sherman, *Time*, 4 July 1960.

116. Review of *Ice Palace*, directed by Vincent Sherman, *Saturday Review*, 23 July 1960.

117. Ferber to Ken McCormick, 22 March 1960, in response to his query of the 21st, box 13, folder 5, Ferber Papers.

118. Advertisements for *Ice Palace* in the *New York World-Telegram*, 28 June 1960, and *New York Sun*, 28 June 1960, box 24, folder 5, Ferber Papers.

119. *Ice Palace* studio accounts, WB Archive.

120. Ferber, *Kind of Magic*, 276.

121. Ferber to Ken McCormick, quoted in Julie Goldsmith Gilbert, *Ferber and Her Circle*, 76.

122. Box 18, folder 5, and box 19, folders 5–7, Ferber Papers.

123. Clark, *Cold Warriors*, 167.

124. Des Jardins, *Women and the Historical Enterprise*, 114.

125. Clark, *Cold Warriors*, 164.

Selected Bibliography

ARCHIVAL SOURCES

Academy of Motion Pictures Arts and Sciences. Margaret Herrick Library, Beverly Hills, California.

Austin, Mary. Papers. Huntington Library, San Marino, California.

Dunne, Irene. Papers. Cinema-Television Library, University of Southern California, Los Angeles.

———. Scrapbooks. Constance McCormick Collection. Cinema-Television Library, University of Southern California, Los Angeles.

Estabrook, Howard. Papers. Academy of Motion Picture Arts and Sciences Library, Beverly Hills, California.

Ferber, Edna. Papers. U.S. MSS 98AN. Archives Division. State Historical Society of Wisconsin, Wisconsin Center for Film and Theater Research, Madison.

———. Miscellaneous Photographs. GSA name files. Archives Division. State Historical Society of Wisconsin, Wisconsin Center for Film and Theatre Research, Madison.

Goldwyn, Samuel. Papers. Academy of Motion Picture Arts and Sciences Library, Beverly Hills, California.

Hellman, Lillian. Letters. Samuel Goldwyn Collection. Academy of Motion Picture Arts and Sciences Library, Beverly Hills, California.

Hurst, Fannie. Papers. Special Collections, Brandeis University, Waltham, Massachusetts.

Jones, Carolyn. Papers. Special Arts Collections. University of California, Los Angeles.

Kaufman, George S. Papers. U.S. MSS 12AN. Archives Division. State Historical Society of Wisconsin, Wisconsin Center for Film and Theatre Research, Madison.

Leech, Margaret. Papers. Houghton Memorial Library, Harvard University, Cambridge, Massachusetts.

MGM Script Collection. Special Collections, Academy of Motion Picture Arts and Sciences Library, Beverly Hills, California.

Moorehead, Agnes. Papers. U.S. MSS 161AN. State Historical Society of Wisconsin, Wisconsin Center for Film and Theatre Research, Madison.

Production Code Administration Files. Special Collections, Academy of Motion Picture Arts and Sciences Library, Beverly Hills, California.

RKO Studios. Script Collection. Special Arts Collections, University of California, Los Angeles.

Selznick, David O. *Duel in the Sun* production material. Harry Ransom Humanities Research Center, University of Texas, Austin.

Sidney, George. Papers. Cinema-Television Library, University of Southern California, Los Angeles.

Stevens, George. Papers. Special Collections, Academy of Motion Picture Arts and Sciences Library, Beverly Hills, California.

Twentieth Century-Fox Papers. University of Southern California Cinema-Television Archive, Los Angeles.

Warner Bros. Archive. Production and legal files. University of Southern California, Los Angeles.

———. Scripts, contracts, press books, and legal files. United Artists Collection, U.S. MSS 99AN, Record Group 1, Series 1.2–1.7. State Historical Society of Wisconsin, Wisconsin Center for Film and Theatre Research, Madison.

Warner, Jack. Papers. Warner Bros. Archive. University of Southern California, Los Angeles.

BOOKS AND ARTICLES

Addams, Jane. *The Long Road of Woman's Memory*. New York: Macmillan, 1916.

Alicoate, Jack, ed. *The 1932 "Film Daily" Year Book of Motion Pictures*. New York: Film Daily, 1932.

Allard, Jack. "Ferber's Big Book on Texas Overdoes Even Zealot's Role." Review of *Giant*, by Edna Ferber. *San Angelo (TX) Standard-Times*, 28 September 1952.

Alpert, Hollis. "It's Dean, Dean, Dean." Review of *Giant*, directed by George Stevens. *Saturday Review*, 13 October 1956, 28–29.

———. "Ten Years of Trouble." *Saturday Review*, 21 December 1957, 9–11.

Altman, Rick. *The American Film Musical*. Bloomington: Indiana Univ. Press, 1989.

———. *Film/Genre*. London: BFI, 1999.

Antler, Joyce. *America and I: Short Stories by American Jewish Women Writers*. Boston: Beacon, 1990.

Archer, Eugene. "George Stevens and the American Dream." *Film Culture* 3, no. 11 (1957): 3–4.

Argran, Edward Gale. *Too Good a Town: William Allen White, Community, and the Emerging Rhetoric of Middle America*. Fayetteville: Univ. of Arkansas Press, 1998.

Armitage, Susan, and Elizabeth Jameson, eds. *The Women's West*. Norman: Univ. of Oklahoma Press, 1987.

Atkinson, Brooks. "Sinister New York." *New York Times*, 6 November 1932.

Atwood, Evangeline. *Anchorage: All American City*. Portland, Ore.: Binford and Mort, 1957.

Auster, Albert. *Actresses and Suffragists: Women in the American Theater, 1880–1920*. New York: Praeger, 1984.

Balio, Tino. *Grand Design: Hollywood as a Modern Business Enterprise, 1930–1939*. Berkeley and Los Angeles: Univ. of California Press, 1996.

Bancroft, H. H. *The History of Alaska, 1730–1885*. San Francisco: Bancroft, 1886.

Banning, Margaret Culkin. "Edna Ferber's America." *Saturday Review of Literature*, 4 February 1939, 5–6.

Barkham, John. "Where It's Biggest and Bestest." Review of *Giant*, by Edna Ferber. *New York Times Book Review*, 28 September 1952, 4–5.

Baym, Nina. *Women's Fiction: A Guide to Novels by and about Women in America, 1829–1870*. Ithaca, N.Y.: Cornell Univ. Press, 1978.

Bazin, Andre. "The Evolution of the Western." In *What Is Cinema?* 2:149–157. Berkeley and Los Angeles: Univ. of California Press, 1972.

Beach, Rex. *The Spoilers*. New York: Harpers, 1906.

Beard, Mary, ed. *America Through Women's Eyes*. New York: Macmillan, 1933.

———. *On Understanding Women*. New York: Grosset and Dunlap, 1931.

———. *Women as Force in History: A Study in Tradition and Realities*. New York: Macmillan, 1946.

Beauchamp, Cari. *Without Lying Down: Frances Marion and the Powerful Women of Early Hollywood*. New York: Scribner's, 1997.

Becker, Carl. *Everyman His Own Historian: Essays on History and Politics*. New York: Appleton-Century-Crofts, 1935.

Beckley, Paul V. Review of *Ice Palace*, directed by Vincent Sherman. *New York Herald Tribune*, 30 June 1960.

Belluscio, Steven J. *To Be Suddenly White: Literary Realism and Racial Passing*. Columbia: Univ. of Missouri Press, 2006.

Berg, A. Scott. *Goldwyn: A Biography*. New York: Knopf, 1989.

Berg, Charles Ramirez. "The Margin as Center: The Multicultural Dynamics of John Ford's Westerns." In *John Ford Made Westerns*, ed. Gaylyn Studlar and Matthew Bernstein, 75–101. Bloomington: Indiana Univ. Press, 2001.

Berkhofer, Robert F., Jr. *The White Man's Indian: Images of the American Indian from Columbus to the Present*. New York: Knopf, 1978.

Berlant, Lauren. "Pax Americana: The Case of *Show Boat*." In *Cultural Institutions of the Novel*, ed. Deirdre Lynch and William B. Warner, 399–422. Durham, N.C.: Duke Univ. Press, 1996.

Bernardi, Daniel, ed. *The Birth of Whiteness: Race and the Emergence of U.S. Cinema.* New Brunswick, N.J.: Rutgers Univ. Press, 1996.

———. *Classic Hollywood, Classic Whiteness.* Minneapolis: Univ. of Minnesota Press, 2001.

Berzon, Judith R. *Neither White nor Black: The Mulatto Character in American Fiction.* New York: New York Univ. Press, 1978.

Bige. Review of *Come and Get It,* directed by William Wyler. *Variety,* 18 November 1936.

Birchard, Robert S. *Cecil B. DeMille's Hollywood.* Lexington: Univ. Press of Kentucky, 2004.

Biskind, Peter. *Seeing Is Believing: How Hollywood Taught Us to Stop Worrying and Love the Fifties.* New York: Pluto, 1983.

Blackman, Ruth Chapin. "Miss Ferber's Alaska." Review of *Ice Palace,* by Edna Ferber. *Christian Science Monitor,* 27 May 1958.

Bloom, Harold, ed. *Jewish Women Fiction Writers.* Philadelphia: Chelsea House, 1998.

Boehnel, William. "*Cimarron,* Beautiful Picturization of Southwest, Hails as Best of All Its Kind." *New York Telegram,* 27 January 1931.

———. Review of *Come and Get It,* directed by William Wyler. *New York World-Telegram,* 12 November 1936.

Bogle, Donald. *Toms, Coons, Mulattoes, Mammies, and Bucks: An Interpretive History of Blacks in American Films.* 1973. Reprint, New York: Continuum, 2003.

Bond, Alice Dixon. "The Case for Books; Edna Ferber Pleads Eloquently for Alaska in Her *Ice Palace.*" Review of *Ice Palace,* by Edna Ferber. *Boston Globe,* 4 June 1958.

Bost, Suzanne. *Mulattas and Mestizas: Representing Mixed Identities in the Americas, 1850–2000.* Athens: Univ. of Georgia Press, 2003.

Briggs, Harold E. "Showboats: The History of an American Institution." *Journal of Southern History* 18, no. 2 (May 1952): 236–237.

Brin, Alexander. "Great American Historian." Review of *Come and Get It,* by Edna Ferber. *Jewish Advocate,* 8 March 1935.

Broun, Heywood. "It Seems to Me." *New York World,* 7 March 1924.

Brown, Dee. *The Gentle Tamers: Women of the Old Wild West.* 1958. Reprint, Lincoln: Univ. of Nebraska Press, 1968.

Brown, Harry Joe. *Injun Joe's Ghost: The Indian Mixed-Blood in American Writing.* Columbia: Univ. of Missouri Press, 2004.

Brown, Sterling. *The Negro in American Fiction.* Washington, D.C.: Association of Negro Folk Education, 1937.

Bruccoli, Matthew J., ed. *A Life in Letters: F. Scott Fitzgerald.* New York: Scribner's, 1994.

Bryant, Billy. *Children of Ol' Man River: The Life and Times of a Showboat Trouper.* Chicago: Donnelley and Sons, 1988.

Bryant, Keith L., Jr. "'An Oklahoma I Had Never Seen Before': Alternative Views of Oklahoma." *Journal of Southern History* 61, no. 3 (August 1995): 644–645.

Burstein, Janet. *Writing Mothers, Writing Daughters: Tracing the Maternal in Stories By American Jewish Women.* Urbana: Univ. of Illinois Press, 1996.

Buscombe, Edward. *"Stagecoach."* London: BFI, 1992.

Bustin, John. "Show World." Review of *Giant*, directed by George Stevens. *Austin Statesman*, 9 November 1956.

Butcher, Fanny. "Edna Ferber Full Length Character Picture in Latest Novel: *So Big*." *Chicago Daily Tribune*, 23 February 1924.

Butler, Judith. *Gender Trouble: Feminism and the Subversion of Identity*. New York: Routledge, 1990.

Byars, Jackie. *All That Hollywood Allows: Rereading Gender in 1950s Melodrama*. Chapel Hill: Univ. of North Carolina Press, 1991.

Cable, George Washington. *Old Creole Days*. New York: Scribner's Sons, 1879.

Cameron, Ian, and Douglas Pye, eds. *The Book of the Western*. New York: Continuum, 1996.

Cameron, Kate. "Bergman's the Show in *Saratoga Trunk*." Review of *Saratoga Trunk*, directed by Sam Wood. *New York Daily News*, 22 November 1945.

———. "Ferber's *Giant* a Giant Film." Review of *Giant*, directed by George Stevens. *New York Daily News*, 11 October 1956.

Campbell, Donna. "'Written with a Hard and Ruthless Purpose': Rose Wilder Lane, Edna Ferber, and Middlebrow Regional Fiction." In *Middlebrow Moderns: Popular American Women Writers of the 1920s*, ed. Lisa Botschon and Meredith Goldsmith, 25–44. Boston: Northeastern Univ. Press, 2003.

Campbell, Randolph B. *An Empire for Slavery: The Peculiar Institution in Texas, 1821–1865*. Baton Rouge: Louisiana State Univ. Press, 1989.

Cantrell, Gregg, and Elizabeth Turner, eds. *Lone Star Pasts: Memory and History in Texas*. College Station: Texas A&M Univ. Press, 2007.

Carroll, Harrison. "*Cimarron* Epochal Smash Hit." *Los Angeles Herald*, 7 February 1931.

———. "Irene Dunne Dons Blackface to Play Scene in *Showboat*." *Motion Picture Herald*, 10 March 1936.

Casper, Drew. *Postwar Hollywood*. Boston: Blackwell, 2005.

Casteñeda, Carlos. *The Mexican Side of the Texas Revolution*. 1928. Reprint, Manchester, N.H.: Ayer, 1988.

Cawelti, John G. *The Six-Gun Mystique*. Bowling Green, Ohio: Bowling Green Univ. Popular Press, 1971.

Chafe, William H. *The American Woman: Her Changing Social, Economic, and Political Roles, 1920–1970*. New York: Oxford Univ. Press, 1972.

Churchill, D. W. "Hollywood Goes Historical." *New York Times Magazine*, 4 August 1940, 6–7.

Clark, Suzanne. *Cold Warriors: Manliness on Trial in the Rhetoric of the West*. Carbondale: Southern Illinois Univ. Press, 2000.

Coben, Stanley. *Rebellion against Victorianism: The Impetus for Cultural Change in 1920s America*. New York: Oxford Univ. Press, 1991.

Cole, Terrence. "Jim Crow in Alaska: The Passage of the Equal Rights Act of 1945." *Western Historical Quarterly* 23 (November 1992): 429–449.

Collier, John. "The Red Slaves of Oklahoma." *Sunset*, March 1924.

———. "The Rich Case of the Poor Indian." *Survey* 3 (June 1916).

Cooper, James Fenimore. *The Last of the Mohicans: A Narrative of 1757*. 1826. Reprint, New York: Viking Penguin, 1986.

Cott, Nancy. *The Grounding of Modern Feminism*. New Haven, Conn.: Yale University Press, 1987.

Countryman, Edward, and Evonne von Heussen-Countryman. *Shane*. London: BFI, 1999.

Courtney, Susan. *Hollywood Fantasies of Miscegenation*. Princeton, N.J.: Princeton Univ. Press, 2005.

Creelman, Eileen. Review of *Saratoga Trunk*, directed by Sam Wood. *New York Sun*, 23 November 1945.

Crewe, Regina. "*Cimarron* Mighty in Cinema Achievement." *New York American*, 27 January 1931.

Cripps, Thomas. *Slow Fade to Black: The Negro in American Film, 1900–1942*. Oxford: Oxford Univ. Press, 1977.

Crowther, Bosley. Review of *Ice Palace*, directed by Vincent Sherman. *New York Times*, 30 June 1960.

———. Review of *Saratoga Trunk*, directed by Sam Wood. *New York Times*, 22 November 1945.

———. "Who Won the West." Review of *Cimarron*, directed by Anthony Mann. *New York Times*, 26 February 1961.

Custen, George. *Bio/Pics: How Hollywood Constructed Public History*. New Brunswick, N.J.: Rutgers Univ. Press, 1992.

Daily Variety, 21 May 1952.

Dalton, David. *James Dean: American Icon*. New York: St. Martin's, 1989.

Darby, William. *Necessary American Fictions: Popular Literature of the 1950s*. Bowling Green, Ohio: Bowling Green State Univ. Press, 1987.

Dardis, Tom. *Some Time in the Sun: The Hollywood Years of Fitzgerald, Faulkner, Nathanael West, Aldous Huxley, and James Agee*. New York: Deutsch, 1976.

Davis, Mary Lee. *Uncle Sam's Attic: The Intimate Story of Alaska*. Boston: Wilde, 1930.

Davis, Tracy C. *Actresses as Working Women: Their Social Identity in Victorian Culture*. London: Routledge, 1991.

Dearborn, Mary V. *Pocahontas's Daughters: Gender and Ethnicity in American Culture*. Oxford: Oxford Univ. Press, 1986.

Debo, Angie. *And Still the Waters Run: The Betrayal of the Five Civilized Tribes*. Princeton, N.J.: Princeton Univ. Press, 1940.

———. *The Rise and Fall of the Choctaw Republic*. Norman: Univ. of Oklahoma Press, 1934.

Delehanty, Thornton. "The New Films." Review of *Cimarron*, directed by Wesley Ruggles. *New York Evening Post*, 27 January 1931.

Dempsey, David. "Tempest in Texas." *New York Times Book Review*, 28 September 1952, 8.

Des Jardins, Julie. *Women and the Historical Enterprise in America*. Chapel Hill: Univ. of North Carolina Pres, 2003.

Dick, Bernard F. *Hellmann in Hollywood*. Rutherford, N.J.: Fairleigh Dickinson Univ. Press, 1983.

Dinnerstein, Leonard. *Anti-Semitism in America*. New York: Oxford Univ. Press, 1994.

Dippie, Brian W. *The Vanishing American: White Attitudes and U.S. Indian Policy*. Lawrence: Univ. of Kansas Press, 1982.

Douglas, Ann. *The Feminization of American Culture*. New York: Doubleday, 1988.

Douglas, Susan. *Where the Girls Are: Growing Up Female with the Mass Media*. New York: Three Rivers Press, 1995.

Drummond, Roscoe. "Alaska—Next to Russia, Yet So Far." *New York Herald Tribune*, 6 July 1958.

Dumenil, Lynn. *The Modern Temper: American Culture and Society in the 1920s*. New York: Hill and Wang, 1995.

Dyer, Richard. *Heavenly Bodies: Film Stars and Society*. New York: St. Martin's, 1986.

———. *White*. London: BFI, 1997.

Edgett, E. F. Review of *Cimarron*, by Edna Ferber. *Boston Transcript*, 29 March 1930.

Eldridge, David. *Hollywood's History Films*. London: Tauris, 2006.

Ellet, Elizabeth. *Pioneer Women of the West*. Philadelphia: Porter and Coates, 1852.

Fadiman, Regina K. *Faulkner's "Intruder in the Dust": Novel into Film*. Knoxville: Univ. of Tennessee Press, 1978.

Farrar, John. "Novelists and/or Historians." *Saturday Review of Literature*, 17 February 1945, 7.

Ferber, Edna. *American Beauty*. Garden City, N.Y.: Doubleday, 1931.

———. *Cimarron*. Garden City, N.Y.: Doubleday, 1929.

———. *Come and Get It*. Garden City, N.Y.: Doubleday, 1935.

———. *Emma McChesney & Co*. New York: Stokes, 1915.

———. *Giant*. Garden City, N.Y.: Doubleday, 1952.

———. *Great Son*. Garden City, N.Y.: Doubleday, 1945.

———. *Ice Palace*. Garden City, N.Y.: Doubleday, 1958.

———. *A Kind of Magic*. New York: Doubleday, 1963.

———. *A Peculiar Treasure*. New York: Literary Guild of America, 1939.

———. *Personality Plus*. New York: Stokes, 1914.

———. "Remedies for Hate." *English Journal* 35, no. 6 (June 1946): 320–322.

———. *Roast Beef, Medium*. New York: Stokes, 1913.

———. *Saratoga Trunk*. Garden City, N.Y.: Doubleday, 1942.

———. *Show Boat*. Garden City, N.Y.: Doubleday, 1926.

———. *So Big*. New York: Grosset and Dunlap, 1924.

Fergusson, Harvey. Review of *Cimarron*, by Edna Ferber. *Books*, 23 March 1930, 7.

Feuer, Jane. *The Hollywood Musical.* London: Macmillan, 1982.

Fiedler, Leslie. *The Return of the Vanishing American.* New York: Stein and Day, 1968.

Finley, James F. Review of *Giant*, directed by George Stevens. *Catholic World*, December 1956, 221–222.

Fitzgerald, Edward J. "Fact, Fiction, or Fantasy." *Saturday Review of Literature*, 17 January 1953, 13.

Foley, Neil. *The White Scourge: Mexicans, Blacks, and Poor Whites in Texas Cotton Culture.* Berkeley and Los Angeles: Univ. of California Press, 1997.

Foster, Gwendolyn Audrey. *Performing Whiteness: Postmodern Reconstructions in the Cinema.* Albany: SUNY Press, 2003.

Gabler, Neal. *An Empire of Their Own: How the Jews Invented Hollywood.* New York: Doubleday, 1988.

Garcia, Ignacio M. *Hector Garcia: In Relentless Pursuit of Justice.* Houston: Arte Publico, 2001.

Garcia, Mario T. *Mexican Americans: Leadership, Ideology, and Identity, 1930–1960.* New Haven, Conn.: Yale Univ. Press, 1989.

Garrett, Oliver H. P. "The Little Brown Men." *Screen Writer* 4 (October 1948): 1–2.

Gehring, Wes D. *Irene Dunne.* Lanham, Md.: McFarland, 2003.

Georgi-Findlay, Brigitte. *The Frontiers of Women's Writing: Women's Narratives and the Rhetoric of Westward Expansion.* Tucson: Univ. of Arizona Press, 1996.

Geraghty, Christine. *Now a Major Motion Picture: Film Adaptations of Literature and Drama.* Lanham, Md.: Rowman and Littlefield, 2007.

Gertner, Richard. Review of *Ice Palace*, directed by Vincent Sherman. *Motion Picture Daily*, 15 June 1960.

Gilbert, Douglas. "Song and Sentiment Pageant in *Show Boat* at Music Hall." *New York World-Telegram*, 15 May 1936.

Gilbert, Julie Goldsmith. *Edna Ferber and Her Circle.* New York: Applause, 1978.

Gomez, Laura. *Manifest Destinies: The Making of the Mexican American Race.* New York: New York Univ. Press, 2007.

Good Housekeeping. "Women and the Box Office." May 1950, 16–17.

Goodwyn, Frank. *Life on the King Ranch.* 1951. Reprint, College Station: Texas A&M Univ. Press, 1993.

Govan, Christine Noble. "Cattle-Rich Texas Family Poses Problems for Bride." Review of *Giant*, by Edna Ferber. *Chattanooga Times*, 5 October 1952.

Graham, Kathleen. Review of *Ice Palace*, by Edna Ferber. *Toronto Leader-Post*, 12 April 1958.

Graham, Philip. *Showboats: The History of an American Institution.* Austin: Univ. of Texas Press, 1951.

Grant, Jack. Review of *Saratoga Trunk*, directed by Sam Wood. *Hollywood Reporter*, 21 November 1945.

Greenberg, Clement. "Avant-Garde and Kitsch." *Partisan Review* 6, no. 5 (1939): 34–49.

Greenebaum, Betsy. "For Better or for Worse." *Chicago Evening Post Literary Review*, 22 February 1924, 6.

Gregory, James. *American Exodus.* Oxford: Oxford Univ. Press, 1989.

Griffin, Sean. "The Gang's All Here: Generic versus Racial Integration in the 1940s Musical." *Cinema Journal* 42, no. 1 (Fall 2002): 21–45.

Griffith, Sally Foreman. *Home Town News: William Allen White and the "Emporia Gazette."* New York: Oxford Univ. Press, 1989.

Griswold del Castillo, Richard, ed. *World War II and Mexican American Civil Rights.* Austin: Univ. of Texas Press, 2008.

Gruening, Ernest. *The Battle for Alaska Statehood.* Anchorage: Univ. of Alaska Press, 1967.

———. "Edna Ferber's Novel of Alaska Dreams and Drama." Review of *Ice Palace*, by Edna Ferber. *New York Herald Tribune*, 20 March 1958.

———. *The State of Alaska.* New York: Random House, 1954.

Guttmann, Alan. *The Jewish Writer in America: Assimilation and the Crisis of Identity.* New York: Oxford Univ. Press, 1971.

Hackett, Alice Payne, and James Henry Burke. *Eighty Years of Best Sellers, 1895–1975.* New York and London: Bowker, 1977.

Hall, Mordaunt. "Oklahoma Then and Now." Review of *Cimarron*, directed by Wesley Ruggles. *New York Times*, 7 February 1931.

———. "Solid Folk." *New York Times*, n.d.

Handley, William R. *Marriage, Violence, and the Nation in the American Literary West.* Cambridge: Cambridge Univ. Press, 2002.

Hansen, Miriam. *Babel and Babylon: Spectatorship in American Silent Film.* Cambridge, Mass.: Harvard Univ. Press, 1991.

Harris, Barbara J. *Beyond Her Sphere: Women and the Professions in American History.* Westport, Conn.: Greenwood, 1978.

Haskell, *From Reverence to Rape: The Treatment of Women in the Movies.* New York: Holt, Rinehart, and Winston, 1973.

Havighurst, Walter. "Big. A." *Saturday Review of Literature*, 29 March 1958, 26.

Haycox, Stephen W. *Alaska: An American Colony.* New York: Hurst, 2002.

Haycox, Stephen, and Mary C. Mangusso, eds. *Alaska Anthology: Interpreting the Past.* Seattle: Univ. of Washington Press, 1996.

Hellman, Lillian. *Scoundrel Time.* Boston: Little, Brown, 1976.

Henderson, Brian. "*The Searchers*: An American Dilemma." In *"The Searchers": Essays and Reflections on John Ford's Classic Western*, ed. Arthur Ekstein and Peter Lehman, 47–73. Detroit: Wayne State Univ. Press, 2004.

Henderson, Daniel. *From the Volga to the Yukon: The Story of the Russian March to Alaska and California, Paralleling Our Own Westward Trek.* New York: Hastings House, 1945.

Hendler, Jane. *Best-Sellers and Their Film Adaptations in Postwar America.* New York: Peter Lang, 2001.

Henriksen, L. L. *Anzia Yezierska: A Writer's Life*. New Brunswick, N.J.: Rutgers Univ. Press, 1988.

Higham, John. *Send These to Me: Jews and Other Immigrants in Urban America*. New York: Atheneum, 1975.

———. *Strangers in the Land: Patterns of American Nativism, 1860–1925*. 1955. Reprint, New York: Atheneum, 1989.

Hitt, Jim. *The American West from Fiction (1823–1986) into Film (1909–1986)*. Jefferson, N.C.: McFarland, 1990.

Hodes, Martha. *Sex, Race, Love: Crossing Boundaries in North American History*. New York: New York Univ. Press, 1999.

Holliday, Carl. "American Showboats." *Theatre Magazine*, May 1917, 246.

Hollywood Citizen-News. 27 August 1957.

Hough, Emerson. *The Passing of the Frontier: A Chronicle of the Old West*. New Haven, Conn.: Yale Univ. Press, 1921.

Howard, Eleanor. Review of *Giant*, by Edna Ferber. *Malibu Times*, 10 October 1952.

Howden-Smith, Arthur D. *Commodore Vanderbilt: An Epic of American Achievement*. New York: McBride, 1927.

Hurst, Fannie. *Back Street*. New York: Cosmopolitan Book, 1931.

———. *Imitation of Life*. London: Harper and Bros., 1933.

Hurston, Zora Neale. *Their Eyes Were Watching God*. Philadelphia: Lippincott, 1937.

Huyssen, Andreas. "Mass Culture as Woman: Modernism's Other." In *After the Great Divide: Modernism, Mass Culture, and Postmodernism*, 44–64. Bloomington: Indiana Univ. Press, 1986.

Hyatt, R. M. "Movies as Historians." *Review of Reviews* 95 (April 1937): 56.

Hyman, Paula E. *Gender and Assimilation in Modern Jewish History: The Roles and Representation of Women*. Seattle: Univ. of Washington Press, 1995.

Ivers, James D. Review of *Giant*, directed by George Stevens. *Motion Picture Daily*, 10 October 1956.

Jackson, Cassandra. *Barriers between Us: Interracial Sex in Nineteenth-Century American Literature*. Bloomington: Indiana Univ. Press, 2004.

Jackson, Helen Hunt. *Ramona*. Boston: Roberts Bros., 1884.

Jackson, Martin, and John E. O'Connor, eds. *American History/American Film: Interpreting the Hollywood Image*. New York: Ungar, 1979.

Jacobson, Matthew Frye. *Whiteness of a Different Color: European Immigrants and the Alchemy of Race*. Cambridge, Mass.: Harvard Univ. Press, 1999.

Jocher, Katharine. "Folk Life in Fiction." *Social Forces* 10, no. 3 (March 1932): 453–455.

Johnson, Kevin R., ed. *Mixed Race Americans and the Law*. New York: New York Univ. Press, 2002.

Johnson, Walter. *William Allen White's America*. New York: Holt, 1947.

Joseph, May, and Jennifer Natalya Fink, eds. *Performing Hybridity*. Minneapolis: Univ. of Minnesota Press, 1999.

Josephson, Matthew. *The Robber Barons: The Great American Capitalists, 1861–1901.* New York: Harcourt, Brace, 1934.

Kahn, Ava F., ed. *Jewish Life in the American West: Perspectives on Migration, Settlement, and Community.* Los Angeles: Heyday, 2002.

Kahn, Nat. "Edna Ferber Story Too Old-Fashioned." Review of *So Big*, directed by Robert Wise. *Hollywood Reporter*, 30 September 1953, 3.

Kammen, Michael G. *The Lively Arts: Gilbert Seldes and the Transformation of Cultural Criticism in the United States.* New York: Oxford Univ. Press, 1996.

Kaplan, Amy. "Manifest Domesticity." *American Literature* 70 (September 1998): 581–606.

Kenaga, Heidi. "Edna Ferber's *Cimarron*, Cultural Authority, and 1920s Western Historical Narratives." In *Middlebrow Moderns: Popular American Women Writers of the 1920s*, ed. Lisa Botschon and Meredith Goldsmith, 167–201. Boston: Northeastern Univ. Press, 2003.

Kibler, M. Alison. *Rank Ladies: Gender and Cultural Hierarchy in American Vaudeville.* Chapel Hill: Univ. of North Carolina Press, 1999.

Kittrell, William. Review of *Giant*, by Edna Ferber. *Saturday Review*, 27 September 1952, 15.

Klein, Kerwin Lee. *Frontiers of the Historical Imagination: Narrating the European Conquest of Native America, 1890–1990.* Berkeley and Los Angeles: Univ. of California Press, 1997.

Klinger, Barbara. *Melodrama and Meaning: History, Culture, and the Films of Douglas Sirk.* Bloomington: Indiana Univ. Press, 1994.

Kluger, Richard. *Simple Justice: The History of "Brown v. Board of Education" and Black America's Struggle for Equality.* New York: Knopf, 1976.

Kolodny, Annette. *The Land before Her: Fantasy and Experience of the American Frontiers, 1630–1860.* Chapel Hill: Univ. of North Carolina Press, 1984.

Konsett, Delia Caporoso. *Ethnic Modernisms: Anzia Yezierska, Zora Neale Hurston, Jean Rhys, and the Aesthetics of Dislocation.* London: Palgrave, 2003.

Korda, Michael. *Making the List: A Cultural History of the American Bestseller, 1900–1999.* New York: Barnes and Noble, 2001.

Kravsow, I. M. "A Gigantic Prejudice." Review of *Giant*, by Edna Ferber. *Hartford Courant*, n.d. [1952].

Kreuger, Miles. *"Show Boat": The Story of a Classic American Musical.* New York: Oxford Univ. Press, 1977.

Kroeger, Brooke. *Fannie: the Talent for Success of Fannie Hurst.* New York: Times Books, 1999.

Kronenberger, Louis. *"Show Boat* Is High Romance." *New York Times Book Review*, August 1926. Reprinted in *Jewish Women Fiction Writers*, ed. Harold Bloom, 20–22. Philadelphia: Chelsea House, 1998.

Kutner, Nanette. "Edna Ferber Today." *Everywoman's Family Circle*, February 1959, 30–31, 57, 59.

Lane, Rose Wilder. *Free Land*. 1938. Reprint, Lincoln: Univ. of Nebraska Press, 1998.

Latham, Aaron. *Crazy Sundays: F. Scott Fitzgerald in Hollywood*. London: Secker and Warburg, 1972.

Lawrence, Margaret. *The School of Femininity*. New York: Stokes, 1936.

Leckie, Shirley. *Angie Debo: Pioneer Historian*. Norman: Univ. of Oklahoma Press, 2000.

Leech, Margaret. *In the Days of McKinley*. New York: Harper and Bros., 1941.

———. *Reveille in Washington, 1860–1865*. New York: Harper and Bros., 1941.

Leisy, Ernest. *The American Historical Novel*. Norman: Univ. of Oklahoma Press, 1952.

Lemons, J. Stanley. *The Woman Citizen: Social Feminism in the 1920s*. 1973. Reprint, Charlottesville: Univ. Press of Virginia, 1990.

Levine, Lawrence W. *Highbrow/Lowbrow: The Emergence of Cultural Hierarchy in America*. Cambridge: Cambridge Univ. Press, 1988.

Lewin, William. "The Effect of Photoplays on Reading." *Publishers Weekly*, 20 October 1934, 1474–1475.

———. "Photoplays of Interest to English Teachers." *English Journal* 21, no. 1 (January 1932): 55–57.

Lewis, Lena Morrow. "A Big Story." *New Leader*, 8 March 1924.

Lichtenstein, Diane. *Writing Their Nations: The Tradition of Nineteenth-Century American Jewish Women Writers*. Bloomington: Indiana Univ. Press, 1992.

Life. "A Tale of a Rich Land and Its Lords." 15 October 1956, 68–70.

Little, Carl Victor. "By-the-way discusses Ferber's New Book, Midget." *Houston Press*, 13 September 1952.

———. "Ferber's Big Bust: She Fills Texas Air with Private 4-Engine Jobs." *Houston Press*, 20 June 1952.

Limerick, Patricia Nelson. *Legacy of Conquest: The Unbroken Past of the American West*. New York: Norton, 1987.

Lott, Eric. *Love and Theft: Blackface Minstrelsy and the American Working Class*. New York: Oxford Univ. Press, 1993.

Luhr, William. *Raymond Chandler and Film*. Tallahassee: Florida State Univ. Press, 1991.

Lynd, Robert S., and Helen Merrell Lynd. *Middletown: A Study in Modern American Culture*. New York: Harcourt, Brace, 1929.

MacDonald, Dwight. "Masscult and Midcult." In *Against the American Grain*, 3–75. New York: Random House, 1962.

MacLeod, William Christie. *The American Indian Frontier*. New York: Knopf, 1928.

Marquez, Benjamin. *LULAC: The Evolution of a Mexican American Political Organization*. Austin: Univ. of Texas Press, 1993.

Mathes, Valerie Sherer. *Helen Hunt Jackson and Her Indian Reform Legacy*. Austin: Univ. of Texas Press, 1990.

Matthews, T. S. "Novels by Weight." Review of *Come and Get It*, by Edna Ferber. *New Republic*, March 1935.

May, Henry. *The End of American Innocence: A Study of the First Years of Our Own Time, 1912–1917*. Chicago: Univ. of Chicago Press, 1964.

Mayer, Arthur. "Myths, Movies and Maturity." *Saturday Review*, 7 April 1956, 7–8.

McCarten, John. Review of *Giant*, directed by George Stevens. *New Yorker*, 20 October 1956, 178–179.

McGinley, Ellen. Review of *Ice Palace*, by Edna Ferber. *Vermont Catholic Tribune*, 18 April 1958.

McLarn, Jack. "A Literary Legend: Edna Ferber Scores Again." Review of *Ice Palace*, by Edna Ferber. *Charlotte Observer*, 30 April 1958.

McManus, John. "Magnolia of the Movies." *New York Times*, 1 May 1936.

McPherson, Tara. *Reconstructing Dixie: Race, Gender, and Nostalgia in the Imagined South.* Durham, N.C.: Duke Univ. Press, 2003.

McWilliams, Carey. *North from Mexico: The Spanish-Speaking People of the United States.* 1949. Reprint, New York: Greenwood, 1968.

———. "Oilmen Invade Hollywood." *Nation*, 16 October 1948, 429.

Meade, Marion. *Bobbed Hair and Bathtub Gin: Writers Running Wild in the Twenties.* New York: Doubleday, 2004.

Mellen, Joan. *Hellmann and Hammett.* New York: HarperCollins, 1996.

Mencke, John G. *Mulattoes and Race Mixture: American Attitudes and Images, 1865–1918.* Ann Arbor, Mich.: UMI Research Press, 1979.

Meyerowitz, Joan. *Not June Cleaver: Women and Gender in Postwar America, 1945–1960.* Philadelphia: Temple Univ. Press, 1994.

Michaels, Walter Benn. *Our America: Nativism, Modernism, and Pluralism.* Durham, N.C.: Duke Univ. Press, 1995.

Miller, Rick. *Photoplay Edition: A Collector's Guide.* Lanham, Md.: McFarland, 2002.

Millichap, Joseph P. *Steinbeck and Film.* New York: Ungar, 1983.

Mitchell, Donald Craig. *Sold American: The Story of Alaska Natives and Their Land, 1867–1959.* Hanover, N.H.: Univ. Press of New England, 1997.

Mitchell, Margaret. *Gone with the Wind.* New York: Macmillan, 1936.

Modleski, Tania. "A Woman's Gotta Do . . . What a Man's Gotta Do? Cross Dressing in the Western." *Signs* 22, no. 3 (Spring 1997): 519–544.

Montejano, David. *Anglos and Mexicans in the Making of Texas, 1836–1986.* Austin: Univ. of Texas Press, 1987.

———. "The Demise of Jim Crow for Texas Mexicans, 1940–1970." *Aztlan* 16, nos. 1–2 (1985): 27–69.

Moore, Colleen. *Silent Star.* Garden City, N.Y.: Doubleday, 1968.

Moss, Marilyn Ann. *Giant: George Stevens, a Life on Film.* Madison: Univ. of Wisconsin Press, 2004.

Movie Secrets. "James Dean: As You Will See Him." October 1956, 26–27.

Mulvey, Laura. *Visual and Other Pleasures.* Bloomington: Indiana Univ. Press, 1989.

Nachbar, Jack, ed. *Focus on the Western.* Englewood Cliffs, N.J.: Prentice-Hall, 1974.

Naremore, James, ed. *Film Adaptation.* New Brunswick, N.J.: Rutgers Univ. Press, 2000.

Neale, Steve. *Genre and Hollywood.* London: Routledge, 2000.

New Republic. "Trouble in Paradise." 24 February 1947, 41.

New York Times. "Envoy Is Victim of Segregation," 24 August 1955.

Nichols, Lewis. "Talk with Edna Ferber." *New York Times Book Review,* 5 October 1952, 30.

Nickles, Shelley. "More is Better: Mass Consumption, Gender, and Class Identity in Postwar America," *American Quarterly* 54, no. 4 (December 2002): 581–622.

Nugent, Frank. Review of *Come and Get It,* directed by William Wyler. *New York Times,* 12 November 1936.

———. Review of *Show Boat,* directed by James Whale. *New York Times,* 15 May 1936.

Nugent, Sam. "Some Think This Giant Not So Big." *Dallas Morning News,* n.d. [1952].

O'Mara, Roger. "Edna Ferber Limns Alaska in Paean of Praise." Review of *Ice Palace,* by Edna Ferber. *New York Star,* 13 April 1958.

Overton, Grant. "The Social Critic in Edna Ferber." *Bookman,* October 1926, 139–143.

Palmer, R. Barton. *Perspectives on Film Noir.* New York: Hall, 1996.

———, ed. *Twentieth-Century American Fiction on Screen.* Cambridge: Cambridge Univ. Press, 2007.

Parker, William R. "A Stranger's Story of Edna Ferber." *English Journal* 19, no. 6 (June 1930): 447–449.

Parsons, Louella. "Edna Ferber in a New Role: Substitutes Talking for Writing." *Los Angeles Examiner,* 21 July 1935.

———. "Saratoga a Woman's Film." *Los Angeles Examiner,* 9 March 1946.

Pascoe, Peggy. *Relations of Rescue: The Search for Female Moral Authority in the American West, 1874–1939.* New York: Oxford Univ. Press, 1990.

Patrick, Arnold. "Getting into Six Figures." *Bookman,* April 1925, 164–168.

Patterson, James T. *"Brown v. Board of Education": A Civil Rights Milestone and Its Troubled Legacy.* Oxford: Oxford Univ. Press, 2002.

Patterson, Martha. *Beyond the Gibson Girl: Reimaging the American New Woman, 1895–1915.* Urbana: Univ. of Illinois Press, 2005.

Peet, Creighton. Review of *Show Boat,* directed by Harry Pollard. *New York Evening Post,* April 1929.

Pelswick, Rose. "Film Lives Up to Its Name in Everything." Review of *Giant,* directed by George Stevens. *New York Journal-American.*

———. Review of *Saratoga Trunk,* directed by Sam Wood. *New York Journal-American,* 23 November 1945.

Perry, George Sessions. *Texas: A World in Itself.* New York: McGraw-Hill, 1942.

Person, Leland S., Jr. "The American Eve: Miscegenation and a Feminist Frontier Fiction." *American Quarterly* 37 (Winter 1985): 668–685.

Phelps, William Lyon. "On American Books of 1931." McClure Newspaper Syndicate for release, 29 November 1931.

Philip, Kenneth R. "The New Deal and Alaska Natives, 1936–1945." *Pacific Historical Review* 50 (1981): 309–327.

Phillips, Gene D. *Fiction, Film, and Faulkner: The Art of Adaptation.* Knoxville: Univ. of Tennessee Press, 2001.

Poore, Charles. Review of *Ice Palace*, by Edna Ferber. *New York Times*, 27 March 1958.

Potamkin, Harry Alan. "*Storm Over Asia* and *Abraham Lincoln*." *New Masses*, October 1930, 16.

Publishers Weekly. "Books into Films: Movies' Acceptance as Integral Part of American Culture." 15 February 1947, 1138.

———. "Current and Forthcoming Movies from Books." 1 February 1936, 618.

———. "Making the Movies Sell Books." 17 September 1932, 1027–1030.

Pyron, Darden Asbury, ed. *Recasting: "Gone with the Wind" in American Culture*. Miami: Univ. Presses of Florida, 1983.

Raimos, Eve Allegra. *The "Tragic Mulatta" Revisited: Race and Nationalism in Nineteenth-Century Anti-Slavery Fiction*. New Brunswick, N.J.: Rutgers Univ. Press, 2004.

Rechy, John. "Jim Crow Wears a Sombrero." *Nation*, 10 October 1959, 212.

Redellings, Lowell E. "*Saratoga Trunk* a Slow Photoplay but Charming." Review of *Saratoga Trunk*, directed by Sam Wood. *Hollywood Citizen-News*, 9 March 1946.

———. "*So Big* an Inspiring Film Version of Pulitzer Prize Novel." Review of *So Big*, directed by Robert Wise. *Hollywood Citizen-News*, 4 November 1953.

Reese, Linda Williams. *Women of Oklahoma, 1890–1920*. Norman: Univ. of Oklahoma Press, 1997.

Review of *Cimarron*, by Edna Ferber. "Miss Ferber's Vivid Tales of Oklahoma's Setting." *New York Times Book Review*, 23 March 1930.

———. *New York World*, 20 March 1930.

Review of *Cimarron*, directed by Anthony Mann. *Motion Picture Daily*, 6 December 1960.

Review of *Come and Get It*, directed by William Wyler. *Daily Variety*, 27 October 1936.

———. *Hollywood Reporter*, 27 October 1936.

———. *Motion Picture Herald*, 7 November 1936.

———. *Time*, 16 November 1936.

Review of *Giant*, by Edna Ferber. "*Giant* Renews Ferber Influence." *Los Angeles Times*, 2 August 1953.

Review of *Giant*, directed by George Stevens. *Ciné Universal* (Mexico), September 1957.

———. *Coventry (UK) Evening Telegraph*, 26 February 1956.

———. *Hollywood Reporter*, 10 October 1956.

———. *Nation*, 20 October 1956, 335.

———. *Newsweek*, 22 October 1956, 112, 114.

———. *Time*, 22 October 1956, 108–112.

———. *Variety*, 10 October 1956.

Review of *Great Son*, by Edna Ferber. *Time*, 5 February 1945, 94, 96.

Review of *Ice Palace*, by Edna Ferber. *San Francisco Chronicle*, 15 June 1958.

———. *Wichita Falls (TX) Times*, 30 March 1958.

Review of *Ice Palace*, directed by Vincent Sherman. *Saturday Review*, 23 July 1960.

———. *Time*, 4 July 1960.

———. *Variety*, 17 June 1960.

Review of *Saratoga Trunk*, directed by Sam Wood. *Daily Variety*, 20 November 1945.

————. *Hollywood Reporter*, 21 November 1945.

————. *Hollywood Review*, 3 December 1945.

————. *Motion Picture Daily*, 21 November 1945.

————. *Variety*, 21 November 1945.

Review of *Show Boat*, directed by Harry Pollard. *Chicago Tribune*, 2 October 1929.

————. *Cleveland Plain Dealer*, 11 February 1929.

Review of *Show Boat*, directed by George Sidney. *Hollywood Citizen-News*, 24 July 1951.

————. *Hollywood Reporter*, 5 June 1951.

————. *New Yorker*, 28 July 1951.

————. *Weekly Variety*, 6 June 1951.

Review of *Show Boat*, directed by James Whale. "The New Dunne." *Detroit News*, 31 May 1936.

————. *Motion Picture Herald*, 18 April 1936, 16.

————. "No Cloud in the Sky." *Picture Play*, August 1936.

————. *Variety*, 20 May 1936.

Review of *So Big*, by Edna Ferber. *New York Evening Post*, 20 February 1924.

————. "So Big the Diminishing Son." *New York Sun and the Globe*, 1 March 1924.

Review of *So Big*, directed by William Wellman. *Motion Picture Herald*, 19 March 1932.

Review of *So Big*, directed by Robert Wise. *Cue*, 24 October 1953.

————. "So Big Mild, But Wyman Strong in Female Lead." *Los Angeles Daily News*, 4 November 1953.

————. *Newsweek*, 9 November 1953, 18.

————. *Variety*, 30 September 1953.

Review of *The Royal Family of Broadway*, directed by George Cukor and Cyril Gardner. *Film Daily*, 28 December 1930.

————. *Variety*, 24 December 1930.

Rivas-Rodriguez, Maggie. *Mexican Americans and World War II*. Austin: Univ. of Texas Press, 2005.

Roediger, David. *The Wages of Whiteness: Race and the Making of the American Working Class*. London: Verso, 1999.

————. *Working toward Whiteness: How America's Immigrants Became White*. New York: Basic Books, 2006.

Rogers, Betty. *Will Rogers*. Garden City, N.Y.: Garden City, 1941.

Rogers, W. G. "In Moonlight and Magnolia the Protest Was Lost." *New York Times Book Review*, 8 September 1963.

Rogin, Michael. "'The Sword Became a Flashing Vision': D. W. Griffith's *The Birth of a Nation*." In Robert Lang, ed., *"The Birth of a Nation,"* 250–293. New Brunswick, N.J.: Rutgers Univ. Press, 1994.

————. *Blackface, White Noise: Jewish Immigrants in the Hollywood Melting Pot*. Berkeley: University of California Press, 1996.

Rose, W. L. *Race and Region in American Historical Fiction: Four Episodes in Popular Culture*. Oxford: Oxford Univ. Press, 1979.

Roth, Sanford. "The Late James Dean." *Colliers*, 25 November 1955, 62–65.

Rotha, Paul. *The Film Till Now*. Rev. ed. London: Spring Books, 1967.

Rubin, Joan Shelley. *The Making of Middlebrow Culture*. Chapel Hill: Univ. of North Carolina Press, 1992.

San Miguel, Guadalupe. "The Struggle against Separate but Unequal Schools." *History of Education Quarterly* 23 (Fall 1983): 343–359.

Sandoz, Mari. *Cheyenne Autumn*. New York: McGraw-Hill, 1953.

———. *Crazy Horse*. New York: Knopf, 1942.

———. *Old Jules*. Boston: Little, Brown, 1935.

Saturday Evening Post. "Texas Tackles the Race Problem." 12 January 1952, 23.

Schallert, Edwin. "Pioneer Days Well Depicted." Review of *Cimarron*, directed by Wesley Ruggles. *Los Angeles Times*, 7 February 1931.

Schatz, Thomas. *Boom and Bust: American Cinema in the 1940s*. Berkeley and Los Angeles: Univ. of California Press, 1997.

———. *The Genius of the System*. New York: Pantheon, 1988.

———. *Hollywood Genres*. New York: Random House, 1981.

Scheick, William J. *The Half-Blood: A Cultural Symbol in Nineteenth-Century American Fiction*. Lexington: Univ. Press of Kentucky, 1979.

Scheuer, Philip K. "*Giant* Looms as Towering Saga of Texas Boom Years." Review of *Giant*, directed by George Stevens. *Los Angeles Times*, 7 October 1956.

Schlissel, Lillian, Vicki Ruiz, and Janice Monk, eds. *Western Women: Their Land, Their Lives*. Albuquerque: Univ. of New Mexico Press, 1984.

School and Society. "Motion Picture Films for the Schools To Be Selected from Hollywood Vaults." Vol. 46 (24 July 1937): 107–108.

Scullin, George. "James Dean: The Legend and the Facts." *Look*, 16 October 1956, 120–124.

Seldes, Gilbert. *The Seven Lively Arts*. New York: Harper and Brothers, 1924. Reprint, New York: Sagamore Press, 1957.

Seymour, Flora W. *The Story of the Red Man*. New York: Longmans, Green, 1929.

Shaughnessy, Mary Rose. *Women and Success in American Society in the Works of Edna Ferber*. New York: Gordon, 1977.

Sherwood, Robert. "The Moving Picture Album." Review of *Cimarron*, directed by Wesley Ruggles. *Hollywood Reporter*, 7 February 1931.

Silverman, Sime. Review of *Show Boat*, directed by Harry Pollard. *Weekly Variety*, 24 April 1929.

Skenazy, Paul. *The New Wild West: Urban Mysteries of Dashiell Hammett and Raymond Chandler*. Boise, Idaho: Boise State Univ. Press, 1980.

Skinner, Constance Lindsay. *Becky Landers, Frontier Warrior*. New York: Macmillan, 1927.

Slotkin, Richard. *The Fatal Environment*. Norman: Univ. of Oklahoma Press, 1985.

———. *Gunfighter Nation*. Norman: Univ. of Oklahoma Press, 1992.

Smith, Bonnie. *The Gender of History: Men, Women, and Historical Practice*. Cambridge, Mass.: Harvard Univ. Press, 1998.

Smith, Harrison. Review of *Ice Palace*, by Edna Ferber. *Saturday Review*, 29 March 1958.

Smith, Henry Nash. *Virgin Land: The American West as Symbol and Myth*. New York: Viking, 1950.

Smyth, J. E. "Classical Hollywood and the Filmic Writing of Interracial Women's History, 1931–1939." In *Mixed Race Hollywood*, ed. Mary Beltran and Camilla Fojas, 23–44. New York: New York Univ. Press, 2008.

———. "James Dean, Jett Rink, Jim Crow: Reconstructing Edna Ferber's *Giant*." *American Studies* 48:3 (Fall 2007) 5–27.

———. "New Frontiers in American Interracial History: Edna Ferber and the Indian Mixed-Blood." *European Journal of Native American Studies* 20, no. 1 (2006): 39–45.

———. *Reconstructing American Historical Cinema from "Cimarron" to "Citizen Kane."* Lexington: Univ. Press of Kentucky, 2006.

Snyder, Robert I. "Ferber's Alaska Novel Lashes 'Robber Barons.'" Review of *Ice Palace*, by Edna Ferber. *Cleveland Plain Dealer*, 30 March 1958.

Sollars, Werner. *Neither Black nor White yet Both: Thematic Explorations of Interracial Literature*. New York: Oxford Univ. Press, 1997.

Spain, Mildred. "See Colleen as Selina." *New York Daily News*, 5 January 1925.

Spearman, Walter. *American History through Historical Novels*. Chapel Hill: Univ. of North Carolina Press, 1952.

Spears, Jack. "The Indian on the Screen." *Films in Review* 10 (January 1959): 18–35.

Stacey, Jackie. *Stargazing: Hollywood Cinema and Female Spectatorship*. London: Routledge, 1994.

Stam, Robert. "Beyond Fidelity: The Dialogics of Adaptation." In *Film Adaptation*, ed. James Naremore. New Brunswick, N.J.: Rutgers Univ. Press, 2000.

Stanfield, Peter. *Hollywood, Westerns, and the 1930s: The Lost Trail*. Exeter, UK: Univ. of Exeter Press, 2001.

Starrett, Vincent. "The Best Loved Books." *New York Herald Tribune*, 23 May 1954.

Stauffer, Helen. *Mari Sandoz, Story Catcher of the Plains*. Lincoln: Univ. of Nebraska Press, 1982.

Stockbridge, Frank Parker. "What are the Popular Books—And Why?" *English Journal* 20, no. 6 (June 1931): 441–449.

Stowe, Charles Edward. *Harriet Beecher Stowe: The Story of Her Life*. Boston: Houghton Mifflin, 1911.

Sundborg, George. "*Ice Palace* Should Insure Early Breakup for Alaska." Review of *Ice Palace*, by Edna Ferber. *Fairbanks News-Miner*, 27 March 1958.

Surmleian, Leon. "It's the Irish in Her." *Motion Picture Story Magazine*, July 1936, 68.

Tarbell, Ida. *The Early Life of Abraham Lincoln*. New York: McClure, 1896.

———. *History of the Standard Oil Company*. New York: McClure, Phillips, 1904.

———. *In the Footsteps of the Lincolns*. New York: Harper and Brothers, 1924.

———. *Life of Abraham Lincoln*. New York: Macmillan, 1917.

———. *The Nationalizing of Business, 1878–1898*. New York: Macmillan, 1936.

Texas Spectator. "Frontier Myth and Texas Politics." Vol. 3, no. 33 (24 May 1948): 3–5, 15.

Teichmann, Howard. *George S. Kaufman.* London: Angus and Robertson, 1972.

Thompson, Stephanie Lewis. *Influencing America's Tastes: Realism in the Works of Wharton, Cather, and Hurst.* Gainesville: Univ. Press of Florida, 2002.

Time. "Great Son." 5 February 1945, 94, 96.

———. "The Power of a Woman." 14 November 1949, 101.

Tinkle, Lon. "Ferber Goes Both Native and Berserk: Parody, Not Portrait, of Texas." Review of *Giant,* by Edna Ferber. *Dallas Morning News,* [1952].

Toplin, Robert Brent. *History by Hollywood: The Use and Abuse of the American Past.* Urbana: Univ. of Illinois Press, 1996.

Tourtellot, Arthur B. "History and the Historical Novel." *Saturday Review of Literature,* 20 August 1940, 3.

TP. "Book of the Week: The Woman Behind the Plough." Review of *So Big,* by Edna Ferber. *TP's and Cassell's Weekly of London,* 5 April 1924.

Trachtenberg, Alan. *The Incorporation of America.* New York: Hill and Wang, 1982.

Trumbo, Dalton. "Minorities and the Screen." *Arts and Architecture,* February 1944, 16–17.

Uffen, Ellen Serlen. "Edna Ferber and the 'Theatricalization' of American Mythology." *Midwestern Miscellany* 8 (1980): 82–93.

Uricchio, William, and Roberta E. Pearson. *Reframing Culture: The Case of the Vitagraph Quality Films.* Princeton, N.J.: Princeton Univ. Press, 1993.

Van Doren, Dorothy. "A Pioneer Fairy Story." Review of *Cimarron,* by Edna Ferber. *Nation,* 23 April 1930, 494.

Variety, 13 May 1953.

———. Review of *Show Boat,* 20 May 1936.

Vestal, Stanley. "Oklahoma Is Setting of Edna Ferber's New Book." Review of *Cimarron. Dallas Morning News,* 30 March 1930.

———. "*Cimarron* Is Readable Account of Early Days in Sooner State." *Saturday Review of Literature,* 22 March 1930, 841.

Wadle, Moe. *The Movie Tie-In Book.* Coralville, Iowa: Nostalgia Books, 1994.

Wagenknecht, Edward. *Cavalcade of the American Novel from the Birth of the Nation to the Middle of the Twentieth Century.* New York: Holt, 1952.

Washington Evening Star. "Scheme to Escape High Taxes Studied by Movie Celebrities," 1 March 1943.

Watts, Jill. *Mae West: An Icon in Black and White.* Oxford: Oxford Univ. Press, 2001.

Webb, Melody. *The Last Frontier.* Albuquerque: Univ. of New Mexico Press, 1985.

Weekly Variety. Obituary of Edna Ferber. 24 April 1968.

Wells, Evelyn. "Author pays San Francisco a Visit." *San Francisco Call-Bulletin,* 8 August 1935.

White, William Allen. "A Friend's Story of Edna Ferber." *English Journal* 19, no. 2 (February 1930): 101–106.

————. Introduction to Edna Ferber's *Cheerful by Request*, reprinted in *So Big*. New York: Grosset and Dunlap, 1925.

Whitehead, John S. *Completing the Nation: The Alaska and Hawaii Statehood Movements*. 1986. Reprint, Albuquerque: Univ. of New Mexico Press, 2004.

Widdemer, Margaret. "Message and Middlebrow." *Saturday Review of Literature*, 18 February 1933, 433–434.

Williams, Linda. *Playing the Race Card: Melodramas of Black and White from Uncle Tom to O. J. Simpson*. Princeton, N.J.: Princeton Univ. Press, 2001.

Williamson, Joel. *New People: Miscegenation and Mulattoes in the United States*. New York: Free Press, 1980.

Wilson, Christopher. *White Collar Fictions: Class and Social Representation in American Literature, 1885–1925*. Athens: Univ. of Georgia Press, 1992.

Winkler, John K. *Morgan the Magnificent: The Life of J. Pierpont Morgan*. Garden City, N.Y.: Garden City, 1930.

Wright, Will. *Sixguns and Society: A Structural Study of the Western*. Berkeley and Los Angeles: Univ. of California Press, 1975.

Yeaman, Elizabeth. "*Cimarron* Proves Thrilling Epic of Early Days." *Hollywood Daily Citizen*, 7 February 1931.

Yerby, Frank. *The Foxes of Harrow*. New York: The Dial Press, 1946.

Yergin, Daniel. "Young Dean's Legacy." *Newsweek*, 22 October 1956, 112, 116.

Yezierska, Anzia. *Children of Loneliness*. New York: Funk and Wagnalls, 1923.

————. *Hungry Hearts*. Boston: Houghton Mifflin, 1920.

————. *Red Ribbon on a White Horse*. London: Virago, 1987.

Zackodnik, Teresa C. *The Mulatta and the Politics of Race*. Jackson: Univ. Press of Mississippi, 2004.

Index